Tax Coordination in the
European Community

# Series on International Taxation

This book, *Tax Coordination in the European Community*, is the seventh in the 'Series on International Taxation' published by Kluwer Law and Taxation Publishers.

This series of books is intended for use by those engaged in the practice of international taxation. The books are of high quality.

Other titles in this series:

# Tax Coordination in the European Community

SIJBREN CNOSSEN

Editor

SERIES ON INTERNATIONAL TAXATION, NO. 7

Kluwer Law and Taxation Publishers
Deventer . Antwerp
London . Frankfurt . Boston . New York

Distribution in the USA and Canada
Kluwer Law and Taxation Publishers
101 Philip Drive
Norwell, Massachusetts 02061
U.S.A.

**Library of Congress Cataloging in Publication Data**
Tax Coordination in the European Community.
(Series on international taxation; no. 7)
Proceedings of a conference held Aug. 22-24, 1985, at Erasmus University, Rotterdam, under the auspices of its Economics Faculty and the International seminar in Public Economics.
Bibliography: p.
Includes index.
1. Taxation — Law and legislation — European Economic Community countries — Congresses. 2. Tax administration and procedure — European Economic Community countries — Congresses. I. Cnossen, Sijbren. II. Erasmus Universiteit Rotterdam. Faculteit der Economische Wetenschappen. III. Series.
KJE7104.95 1986    343.404    86-18526
ISBN 90-6544-272-3    344.034

D/1987/2664/15
ISBN 9065442723

# Preface

The results of the work of the Conference on Tax Coordination in the European Community appear at a time when the Community has undertaken, as a priority task, the completion of the internal market. The Commission's programme and proposed timetable for the achievement of that goal are spelt out in the White Paper, which was endorsed by the European Council at Milan in June 1985, an endorsement which was repeated at the Council's subsequent meeting in Luxemburg in December 1985.

The Commission wholly endorses the views of the Conference as regards the need for urgent action to remove the grave restrictions on the free movement of the factors of production which continue to exist within the Community. It is the Commission's firm view that only a true dismantling of fiscal frontiers can permit the creation of an area without internal frontiers for which the Single European Act provides. To that end a certain approximation of rates of indirect taxation is indispensable if unacceptable distortion of competition is to be avoided.

It is noteworthy that the Conference attaches great importance to the Community's problems in the field of direct taxation. This work will be particularly useful to the Commission, which intends to produce a further White Paper on company taxation in the near future. As the Conference rightly notes, action in this field is important for equalisation of the conditions of competition necessary for the completion of the internal market.

The high quality of the contributions to the Conference and the breadth of the field covered have resulted in a comprehensive and thought-provoking document, which will without doubt enrich the debate as the Community completes the present decisive phase of the European construction.

Jacques Delors
President
Commission of the European Communities

# Contents

# Introduction

## Sijbren Cnossen

Little scholarly research has been undertaken in recent years on tax harmonization issues in the European Community (EC). Although the EC Commission in Brussels labors hard to obtain agreement and implement the tax objectives of the Treaty of Rome, the academic world has left the field largely unworked since Professor Carl Shoup, member of the famous Neumark Committee, edited two volumes on *Fiscal Harmonization in Common Markets* nearly twenty years ago. Therefore, a fresh look at what has been achieved and especially at what is still required to meet the Treaty's ultimate objectives seems desirable. For that purpose, a conference was held on August 22-24, 1985 at Erasmus University Rotterdam under the auspices of its Economics Faculty and the International Seminar in Public Economics. A major objective of the organizers was to bring together leading overseas specialists with EC economists and lawyers to further public and academic discussion of basic tax coordination issues through publication of the conference papers. This introduction explains the workings and objectives of the Community and summarizes the papers and discussions of the conference.

### I. The European Community

'Determined to lay the foundations of an ever closer union among the peoples of Europe', Belgium, France, Germany, Italy, Luxembourg, and the Netherlands signed a Treaty in Rome on March 25, 1957 establishing the European Economic Community. The Treaty, which came into force at the beginning of 1958, is of unlimited duration. By accession treaties, Denmark, Ireland, and the United Kingdom joined the Community on January 1, 1973, and Greece became a member at the beginning of 1981. Following the entry of Portugal and Spain, effective January 1, 1986, the Community at present has 12 Member States encompassing some 320 million people and generating a combined gross domestic product (GDP) of ECU (European Currency Units) 2,800 billion in 1983. In comparison, the United States (US) had 235 million inhabitants in that year and its GDP was ECU 3,600 billion. The Community's

1

combined exports of industrial and agricultural commodities account for 19 percent of world exports compared to a US share of 15 percent. Through the Treaty of Lomé, the Community maintains trade and other relations with a large number of developing countries of which it is the major importer.

The objectives of the Treaty of Rome go far beyond purely economic considerations. As opposed to ordinary international agreements, the Treaty established its own legal order distinct from international law and from the internal law of the Member States. The Community has legal personality and enjoys extensive legal capacity in each of the Member States. The tasks entrusted to the Community are carried out by an Assembly, a Council, a Commission, and a Court of Justice. The acts of these institutions are binding, as they are applicable, on the Member States, their citizens, or other institutions. The Assembly, which took to itself the name of European Parliament, exercises the advisory and supervisory powers conferred upon it by the Treaty. On a roughly proportional basis, it is directly elected by the citizens of the Member States. The Council of Ministers consists of representatives of the Member States (the individual representatives varying depending upon the subject matter, e.g. agriculture, economic affairs, finance, foreign affairs), each bearing a mandate from his Government; it is charged with the duty of ensuring that the objectives set out in the Treaty are attained. While the Council represents the interests of the various Member States, the Commission is required to show complete impartiality towards the Common Market. The Commission has 17 members, each with his specific portfolio, who are appointed by agreement among the member governments. Finally, the Court of Justice ensures that in the interpretation and application of the Treaty the law is observed.

In order to carry out their task, the Council and the Commission make regulations, issue directives, take decisions, make recommendations and deliver opinions. A regulation has general application; it is binding in its entirety and is directly applicable in all Member States in exactly the same way as a national law. A directive is binding, as to the result to be achieved, upon each Member State to which it is addressed, but leaves to the national authorities the choice of form and methods. A decision is binding upon those to whom it is addressed. Recommendations and opinions have no binding force. Generally, Commission proposals for legislation go first to the European Parliament and, in some cases, to the Economic and Social Committee (which consists of representatives from bodies such as trade associations and consumer groups in the Community) for an opinion. In the light of the opinion(s), the Commission may amend its proposal and subsequently submit it to the Council of Ministers which decides whether the proposal should become Community law or policy. The work of the Council is prepared by the Committee of Permanent Representatives, consisting of ambassadors of the Member States to the Community.

## II. Tax Coordination

Tax coordination in the EC may be defined as any change in the tax systems of the Member States that is intended to forward the aims of the Community. As set out in Article 3 of the Treaty, the aims clearly include the creation of a single integrated market free of restrictions on the movement of goods, the abolition of obstacles to the right of establishment of businesses and employment and to the free movement of persons, services and capital, and the institution of a system ensuring that competition is not distorted. Among other things, these goals have a number of consequences for the tax systems of the Member States, including the abolition of customs duties, the coordination of the major indirect taxes, and the approximation of some direct tax laws as required for the proper functioning of the Common Market.

First, and most obviously, in 1968 customs duties imposed on goods moving from one Member State to another were abolished and a common customs tariff was established with respect to imports from third countries. Although an indispensable step toward achieving a single integrated market, a few quantitative restrictions on the import and export of goods remain, as well as a great many other measures having equivalent effect. The latter, called technical barriers, include different industrial standards and varying health and safety regulations, as well as competitive impediments such as protectionistic state aids and procurement policies. Three hundred and forty-four official steps must still be taken to get butter from a Dutch farm to a Paris market stall.

Second, the aim of instituting a system ensuring that competition is not distorted, *inter alia*, required that the product taxes of the Member States be revamped in such a way that precise rebates are given upon export of goods from one Member State to another and that precise compensating taxes are levied on imports by one Member State from another. These rebates and compensating taxes, called border tax adjustments, were made uniform through the Community-wide introduction of a destination-based, tax-credit value-added tax of the consumption type. Perhaps the most notable achievement to come out of this development was the adoption and implementation of the Sixth Directive on Value-Added Tax in 1977 which prescribed a uniform basis of assessment for Member States. Furthermore, agreement was reached in 1973 on the partial harmonization of the structure and basis of assessment of the excise duties on cigarettes.

Third, a common market will not have all of the characteristics of a single domestic market if physical barriers such as customs posts between Member States are not abolished. The recent agreement on a single customs document for the whole Community should facilitate this goal, but in the Commission's view much closer approximation of the indirect tax systems is also required, including the alignment of value-added tax rates and excise taxes. Furthermore, a system of shifting border tax adjustments to books of account is necessary, as

3

well as Community-wide procedures for excise suspension. Alternative ways must also be found of dealing with public security, immigration and drug controls at borders.

Fourth, approximation is required of effective tax rates on the use of capital. Substantial coordination has already been achieved through unilateral exemptions and tax credits and bilateral tax treaties, but harmonization, particularly of the corporation taxes, is essential if free movement of capital is to occur without distortion of the structure of production. In line with its philosophy that agreement on the type of tax should precede agreement on the basis of assessment and the rate structure, in 1975 the Council of Ministers, upon the recommendation of the Commission, adopted a draft directive on the inter-state integration of the corporation and individual income taxes, as well as on a harmonized system of withholding taxes on dividends. Furthermore, three directives were adopted on the harmonization of capital duty payable by companies. Coordination of the personal income taxes and social security systems has not been viewed as being urgent, although continuing efforts are made to further the freedom of labor by ensuring that double taxation, especially of frontier and migrant workers, does not occur.

Broadly, then, while competition is the allocating mechanism in the Common Market, tax coordination is its corollary in so far as it aims at ensuring that equal conditions for competitors are not distorted. The freedoms of movement and establishment mentioned above and the absence of discriminatory measures or actions by governments and businesses alike characterize the Common Market. The Common Market is one of the means to achieve the primary objective of the Community: a fuller and better life for its inhabitants. The concept is laid out in Part Two of the Treaty: 'Foundations of the Community'. The second means to achieve that objective is the approximation of the economic policies of the Member States, set forth in Part Three of the Treaty: 'Policy of the Community'. Ultimately this policy should lead to an Economic and Monetary Union. Although the Treaty does not provide for any specific rules to achieve this Union, its true mark would be a common currency. The European Monetary System (EMS), which seeks to maintain a set of fixed, if adjustable, exchange rates between the participating Member States, is an important first step toward the closer alignment of the various economic policies.

A large number of expert reports and Commission studies have analyzed the tax systems of the various Member States and made recommendations for harmonizing them. Most notable among the reports is that of the Neumark Committee recommending the introduction of a common value-added tax. While the enthusiasm of the early days led to far-reaching proposals for aligning the various tax systems, recent Commission reports are more cautious and limited in scope. In its 1980 'Report on the Scope for Convergence of Tax Systems in the Community', the Commission identifies two fundamental

4

objectives at which all efforts must be directed, viz. the elimination of border controls and the alignment of company tax burdens. The recommendations of the Report were endorsed in a resolution of the European Parliament passed November 17, 1983. Furthermore, in a closely argued 1985 White Paper to the European Council on 'Completing the Internal Market', commonly referred to as the Cockfield Report, the Commission focuses on the removal of border controls through the alignment of value-added tax rates and excises, as well as a shift of border tax adjustments to domestic stages of production and distribution.

Against this background, the conference steering committee invited 13 papers on a great variety of subjects, including the coordination of product taxes, taxes on motoring, taxes on capital income and corporations, personal income taxes, and on the interaction between fiscal and monetary policies. In the terms of reference, a number of points were stressed. Thus, it was pointed out that with national monetary policies becoming more aligned, the weight on tax (and expenditure) policies for short-term stabilization and long-term structural adjustments in individual Member States would increase. This implied, *inter alia*, that tax *equalization*, i.e. complete uniformity of tax bases and especially of tax rates, apart from its political ramifications, did not appear desirable. Rather, the focus might be on tax *coordination* allowing Member States maximum flexibility in arranging their tax systems without, of course, interfering with the establishment of a common market. In this connection, it seemed that flexibility in taxation should probably be achieved through variations in rate structures; differences in types of tax and bases of assessment might obscure and perpetuate competitive distortions, as well as jeopardize agreement on compensation mechanisms, if required. Finally, the authors were invited to adopt a pragmatic, institution-oriented approach and to try to learn from the experience of federal countries, such as the United States and Canada, where subnational tax systems differ widely one from another.

### III. Summary of Papers

#### A. Developments and Issues

Extending the previous statement of issues, Part One of the volume begins with a survey, by Sijbren Cnossen, of the major tax structure developments in the EC since its inception until the present time. The paper shows that the role of taxation, as reflected by the ratio of total tax revenues to GDP, has grown enormously in recent years. For the EC as a whole, this ratio, on a weighted basis, rose from some 29 percent in 1955 to about 40 percent in 1983, mainly on account of increases in income tax collections and social security contributions. Broad contemporary influences, including the increased effective demand for income redistribution through the budget, are noted to explain this trend. Whatever the causes, the potential effects of the large public sectors on resource allocation emphasize the need for tax (and expenditure) coordination.

In subsequent sections on product taxes and income taxes, the paper introduces the main issues that are taken up in more detail in other papers. Drawing on earlier work by Professor Richard Musgrave, the paper summarizes the major implications that follow from two fundamental tax coordination criteria, viz. tax neutrality and tax base entitlement, that should govern discussions of and efforts at tax coordination. Tax neutrality requires that relative prices between home-produced and foreign-made goods are not distorted, thus establishing the case for the abolition of customs duties and precise border tax adjustments under the value-added taxes and the excises. Less coordination seems required for those tax bases that have low intra-Community mobility, including employment income and social security contributions. On the other hand, since the capital base is highly mobile, special coordination efforts are required in the field of corporation taxes and capital income covered by individual income taxes. The paper's main conclusion is that product tax coordination has probably been carried as far as it should go and that the focus should now be on the removal of border controls and non-tariff barriers. Beyond that, efficiency gains may be reaped from greater coordination of the various corporation taxes.

## B. Product Taxes

Part Two contains three papers dealing with product tax coordination. Following the abolition of customs duties, the Community's attention turned to internal taxes, such as turnover taxes, that might be used to discriminate, intentionally or inadvertently, against products from other Member States, because appropriate border tax adjustments for such taxes are inherently indeterminable. The replacement of the turnover tax by a destination-based value-added tax extending through the retail stage rectified this shortcoming so that manufacturing location decisions are not distorted on account of the sales tax. For years it was thought, however, that border tax adjustments required the maintenance of border controls (that is, customs posts) to ensure that imports are actually taxed and that exports enter intra-Community trade free of tax. To abolish border tax adjustments and by extension border controls, it has been suggested that a uniform-rate, origin-based value-added tax on trade internal to the EC be combined with a destination-based value-added tax applied to trade with third countries.

The first paper, by Sijbren Cnossen and Carl Shoup, argues that the change-over to the origin principle within the EC would violate neutrality, because the conditions for the equivalence theorem, viz. full domestic price and exchange

6

rate flexibility, as well as full tax coverage and uniform rate application, are far from being met in practice. Furthermore, the origin principle is administratively infeasible because exports and imports must be valued: exports in order to ensure that they are fully taxed, and imports so that a notional tax credit can be attached to them to avoid double taxation in domestic stages. A uniform rate throughout the EC would also sacrifice substantial fiscal autonomy. Based on their earlier work, the authors then proceed to show that a shift to the origin principle is unnecessary, because border controls can simply be removed by shifting border tax adjustments to books of account in the form of either a tax deferral method or, preferably, a tax credit clearance system. Basically, this would leave Member States free to determine their own rates of value-added tax in line with their revenue needs and social and economic policy objectives.

In similar fashion, border tax adjustments for the excises might be shifted to factory gates and retail outlets in conjunction with the introduction of an EC-wide system of in-bond transportation of excisable products. The high rates of tax on such commodities raise particular economic and administrative problems. In the second paper, on tobacco and alcohol taxes, John Kay and Michael Keen argue that it is untenable to attach significance only to the process and fact of harmonization and none to the criteria and ultimate objectives of Community tax harmonization. They proceed to identify two issues for consideration: first, the need to secure agreement on the relative rates of tax to be imposed on beer, wine and spirits, so that tax structures cannot be used as non-tariff protective devices; and second, the establishment of an appropriate balance between specific and ad valorem components in the overall tobacco excise mix. In a closely argued exposition, the authors show that high-rate excises should primarily be based on product characteristics (and on quantity over quality) rather than on the commodities themselves. Medical arguments and the association, in consumption, of alcohol and tobacco with leisure both point toward heavy reliance on specific rates, which, unlike ad valorem rates, do not degrade quality with resulting welfare and revenue losses.

The papers on value-added and excise taxes argue that uniformity of rates is not necessary or desirable for tax coordination. This is also the conclusion of a third paper, by Professor Manfred Rose, that applies the theory of optimal taxation (which seeks to devise rate structures to minimize excess burdens) to commodity taxes in the EC. Relying on duality theory, the author derives optimal tax rates for the situation of national as well as that of joint welfare maximization. Without further empirical information, explicit rate structures cannot be designed, but the general equilibrium model produces no evidence that a closer alignment of product tax rates would improve social welfare in the Community.

## C. Taxes on Motoring

Motor vehicle taxes, viz. fuel excises, purchase taxes, registration duties, tolls and other charges, may either be related to cars, which are industry products in the same way as other products, or to buses and trucks, which must be viewed as representative of the passenger and road freight industry. It is the role of tax policy to ensure that infrastructure costs are correctly borne and that externalities, e.g. congestion and pollution, are internalized. Furthermore, tax coordination must ensure equal conditions of competition between operators and producers from different Member States, between different modes of transport, and between the transport sector and other sectors of the economy. In Part Three two papers deal respectively with motor vehicle tax harmonization and with price discrimination and tax differences in the European motor industry.

In a broad-ranging paper, Roger Smith reviews EC policy objectives with respect to motor vehicle taxation, noting that the failure to establish a common transport policy limits the degree of meaningful discussion on tax coordination in this field. However, since there is no evidence that existing differences in motor vehicle taxation are related to differing costs, movement toward a common market in road freight and private passenger transportation services, and in the production and sale of cars, suggests that convergence of motor vehicle taxes is a good thing. Having reviewed the different types of car and truck taxes, Professor Smith concludes that in the case of road haulage there is evidence of convergence of taxes on diesel fuel. Moreover, the real value of registration and fuel taxes on commercial vehicles fell by 30 percent between 1972 and 1984, thus reducing the impact that tax differences may have on competition. In his opinion, the greater awareness of such differences results from more rapid growth in the movement of goods between Member States than within States. There has been little, if any, convergence of taxes on cars, thus inhibiting rationalization of EC car production and blurring the focus on larger international markets.

With respect to the car market, different forms of taxation interact with the development of different types of car industry. Italian taxes on gasoline, relative to other Member States, discourage the purchase of larger cars; German taxes do the reverse. Similarly, combined registration taxes and purchase taxes in Italy and France provide a much greater incentive to purchase a small car than is true in Germany or the United Kingdom. In a companion paper, Andy Murfin examines the structure of price levels and product taxes (value-added tax and special excises) in the European car market. It appears that it is not only differences in product taxes which explain the differences in pre-tax car prices in various Member States. Other factors of major importance are differences in the price elasticity of demand, variations in the level of industrial concentration, dealer structure and regulation, and in the degree of collusion between firms. The author concludes that market segmentation is leading to welfare losses for certain European consumers. Other action than tax coordination may be necessary to curb the exploitation of this monopoly power.

## D. Taxes on Capital Income and Corporations

The conceptual basis for a separate corporation income tax has generally been considered weak by economists, although there is agreement that the tax serves as a suitable instrument for taxing foreign direct investment and as a useful proxy for the inclusion of capital gains through the tax on retained profits. There is much debate and disagreement, however, on the extent to which the tax on distributed corporate profits should be integrated with the personal income tax of shareholders. Furthermore, numerous tax preferences under the various corporation taxes distort saving and investment decisions and cause wide variations in effective rates of return to capital. Tax coordination in this area may have some urgency, but clearly the principles, issues and effects require careful exposition and analysis before that task is undertaken. Part Four contains three papers on the subject.

The first paper, by Peggy Musgrave, focuses on the broad principles and criteria that should govern the interjurisdictional coordination of taxes on capital income. The choice is between the source (territoriality) principle and the residence (allegiance) principle. The problems include the appropriate taxation of income earned by foreign investors (interjurisdictional equity), tax neutrality with respect to the location of investment (locational neutrality), and inter-taxpayer equity. In the EC, locational neutrality has been considered of paramount importance. Professor Musgrave concludes that the adoption of a source-based, equal flat-rate corporation tax applied to a uniformly defined base to implement interjurisdictional equity among the Member States would also be helpful in the achievement of locational neutrality within the Community. If effective rates of corporation tax were equalized, the need for a uniformly applied imputation system would disappear, although a dividend-received credit remains desirable on taxpayer equity grounds. Uniformity in type, base and rates of corporation taxes would sacrifice some tax sovereignty, but fortunately the previous discussion on product tax coordination showed that full equalization in that field is not necessary, thus leaving substantial revenue flexibility.

Richard Bird continues the analysis with a review of the complicated issues involved in corporate-personal tax integration, a subject for which interest has waxed and waned in the EC since the early 1960s. The imputation systems introduced in seven Member States show a very diverse picture of rates, and size of tax credits, as well as the treatment of intra-Community income flows and

9

foreign-source income in recipient countries. This uneven approach to integration in the Community has been paralleled in other industrial countries, including the United States, Canada and Australia. The systems reflect the diversity of domestic considerations rather than Community or international concerns. Professor Bird argues that the spread of imputation systems in the EC may have to be attributed to some 'emulation effect', because the present state of knowledge on the effects of the corporation tax is not really such that a strong case can be made for requiring all Member States to adhere to a particular corporate-personal tax structure. In his opinion, the most useful way to approach the analysis of tax relations in the Community may not be with the normative tool of economic efficiency, which dominates the professional literature, but rather with the tool of the new economic theory of politics. In the end, therefore, the real significance of any future progress towards interjurisdictional integration of corporate and personal income taxes may be its political symbolism rather than its economic effect.

Extending his own work and that of others, Julian Alworth's paper provides a cross-country comparison of the extent to which the taxation of savings and investment differs amongst EC Member States in terms of simulated 'average marginal tax rates'. These rates are derived as weighted averages from the 'tax wedge' between the pre-tax rate of return on investments and the post-tax rate of return on savings for a series of hypothetical projects. Wide divergencies in effective tax rates on capital income are shown to exist across countries. The divergencies are attributable to differences in nominal company tax rates, in the definition of the tax base, in the provision of various tax and other fiscal incentives, and in personal income and wealth taxes. The effects of harmonizing nominal company tax rates in approximating effective rates of tax on capital income appear to be very small. Thus, harmonization must be extended to the tax base if effective rates are to be harmonized. Moreover, effective tax rates vary widely across sectors within each Member State, suggesting that the coordination of taxes on capital income is a domestic as well as a Community issue.


### E. Other Issues in Income Taxation

It is important that flesh be put on the bare bones of tax policy. The proposal for closer coordination of the various corporation taxes requires harmonization of the way in which company profits are determined. In the first paper of Part Five, Norbert Andel provides a thorough review of the Commission's endeavors to harmonize tax legislation in this field. He discusses successively various issues and reports concerning the computation of business profits for tax purposes, including depreciation, the carry-over of losses, the treatment of capital gains and losses, and the valuation of stock-in-trade. Related proposals in the field of company law, mergers, measures to avoid international double taxation, and mutual assistance matters are also treated. Noting that differences in company taxation are large indeed, Professor Andel concludes that the subject should be given a higher priority than has hitherto been the case.

In the second paper, David Ulph examines the impact of tax harmonization on labor mobility in the EC. He notes that there are crucial features of labor, such as individuals having preferences about where to work and form family units, which, unlike capital, effectively limit the scope and possibly even the desirability of tax harmonization in this field. Nevertheless, as Professor Ulph points out, the Commission's proposals with respect to frontier and migrant workers do go some way to eliminating distortions, though they may have complex distributional consequences. He finds it difficult to understand why it is proposed to assess the income of other non-resident workers on the basis of employment instead of residency.

Drawing upon the results of a multinational study group on tax expenditures, the third paper, by Paul McDaniel, explores a new approach to chart the differences in personal and business income tax systems for tax coordination purposes. His somewhat non-traditional view is that tax preferences in fact do not erode the tax base because, under the tax expenditure construct, a taxpayer in effect may be considered to pay the tax based upon economic income (normatively defined) and then receive back a tax subsidy check for the amount of the tax expenditures for which he is qualified. Given this construct, all that is required for tax coordination is that the tax expenditures themselves be treated according to the normative income definition principle adopted. According to Professor McDaniel, it is then quite a separate question whether the tax expenditure provisions violate the rules or principles of the Treaty of Rome with respect to expenditure coordination and the prohibition against subsidies which distort competition.


### F. European Monetary System

As is well-known in economic theory, product taxes and possibly also income taxes interact with exchange rates which are an important indicator of the nature and performance of a country's monetary policies. Coordination in taxation might be to no avail if different monetary policies lead to different inflation rates resulting in distortions that would promote tax-induced capital movements. More generally, tax policy coordination must be rooted in monetary policy coordination and vice versa. In 1978, the European Council agreed that closer monetary cooperation between the Member States should be promoted through the creation of the European Monetary System (EMS) which seeks to establish a greater measure of monetary stability through a system of fixed but adjustable exchange rates. The European Currency Unit plays a central role in the EMS and may be viewed as the precursor of a common currency.

The paper by Vito Tanzi and Teresa Ter-Minassian in Part Six of the volume examines the extent to which participation in the EMS has contributed to promoting mutually consistent monetary and fiscal policies, as well as the consequences of differences in the mix of those policies among the participants. The analysis is based on a robust theoretical framework of a two-country world with fixed exchange rates, substantial capital mobility, significantly differing fiscal policies, but well-coordinated and conservative monetary policies that place the burden of adjustment primarily on the Member State with the highest inflation. It is shown that the latter will drift into a situation in which its debt, interest payments, and deficits feed on each other. Monetary policy will not be able to hold the line, inflation will increase, and so will instability. Ultimately, the fixed exchange rate will have to be adjusted. Confronting the actual behavior of the EMS Member States with this framework, the authors conclude that the EMS has brought about more coordinated monetary policies, but that so far its impact on fiscal policies has been much more limited. This is unfortunate because, in the longer run, an expansionary fiscal policy may undermine monetary policy and the performance of the real economy, and thus also the ability to maintain fixed exchange rates.


## IV. CONFERENCE DISCUSSION

In a closing session, the participants reviewed four major themes that had loomed large in previous discussions on tax coordination. These themes were: tax reform versus tax harmonization, uniformity versus diversity, direct taxes versus indirect taxes, and tax harmonization versus fiscal harmonization. Although a vote was not taken, the consensus of the conference was that tax reform was an important, indispensable part of the tax coordination process, that diversity among tax systems, provided it did not interfere with the establishment of a true community, was to be preferred to uniformity, that personal direct taxes should not be played down in favor of indirect taxes, and that tax harmonization should be viewed in the broader context of tax *and* expenditure coordination, i.e. fiscal harmonization.

On tax reform versus tax harmonization, the participants agreed that tax harmonization should not be considered of such importance in itself that the objective would be to find that average of existing practices on which Member States could be induced to agree. Rather, the tax structure of each Member State, in conjunction with that of other Member States, should be judged in light of the underlying criteria and objectives concerning revenue, equity, efficiency, and administrative feasibility. Tax reform and tax coordination should go hand in hand. Basically, convergence should be measured by points of departure rather than by points of arrival. Certainly, no contribution would be made to the welfare of the Community's citizens if inequitable and distortionary tax structures of some Member States were imposed on other Member States. It was also agreed that harmonization of rate structures made no sense without reference to the bases on which the rates were levied.

With respect to uniformity versus diversity, the conference participants expressed a strong preference for diversity commensurate with the goal of achieving a true common market and beyond that an economic and monetary union. It was held that uniformity made no sense if conditions and preferences of the parties to the tax coordination process were as different as they are. Indeed, it might even be counterproductive to impose uniform institutions on very diverse realities. Diversity is the end and purpose of all economics and people's interests in peculiar national and local things should not be constrained. In a broad sense, the European Community is but an instrument to achieving a fuller and better life for its citizens; it should not be considered a goal in itself. Diversity might entail economic and administrative costs, but these should be acceptable, particularly if those whose interests are being served pay the price. In this philosophy, tax coordination would come about as people saw it as in their interest to bring it about. It was also pointed out that in the United States, for example, subnational tax systems differ widely one from another, yet this does not seem incompatible with the proper functioning of the domestic market. Probably greater weight should be attached to devising processes in which participants have equal chances of influencing the results rather than to the results themselves. The increasingly crucial and constructive role of the European Court of Justice seems to augur well for the equitable resolution of future conflicts.

This having been said, however, it was agreed that selective coordination is desirable to reduce trade, location, capital market and employment distortions, to be able to remove border controls, and more generally to eliminate unjustified differences in taxpayer obligations and accounting requirements. As regards the value-added taxes, the participants shared the view that trade and location distortions were no longer significant. In essence, rate approximation is largely irrelevant to the objective of removing border controls, because border tax adjustments could be shifted to books of account. Much of the resistance to abolishing customs posts is probably political and psychological rather than administrative and more concerned with the policing functions instead of the taxing functions of the various national authorities. In this connection, it was noted that the establishment of a common customs service, operating at external frontiers, might do more to further the removal of internal customs posts than such things as rate approximation of the value-added taxes. Some approximation and particularly more coordinated administration appeared to be required for the excises on tobacco products, alcoholic beverages, and petroleum derivatives. However, the taxing principles to be applied should be sorted out first. Closer coordination is also required of the taxes on corporations and capital income. Existing differences create very diverse patterns of incentives, disincentives and shares in non-resident income across the Community. Such a move would diminish tax competition for foreign capital if accompanied by the equalization of withholding taxes on investment income, such as royalties, dividends and interest, paid to investors from outside the Community.

Most of the conference participants expressed a preference for direct, personal taxes, such as the individual income tax or an expenditure tax, over indirect, impersonal taxes, such as the value-added tax. The individual income tax, it was argued, closely reflects the ability-to-pay philosophy which plays an important role in political thinking. The income tax can be designed to take account of personal and special circumstances, is adaptable to progressive rates, and exhibits substantial built-in flexibility or elasticity which is important for revenue and economic policy purposes. Unfortunately, its transparency is largely obscured by pervasive withholding systems. In the view of these participants, moves to heavier reliance on indirect taxes should be resisted. Other participants, however, did not agree. Citing fresh insights brought to the fore by the new supply-side economics, they emphasized that savings, capital formation, economic growth, and employment would be promoted through a shift from direct to indirect taxes.

On the theme of tax harmonization versus fiscal harmonization, the participants agreed that the implications of different expenditure levels and structures should be taken into account in assessing the impact of governments' intervention in the functioning of the Common Market. Ideally, benefit levies provide an appropriate link between taxes as proxies for prices paid for government-provided services and the costs of those services, but the extent of their application is limited. For the majority of taxes, diverse patterns of tax-induced incentives and disincentives might be offset or accentuated by unneutralities on the expenditure side of the budgets of the Member States. Thus, protectionistic import duties might take the form of free services to industries rather than taxes collected at borders. Similarly, export subsidies might be given in the form of highways leading to harbors. As another example, it was pointed out that tax differentials affect capital flows, but so do cost differentials due to expenditure benefits in the form of education, infrastructure, and similar government services. Furthermore, social expenditures might be more important for labor mobility than tax differentials. What matters in this context are differences in net wages, defined as gross wages minus taxes but plus transfer benefits. As was increasingly being realized in the Community, viz. the concern with non-tax and non-tariff barriers, in the final analysis it is net burdens and benefits that matter in evaluating the distortionary effects of taxes and expenditures.

14

In closing, it was noted that the Community had often been compared to a tortoise that never seemed to move, but that had covered a remarkable amount of ground since its birth in the late 1950s. As evidenced by the experience of federal countries, tax coordination and harmonization would continue to be a slow, arduous process, even after the Common Market would have attained most of the characteristics of a single, domestic market. In terms of political significance, the single most important next step would be the elimination of border controls. Given the political will, this step could be taken forthwith if Member States would agree to shift border tax adjustments to books of account. Close integration of the various customs and excise services would also be helpful. In terms of economic effect, substantial gains would be reaped from pulling down the various technical barriers, such as different product regulations and standards, that effectively impede entry. Thus, in the words of the European Council, a single large market would be achieved 'thereby creating a more favorable environment for stimulating enterprise, competition and trade'.

In an undertaking of this kind, the organizer/editor must rely on assistance from a variety of sources. As members of the steering committee, John Kay, Richard Musgrave and Carl Shoup provided many useful suggestions for subjects and contacts with contributors and discussants. The idea for the conference arose in discussions with Richard Musgrave, President of the International Seminar in Public Economics, in Canberra, Hamburg and Rotterdam. The European Commission, the Fund of Erasmus University, its Economics Faculty and Rabobank Nederland, were the chief financial sponsors of the conference; without their generosity the conference would not have been possible. The editor is especially grateful to the authors who responded enthusiastically to the call for papers and to the discussants who agreed that their commentaries be taken into account in revising the main contributions rather than be published separately. Special thanks are due to Peter Kavelaars, Ada van Krimpen, and Jeannie de Nijs who bore the brunt of the heavy administrative burden associated with the organization of the conference. Judith Payne gave valuable assistance in editing and preparing the manuscript for publication. The responsibility for whatever faults remain rests, of course, with the editor.

*Sijbren Cnossen*

Erasmus University Rotterdam

June, 1986

# Part One

# Developments and Issues

# 1

## Tax structure developments

*Sijbren Cnossen* *

### I. Introduction

According to folk wisdom, people joined in matrimony tend to look more like each other as time passes by. There is a presumption that this should also happen to the tax structures of the member states of a common market, such as the European Community (EC). As barriers to trade and factor movements are broken down, individual economies become more closely integrated. As a result, the nature and size of the major tax bases should become more aligned and with it the various tax handles to which individual taxes are attached. Moreover, increased competition in product and factor markets may enhance rivalry in taxation. By definition, discriminatory border taxes, such as import duties, are prohibited in the Common Market. As border controls are further relaxed, effective product tax rates of adjoining states and, by extension, of the whole Common Market might move closer to the Community's average. Furthermore, differences in factor tax treatment should induce capital to move to countries with lower rates, which should act as a brake on too great a divergency in tax levels of individual Member States. Although differences in language and cultural traditions are important barriers, over time substantial differentials in the taxation of labor income might induce people to vote with their feet. Discretionary action, whether jointly or unilaterally, may accelerate these trends.

Against this background, this paper surveys and evaluates tax structure developments in the EC from its inception in 1957 until the present time. The second section looks at trends in the total level and overall composition of tax revenues. General contemporary influences have resulted in significant increases in tax burdens, particularly of the income taxes and social security contributions. The third section examines developments in the field of product taxes: the elimination of customs duties, the introduction of a common value-added tax, and the harmonization of excise duties. From the beginning, the fear of export subsidies or import taxes hidden in internal product tax systems has

* I am indebted to Emile a Campo, Ken Messere and Carl Shoup for their perceptive comments on an earlier draft. Johan van der Sluis assisted with the statistics.

19

been of overriding concern in the Community. The fourth section reviews taxes on income and profits and social security contributions which have received much less attention, but which may become more important if equity and administration come to the fore as major areas of common concern. Finally, a concluding section considers the tax structure developments in the light of tax theory and attempts to place them in a broader social and political context. It argues that greater uniformity of tax systems is not necessarily conducive to the formation of a 'good' community, just as closer resemblance in matrimony is not a litmus test for a happy marriage.

Tax revenue statistics, covering central, provincial, and local governments have been drawn from publications of the Organisation for Economic Co-operation and Development (OECD).[1] The term tax ratio is used to express tax revenues (including social security contributions) as a percentage of gross domestic product (GDP) at market prices, while the term tax share is defined as the percentage contribution of a particular tax to total tax revenues. Throughout the paper, brief references are made to the tax situation in the United States (US) that has a comparable large market and that faces similar fiscal coordination issues as the EC. In 1983, the populations of the Member States of the EC totaled 320 million and their GDPs US $ 2,500 billion, yielding a per capita income of US $ 7,800. In the same year, the US had 235 million inhabitants, its GDP was US $ 3,200 billion, and its per capita income US $ 13,600. Detailed data are shown in an Appendix.

## II. LEVELS OF TAXATION

Total tax levels have increased significantly in all Member States during the period under review. An examination of the overall composition of tax revenues indicates that this development is mainly attributable to increases in income taxes and social security contributions. References are made to explanatory factors for these trends.

### A. Increase in Total Tax Ratios

From 1955 to 1983, total levels of taxation in all EC Member States rose at historically unprecedented rates, as shown in Table 1.1. The weighted tax ratio for the EC as a whole increased from 29 to 40 in the period under review, or at an average rate of 0.4 percentage points per annum. By comparison, the tax ratio in the US increased on average by 0.2 points per annum from 24 to 29,

---

1. For a note on the conceptual and practical pitfalls in making international comparisons of tax levels, see Messere and Owens (1985).

20

positioning it at the same level in 1983 as the EC was at in 1955. In 1983, three EC Member States collected 45-47 percent of GDP in the form of tax revenue. In six other countries the ratio varied from 37 to 45. In later years, the tax ratio appears to be leveling off in the high-tax states (Messere, 1983). The figures suggest that the tax ratios of individual countries moved closer to the Community's average.[2] For three recent members – Greece, Portugal and Spain – that are distinctly less industrialized than most other states, the tax ratio was 33 or less in 1983, but the rate of increase since 1975 was greater than in other Member States.

*Table 1.1 EC: total tax revenues as percentage of gross domestic product*

| Country[a] | 1983 | 1975 | 1965 | 1955[b] | Tax Buoyancy Ratio[c] | Marginal Tax Ratio[d] |
|---|---|---|---|---|---|---|
| *European Community*[e] | *39.7* | *34.7* | *30.4* | *28.9* | *1.37* | *41.9* |
| Netherlands | 47.3 | 43.6 | 33.6 | 26.3 | 1.50 | 50.5 |
| Denmark | 46.2 | 41.4 | 29.9 | 23.4 | 1.63 | 48.8 |
| Belgium | 45.4 | 41.1 | 30.8 | 24.0 | 1.59 | 49.1 |
| France | 44.6 | 37.4 | 35.0 | 32.4 | 1.31 | 45.9 |
| Luxembourg | 42.5 | 36.7 | 30.5 | ... | 1.47 | 45.0 |
| Italy | 40.6 | 29.0 | 27.3 | 30.5 | 1.53 | 41.6 |
| Ireland | 39.2 | 31.6 | 26.0 | 22.5 | 1.54 | 40.1 |
| United Kingdom | 37.8 | 35.5 | 30.6 | 29.8 | 1.27 | 38.8 |
| Germany | 37.4 | 36.0 | 31.6 | 30.8 | 1.25 | 39.6 |
| Greece | 32.9 | 24.6 | 20.6 | 18.6 | 1.63 | 33.7 |
| Portugal | 32.9 | 24.7 | 18.4 | 15.4 | 1.83 | 33.6 |
| Spain | 27.2 | 19.6 | 14.7 | ... | 1.91 | 28.0 |
| *United States* | *29.0* | *29.6* | *26.3* | *23.6* | *1.13* | *29.7* |

*Notes:*  a. Listed in descending order of total tax revenue to GDP ratio in 1983.
   b. Provisional estimates.
   c. Percentage increase in taxes divided by percentage increase in GDP for the period 1965-83.
   d. Increase in taxes divided by increase in GDP, expressed in percent for the period 1965-83.
   e. Weighted averages.

*Sources:* Organisation for Economic Co-operation and Development (1985), Tables 3 and 113; 1955 figures for France and Greece: *idem* (1966).

2. The coefficient of variation (the standard deviation divided by the unweighted average, in percent) fell from 23.1 in 1965 to 15.7 in 1983. Broadly, the ranking in terms of total tax to GDP ratio altered little between 1955 and 1983. The Spearman coefficient is 0.685 with a significance at the 95 percent level. Weighted tax ratios are computed by converting absolute figures for tax collections and domestic products denoted in national currencies into figures denoted in US dollars.

Basically, as pointed out in the public finance literature, the reasons for the acceptance of high levels of taxation must be sought on the expenditure side of the budget, as epitomized in Wagner's law of the 'expanding scale of state activity'.[3] A detailed explanation of the underlying forces is beyond the scope of this paper, but some broad economic, social, and political factors may be noted. Major upheavals, such as the two world wars and the great depression, interrupted the steady path of fiscal development and facilitated the acceptance of a larger role of the public sector (Peacock and Wiseman, 1961). Moreover, these events profoundly affected cultural values and social philosophies, resulting in, among other things, an increased effective demand for income redistribution through the budget. Following the last war, high levels of defense expenditures were replaced by increased public outlays on economic rehabilitation and subsequently transfer programs for the aged, sick, unemployed and other less privileged groups. No doubt, universal suffrage and the rise of participatory democracy strengthened these trends.

A similar set of general contemporary influences has probably been at work on the tax side of the budget in the various Member States of the Community. The re-assessment of the role of the state involved the acceptance of higher levels of taxation than before. This and the effective spread of representative government made it possible to place greater reliance on taxpayer cooperation and voluntary compliance. Moreover, as economic development proceeded, the nature and accessibility of the various tax bases changed and with it the tax handles to which individual taxes are attached. Economies became highly monetized with virtually all income and output moving through the market. The size of production and distribution establishments increased and employment became more concentrated. At the same time, business accounting practices improved and government collection and assessment methods were modernized. Withholding techniques, of paramount importance for the successful administration of the income tax and social security schemes, were introduced in most countries. In short, the two major tax bases − income and consumption − could be broadened considerably and hence their revenue productivity increased. To be sure, the emergence of large underground economies (Tanzi, 1982) may have helped to check these increases in some Member States.

As has been noted before (Goode, 1968), the feasibility of diverting a rising share of GDP to the public sector through taxation may be explained by the high rates of economic growth in the Community, particularly in the earlier years. As per capita income increased, nearly quintupling in nominal terms since 1965 (see Appendix), the proportion of income required for food and shelter diminished. Hence, it may be postulated, the 'ability-to-pay' for public

---

3. This and the following paragraph draw heavily on Musgrave (1969), Chapter 5. For a recent analysis of expenditure growth in industrial countries, see also Tanzi (1986).

sector outlays increased. Table 1.1 shows two measures of the change in total tax revenue to GDP. First, the tax buoyancy ratio denotes the relationship between the percentage increase in total tax revenue to the percentage increase in GDP. This ratio is above 1 in all EC Member States. Particularly high figures are shown for the high-tax countries and the low-tax countries. Secondly, the marginal tax ratio measures the fraction of the increase in GDP absorbed by taxes. This ratio is particularly high in the high-tax states, but not in the low-tax countries.

The unprecedented increase in the size of the public sector in the EC has not been matched in the US. Whereas the weighted tax ratio in the EC was 16 percent ahead of the US ratio in 1965, the difference had grown to 37 percent in 1983. This image is altered little when non-tax revenues are taken into account. The weighted non-tax revenue ratio for the EC was 4.8 in 1982 against 6.2 for the US.[4] If these ratios are added to the total tax revenue ratios, the weighted average public sector 'burden' in the EC is one and a quarter times that in the US. Apparently, political resistance to public spending and heavy taxes and charges is stronger in the US than in the EC. Lately, however, there is a growing awareness in the Community of the disincentive effects associated with excessively generous entitlement programs and high marginal tax rates, as well as the stimulus that high taxes give to underground economic activities (De Clercq, 1985; Tanzi, 1986; OECD, 1986a).

### B. Overall Composition of Tax Revenues

The time trend of economic, social and political forces sketched above may now be extended to broad categories of taxation: product taxes, income taxes, social security contributions, property and other taxes. Thus, the pervasive rise of egalitarianism has been a driving force behind the increased use of the progressive income tax as the best available indicator of economic power and social status. Similarly, the growing sense of social responsibility for the welfare of individuals has resulted in greater reliance on social security contributions to finance related transfer programs. At the same time, these social and political factors should have diminished the relative role of product taxes whose burden distribution is generally perceived as regressive with respect to income.

---

4. In 1982, non-tax revenue ratios for individual Member States were – Ireland: 7.2; United Kingdom: 7.1; Denmark: 6.8; Netherlands: 6.7; Germany: 6.5; Luxembourg (1981): 6.0; France: 3.3; Greece: 3.1; Belgium: 2.6; Spain (1981): 2.3; and Italy: 2.0. In addition, of course, aspects such as the extent of tax expenditures (doing things through the tax side rather than the expenditure side of the budget), public borrowing and the effect of underground economies have to be taken into account in evaluating the size of the public sector.

*Table 1.2 EC: composition of total tax revenues*

| Country[a] | Product Taxes | | | Income Taxes | | | Social Security Contributions | | | Property and Other Taxes | | |
|---|---|---|---|---|---|---|---|---|---|---|---|---|
| | 1983 | 1975 | 1965 | 1983 | 1975 | 1965 | 1983 | 1975 | 1965 | 1983 | 1975 | 1965 |
| | As Percentage of Gross Domestic Product | | | | | | | | | | | |
| *European Community[b]* | *11.1* | *9.9* | *10.8* | *12.4* | *10.7* | *8.4* | *13.6* | *11.8* | *8.1* | *2.6* | *2.3* | *3.1* |
| Netherlands | 11.4 | 10.5 | 9.6 | 13.0 | 15.2 | 12.0 | 21.3 | 16.7 | 10.3 | 1.6 | 1.2 | 1.7 |
| Denmark | 16.5 | 13.9 | 12.2 | 25.4 | 24.4 | 13.7 | 1.8 | 1.0 | 1.6 | 2.5 | 2.1 | 2.4 |
| Belgium | 12.0 | 10.9 | 11.4 | 18.6 | 16.1 | 8.5 | 13.9 | 13.1 | 9.7 | 0.9 | 1.0 | 1.2 |
| France | 12.9 | 12.3 | 13.4 | 7.9 | 6.6 | 5.6 | 19.6 | 15.3 | 11.9 | 4.2 | 3.2 | 4.1 |
| Luxembourg | 10.1 | 7.6 | 7.6 | 18.9 | 15.8 | 10.9 | 10.6 | 11.1 | 9.9 | 2.9 | 2.2 | 2.1 |
| Italy | 9.5 | 8.5 | 10.8 | 14.9 | 6.2 | 4.9 | 14.6 | 13.3 | 9.3 | 1.6 | 1.0 | 2.3 |
| Ireland | 18.1 | 14.7 | 13.7 | 13.0 | 9.5 | 6.7 | 5.8 | 4.4 | 1.7 | 2.3 | 3.0 | 3.9 |
| United Kingdom | 11.3 | 9.0 | 10.1 | 14.6 | 15.8 | 11.3 | 6.7 | 6.2 | 4.7 | 5.2 | 4.5 | 4.5 |
| Germany | 10.3 | 9.7 | 10.4 | 12.5 | 12.4 | 10.7 | 13.3 | 12.3 | 8.5 | 1.3 | 1.6 | 2.0 |
| Greece | 14.3 | 11.9 | 10.7 | 5.4 | 3.4 | 2.0 | 11.7 | 6.7 | 5.5 | 1.5 | 2.6 | 2.4 |
| Portugal | 14.4 | 10.1 | 8.2 | 8.1 | 4.3 | 4.5 | 8.5 | 8.5 | 4.0 | 1.9 | 1.8 | 1.7 |
| Spain | 6.5 | 4.7 | 6.0 | 7.1 | 4.3 | 3.6 | 12.2 | 9.3 | 4.2 | 1.4 | 1.3 | 0.9 |
| *United States* | *5.2* | *5.5* | *5.8* | *12.4* | *13.0* | *12.2* | *8.3* | *7.3* | *4.3* | *3.1* | *3.8* | *4.0* |

*Notes:*    a. Listed in descending order of total tax revenue to GDP ratio in 1983.

           b. Weighted averages.

*Source:*   Organisation for Economic Co-operation and Development (1985): Table 24 (heading 5000); Table 8 (heading 1000); Table 14 (heading 2000); and the difference between the figures shown in Table 1.1 of this paper and the sum of the figures shown in this table for product taxes, income taxes and social security contributions.

Generally, this line of reasoning is borne out by the figures shown in Table 1.2. The weighted product tax ratio in the EC rose only slightly from just below 11 in 1965 to just above 11 in 1983. In view of the substantial increase of 31 percent in the overall tax ratio, this implies that the share of product taxes in total tax revenue declined. Substantial increases in the product tax ratio took place in Denmark (that has one of the highest tax buoyancy ratios of all Member States), Luxembourg, Ireland, and the low-tax countries Greece and Portugal. As expected, the ratios of the income taxes and social security contributions rose markedly. For the income taxes, the weighted average ratio increased by 48 percent, and for social security contributions the increase was 68 percent; both figures are well above the rise in the overall tax ratio. For the income taxes, above average increases in the ratios were recorded in Denmark, Belgium, Luxembourg, Italy, Ireland, Greece, Portugal and Spain. In the Netherlands, Ireland, Greece, Portugal and Spain, revenues from social security contributions increased by more than 68 percent.

These trends were much less pronounced in the US. Although the ratio for

24

social security contributions nearly doubled, it remained well below the EC average. Moreover, the income tax ratio rose only slightly and the product tax ratio dropped some 10 percent.

An issue which has preoccupied the Community from time to time (Neumark, 1963; Deringer, 1964; Fredersdorf, 1978) is the 'proper balance' between direct and indirect taxes. (For this purpose, direct taxes are defined to include the individual income tax, the corporation tax, social security contributions from employers and employees, and various taxes on property; indirect taxes, on the other hand, comprise the value-added tax, excises, and customs duties.) As a closer economic union developed, it was argued, tax harmonization would be facilitated if Member States were to align their direct: indirect tax ratios in the meantime. Direct-tax Member States should reduce their reliance on the income taxes and social security contributions, while indirect-tax states should put less emphasis on revenues from the value-added tax and excises. Whatever the merits of this line of thought, such a trend can hardly be discerned from Table 1.2. In 1965, the Netherlands, Luxembourg, the United Kingdom and Germany were direct-tax countries, in the sense that their direct-tax ratio exceeded the Community's (unweighted) average ratio. The first two countries had clearly maintained that status in 1983, but had been joined by Belgium, Italy and Spain.

## III. COORDINATION OF PRODUCT TAXES

The formation of a true common product market was the most essential objective of the Treaty of Rome. This meant that the Community should ensure both the free movement of goods and equality of competition. Firstly, this involved the elimination of all remaining customs duties and the establishment of a common external tariff. Secondly, the complementary goal of equality of competition meant that Member States should not be allowed to use their internal product taxes, such as sales taxes and excises, to discriminate against goods from other Member States. To this end, unequivocal border tax adjustments based on the destination principle were required. But these adjustments implied that border controls could not be dispensed with forthwith, leaving the Community with the task of removing customs posts.

### A. Abolition of Customs Duties

One of the foremost objectives of the Treaty of Rome was the creation of a true customs union in which all duties on imports and exports would be prohibited and abolished and a common customs tariff adopted with respect to third countries. Essentially, this goal was achieved in 1968, 18 months ahead of

25

*Table 1.3 EC: importance of customs duties revenue*

| Country[a] | 1983 | 1975 | 1965 |
|---|---|---|---|
| | | As Percentage of Gross Domestic Product | |
| *European Community*[b] | *0.5* | *0.6* | *1.1* |
| Portugal | 1.4 | 2.4 | 3.8 |
| Belgium | 0.9 | 0.6 | 1.3 |
| Greece | ... | 1.4 | 2.2 |
| Spain | 0.7 | 0.8 | 1.0 |
| Ireland | 0.6 | 0.5 | 0.8 |
| Netherlands | 0.6 | 0.7 | 2.2 |
| United Kingdom | 0.4 | 0.5 | 1.0 |
| Germany | 0.4 | 0.4 | 0.7 |
| Italy | 0.3 | 0.1 | 0.7 |
| Denmark | 0.3 | 0.4 | 0.8 |
| France | 0.2 | 0.2 | 0.6 |
| Luxembourg | 0.1 | ... | 0.1 |
| *United States* | *0.3* | *0.2* | *0.2* |

*Notes:* a. In descending order of customs duties revenue to GDP ratio in 1983.
b. Weighted averages.
*Source:* Organisation for Economic Co-operation and Development (1985), country tables (heading 5123).

schedule, although, as discussed below, various infringements linger on. Not surprisingly, therefore, the revenue role of customs duties greatly decreased in the period under review. As shown in Table 1.3, the weighted ratio was halved between 1965 and 1983; the coefficient of variation decreased from 80 percent to 69 percent. In the latter year, on average the duties contributed some 1 percent to total tax revenues. Above or below average ratios in some Member States simply mean that more or less external imports enter through them. The revenue role of customs duties in Portugal, Greece and Spain should decrease further as these countries' tariffs are harmonized with that of the Community.

The loss of revenue from the elimination of internal tariffs in the EC might have been made up by an increase in the common external tariff. This did not happen, however, because various general import duty reductions were negotiated among industrial countries under the auspices of the General Agreement on Tariffs and Trade (GATT), lowering tariff levels on non-agricultural goods from some 15 percent in the 1950s to about 5 percent now. As a result, the revenue role of customs duties in the EC and the US moved closer together. In the industrial world, customs duties have become a minor source of revenue. In the EC, proceeds from customs duties collected by the Member States are paid into the common fund as they are considered part of the Community's 'own resources', along with receipts from agricultural levies and a 1.4 percent charge on a uniformly determined value-added tax base (Council, 1972, as amended).

For the internal market, Article 3 (a) of the Treaty requires the elimination not only of customs duties, but also of quantitative restrictions on the import and export of goods, and of all other measures having equivalent effect. The European Court of Justice, called upon to rule on this provision, has broadly interpreted the meaning of this clause. Thus, in Dassonville (Case 8/74), the Court declared that '. . . all trading rules enacted by member states which are capable of hindering, directly or indirectly, actually or potentially, intracommunity trade are to be considered as measures having an effect equivalent to quantitative restrictions.' Derogations from the Article are to be construed strictly, i.e. subject only to those permitted under Article 36 for reasons of public morality, public policy, public security, and the protection of health. Similarly, strict interpretations have been accorded to the prohibition upon charges having an equivalent effect. Thus, the Court has declared to be invalid the imposition of various fees and charges for the issue of import licenses, unloading at borders, the compilation of statistics, and public health, phytosanitary and veterinary inspections carried out at internal borders upon imported or exported products.[5]

To be sure, Article 17(3) permits Member States to convert a customs duty formerly imposed for the purpose of raising revenue into a non-discriminatory excise tax on the same product, but even then the Court will look beyond its mere form and have regard to the substance of the new tax. For example, in Capolongo (Case 77/72), the Court ruled invalid the imposition of an excise tax on cardboard and cellulose containers, whether imported or domestically produced, the proceeds of which were paid into a public corporation that had as its sole purpose the promotion of the domestic production of such products. More generally, the Court has not taken a constructionist attitude to the prohibition of discrimination, but extended its authority beyond a literal examination of the national law, to the nature and economic effects of the tax, the actual characteristics of the product, the economic circumstances of a particular industry, as well as the uses to which the proceeds are put.

When in doubt, the Court has chosen to favor the imported product by ruling that it should not be taxed at a rate higher than the lowest rate applicable to a similar domestic product (Case 148/77). Furthermore in a number of cases (7/68; 51/74), the Court has ruled that Member States are not permitted to tax exports more heavily than goods destined for the domestic market. Finally, a review of the various cases suggests that 'the Court does not ever seem to have taken the view that an action which offends the Treaty becomes less offensive if it is widely practised' (Easson, 1980, para. 16).

---

5. For a detailed description and analysis on which these paragraphs draw, see Easson (1980), paras 9-23, and the literature cited there.

## B. Introduction of Common Value-Added Tax

The founding fathers of the Community clearly realized that the removal of tariffs, quotas, subsidies and other customs barriers would not create a truly common market, if Member States were allowed to maintain or restore through their internal tax systems the discriminatory treatment of trade with other members (Sullivan, 1967). In addition to the prohibition of customs duties, Article 95 therefore prescribes that 'no Member State shall impose, directly or indirectly, on the products of other Member States any internal taxation of any kind in excess of that imposed directly or indirectly on similar domestic products.' This provision reinforces the ban on customs duties, prohibiting the imposition of discriminatory taxes having the same effect (see above) and, more broadly, seeks to ensure conditions of free competition between Community products by removing distortions emanating from national tax systems.

As succeeding articles make plain, free competition of goods crossing intra-Community borders is sought to be achieved through the unequivocal application of the destination principle which holds that goods should be taxed at the rate prevailing in the country in which they are consumed rather than at that in the country in which they are produced (origin principle). To place imports on an equal tax footing as domestic goods, the destination principle entails border tax adjustments under which previously imposed taxes on exports are fully rebated and compensatory taxes are placed on imports equivalent to the internal taxes on domestic goods. As a result, internal taxes do not distort the relative costs between home-produced and foreign-made products. Hence, they are neutral with respect to manufacturing location decisions, an efficiency requirement that is one of the fundamental principles of the Treaty.

Non-discriminatory border tax adjustments could not be applied unambiguously under the cumulative turnover taxes that were levied in all but one of the six original Member States at the time the Treaty was signed in 1957, because the amounts of the export rebates and the compensatory import taxes depended not only on the rate of tax, but also on such unknown factors as the number of times a product had been traded and the amount of value added in various stages. Therefore, border tax adjustments had to be computed on the basis of estimated average rates that might incorporate protectionistic elements. To implement a proper system of border tax adjustments, Article 99 placed a mandatory call upon the EC Commission to submit proposals for the harmonization of turnover taxes, excises, and similar forms of internal taxation.

As described elsewhere in this volume (Cnossen and Shoup), the harmonization of the various turnover taxes was pursued through the Community-wide adoption of a destination-based, tax credit type of value-added tax extending through the retail stage. The tax credit mechanism, permitting sellers a full credit for taxes invoiced by suppliers, ensured that export rebates could be ascertained unambiguously. Furthermore, the value-added tax treated imports in the same way as domestic goods by taxing the former at the same rate and allowing such tax to be offset against the tax payable in succeeding stages. In the case of registered traders, the effective tax rate would always be determined at the retail stage where imports and domestic products would be treated alike.

As shown in Table 1.4, 9 Member States introduced the common value-added tax between 1967 and 1973. Portugal and Spain followed in 1986 and the introduction date for Greece has been set for 1987. The value-added tax has become an important source of revenue, contributing on average 17 percent to total tax revenues, or 6.6 percent of GDP. The revenue role differs widely in various Member States ranging from 5.1 percent of GDP in Luxembourg which imposes a comparatively low standard rate of 12 percent, to 9.8 percent of GDP

*Table 1.4 EC: role of value-added taxes*

| Country[a] | Year VAT Introduced | Standard VAT Rate[b] | | Receipts as Percent of Gross Domestic Product | | | |
|---|---|---|---|---|---|---|---|
| | | 1986 | Year VAT Introduced | 1983 | Year VAT+1 | Year VAT-1 | 1965 |
| *European Community*[c] | – | *17.1* | *12.6* | *6.6* | – | – | *4.6* |
| Denmark | 1967 | 22 | 10 | 9.8 | 6.8 | 3.0 | 2.7 |
| France | 1968 | 18.6 | 16.7 | 9.1 | 9.7 | 8.2 | 8.1 |
| Ireland | 1972 | 23 | 16.4 | 8.3 | 5.1 | 4.3 | 1.5 |
| Belgium | 1971 | 19 | 16 | 7.6 | 6.9 | 7.4 | 6.5 |
| Netherlands | 1969 | 19 | 12 | 7.0 | 5.5 | 5.5 | 4.2 |
| Germany | 1968 | 14 | 10 | 6.4 | 5.7 | 5.0 | 5.2 |
| Italy | 1973 | 18 | 12 | 6.1 | 4.9 | 3.2 | 3.5 |
| United Kingdom | 1973 | 15 | 10 | 5.2 | 3.2 | 2.2 | 1.8 |
| Luxembourg | 1970 | 12 | 8 | 5.1 | 4.1 | 3.0 | 3.8 |
| Greece[d] | – | – | – | 5.0 | – | – | 2.3 |
| Portugal[e] | 1986 | 16 | 16 | 4.7 | – | … | … |
| Spain[f] | 1986 | 12 | 12 | 3.3 | – | … | 3.3 |
| *United States*[g] | – | *4-8* | – | *2.0* | – | – | *1.2* |

*Notes:* a. Listed in descending order of value-added tax revenue to GDP ratio in 1983.
  b. Rates are exclusive of value-added tax.
  c. Weighted averages for GDP ratios.
  d. Revenue figures refer to turnover and manufacturers sales taxes.
  e. Revenue figures refer to previously imposed wholesale tax.
  f. Revenue figures refer to previously imposed turnover tax.
  g. Refers to retail sales taxes levied by 45 states and the District of Columbia.
*Source:* Organisation for Economic Co-operation and Development, *Revenue Statistics*, various years, Table 28 (heading 5100).

in Denmark which applies a high, single rate of 22 percent. The ranking of the tax ratios is not necessarily the same as that of the standard tax rates, because all Member States, except Denmark, also levy reduced and some increased rates of value-added tax on different categories of goods and services. Ireland, for example, has the highest standard rate, but its GDP ratio ranks third, because a broad range of goods and services are zero-rated, as is the case in the United Kingdom. Reportedly, in Italy which also has a high standard rate, a substantial part of the value-added tax is evaded (Pedone, 1981, p. 35). Judging by the increase in the spread of the standard rates, the once expressed goal of rate approximation has become more elusive. The coefficient of variation increased from 21.5 to 26.3.

It may be surmised that the value-added tax has become a mainstay of the revenue structures of various Member States, precisely because agreement has been reached on a uniform basis of assessment. Derogations from this basis are not permitted, implying that the tax base is not subjected to the usual national political forces of erosion. (Admittedly, Ireland and the United Kingdom still retain a zero rate for certain domestic products, but eventually this rate has to be phased out.) There is a weak presumption, therefore, that Member States may exploit the value-added tax base more fully than that of other taxes, thus enlarging the role and scope of their public sector. Some evidence for this proposition may be found in the increase in the average standard rate by 4.5 percentage points, or 36 percent of the average starting rate. Moreover, the weighted ratio of sales tax receipts to GDP since 1965 increased by 43 percent, well in excess of the increase in the total tax ratio of 31 percent. Although nearly all governments professed that the changeover to the value-added tax would be revenue-neutral, on average, revenues increased by 24 percent after the change.[6] The revenue role of the retail sales taxes that are levied in 45 out of 50 states (and the District of Columbia) in the US is much more modest than that of the value-added tax in the EC.[7]

### C. Excise Tax Developments

Developments in the excise tax field have been very different from those of the value-added tax. As shown in Table 1.5, excise revenues decreased on average from some 5 percent of GDP in 1965 to about 3 percent in 1983. Ninety percent of such revenues derives from three products: tobacco, alcohol and mineral oil. The tobacco excise ratio dropped sharply, but the other two ratios decreased too. A similar trend occurred in the US, suggesting that some common

---

6. For a view that the value-added tax did not necessarily increase government spending, see Stockfish (1985).
7. For a survey and analysis of sales taxes in OECD member countries, see Cnossen (1983c).

*Table 1.5 EC: importance of excise tax revenues*

| Country[a] | Total | | Tobacco | | Alcohol | | Petroleum Products | | Other[b] | |
|---|---|---|---|---|---|---|---|---|---|---|
| | 1983 | 1965 | 1983 | 1965 | 1983 | 1965 | 1983 | 1965 | 1983 | 1965 |
| | As Percentage of Gross Domestic Product | | | | | | | | | |
| *European Community*[c] | *3.2* | *4.7* | *0.8* | *1.4* | *0.5* | *0.7* | *1.6* | *1.9* | *0.2* | *0.5* |
| Ireland | 8.0 | 10.2 | 1.7 | 4.1 | 2.6 | 2.9 | 2.7 | 2.5 | 0.2 | 0.1 |
| Denmark | 5.7 | 7.8 | 1.1 | ... | 1.1 | ... | 1.1 | ... | 1.1 | ... |
| United Kingdom | 4.7 | 6.6 | 1.2 | 2.8 | 1.2 | 1.7 | 2.0 | 2.0 | – | – |
| Luxembourg | 4.3 | 3.0 | ... | ... | ... | ... | ... | ... | ... | ... |
| Italy | 3.3 | 5.5 | 0.7 | 1.4 | 0.1 | 0.2 | 2.2 | 2.5 | 0.3 | 1.4 |
| Germany | 2.7 | 3.5 | 0.8 | 1.0 | 0.4 | 0.6 | 1.4 | 1.6 | 0.1 | 0.3 |
| Netherlands | 2.6 | 2.7 | 0.6 | 0.9 | 0.5 | 0.5 | 1.0 | 1.1 | 0.1 | 0.1 |
| Belgium | 2.4 | 2.5 | 0.7 | 0.6 | 0.4 | 0.5 | 1.2 | 1.3 | 0.1 | 0.1 |
| France | 2.4 | 3.8 | 0.3 | 0.7 | 0.3 | 0.2 | 1.5 | 2.0 | 0.2 | 0.8 |
| *United States* | *2.0* | *3.3* | *0.3* | *0.5* | *0.3* | *0.7* | *0.3* | *0.7* | *0.8* | *0.8* |

*Notes:* a. In descending order of total excise tax revenue to GDP ratio in 1983.

b. Excluding revenues from special excises on the purchase of automobiles (which are subject to higher value-added tax rates elsewhere) and user charges in Ireland, Denmark, the United Kingdom, the Netherlands and the United States. However, these revenues are included in total excise tax revenues.

c. Weighted averages.

*Source:* Organisation for Economic Co-operation and Development (1985), country tables, headings 5121 and 5122.

influences have been at work. Awareness of the harmful effects of smoking has resulted in a decline of per capita tobacco consumption. Per capita consumption of alcohol, on the other hand, doubled in the period under review as social bans on drinking were relaxed and retail outlet policies liberalized (Cnossen, 1981). To cushion the effects of major price increases in mineral oil products, the real value of the related excises declined more sharply (Tait and Morgan, 1980). With the exception of part of the duty on cigarettes, most excises are specific. In the absence of periodic discretionary adjustments, therefore, inflation has eroded their real value. Furthermore, several EC Member States are major producers of wine, beer and spirits, creating political pressures to keep duties low.

Although Article 99 of the Treaty of Rome mentions excises in the same breath as sales taxes as prime candidates for harmonization, so far progress has been excruciatingly slow. A working party was established as early as 1960 and the Neumark Report (1963, p. 127) emphasized that excises should be harmonized in step with the sales tax, but it was not until 1972 that the EC Commission issued a framework-directive outlining the features of a possible harmonization policy. The Commission classified the excises in the Member States into four main groups:

(1) Harmonized excises to be levied in all Member States on tobacco products, alcoholic beverages, and petroleum products; agreement on common definitions for the various bases of assessment should be followed by rate unification.

(2) Excises, e.g. on matches, playing cards, and gramophone records, to be incorporated in increased value-added tax rates, and thereby eliminated; of course, this begged the question of the eventual removal of border controls.

(3) Excises, e.g. on entertainment and betting, that might be retained because they do not involve border tax adjustments or affect trade between Member States.

(4) Excises to be abolished, because their contribution to revenue is negligible, because they are levied on products imported from developing countries (e.g. coffee), or because they are in large part a raw material for industry (e.g. sugar).

From the beginning, the concern has mainly been with the traditional excises on tobacco products, alcoholic beverages, and petroleum products (and related taxes on motoring). Since nearly all these products are processed in large manufacturing establishments that are integrated forward with the export stage, the application of proper border tax adjustments has not been a problem, but rather the focus has been on infringements of the non-discrimination principle of Article 95.[8] According to the Commission (1980, pp. 31 and 57), 'the symbiotic relationship between national industries and national excises has resulted in excise structures that discriminate against products of other Member States.' And in the same vein, real or feigned concern with national social and health policies 'generally result in preferential treatment of domestic production.'

Until a few years ago, for instance, France and Italy imposed substantially higher excises on spirits made from cereals, such as gin, whisky and vodka, than on spirits distilled from wine, such as cognac, armagnac and calvados. Since the cereal distillates were all imported, in effect the excise structures of these countries favored domestic products, although there was no open discrimination on the basis of origin. Similarly, Denmark had a separate rate for akqavit, which was taxed at only two-thirds the rate imposed on brandy, gin, rum and whisky, which were mostly imported. Upon complaints filed by the EC Commission, the Court of Justice (Cases 168-171/78) ruled that all these products stood in a competitive relationship to each other. Hence, the non-discrimination principle of Article 95 implied that the tax on an imported product could not exceed the tax on a comparable domestic product. In another case (55/79), it was held that Ireland discriminated against imported products by affording Irish producers preferential treatment with regard to the time

8. For an analysis of the non-discrimination principle of Article 95, see Easson (1980), paras 23-66. For a description of excise tax harmonization, also paras 218-51.

*Table 1.6 EC: examples of excise taxes, March 1985*

| Member State | 20 Cigarettes[a] | 1 Liter of Beer | 1 Liter of Wine | 0.75 Liter of 40% Spirits | 1 Liter of Premium Petrol |
|---|---|---|---|---|---|
| | | | In European Currency Units | | |
| Ireland | 1.14 (75) | 1.14 | 2.74 | 7.84 | 0.36 |
| Denmark | 1.96 (87) | 0.65 | 1.35 | 9.58 | 0.28 |
| United Kingdom | 1.25 (75) | 0.70 | 1.60 | 7.70 | 0.29 |
| Luxembourg | 0.54 (67) | 0.06 | 0.13 | 2.54 | 0.20 |
| Italy | 0.57 (72) | 0.18 | – | 0.75 | 0.49 |
| Germany | 1.02 (74) | 0.07 | – | 3.43 | 0.23 |
| Netherlands | 0.74 (72) | 0.23 | 0.33 | 3.79 | 0.28 |
| Belgium | 0.73 (71) | 0.13 | 0.33 | 3.78 | 0.25 |
| France | 0.31 (75) | 0.03 | 0.03 | 3.37 | 0.36 |
| *Unweighted Average* | *0.92 (74)* | *0.35* | *0.93* | *4.75* | *0.30* |

*Note:* a. Figures in parentheses indicate the proportion of excise and value-added tax in consumer price of the most popular price category of cigarettes.
*Source:* Commission of the European Communities (1985).

limits for payment of the excises. The United Kingdom lost its case (170/78) against the Commission on the relative tax burdens to be imposed on wine and beer. The Commission took the view that the ratio of the two excises should not exceed that of the alcoholic strength of an average table wine and the most popular beer. This pointed to a ratio of 3:1, since table wine is typically 11 percent alcohol by volume and beer about 3.5 percent.

Although the Court's decisions may have eliminated the most obvious forms of discrimination, considerable differences continue to exist in the level and the structure of the various excises on alcoholic drinks. As shown in Table 1.6, duty levels are particularly high in Denmark, Ireland and the United Kingdom. Furthermore, Italy (and Greece) do not levy a wine excise at all and Germany confines its excise to sparkling wine. National vinicultures are further protected by rate structure distinctions between wine from fresh grapes and fruits, ordinary and fortified wines, and still and sparkling wines. In vain the Commission has attempted to reach agreement on common bases of assessment and collection, let alone the different rate structures. Basically, harmonization is still where it stood in 1972 when the Commission formulated as points of departure: (a) all Member States to impose some excise on wines; (b) spirits to be taxed on the basis of alcoholic strength; (c) both wine and beer to be taxed by volume (possibly at different rates within as well as between the two categories); and (d) tax on beer to be assessed at the product stage rather than on the wort which requires discretion in the taxation of imports.

More progress has been made with the harmonization of the various tobacco excises, possibly because most raw tobacco is imported, production is highly concentrated, cost differentials are small, and there is a widespread consensus on the harmful effects of smoking. Common definitions of manufactured tobacco products have been agreed upon (an important prerequisite for excise harmonization), as well as a phased reduction of the specific element (a fixed monetary amount per weight unit) in the excise (allegedly favoring expensive imported blond tobaccos), from 5-75 percent in 1972, to 5-55 percent in 1977, and further to 10-35 percent as proposed in 1980. Eventually a target ratio of 20 percent is envisaged, resulting in a predominantly ad valorem regime. But agreement will probably be hard to reach. The ratio of specific to total tax is 5 in southern EC-countries, but above 40 in most northern Member States. Here, tax principle and politics are clearly at loggerheads (Kay and Keen, this volume). Retail prices of representative brands of cigarettes differ considerably in the EC, but this should primarily be attributed to the differences in quality. Effective tax rates (defined as the sum of excise and value-added tax, expressed as a percentage of the tax-inclusive retail price) lie within the fairly narrow range of 67-75 percent, excepting Denmark (Table 1.6).

In contrast, progress in harmonizing the taxes on motoring has been very slow. The Commission has attempted in vain to reach agreement on a draft directive for a uniform basis of assessment for the fuel excises. Also it has submitted proposals to the Council of Ministers to eliminate any double taxation of motor vehicles, to standardize national systems of taxes on lorries, to exempt the temporary importation of certain means of transport, and to standardize the tax-free admission of fuel in fuel tanks. Thus far only the draft directive exempting 50 liters of fuel in motor vehicle tanks has been approved, although the harmonization of the excises on diesel oil and liquified petroleum gas, as well as the exemptions and special-purpose reduced rates applied in some Member States, is of special importance (Commission, 1980). Except in Italy and Luxembourg, petrol excises are fairly closely aligned in the EC, ranging from 0.23 ECU in Germany to 0.36 ECU in France and Ireland (Table 1.6).

The Commission has not issued any specific directives for the harmonization of the nuisance excises levied in various Member States: for revenue purposes (sugar, soft drinks), as proxies for taxpaying capacity (consumer durables, cosmetics), or as relics of the past (salt, matches, playing cards). Judged by their contribution to GDP, it is surprising that these excises have not been eliminated long ago; the yield of most does not exceed 1/10 of 1 percent of GDP. They might be harmonized spontaneously if border controls for the major excises were removed (Cnossen, 1983b).

### D. Removal of Border Controls and Non-Tariff Barriers

The abolition of customs duties, the adoption of a common value-added tax with appropriate border tax adjustments, and some small steps toward excise harmonization have had little, if any, effect on the removal of internal border controls. Customs posts, mainly engaged in collecting and rebating national taxes, still straddle nearly every internal frontier. As the Deringer Report (1964) prophetically observed more than 20 years ago: 'On this basis, it will still be necessary in twenty years' time to open one's case between Emmerich and Arnhem, Wasserbillig and Trier, between Erquelines and Jeumont, between Strassbourg and Kehl, Ventimiglia and Menton, to prove to customs that one has not wrapped cigars inside one's pyjama's.'

To prevent this prophecy from having another 20 years' validity, the EC Commission (1985) has recently submitted a White Paper with a large number of clear and concise proposals (together with a detailed timetable for action) for removing physical, technical, and fiscal barriers between the Member States. Fiscal barriers comprise the border controls to implement the border tax adjustments for the value-added tax and the excises. To eliminate these controls for the value-added tax, initially a deferred payment system is to be introduced under which export rebates are granted on the basis of documentary evidence and the collection of the compensatory import tax is shifted inland to the first production or distribution stage. In a following phase – marking a major departure from earlier insistence on the adoption of the origin principle – a Community-wide destination principle would be maintained by mutual recognition of each Member State's tax credits shown on exporters' invoices, balances being settled through a common clearing house. For the excises, border controls would become unnecessary by linking national systems of excise suspension.

If fiscal barriers are removed by shifting border tax adjustments to books of account and linking the bonded warehouse systems for excisable products in individual Member States, cross-border shopping would become advantageous if tax rates differed widely, especially between adjoining Member States. Some 40 million people in the EC live along intra-Community borders. The abolition of customs posts might have unacceptable revenue consequences, the Commission believes, if some approximation of rates were not achieved. With the exception of Denmark and Ireland, this should be possible if the revenue picture for the value-added taxes and the excises is considered jointly. Variations in the total yield of these two major indirect taxes are considerably smaller than variations in the yield of either tax category.

Costs having the same effect as customs duties would, of course, continue to divide the Community if different product regulations and standards for health or safety reasons, environmental or consumer protection, that effectively impede entry, are permitted to remain in place.[9] To remove these technical, non-tariff barriers, the Commission (1985) proposes to accept as the guiding principle that if a product is lawfully manufactured and marketed in one

9. For an analysis of the various non-tariff barriers in the EC whose removal is desirable for completing the internal market, see Pelkmans and Vanheukelen (1986).

Member State, it should be allowed to be sold freely throughout the Community. Essential health and safety requirements should be harmonized, as well as industrial standards in the fields of technology and telecommunications, construction, and the production of foodstuffs. Furthermore, public procurement, which covers a sizeable part of each Member State's GDP, should be liberalized and the Community's restrictive policies on state aids vigorously enforced. Finally, physical barriers would be done away with through the implementation of the single administrative (customs) document, the coordination of immigration policies and the adoption of common public health standards, the liberalization of the transport quota system and the enforcement of common protective measures relating to terrorism, drugs and crime.

## IV. COORDINATION OF INCOME TAXES

Although the founding fathers of the EC were concerned chiefly with the removal of competitive distortions in product markets, the free movement of persons, services and capital is also one of the fundamental aims of the Treaty of Rome. According to Title III, such free movement includes freedom of establishment, the abolition of restrictions on the movement of capital belonging to residents of other Member States and of discrimination based on the nationality or residence of persons or firms. It was recognized that, as with product taxes, differences in income taxes might distort competitive conditions. Therefore, Article 220 requires that Member States enter into negotiations with a view to abolishing any double taxation of residents and firms of other Member States. Furthermore, Article 221 provides that Member States shall accord nationals of other States the same treatment as their own nationals with respect to the participation in the capital of companies or firms.

As the Neumark Report (1963) stood at the beginning of the formation of an integrated product market, so the Segré Report (1966) stands at the cradle of the establishment of an integrated capital market. According to the Report, tax considerations should not influence the choice of investment location, or the choice between direct and branch investment. International double taxation of investment income, various tax incentives, and the differential treatment of non-resident and corporate investments were identified as the chief obstacles to the free movement of capital. Many of the recommendations of the Segré Committee Report were adopted in the Commission's (1967) 'Programme for the Harmonisation of Direct Taxes'. It envisaged the liberalization of capital movements, among others through the introduction of the same type of corporation tax, based upon broadly similar methods of assessment and rates. Beyond this, a single comprehensive individual income tax should be introduced which, however, would continue to differ from one Member State to another for a long time to come.

## A. Approximation of Corporation Taxes

Table 1.7 shows the various corporation tax systems in the EC, related tax ratios, effective standard tax rates, the extent to which corporation taxes are integrated with individual income taxes, and dividend withholding rates. Since the Treaty of Rome, 7 Member States have introduced an imputation system that permits shareholders a partial or full credit (if local taxes are not taken into account) for the corporation tax that can be attributed to the dividends received by them. Three members – Luxembourg, the Netherlands and Spain – still regard the corporation as an entity entirely separate from its shareholders and consequently tax distributed profits again in the hands of shareholders (classical system). Like Germany under its imputation system, Portugal has a split-rate system under which a lower rate of tax is levied on distributed profits, and Greece's corporation tax permits a deduction for dividends from taxable profits, as is commonly done for interest. The United States has a classical system of corporation tax.[10]

In 1983, the weighted average corporation tax ratio was 2.6 in the EC, up from 2.1 in 1965. Apart from a possible relative rise in corporate profits and rate increases, several special factors may have influenced these developments. In the Netherlands, for instance, incorporation rules were substantially liberalized in 1970 and nearly half of corporation tax revenue derives from natural gas operations. The general rise in the ratios since 1975 contrasts with earlier research (Conrad, 1974) that concluded that corporation taxes were a declining source of revenue due to erosion of the tax base (tax incentives), increased capital-intensity of manufacturing (higher initial write-offs), and a shift in economies to service industries (larger wage bills). On the other hand, this trend is clearly observable in the US where the corporation tax ratio decreased from 4.2 in 1965 to 1.6 in 1983, because of numerous special concessions to industry. The increased revenue importance of the corporation tax levied in various US states was more than offset by the declining importance of the federal tax.

For imputation countries, corporation tax ratios differ widely in the EC, ranging from 1.4 in Denmark that levies a low rate of 40 percent on company profits, to 4.1 in the United Kingdom where the rate is 52 percent. In comparing these ratios with those of other systems of corporation tax, it should be noted that the yields of the imputation systems include the creditable 'income tax portion', whereas other systems, of course, leave the income tax out of account. Substantial differences exist also in the rates of tax credit permitted under imputation systems, ranging from 34 percent of the corporation tax rate in Italy to 64 percent in Germany. Similarly, withholding rates on distributed profits differ widely.

---

10. For a description and analysis of the various corporation tax systems in the EC and other industrial countries, see Cnossen (1983a, 1984). For an early treatment of the international implications, also Sato and Bird (1975), and for the classic analysis, McLure (1979).

## Table 1.7 EC: role of corporation taxes

| Country[a] | Revenues as Percent of GDP | | | Statutory Tax Rate [b,c,d] | Tax Credit as Percent of Statutory Tax Rate[e] | Dividend Withholding Rate |
|---|---|---|---|---|---|---|
| | 1983 | 1975 | 1965 | | | |
| *European Community* | *2.6* | *1.9* | *2.1* | | | |
| A.  Imputation System | | | | | | |
| United Kingdom | 4.1 | 2.2 | 2.2 | 52 | 39.6 | 0/15 |
| Italy | 3.8 | 1.8 | 1.9 | 40.5 | 34.2 (100) | 0/30 |
| Belgium | 2.7 | 3.0 | 1.9 | 45 | 49.9 | 15 |
| France | 1.9 | 2.0 | 1.8 | 50 | 50 | 0/25 |
| Germany | 1.9 | 1.6 | 2.5 | 63.3/46.7 | 64.1 (100) | 5/25 |
| Ireland | 1.5 | 1.5 | 2.4 | 50 | 42.9 | 0 |
| Denmark | 1.4 | 1.3 | 1.4 | 40 | 37.5 | 15 |
| B.  Other Systems | | | | | | |
| Luxembourg | 7.4 | 5.7 | 3.4 | 47.3 | – | 0/15 |
| Netherlands[f] | 2.9 | 3.4 | 2.7 | 43 | – | 0/25 |
| Spain | 1.3 | 1.4 | 1.4 | 35 | – | 10/18 |
| Greece[g] | 0.8 | 0.9 | 0.4 | 48.5 | – | 25/42 |
| Portugal | ... | ... | ... | 52/40 | – | 10/15 |
| *United States[f,h]* | *1.6* | *3.2* | *4.2* | *50.3* | – | *30* |

*Notes:*  a. Listed in descending order of corporation tax revenue to GDP ratio in 1983.

b. In computing the total standard rate –
  (i)  local corporation tax rates (on an average basis if differentiated) are included in Germany, Italy, Luxembourg, and the United States;
  (ii)  surcharges or surtaxes are included in Italy, Luxembourg, and Portugal;
  (iii)  the statutory tax-exclusive local tax rates in Germany and Luxembourg have been converted to tax-inclusive rates as follows: $t_i = t_e/(1 + t_e)$ where $t_i$ is the tax-inclusive rate and $t_e$ the tax-exclusive rate;
  (iv)  local taxes on corporate profits are deductible in computing taxable profits for the national corporation tax in Germany, Italy, Luxembourg, and the United States; the effective total corporation tax rate then equals $t_s(100 - t_i) + t_i$ where $t_s$ is the statutory national tax rate and $t_i$ the (effective) tax-inclusive local tax rate.

c. Some countries levy higher corporation tax rates on specified mining (petroleum) companies (Netherlands, Spain), higher rates on non-resident companies (Belgium), or lower rates on manufacturing and processing operations (Ireland).

d. Lower corporation tax rates on small profits or, sometimes, small corporations are levied in Belgium, Ireland, Luxembourg, Portugal, the United Kingdom, and the United States.

e. Figures in parentheses indicate tax credit percentages without taking account of local taxes.

f. The Netherlands, France, and the United States exempt a small amount of dividend income in the shareholder's hands.

g. At the shareholder's option, dividend income is exempt.

h. In addition to the regular corporation tax, a tax of 15 percent, called an add-on minimum tax, is imposed on preference items.

*Sources:*  Organisation for Economic Co-operation and Development (1985), Table 12; Cnossen (1984); Berger (1985); and Alworth (this volume).

Although the corporation tax is not a major source of revenue in any EC Member State, even corporations that pay little or no tax are still subjected to all its complexities, attendant compliance costs and excess burdens, causing a substantial misallocation of resources in Member States themselves, as well as throughout the Community. Evidence for this may be found in a recent study (Kopits, 1982) dealing with factor prices in industrial countries. Based on 1978 data, the study estimated that 'required' rates of return, which incorporate the effects of inflation and interest rates, ranged from a low of 5 percent in Italy to almost 18 percent in Germany. These figures indicate that the need to coordinate the systems of taxing company profits and distributions, as well as the removal of various non-tax barriers, are at least as important as in the case of the sales taxes and excises (also Neumark, 1963).

In line with its 1967 Programme, the Commission directed its attention first to the choice of the most appropriate type of corporation tax, focusing specifically on reducing the so-called economic double taxation of dividends arising under the classical system, and the coordination of the systems of withholding tax charged on dividends. In 1975, the Commission issued a draft directive calling for the adoption of an imputation system with a normal, single rate of corporation tax ranging from 45 percent to 55 percent, together with a 45-55 percent income tax credit on grossed-up dividends. Whether directly or through a subsidiary, source countries should extend their tax credit to shareholders in other Member States and bear its cost through a so-called clearing-house mechanism. Furthermore, dividend withholding tax rates were to be set at a uniform rate of 25 percent. The draft-Directive got stranded in the European Parliament (1979), however, which argued that it made little sense to harmonize corporation tax rates and the tax treatment of profit distributions as long as, possibly large, differences in the rules for computing taxable company income continued to exist between Member States. This will be the subject of a White Paper which the Commission intends to publish shortly (see Andel, this volume).

### B. Individual Income Taxes

For reasons broadly explained earlier, the role of the individual income tax in the tax structure of the various Member States has greatly increased in importance in recent decades. As shown in Table 1.8, the weighted average income tax ratio rose from 6.4 in 1965 to 9.8 in 1983, or by 53 percent. Apart from the wide acceptance of income as the most equitable tax base, various administrative and technical reasons account for the prominent place of the income tax. Thus, the universal expansion of wage withholding schemes in conjunction with the concentration of employment in larger and better organized production units has made PAYE the mainstay of income tax

*Table 1.8 EC: role of individual income taxes*

| Country[a] | Revenue as Percent of GDP | | | Effective Tax Rate 1984[b] | | Rate Band 1983 |
|---|---|---|---|---|---|---|
| | 1983 | 1975 | 1965 | Single People | Two-Child Family | |
| *European Community[c]* | *9.8* | *8.8* | *6.4* | | | |
| Denmark | 24.0 | 23.1 | 12.4 | 39.6 | 33.8 | 14.4 - 39.6 |
| Belgium | 15.9 | 13.1 | 6.3 | 21.4 | 13.6 | 17  - 72[d] |
| Ireland | 11.6 | 8.0 | 4.3 | 25.9 | 15.6 | 25  - 65 |
| Luxembourg | 11.6 | 10.1 | 7.6 | 17.3 | 2.6 | 12  - 57[d] |
| Italy | 11.3 | 4.4 | 3.0 | 17.4 | 14.0 | 18  - 65 |
| Germany | 10.6 | 10.8 | 8.2 | 17.6 | 10.7 | 22  - 56[d] |
| United Kingdom | 10.5 | 13.6 | 9.1 | 22.1 | 17.6 | 30  - 60 |
| Netherlands | 10.1 | 11.8 | 9.3 | 11.8 | 9.3 | 17  - 72 |
| France | 6.0 | 4.6 | 3.7 | 7.7 | 0.0 | 5  - 65[d] |
| Spain | 5.8 | 2.8 | 2.1 | 13.4 | 8.9 | 15.72- 65 |
| Greece | 4.3 | 2.3 | 1.5 | 3.3 | 1.7 | 11  - 63.4[d] |
| Portugal | ... | ... | ... | 7.1 | 6.0 | 4  - 80 |
| *United States* | *10.8* | *9.8* | *8.0* | *22.9* | *15.2* | *11  - 50[d]* |

*Notes:* a. In descending order of income tax revenue to GDP ratio in 1983.

b. Imposed on average earnings of an adult full-time production worker in the manufacturing sector after making allowance for standard tax reliefs unrelated to the actual expenses incurred by taxpayers.

c. Weighted averages.

d. Countries with zero-rated first brackets.

*Sources:* Organisation for Economic Co-operation and Development: (1985), Table 10; (1986a), Table 1; and (1986b), Table 1.10.

revenues. Like the value-added tax, the income tax has become less visible, reducing taxpayer resistance. In the Netherlands, for instance, wage withholding now accounts for 82 percent of income tax collections against 49 percent in 1965.

Furthermore, as pointed out by Messere (1983), the sharp rise in the income tax ratio between 1965 and 1975 should probably be attributed to uncorrected fiscal drag. With incomes growing in real terms, taxpayers were pushed into higher brackets. This effect was exacerbated by inflation which lowered real income brackets and eroded the real value of tax allowances. The income tax ratio has also been pushed up by a switch in aid to families from tax allowances to cash transfers, as well as by limitations in various Member States on the deductibility of mortgage interest, especially for second homes. From 1975 onwards, on the other hand, the upward effect of inflationary fiscal drag was substantially offset by automatic rate adjustments (indexation) and discretionary changes in most Member States, except Italy and to a lesser extent Belgium and Spain (OECD, 1986c). Similarly, the switch from joint to separate taxation of two-earner couples may have slowed down the increase in the ratio. Last but not least, the increase in social security contributions, which in most Member States are deductible in computing taxable income (Table 1.9), must have acted as a brake on the rising income tax ratio.

Even a perfunctory glance at one of the tax summary handbooks issued by various accounting firms indicates that the determination of taxable income and the rate structures that are applied differ greatly from one Member State to another. Numerous special allowances and credits exist for small and unincorporated firms. Capital gains, not arising in the course of business, either are not taxable or are subject to a preferential rate. Furthermore, there are substantial differences in various deductions and personal allowances, the aggregation or separate taxation of family income, the initial and maximum rate of tax, and the comparable income brackets to which they are applied (for a full treatment, see OECD, 1986b). Consequently, the effective tax rate applicable to a single person earning the average industrial wage of a Member State may range from as little as 3 percent of his earnings in Greece to nearly 26 percent in Ireland.[11] Similarly, when deductions are made for family benefits, a married couple with two children may pay no tax in France but 18 percent in the United Kingdom. Not surprisingly, income tax ratios range from 4 in Greece to 16 in Belgium.

In view of the overriding concern with ensuring the free movement of goods and to a lesser extent capital, the harmonization of the individual income tax has received far less attention than the proper coordination of the product taxes and the corporation tax. To be sure various committees (e.g. Neumark, 1963) have advocated the introduction of a similar type of global income tax with a similar bracket structure (but not similar rates) and in its 'Programme for the Harmonisation of Direct Taxes', the Commission (1967) envisaged a single comprehensive personal income tax, but in the same breath it was stated that such a tax would differ from one Member State to another for a long time to come. Apparently, considerations of competitive distortions on account of wage-tax-induced labor costs, the free movement of workers and executives, as well as the requirements of a free capital market, did not feature as prominently in the income tax field as in other areas of taxation. More recently, the Fredersdorf Report (1978) concluded that it was not essential to harmonize the income tax. More fundamentally, Burke (1979), then a member of the Commission, stated: 'it is not our ambition to harmonise the personal income tax in general, which is an important instrument of national policy and should be left to the Member States even when the Community achieves a much higher degree of integration than at present'.

11. The effective tax rate is 40 in Denmark, but since this country in effect has integrated the social security contributions with the income tax, the figure is not comparable with those in other Member States.

However, a notable exception has always been made for the (wage) income tax of frontier and migrant workers. Although double taxation both in the resident state (where the employee would have his home and family) and the source state (where he derives income from employment) is generally avoided under tax agreements, troublesome questions remain with respect to the (non-) aggregation of income, applicable rates, deductions and allowances. Various cases, for instance, Sotgiu (Case 152/73), involving the denial of allowances for non-resident family members, have been referred to the European Court of Justice which has considered that a rule based upon residence may conceal a discrimination based upon nationality. But granting an allowance to a non-resident worker may involve a double concession if the same allowance is extended by the resident country. Generally, full taxation in the resident country with a credit for tax paid in the source country would be the solution.

## C. Social Security Contributions

Revenues from social security contributions rose as sharply between 1965 and 1983 as revenues from the individual income tax with which they are usually closely associated. The base on which both levies are imposed is often the same. Generally, employees' social security contributions are withheld along with the wage tax that forms a prepayment for the income tax. The major difference between the two levies concerns the rate structure and the assumed tax burden distribution. Social security contributions are payable on the first unit of earnings. Based on the insurance philosophy, moreover, rates are usually proportional and vanish beyond a prescribed income ceiling.[12] Ignoring benefits, therefore, the burden distribution should be regressive.

As shown in Table 1.9, the weighted average ratio of total social security contributions in the EC was 13.6 in 1983. This is nearly 40 percent above the average income tax ratio of 9.8. The Netherlands and France, which adhere strongly to the insurance view, collect some 20 percent of GDP in the form of social security contributions. In Ireland and the United Kingdom on the other hand, ratios are respectively 6 and 7. In Denmark, contributions are virtually indistinguishable from the individual income tax with which they are nearly fully integrated.

Employers' contributions, usually significantly higher than employees' contributions, have increased at a somewhat greater rate than employees' contributions, possibly because they are even less visible and their incidence is even more uncertain. Employers' contributions are particularly high in Italy and France where they account for over 40 percent of the wage bill for an

12. For arguments that most industrial countries have moved away from the insurance principle to the perception that contributions are just another tax, see Messere (1983).

*Table 1.9 EC: role of social security contributions*

| Country[a] | Revenues as Percent of Gross Domestic Product | | | | | | | | Effective Rate Employees' Contri- bution 1984[c] | Deductible from Income |
|---|---|---|---|---|---|---|---|---|---|---|
| | Total | | Employees | | Employers | | Other[b] | | | |
| | 1983 | 1965 | 1983 | 1965 | 1983 | 1965 | 1983 | 1965 | | |
| European Community[d] | *13.6* | *8.1* | *4.5* | *2.7* | *8.2* | *4.9* | *1.0* | *0.5* | | |
| Netherlands | 21.3 | 10.3 | 9.4 | 5.1 | 8.4 | 4.2 | 3.5 | 1.0 | 27.4 | Yes[e] |
| France | 19.6 | 11.9 | 5.2 | 2.3 | 13.0 | 8.9 | 1.4 | 0.7 | 14.8 | Yes |
| Italy | 14.6 | ... | 2.9 | ... | 10.4 | ... | 1.3 | ... | 9.5 | Yes |
| Belgium | 13.9 | 9.7 | 4.8 | 2.7 | 7.9 | 6.3 | 1.2 | 0.7 | 12.1 | Yes |
| Germany | 13.3 | 8.5 | 5.9 | 3.7 | 7.2 | 4.6 | 0.2 | 0.2 | 16.8 | Yes[f] |
| Spain | 12.2 | 4.2 | 2.4 | 1.0 | 9.1 | 3.2 | 0.7 | – | 6.0 | Yes |
| Greece | 11.7 | ... | 5.0 | ... | 5.0 | ... | 1.7 | ... | 13.2 | Yes |
| Luxembourg | 10.6 | 9.9 | 4.5 | 3.6 | 5.5 | 5.7 | 0.6 | 0.6 | 12.2 | Yes |
| Portugal | 8.5 | 4.0 | 3.3 | 1.6 | 5.0 | 2.4 | 0.2 | – | 11.5 | Yes |
| United Kingdom | 6.7 | 4.7 | 3.1 | 2.2 | 3.5 | 2.3 | 0.1 | 0.2 | 9.0 | No |
| Ireland | 5.8 | 1.7 | 2.1 | 0.8 | 3.7 | 0.9 | – | – | 8.5 | Fixed |
| Denmark | 1.8 | 1.6 | 0.9 | 1.1 | 0.9 | 0.5 | – | – | 5.5 | Yes[g] |
| *United States* | *8.3* | *4.3* | *3.2* | *1.7* | *4.9* | *2.5* | *0.2* | *0.1* | *6.7* | *No* |

*Notes:*
  a. In descending order of social security contributions to GDP ratio in 1983.
  b. Self-employed or non-employed and unallocable receipts. Does not include voluntary contributions to government and/or compulsory contributions to the private sector. See Part C of OECD (1985) on the financing of social security benefits.
  c. Expressed as a percentage of gross earnings of two-child families. This percentage is the same as for single people, except in Denmark (6.2) and Greece (13.3).
  d. Weighted averages.
  e. Except health insurance contributions.
  f. Subject to a ceiling.
  g. If within heading 2100 of OECD classification.

*Sources:* Organisation for Economic Co-operation and Development: (1985), Tables 16 and 18; (1986a), Table 3; and (1986b), Table 1.6.

average worker (OECD, 1983). As a percentage of gross earnings, employees' contributions range from 6 percent in Spain to 27 percent in the Netherlands (Table 1.9).[13]

Although the Treaty of Rome envisages some approximation of social policies and the Commission's 'Social Action Programme' (1974) mentions social security contributions and the benefits they are meant to finance, generally harmonization of the various systems is not perceived as necessary or considered feasible at the present stage. The issues involved are probably even more intractable politically than in the case of the individual income tax. Again, an exception has been made for the taxation of social security benefits of

13. See footnote 11.

frontier and migrant workers. To ensure that they are treated the same as residents, the Community has attempted to provide for the aggregation of qualifying periods and for the payment of benefits to persons anywhere in the Community. Double taxation is avoided under bilateral agreements.

## D. Removal of Non-Tax Barriers

The Commission (1985) believes that the economies of scale offered by a large common market cannot be reaped readily if various obstacles to industrial cooperation remain in place. National laws and administrative practices hamper the development of cross-border activities by companies of different Member States. For this purpose, the European Economic Interest Grouping, governed by Community legislation, is being set up and a proposed statute for a European Company has been put up for a Council decision. Furthermore, national legislation on limited companies will be coordinated and the legal position of branches and subsidiaries clarified. The acquisition of holdings in companies in other Member States and cross-border mergers are to be facilitated. In turn, of course, these proposals have tax aspects that may well be the most important obstacle to eventual agreement. So far anyway, fear of revenue loss, either directly or through emigration of companies to lower-tax Member States, have stalled progress.

In the Commission's view, the liberalization of financial services would be a necessary adjunct to achieving greater industrial cooperation and integration. 'Financial products' provided by the banking and insurance sectors should move as freely as 'physical products'. Harmonization measures in this area should be based on the principale of 'home-country control', but standards of financial stability, accounting rules, and rules of supervision should be coordinated. Similar coordinating activities are developed in the areas of securities, savings contracts, consumer credits, etc. Beyond this, measures are planned to open up new service areas in information marketing and audiovisual services.

Nearly complete free movement of employees has already been achieved. Only government posts may be reserved for nationals. However, cumbersome administrative procedures relating to residency permits are still in effect and the rights of establishment for the self-employed are constrained by wide differences in vocational and professional qualifications. For universities the mutual recognition of degrees and diplomas is envisaged. The mobility of students will be promoted through the establishment of a Community scholarship scheme.

## V. Summary and Evaluation

In conclusion, there remains the question of evaluating the EC's efforts to coordinate and harmonize the tax systems of its Member States in the light of the theory of tax coordination and assignment and the special institutional context in which the Community takes shape.

### A. Summary of Survey

This paper has shown that the role and scope of the public sector in the various Member States of the EC is very large indeed. The weighted total tax ratio averages 40 percent of GDP. If non-tax revenues and other sources of finance are taken into account, on average close to half of Member States' income may be allocated through the budget mechanism. As recognized in the Treaty of Rome, these figures emphasize that it is clearly to the mutual advantage of Member States to agree on common tax rules for efficient trade and factor utilization and fair entitlement of revenues. Such rules become more urgent as the EC moves closer to a confederation, a joining of independent jurisdictions for limited common purposes, including the completion of the Common Market and beyond that the creation of a monetary and economic union.

Substantial progress has been made in coordinating various product taxes. Customs duties have been abolished, some remaining quantitative restrictions are being phased out, and charges having an equivalent effect are prohibited. Furthermore, a destination-based common value-added tax with appropriate border tax adjustments has been introduced. Little progress has been made in the excise field, but some forms of blatant discrimination have been prohibited by the European Court of Justice which is increasingly establishing itself as a truly supra-national institution. Possibly substantial non-tariff barriers that may be compared to charges having equivalent effect as customs duties remain. Technically, however, it should be possible to remove border controls fully by shifting border tax adjustments for the value-added tax to books of account and by providing for a Community-wide system of excise suspension. As evidenced by the enormous growth of intra-Community trade, substantial progress has been made towards the objective of the free movement of goods based on the principle of non-discrimination.

There is little, if anything, to report on the coordination of the income taxes and social security contributions. Source Member States cling to their traditional rights to fully tax the profits of foreign-owned corporate activities. Substantial differences in the computation of the tax base, the rate structures, and the degree to which the corporation tax is (not) integrated with the individual income tax of shareholders remain; they should distort capital movements. Tax liability for the individual income tax is based on residence

45

and rates are applied to a global income concept without, however, tax administrations in different Member States being able effectively to reach income earned abroad. There are many practical problems in processing exchanges of information and a common stand on the treatment of income arising outside the Community has not been developed. Generally, the same applies to social security contributions. Infringements on tax neutrality between Member States are largely ironed out through bilateral agreements for the avoidance of double taxation and special arrangements are hammered out for frontier and migrant workers.

Clearly, the founding fathers of the EC were foremost concerned with the removal of competitive distortions in product markets. In their view these were caused by indirect taxes which therefore should be harmonized in the interest of the Common Market. Apparently, the eventual removal of border controls as the most visible indication that the Common Market did not have the characteristics of a domestic market was foremost in their minds. To be sure, the free movement of capital and persons is also an explicit objective of the Treaty, but the approximation of the relating direct taxes is required only to the extent that they directly affect the establishment or functioning of the Common Market. The distinction between direct and indirect taxes that was made may have been influenced by naive views on incidence and the belief that distortions in factor markets would not affect product markets.

## B. Theory of Tax Coordination and Assignment

As Musgrave (1983) points out, the wish or necessity to establish intra-Community rules of good tax manners arises from the contingency to deal with tax burden exports and tax base flights. In the absence of an operational framework for basing taxes on the benefit principle (they would then represent cost-reducing payments for intermediate goods supplied by government), two criteria may be postulated for tax coordination. The first basic rule, deeply anchored in the Treaty of Rome, is tax neutrality: Member States should (re-)arrange their tax systems in such a way that the free flow of trade and factors is not distorted. More positively, tax coordination and harmonization is required for 'creating a more favourable environment for stimulating enterprise, competition and trade' (Commission, 1985). The second, and really prior, requirement, to which much less thought has been given, is that entitlements to, or property rights in, tax bases should be established, based on the allegiance or residency principle, and the territoriality or source principle. To be sure, trade-offs must be made and administrative considerations should be taken into account.

Based on Musgrave's criteria of efficient resource mobilization and fair entitlement, the following principles of tax coordination and assignment,

46

modified to suit EC arrangements, may be formulated.

(1) In analogy to the case for free trade, Community welfare was promoted following the abolition of import and customs duties between Member States and the establishment of a common external tariff. This prevents tax burden export, made feasible if the demand and supply for traded goods is inelastic and exchange rates are fixed. Moreover, there is a strong case for allocating the import tax base or the proceeds from import duties to the Community. Harmonized import duties imposed and retained by the Member State through which goods enter the Community would give rise to inefficiencies in resource utilization. Of course, some destination-based inter-treasury transfer system would also achieve tax neutrality, as do present arrangements under which import duties are collected by national customs administrations but remitted to the Community. Eventually, a common customs service operating only at external frontiers may be envisaged.

(2) In view of the very high tax rates, the case for harmonizing the excises on tobacco products and alcoholic beverages is also urgent if border controls are to be abolished. Arguably, the proposed common customs service might also be charged with the administration of these major excises as Community sources of revenue. Linking systems of excise suspension seems to require close control of retail outlets which may not always be feasible. As regards oil and natural gas deposits, thus far Member States have jealously guarded their patrimony (as have US states). In the EC, tax-inclusive export prices are permitted, provided owner Member States charge their own consumers and producers the same tax-inclusive price. Therefore, inefficiencies in the provision of public services financed by the additional revenues are accepted.

(3) Tax neutrality requires that relative prices between home-produced and foreign-made goods should not be distorted, establishing the case for precise border tax adjustments under the various value-added taxes. When border controls are abolished, some inter-treasury clearing-house arrangement is necessary if the destination principle is retained. To minimize tax base flight through cross-border shopping, some approximation of the value-added tax rates of adjoining Member States would be desirable and use taxes on (registered) durable consumer goods may have to be introduced. But as evidenced by the experience with state and provincial retail sales taxes in the US and Canada, there is no compelling reason why the sales tax base should be ceded to the Community.

(4) Less coordination is required for those tax bases that have low intra-Community mobility. Taxes on employment income, representing by far the largest share of total income, are inherently less open to tax base flight and burden export than import duties and excises. Mobility is restrained by

language and cultural barriers, which largely coincide with territorial borders. This applies not only to the wage income tax, but also to social security contributions. However, efficiency losses may occur to the extent that such taxes affect product prices. Furthermore, tax burdens may be imported if, in the absence of nationality requirements, the poor move to countries with generous social security benefits. In analogy to cross-border shoppers, special arrangements are required for frontier and migrant workers.

(5) Since the capital base is highly mobile, special coordination efforts are required in the field of corporation taxes and capital income covered by individual income taxes. Distorting location effects of tax differentials between Member States would be avoided under the allegiance (residency) rule, but, as Musgrave (1983) points out, for this approach to be effective, it must be assumed that Member States are in fact able to reach the income and profits of their residents in other Member States. If not, the territoriality principle has to be used, but to secure Community-wide efficiency in the location of resource use, it is then necessary to require uniform bases of assessment and rates across Member States. This is increasingly being appreciated with respect to the corporation tax (see Musgrave, this volume).

(6) No such *in rem* solution is available for personal income taxes with progressive rates. A comprehensive personal tax can be pursued under the allegiance rule only if all income can be reached effectively and a full credit is given for all income taxes paid in other Member States. But this implies a full exchange of information pertaining to income tax liabilities and compliance control at Community level, so close that the contours of a central tax administration emerge. Moreover, the non-wastable foreign tax credit means that capital-exporting states are held hostage by capital-importing states. The requirement of a Community-level personal income tax becomes more urgent if the corporation tax is to be integrated with the income tax. In the absence of a central tax administration, the base of the personal income tax will not be truly global and it will not be possible to use the tax to secure inter-individual redistributional objectives on a Community-wide basis.

(7) Little, if any, coordination is required for benefit taxes and user charges that are closely attached to residency and territoriality characteristics. In view of the inherent immobility of the base, this is also true of property taxes.

Judging by the theory of tax coordination and assignment, the Commission's tax harmonization efforts seem to be on the right track. Technically, border controls can be removed without substantial further adjustments to the various indirect tax systems. A genuine single product market without internal customs posts is within reach and the main focus should be shifted to the removal of non-tariff barriers, such as regulations and standards, government procurement policies and subsidies. Furthermore, as indicated by the Commission's activities, the closer alignment of company tax burdens to ensure fair competition and eliminate tax-induced capital movements is rightly given high priority. Coordination of wage income taxation and social security contributions, as well as progressive income taxation, if really desired, might be left to a later stage, following the creation of a monetary and economic union. In the meantime, work should proceed on the approximation of legal requirements and licensing procedures.

## C. Concluding Remarks

As the Commission (1980) recognizes, tax sovereignty is one of the basic components of national sovereignty. Difficulties in the field of tax harmonization are compounded by deep-rooted differences in economic and social structures, different perceptions on the role of taxation, differences in the acceptability of various taxes, the technical complexity of tax harmonization, and complications arising from further enlargement of the Community. These difficulties are magnified as national monetary policies become more closely aligned, thereby increasing the weight on tax (and expenditure) policies for short-term stabilization and long-term structural adjustments in individual Member States.

More generally, differences in tax systems did not come about at random, but rather reflect social and political preferences that should not be ignored. It may be that after the removal of border controls, the introduction of a destination-based clearing mechanism for rate-differentiated value-added taxes and excises, and the approximation of the various corporation tax systems, the EC tax coordination process has been carried as far as it should go. Individuals in Member States are entitled to their national identity, cultural values, and the desire to spend as much of their own tax revenue on national goals, including redistribution, as they see fit. The Member States are in no sense the creation of the Community, but rather should retain at least as independent an existence as the Community seeks to achieve.[14] Under this view, efficiency losses, likely to be borne anyway by the Member State incurring them, may be an acceptable price to pay for retaining national diversity and autonomy. It is this new sense of realism that is a distinguishing characteristic of the Commission's latest White Paper (1985) which repeatedly asserts that the general thrust of the

---

14. For an excellent review of recent thinking on issues of federal finance suggesting that the process of reaching decisions is as important as or possibly more important than their substance, see Bird (1984).

49

Commission's approach will be to move away from the concept of harmonization, understood as uniformity, towards that of mutual recognition and equivalence.

# APPENDIX

EUROPEAN COMMUNITY AND UNITED STATES:
GROSS DOMESTIC PRODUCT, POPULATION AND PER CAPITA INCOME, 1983 AND 1965

| Country[a] | Gross Domestic Product (In Billions of US Dollars) | | Population (In Millions) | | Per Capita Income[b] (In US Dollars) | |
|---|---|---|---|---|---|---|
| | 1983 | 1965 | 1983 | 1965 | 1983 | 1965 |
| *European Community* | *2,483.8* | *458.8* | *320.4* | *293.3* | *7,752* | *1,564* |
| Germany | 653.1 | 114.8 | 61.4 | ·58.6 | 10,633 | 1,959 |
| France | 516.3 | 97.9 | 54.4 | 48.8 | 9,486 | 2,007 |
| United Kingdom | 454.9 | 100.3 | 56.4 | 54.3 | 8,069 | 1,846 |
| Italy | 352.8 | 62.6 | 56.8 | 52.0 | 6,209 | 1,204 |
| Spain | 158.8 | 23.3 | 38.2 | 32.1 | 4,155 | 726 |
| Netherlands | 132.0 | 19.7 | 14.4 | 12.3 | 9,191 | 1,603 |
| Belgium | 81.9 | 16.8 | 9.9 | 9.5 | 8,314 | 1,778 |
| Denmark | 56.4 | 10.2 | 5.1 | 4.8 | 11,020 | 2,141 |
| Greece | 34.8 | 6.0 | 9.8 | 8.6 | 3,534 | 700 |
| Portugal | 20.7 | 3.7 | 10.1 | 9.2 | 2,056 | 408 |
| Ireland | 18.0 | 2.7 | 3.5 | 2.9 | 5,118 | 935 |
| Luxembourg | 4.0 | 0.7 | 0.4 | 0.3 | 10,954 | 2,118 |
| *United States* | *3,195.1* | *658.4* | *234.5* | *194.2* | *13,626* | *3,390* |

*Notes:*  a. In descending order of GDP size in 1983.
  b. Figures may not exactly equal GDP divided by population because of rounding. In interpreting the value figures, allowance should be made for the fact that the exchange rates that have been used are but snapshots for 1983 and 1965.
*Source:* Computed from Organisation for Economic Co-operation and Development (1985): Tables 32, 34, 36 and 37.

Alworth, Julian. 'Taxation and the Cost of Capital: A Comparison of Six EC Countries.' Chapter 9, this volume, 1986.

Andel, Norbert. 'Determination of Company Profits.' Chapter 10, this volume, 1986.

Berger, Alexander. (ed.). *International Tax Summaries 1984*. New York: Published for Coopers and Lybrand by John Wiley, 1985.

Bird, Richard M. 'Tax Harmonization and Federal Finance: A Perspective on Recent Canadian Discussion.' *Canadian Public Policy*, 10, 3, 1984.

Burke, R. 'Harmonisation of Taxation in Europe.' *Intertax*, 46, 1979.

Cnossen, Sijbren. 'Issues in Excise Taxation: The Alcohol Problem.' In Roskamp, Karl W. and Forte, Francesco (eds). *Reforms of Tax Systems*. Detroit: Wayne State University Press, 1981.

Cnossen, Sijbren. 'The Imputation System in the EEC.' In Cnossen, Sijbren (ed.). *Comparative Tax Studies: Essays in Honor of Richard Goode*. Amsterdam: North-Holland, 1983a.

Cnossen, Sijbren. 'Harmonization of Indirect Taxes in the EEC.' In McLure, Charles E. Jr (ed.). *Tax Assignment in Federal Countries*. Canberra: ANU Press, 1983b. Reprinted in *British Tax Review*, 4, 1983b.

Cnossen, Sijbren. 'Sales Taxation: An International Perspective.' In Head, John G. (ed.). *Taxation Issues in the 1980s*. Sydney: Australian Tax Research Foundation, 1983c. Reprinted as 'Sales Taxation in OECD Member Countries.' *Bulletin for International Fiscal Documentation*, 37, 4, 1983c.

Cnossen, Sijbren. 'Alternative Forms of Corporation Tax.' *Australian Tax Forum*, 1, September 1984. Reprinted as 'Corporation Taxes in OECD Member Countries.' *Bulletin for International Fiscal Documentation*, 38, 11, 1984.

Cnossen, Sijbren and Shoup, Carl S. 'Coordination of Value-Added Taxes.' Chapter 2, this volume, 1986.

Commission of the European Communities. 'Programme for the Harmonisation of Direct Taxes.' *Bulletin of the European Economic Community*, Supplement 8, 1967.

Commission of the European Communities. 'Proposed Council Directives on Excise Duties and Similar Taxes.' *Bulletin of the European Communities*, Supplement 3, 1972.

Commission of the European Communities. 'Social Action Programme.' *Bulletin of the European Communities*, Supplement 2, 1974.

Commission of the European Communities. 'Proposal for a Directive of the Council concerning the Harmonisation of Systems of Company Taxation and of Withholding Taxes on Dividends.' *Bulletin of the European Communities*, Supplement 10, 1975.

Commission of the European Communities. 'Report on the Scope for Convergence of Tax Systems in the Community.' *Bulletin of the European Communities*, Supplement 1, 1980.

Commission of the European Communities. 'Completing the Internal Market.' White Paper from the Commission to the European Council. Brussels, 1985.

Conrad, Ernst-Albrecht. 'Trends in the Level of Corporate Taxation.' *Finanzarchiv*, 32, 1974.

Council of the European Communities. 'Decision of 21 April 1970 on the Replacement of Financial Contributions from Member States by the Communities Own Resources.' *Official Journal of the European Communities*, Special Edition 1970 (1), December 1972.

Court of Justice of the European Communities.

Case 7/68: Commission v. Italy. *Recueil*, XIV-5, 1968.

Case 77/72: Capolongo v. Maya. *Reports* 5, 1973.

Case 152/73: Sotgiu v. Deutsche Bundespost. *Reports* 1, 1974.

Case 8/74: Fourcroy S.A. v. Dassonville. *Reports* 5, 1974.

Case 51/74: Van der Hulst's Zonen v. Produktschap voor Siergewassen. *Reports* 1, 1975.

Case 148/77: Hansen & Balle v. Hauptzollamt Flensburg. *Reports* 10, 1978.

Case 168/78: Commission v. France. *Reports* 2, 1980.

Case 169/78: Commission v. Italy. *Reports* 2, 1980.

Case 170/78: Commission v. United Kingdom of Great Britain and Northern Ireland. *Reports* 7, 1983.

Case 171/78: Commission v. Denmark. *Reports* 2, 1980.

Case 55/79: Commission v. Ireland. *Reports* 8, 1979.

De Clercq, W. 'Some Remarks on the Trend of Public Finance in the Western Industrialized Countries.' Paper presented at the 41st Congress of the International Institute of Public Finance. Madrid, August 26-30, 1985.

Deringer Report. 'Rapport fait au nom de la Commission du Marché Intérieur sur la proposition de la Commission de la CEE au Conseil concernant une Directive en matière d'harmonisation des législations des Etats Membres relative aux taxes sur le chiffre d'affaires.' European Parliament, *Documents 1963-64*, 56, 1964.

Easson, A.J. *Tax Law and Policy in the EEC*. London: Sweet & Maxwell, 1980.

Fredersdorf Report. 'Information Report of the Section for Economic and Social Questions of the Economic and Social Committee on Tax Harmonization.' Economic and Social Committee, 1978.

Goode, Richard. 'The Tax Burden in the United States and Other Countries.' In *Financing Democracy: The Annals of the American Academy of Political and Social Science*. Philadelphia, 379, 1968.

Kay, John and Keen, Michael. 'Alcohol and Tobacco Taxes: Criteria for Harmonisation.' Chapter 3, this volume, 1986.

Kopits, George. 'Factor Prices in Industrial Countries.' *IMF Staff Papers*, 29, 3, 1982.

McLure, Charles E. Jr. *Must Corporate Income Be Taxed Twice?* Washington DC: The Brookings Institution, 1979.

Messere, Ken. 'Trends in OECD Tax Revenues.' In Cnossen, Sijbren (ed.). *Comparative Tax Studies: Essays in Honor of Richard Goode.* Amsterdam: North-Holland, 1983.

Messere, Ken and Owens, J.P. 'International Comparisons of Tax Levels: Pitfalls and Insights.' Paper presented at the 41st Congress of the International Institute of Public Finance. Madrid, August 26-30, 1985.

Musgrave, Peggy B. 'Interjurisdictional Coordination of Taxes on Capital Income.' Chapter 7, this volume, 1986.

Musgrave, Richard A. *Fiscal Systems.* New Haven: Yale University Press, 1969.

Musgrave, Richard A. 'Who Should Tax, Where, and What?' In McLure, Charles E. Jr (ed.). *Tax Assignment in Federal Countries.* Canberra: ANU Press, 1983.

Neumark Report. 'Report of the Fiscal and Financial Committee.' In *The EEC Reports on Tax Harmonization.* Amsterdam: International Bureau of Fiscal Documentation, 1963.

Organisation for Economic Co-operation and Development (OECD). *National Accounts Statistics 1955-1964.* Paris, March 1966.

Organisation for Economic Co-operation and Development (OECD). *The 1982 Tax/Benefit Position of a Typical Worker in OECD Member Countries.* Paris, 1983.

Organisation for Economic Co-operation and Development (OECD). *Revenue Statistics of OECD Member Countries 1965-1984.* Paris, 1985.

Organisation for Economic Co-operation and Development (OECD). *The Tax/Benefit Position of a Typical Worker in OECD Member Countries.*

Organisation for Economic Co-operation and Development (OECD). *Personal Income Tax Systems Under Changing Economic Conditions.* Report by the Committee on Fiscal Affairs of OECD. Paris, 1986b.

Organisation for Economic Co-operation and Development (OECD). *An Empirical Analysis of Changes in Personal Income Taxes.* Report by the Committee on Fiscal Affairs. Paris: OECD Studies in Taxation, 1986c.

Parliament of the European Communities. 'Resolution on the Harmonization of Systems of Company Taxation and of Withholding Taxes on Dividends.' *Official Journal of the European Communities* C 140, 5.6.79, 1979.

Peacock, Alan T. and Wiseman, Jack. *The Growth of Public Expenditures in the United Kingdom.* Princeton University Press for the National Bureau of Economic Research, 1961.

Pedone, Antonio. 'Italy.' In Aaron, Henry J. (ed.). *The Value-Added Tax: Lessons from Europe.* Washington DC: The Brookings Institution, 1981.

Pelkmans, Jacques and Vanheukelen, Marc (eds). *Coming to Grips with the Internal Market*. Maastricht: European Institute of Public Administration, 1986.

Sato, Mitsuo and Bird, Richard M. 'International Aspects of the Taxation of Corporations and Shareholders.' *IMF Staff Papers*, 22, 1975.

Segré Report. *Le Développement d'un Marché Européen des Capitaux*. Brussels: Commission of the European Communities, 1966.

Shoup, Carl S. (ed.). *Fiscal Harmonization in Common Markets*. Vols 1, 2. New York: Columbia University Press, 1967.

Stockfish, J.A. 'Value-Added Taxes and the Size of Government: Some Evidence.' *National Tax Journal*, 4, 38, 1985.

Sullivan, Clara K. 'Indirect Taxation and Goals of the European Economic Community.' In Shoup, Carl S. (ed.). *Fiscal Harmonization in Common Markets*. Vols 1, 2. New York: Columbia University Press, 1967.

Tait, Alan A. and Morgan, David A. 'Gasoline Taxation in Selected OECD Countries, 1970-1979.' *IMF Staff Papers*, 27, 2, 1980.

Tanzi, Vito (ed.). *The Underground Economy in the United States and Abroad*. The Lexington Press, 1982.

Tanzi, Vito (ed.). 'The Growth of Public Expenditure in Industrial Countries: An International and Historical Perspective.' *Mimeograph*. Washington DC: International Monetary Fund, February 11, 1986.

# Part Two

# Product Taxes

# 2

# Coordination of value-added taxes

*Sijbren Cnossen and Carl S. Shoup**

## I. INTRODUCTION

'Parking place Europe', read the headline of an editorial in *NRC-Handelsblad*, a Dutch newspaper, on February 23, 1984 when more than two thousand trucks were stranded in the Alps because of striking French truckers and Italian customs officers. Although the European Community (EC) has been tariff-free since 1968, there are still customs posts at nearly every inter-Member State border, regularly causing queues of lorries and automobiles even when there is no strike. The principal revenue job of customs personnel at internal border crossings is to process value-added tax payments and rebates on goods traded inside the EC. In addition, officers are involved in the control and collection of excises on tobacco, alcohol and petroleum products, the imposition of monetary compensatory levies on farm trade, the verification of customs documents, and the search for drugs. The costs of internal customs, including administration and delays, has been put at some 5-7 percent of the value of goods traded inside the Community every year.

No doubt this is not what the founding fathers of the EC had in mind when they signed the Treaty of Rome in 1957 calling for the establishment of a common market with characteristics similar to those of a domestic market, that is, without customs posts. In an attempt to reach that goal, this paper focuses on the elimination of border controls for the value-added taxes. Allegedly, such controls are necessary to effect border tax adjustments, in turn required because in the EC, as is generally accepted in international trade, goods are taxed in the country of consumption (destination principle) rather than the country of production (origin principle). To implement the destination principle properly, imports should be taxed on the same footing as domestic goods, and exports should leave a country free of tax. To eliminate discrimination of internal trade from the various cumulative turnover taxes, the Community's first task at the time of its formation, therefore, was to introduce a common sales tax allowing unambiguous and expeditious border tax adjustments. This task was achieved through the adoption by every Member

* The authors are grateful for the comments received from Francesco Forte, Malcolm Gillis and Satya Poddar who, of course, should not be held responsible for any remaining shortcomings.

State of a harmonized value-added tax. Section II reviews its history and role in the Community.

The next step, still to be taken, will be to eliminate border controls. It is often asserted that such controls cannot be done away with without at the same time abolishing border tax adjustments. This would appear to imply an EC-wide shift to the origin principle under which each Member State would only tax the value added within its own boundaries. Exports would be taxed, and imports would be exempt. Section III highlights the benefit, efficiency, fairness, and administrative considerations that affect the choice between the destination and the origin principle. The destination principle, already in place, appears to come out ahead. The next question, therefore, is whether border controls can be eliminated while border tax adjustments are retained. Section IV shows that this can be achieved either by a deferred payment scheme under which imports are taxed at the first inland production or distribution stage, or, preferably, by an EC-wide tax credit clearance system under which credit for tax on exports is provided by the importing country's tax administration, but paid by the exporting country. A highly important implication of these arrangements is that Member States remain free to set their own value-added tax rates. This conclusion is underlined in Section V.

## II. BACKGROUND OF COMMON VALUE-ADDED TAX

This section briefly reviews the history of the value-added tax in the EC and surveys its role in the tax structures of the respective Member States. It shows that the base of the tax is harmonized and that proper border tax adjustments can easily be made, but also that rates are far from converging to some EC average.

### A. History

When calling for the creation of a common market in which distortions of competitive conditions would be prevented and the free movement of goods and services ensured, the founding fathers of the EC recognized that the elimination of import duties (completed on July 1, 1968) would not be sufficient for these goals to be achieved if sales taxes (and excises) were to continue to be allowed to function as trade barriers.[1] There was ample reason for such fear. At the time the Treaty was signed in 1957, five out of six original Member States were levying a 'cascade' type of turnover tax which applied to

---

1. In addition, of course, persons and capital were to move freely within the Common Market. See Commission (1980, p. 6) as well as Neumark Committee (1963, p. 101).

60

every sale at nearly every stage of production and distribution with no allowance for tax already paid at earlier stages. As a result, the tax was cumulative and capricious in its effects on prices. The total amount of tax included in consumer prices varied widely, even for products taxed at the same nominal rate.

More specifically, border tax adjustments could not be ascertained reliably and unambiguously. Simple exemption of export sales took no account of turnover tax collected at earlier stages. A rebate of such tax could only be approximate, given the differing number of selling stages that different goods went through before being exported and the differing values added at those stages. The same applied to imports. To match the cumulative burden of the tax imposed on goods produced domestically, the compensating rate of tax should in principle be higher the closer the good was to its final form. On the whole, however, this was not and could not be done.[2] In most countries the situation was compounded by the use of rate structures that were differentiated across products and stages of production and distribution. In short: border tax adjustments were at best guesstimates and it was tempting to use them for protective purposes.

To prevent Member States from using their indirect tax systems to discriminate against products from other Member States, the EC Commission was instructed to formulate proposals for the harmonization of the sales taxes (and excises) in the interest of the Common Market. Two committees were formed which were to indicate the principles and procedures, including the types of tax, that would ensure the exact computation of border tax adjustments and eventually the removal of border controls. Noting that existing turnover taxes distorted competitive conditions among domestic products as well as between domestic and foreign goods, the Fiscal and Financial Committee (the Neumark Committee, 1963) and the Sub-Groups A, B and C (the Jansen Committee, 1963) both proposed to replace the turnover taxes by a value-added tax of the type already in place in France and under active consideration in Germany.[3]

But for the elimination of border controls, the proposed value-added tax had

2. These and other problems were already noted by Shoup (1930, pp. 133, 181). To escape the difficulties in applying correct border tax adjustments, discrimination against specialized firms, as well as the attendant administrative problems, several countries consolidated the turnover tax for various products at a single stage: *taxe unique*. But this resulted in several different taxes on several different classes of commodities, each at some single stage in the production/marketing process.

3. France proved a prime innovator in the sales tax field. First, a uniform-rate production tax was introduced for certain commodities in 1936. Second, in 1948, this tax was transformed into a value-added tax, income type, on producers, using the tax-credit technique. Third, in 1953-55, the cascade tax was completely abandoned, and the production tax was changed to a consumption type of value-added tax giving full credit for tax on investment goods.

the answer to all the problems raised by the old 'cascade' type of turnover tax. Most importantly from an EC point of view, it was precise in fully freeing exports from tax and in levying an equivalent compensatory tax on imports. The proposed value-added tax would permit each taxpayer a credit for the tax charged by suppliers against his own tax payable on sales. Since the tax would have to be explicitly stated on invoices, at each stage, including the export stage, the amount of tax paid at previous stages and therefore to be rebated could be reliably ascertained.

Similarly, the value-added tax imposed an equivalent compensatory tax on imports even if import values were understated, because any underpayment would be automatically caught and corrected in the following stage. Last but not least, a value-added tax extending through the retail stage would not distort consumer and producer choices unintendedly, as the sum of the net taxes collected at all stages would exactly equal the tax rate times the consumer price before tax.

In 1967 the Committees' proposal was accepted by the Council of Ministers of the EC, which started issuing a number of directives ensuring the adoption and proper coordination of the common value-added tax. The First Directive required all Member States, except France which already levied the tax, to introduce the value-added tax before the beginning of 1970. A Second Directive, issued at the same time, specified the basic structure of the tax and defined important concepts, as well as the treatment of exports and imports. Member States were still permitted a choice of the consumption type (immediate credit for tax on capital goods) or the income type (tax credit based on useful lives) of value-added tax, but all Member States opted for the consumption type.[4] Although the implementation date was postponed a few times, by 1973 all States, including the late entrants Denmark, Ireland and the United Kingdom, had introduced the tax.[5] Greece, which joined the EC in 1981, undertook to do so before 1987, and the recent Members, Portugal and Spain, have also agreed to this condition.

List 2.1 presents dates and details of the various approved and draft directives. Noteworthy is the Sixth Directive which substantially narrowed the wide latitude in legal definitions, exemptions, and administrative procedures

---

4. For a treatment of the various forms of value-added tax, see Musgrave and Musgrave (1980, pp. 458-63) and Shoup (1969, pp. 250-69). For a review of value-added taxes and other sales taxes in countries that are members of the Organisation for Economic Co-operation and Development, see Cnossen (1983b). For the original distinction between income type and consumption type of value-added taxes, see Shoup (1955).
5. Denmark had already introduced a value-added tax in 1967, long before it became a member of the Community. Non-EC European countries that have adopted an EC-type value-added tax are Austria, Norway and Sweden. For a critical assessment of the equity, economic, and administrative aspects of the various value-added taxes, see the contributions in Aaron (1981); for a detailed account of the experience in the Netherlands, see Cnossen (1981).

still allowed under the earlier directives. A uniform basis of assessment was agreed upon through the adoption of common definitions for such important concepts as taxable persons, taxable transactions and taxable amounts. The Directive also listed the allowable exemptions. These include health-care, educational, social and cultural activities, postal services, non-commercial radio and television broadcasts, insurance, banking, and financial transactions. Furthermore, all Member States, except the United Kingdom, agreed to tax the sale of new buildings, but exempt the sale of previously occupied residential property. Generally, governments are treated as final consumer households and special schemes are permitted for small businesses and farmers.[6]

List 2.1
EC DIRECTIVES ON VALUE-ADDED TAX

| Number | | |
| --- | --- | --- |
| Approved Draft | Date | Description |
| | Day.Mth.Year | |
| 1 | 11.04.67 | Introduction of general, multistage, non-cumulative sales tax, if possible through the retail stage, before January 1, 1970. Member States remain free to determine rates and, to a lesser extent, exemptions. |
| 2 | 11.04.67 | Structure of tax: definitions of tax base (domestic deliveries of goods and services plus imports), taxpayer, taxable event, taxable price, tax credit or invoice method, treatment of investment goods *(pro rata temporis* credit, if desired) and of imports and exports (destination principle). |
| 3 | 09.12.69 | Extension of introduction date until January 1, 1972. |

6. For reviews of the Sixth Directive, see Georgen (1977) and Guieu (1977); for a detailed analysis of its implications for the legislation of individual Member States, see Timmermans and Joseph (1980); for a progress report, see Commission (1983). In the EC, sales of exempt firms are not taxed but, as distinct from zero rating, neither do exempt firms receive a credit for tax invoiced by their suppliers. Early on, exemptions rather than zero rates were favored, because they are less costly to the treasury. A cumulative element arises, however, when intermediate and capital goods bought by exempt firms are resold to taxable firms.

| Number | | | |
|---|---|---|---|
| Approved | Draft | Date | Description |
| | | Day.Mth.Year | |
| 4 | | 20.12.71 | Extension of introduction date until July 1, 1972. |
| 5 | | 04.07.72 | Further respite for Italy until January 1, 1973. |
| 6 | | 17.05.77 | Common basis of assessment, definitions, and rules with respect to agriculture, the retail stage, exemptions, immediate tax credit for investment goods, placc of service. |
| | 7 | 11.01.78 | Anti-cumulation provisions for works of art, collector's items, antiques, and used goods. |
| 8 | | 06.12.79 | Refunds for non-resident taxpayers in the EC. |
| 9 | | 19.06.78 | Extension of introduction date of the Sixth Directive until January 1, 1979. |
| | 10 | 31.07.84 | Place of service for the rental of movable goods (except means of transport). |
| 11 | | 26.03.80 | Exclusion of French overseas departments from Sixth Directive. |
| | − | 23.01.80 | Zero-rating of provisions for ships, airlines, and international trains. |
| | − | 28.03.83 | Exemption of the final importation of specified goods, the temporary importation of specified means of transport, and the definitive importation of personal effects. |
| | 12 | 25.01.83 | Prohibition of tax credit for specified business expenditures on cars, yachts, airplanes, motor cycles, travel, food, accommodation, entertainment, and luxury items. |
| | 13 | 19.07.82 | Refunds for non-resident taxpayers outside the EC. |
| | 14 | 09.07.82 | Deferred payment scheme for tax on imports. |

64

| Number | | | |
|---|---|---|---|
| Approved Draft | | Date | Description |
| | | Day.Mth.Year | |
| 15 | | 19.12.83 | Extension of introduction date for Greece until January 1, 1986. |
| | 16 | 23.07.84 | Avoidance of double taxation of goods imported by consumers. |
| | 17 | 17.08.84 | Temporary importation of goods other than means of transport. |
| | 18 | 04.12.84 | Phasing out of certain derogations permitted under the Sixth Directive. |
| | 19 | 05.12.84 | Clarifications and amendments of the Sixth Directive. |
| | 20 | 17.07.84 | Derogations in connection with aid granted to German farmers to compensate for abolition of monetary compensatory amounts. |

Adoption of the Sixth Directive was stimulated by the 1970 decision of the EC Council to replace the financial contributions of individual Member States with the EC's own resources. These resources comprise: agricultural levies, import and customs duties, and a one percent levy on a uniform value-added tax base. By 1979, the Sixth Directive had been implemented by all Member States. In 1983 the EC Commission submitted a draft decision to the Council proposing to raise the value-added tax contribution to 1.4 percent of the base. A suggestion was that each Member State's contribution should vary on the basis of certain economic indicators, including Gross Domestic Product (GDP) per capita and the share of agriculture in GDP. In May 1985, the Council approved the raise, effective from 1986, but the method by which the own resources base would be determined was not changed (*Official Journal*, L 128, May 14, 1985, p. 15).

## B. Review

As a broad-based tax that includes the retail stage, the value-added tax plays an important role in the tax structures of individual Member States, as shown in Table 2.1. Value-added tax receipts average 17 percent of total tax revenues in the EC, with individual country shares ranging from 12 percent in Luxembourg to 22 percent in Denmark. Expressed as a percentage of GDP, the average contribution is 7 percent, and those of Luxembourg and Denmark 5.1 percent and 9.8 percent, respectively. In many Member States, the value-added tax is the single most important source of tax revenue.

Since the tax base is largely uniform, if not identical, throughout the Community, differences in revenue contributions can be attributed to differences in the level and structure of the various rates which, as shown in Table 2.1 are far from harmonized. The standard rate ranges from a low 12 percent in Luxembourg to a high 23 percent in Ireland. Furthermore, all Member States, except Denmark, impose one or two reduced rates on items regarded as essential, such as food products, medical goods, books, newspapers, and public transportation. Ireland, Italy and the United Kingdom extend their reduced rates to other items, including clothing, footwear, electricity, and household fuels. In fact, all these goods are zero-rated in Ireland and the United Kingdom. France, Belgium and Italy impose increased rates on items such as motor cars, audio-visual aids, jewelry, furs, perfumery, cosmetics, and various excisable goods. The value of the goods and services subject to reduced rates comprises a sizable proportion of the total actual tax base, ranging from 20 percent in Germany to 40 percent in the United Kingdom. The coverage of the increased rates is relatively small: some 5-7 percent (Commission, 1980, pp. 25-26).

*Table 2.1 Value-added taxes in the EC, 1986*

| Country (Year of Introduction) | Statutory Rates (Percent) | | | Revenue Contribution (1983) | |
|---|---|---|---|---|---|
| | Standard | Reduced | Increased | As Percentage of Total Tax Revenue | As Percentage of GDP |
| Luxembourg (1970) | 12 | 3 and 6 | – | 12.1 | 5.1 |
| Spain (1986) | 12 | 6 | 33 | ... | ... |
| Germany (1968) | 14 | 7 | – | 17.0 | 6.4 |
| United Kingdom (1973) | 15 | 0 | – | 13.9 | 5.2 |
| Portugal (1986) | 16 | 0 and 8 | 30 | ... | ... |
| Italy (1973) | 18 | 2 and 9 | 38 | 14.9 | 6.1 |
| France (1968) | 18.6 | 5.5 and 7 | 33 1/3 | 20.5 | 9.1 |
| Belgium (1971) | 19 | 6 and 17 | 25 and 33 | 16.7 | 7.6 |
| Netherlands (1969) | 19 | 5 | – | 14.8 | 7.0 |
| Denmark (1967) | 22 | – | – | 22.1 | 9.8 |
| Ireland (1972) | 23 | 0 and 10 | – | 21.1 | 8.3 |
| Unweighted Average | 17.1 | | | 17.0 | 7.2 |

*Sources:* Rates: Commission (1985, p. 49); revenue contribution: OECD (1985). Rates are tax-exclusive, that is, based on sale price before tax.

Clearly, from this review, on revenue grounds Member States will be extremely averse to any steps that would jeopardize the yield of their value-added taxes. The high rates also emphasize the pivotal role of proper border tax adjustments, as well as the potential difficulties involved in removing border controls. Moreover, the rate structures reflect potentially contentious policy issues with respect to the tax burden distribution. Equalization of rates across Member States does not appear feasible; fortunately, as will be shown below, it is not necessary either.

## III. DESTINATION VERSUS ORIGIN PRINCIPLE

Taxes on goods entering intra-Community or international trade can be levied according to either of two principles. If a commodity is taxed in the country where it is consumed, it is said to be taxed on the basis of its location of consumption or destination. Alternatively, if a commodity is taxed in the country where it is produced, it is said to be taxed on the basis of its place of production or origin. In principle, a value-added tax can be imposed on either of these bases. Application of the destination principle requires border tax adjustments. To ensure that goods are taxed only in the country of consumption, exports must leave the exporting country free of tax and a compensating tax is required on imports so that they compete on an equal tax footing with domestically produced goods. No visible adjustments are necessary under the origin principle: imports are not taxed and no rebate is given with respect to exports. Invariably, goods moving in international trade are taxed under the destination principle.[7] Within a federal country with local, provincial, or state taxing jurisdictions, goods are in some instances taxed on the basis of origin.

Thus far the EC has applied the destination principle with respect to intra-Community trade, but consideration has been given to the origin principle as a means of avoiding border controls that appear to be required to administer border tax adjustments.[8] This section attempts to provide some guidance in choosing between the two principles. First, the discussion thus far is summarized, then benefit considerations are examined, followed by some arguments on economic efficiency and fairness, and an evaluation of administrative aspects. Although the origin principle – since it appears to make border tax adjustments and hence controls redundant – is given the benefit of the doubt, the destination principle is the preferred choice.

7. For the principles of indirect tax coordination in the international setting, see Musgrave (1969, pp. 270-91); Shoup (1969, pp. 262-64, 644-47); and Musgrave and Musgrave (1980, pp. 776-80).
8. For the theory of tax harmonization, see Shibata (1967, pp. 145-264) and Dosser (1967, pp. 1-41 and 1973, pp. 1-20).

## A. Discussion

Shoup, the non-European member of the Neumark Committee (1963), recalls that in the seven meetings held during the period July, 1960 to July, 1962 there was initially some sentiment among a few members for changing to the origin basis for intra-Community trade, on which exports would be taxed and imports made tax-free, just as within a true single trading market (where, indeed, there are no 'exports' or 'imports'). Experience with *Gewerbesteuern* in Germany and Luxembourg indicated that goods could be taxed on the basis of their place of production without serious distortion of competitive conditions or revenue contention between production and consumption states.

But the sentiment favoring the origin principle dwindled under the pressure of two considerations. First, uniform rates across countries in the EC would clearly be too much to expect initially, if indeed ever. With unequal rates, competition would *appear* to be unequal: Member A might be selling automobiles bearing only say a 10 percent tax to consumers in Member B where the tax rate was 20 percent. Second, the origin tax is a tax on production − the tax money levied up to the export stage goes to the country of production − and the general sales tax, whatever its form, was deemed to be one on consumption, the proceeds to go to the country of consumers.

At the same time, the Committee was reluctant to recommend continued use within the EC of the destination principle (exports exempt, imports taxable), because it believed that border controls were needed to ensure that the exempted (zero-rated) goods were actually exported, and the imported goods actually taxed. On balance, the Committee opted for retaining the destination principle, with border tax adjustments and controls, expressing the hope, however, that eventually rates would become uniform enough, and the distinction between taxing producers and taxing consumers unimportant enough, for the origin principle to be applied to trade within the EC and, thus, for border controls to be abolished.

In the event, all Member States, at the direction of the EC Council, adopted a destination-principle value-added tax. But the vision of a truly free internal market without the nuisance of border controls found its way into the preamble and Article 4 of the First Directive, which call explicitly for the abolition of export rebates and compensating import taxes.[9] The origin principle for intra-Community trade has also been widely recommended in the economic literature as the key to getting rid of border controls. In fact, the principle has become a

---

9. Perhaps in line with this sentiment, the Commission (1980, p. 54) began to call for an alignment of value-added tax rates. It suggested that agreement should be sought on a dual rate structure comprising a standard rate band of 15-17 percent and a reduced rate band of 3-5 percent. Recently, however, the Commission (1985) came out in favor of retaining the destination principle. See below.

standard tenet in public finance textbooks.[10] The argument is that internal border controls are not necessary, if only each Member State confined the tax to the value added within its own jurisdiction.

## B. Benefit Considerations

Under the origin principle, the revenue from the value-added tax on a traded good up to the time it is exported goes to the exporting country, that is, the country in which the good has been produced. Such allocation of revenue can be defended if that exporting country has rendered particular services to the firms that produced and exported the good. Perhaps certain infrastructure has been supplied without charge, or, more generally, the climate of law and enforcement of contracts that has made production and export possible has been given without specific user charges attached. For efficiency in future allocation of resources, those who have benefited should pay the charge for the use of intermediate goods and services supplied by government.

If the origin principle is adopted here, presumably the consumers of the good in the importing country would pay the tax in the price, and, quite properly, they would ultimately defray the cost of goods and services that the exporting country's government has rendered to the producing firms. Under the destination principle, the consumers would pay just as much, but all of the value-added tax included in the price, not just the tax on the value added in the importing country, would go to the importing country's government. This seems unfair, or inefficient, or both. The ideal case for the destination principle, by that reasoning, would be one in which the exporting country's government supplied few or no services to the firms involved, while the importing country was heavily engaged in supplying services to consumers: an extreme and unlikely situation.

In the real world, the appropriate system would seem to be to hold a middle course between the origin and the destination principles. At least, it seems a bit extreme for one country, the country of importation, to get all the tax revenue from a traded good; surely the country of exportation did give some services to the producer. Except for direct mail order sales to final consumers, the importing country's government will get at least some of the total value-added tax revenue, even under the origin principle, since the imported good must pass through the retail (and maybe also wholesale) stage, where a great deal of taxable value is added. An argument against the benefit approach is that value

10. See Due and Friedlaender (1975, p. 519); Musgrave and Musgrave (1980, p. 779); and Shoup (1969, p. 644). For an analysis in the US setting, see also McLure (1980, pp. 127-39). As shown below, however, while the tenet may be of interest to the theory of tax harmonization, it has no relevance to the real world; a much better, practical solution is available.

added is not a good proxy for measuring benefits received. Rather, if rendered, benefits should be taxed through approximate user charges. Furthermore, some benefits, such as a good legal system, cost next to nothing, which renders taxes of the user-charge type hardly justifiable. Benefit-based value-added taxation finds little or no support in the real world (Musgrave, 1969, p. 242).


## C. Efficiency and Fairness

Aside from the allocation of the tax revenue, is economic efficiency – in the usual hypothetical sense of being able to make someone better off without making anyone else worse off – enhanced by applying the origin principle or rather by using the destination principle? As is well known, economic theory has an easy answer: under certain conditions it makes no difference which method is used (Shoup, 1969, p. 209, and sources cited there). If the origin principle is substituted for the destination principle, exports will be taxed and imports exempt, resulting in a change in the foreign exchange rate and/or domestic prices such that the flow of goods will be the same as under the previous principle.

This conclusion is gratifying until attention is paid to the conditions: trade between the countries is balanced initially; no net transfer payments from one country to the other (e.g. interest on debt); no net flow of capital to one country. These conditions, plus that of perfectly flexible exchange rates and prices, as well as a truly comprehensive and completely uniform value-added tax, are so far from being met, in practice, that pending further study, the general application, under all conditions, of the equivalence theorem had better be refrained from (Shoup, 1953, p. 93). That may seem too abrupt a dismissal of the issue, but in fact policymakers have not assumed that the two systems are equal in efficiency. Rather, they have not seriously considered the question. They are more concerned with the division of the tax revenue, as discussed above, and with what may be termed 'perceived fairness' or 'perceived equality' or even 'perceived efficiency'.[11]

The notion 'perceived fairness' may be illustrated as follows, using the example above. If Member A imposes a value-added tax of 10 percent, and Member B a tax of 20 percent, and if A exports automobiles to B that compete with similar, but more highly taxed, automobiles produced in B, then, under

11. A tax measure may be perceived as unfair or inefficient economically even though economic analysis demonstrates, at least to the satisfaction of economists, that it is not. But perceived (even though not real) unfairness and perceived inefficiency count heavily against a tax proposal. Indeed, such perceptions will probably be decisive in policy formulation. Admittedly, such conjectures are matters not so much of economic analysis as of social psychology. At any rate, no one, economist or other, can responsibly support a policy proposal unequivocally without taking perceptions into account.

the origin principle, a customer in B buys a foreign car with only a 10 percent tax on it (aside from the value added in B by marketing the car there), compared with the 20 percent tax on a domestically produced car. (To be sure, the law might require that the tax not be shown separately in the breakdown of the sales price, but the word would get around.) An analysis of alterations in exchange rates upon adoption of the origin principle is unlikely to convince the domestic automobile producer that no unfairness or inefficiency arises from the difference in tax rates. If the tax rate differential is reversed − high tax rate in the exporting country − the origin principle will be perceived as unfair to the producer in A, whose cars must now sell at a higher price in B than B-produced cars.

Under the destination principle these perceived injustices disappear, but in their place arises a perceived unfairness against producers of non-traded goods or importers in the exporting country in favor of those who produce traded goods and therefore seem to benefit from the exemption of exports. Similarly, if two countries have different destination-based sales tax rates, the domestic producer in the low-tax country may feel that he has to pay a higher 'price of admission' to the high-tax country than the foreign producer has to pay for admission to the low-rate domestic market. In practice, however, these forms of unfairness seem to be regarded as less unfair, or at least to receive less attention, than the perceived unfairness of rate differences under the origin principle.

### D. Equal Rates?

Might the origin principle get a stronger hearing if rates of value-added tax were closely aligned within the Community? In the automobile case above, competition or the perception of fairness might not appear impaired if rates were uniform. The destination principle might then be used for trade with non-Members, while the origin principle was applied to trade among Member States, in order to avoid border tax adjustments and border controls. The analysis of such a mixed system, which goes by the name of 'restricted origin principle', was pioneered by Shibata (1967, pp. 206-24).

Shibata demonstrated that the differences in value-added tax rates among origin-principle countries would not, under certain conditions, lead to a reallocation of production among Member States and hence to economic inefficiency. In addition, he showed that differences in rates would lead to income redistribution among origin-principle countries. His careful step-by-step analysis has been supplemented and modified by further analytical contributions in recent years by Whalley (1979, 1981) and Berglas (1981). The chief points that emerge are the following.

(1) 'The claim that origin-based taxation at unequal rates is not distorting is

derived from models where factors do not move across countries; if movement is costless, some revision is necessary' (Berglas, 1981, p. 386). But such movement is precisely one aim of a true common market, even though beyond some point it will no doubt cease to be 'costless'.

(2) Even a uniform value-added tax rate throughout the EC will not (save under certain unlikely conditions) prevent income transfers among Member States under the restricted origin principle. Whalley (1979) demonstrated this, and Berglas agrees, except that he does not want to term this a 'distortion', reserving that term for allocational inefficiency, not income transfers.

(3) The equivalence of the destination and origin principles for intra-Community trade depends crucially on flexibility of exchange rates and prices. The condition of exchange rate flexibility is inconsistent, however, with the goal of establishing an economic union. Even if exchange rates would adjust, prices might not be so flexible. As money wages are downward rigid, tax-induced price responses tend to be upward. In such a situation, origin-based taxes are not attractive (Cnossen, 1983a, pp. 240-41).

(4) Similarly, the condition of a truly comprehensive and completely uniform value-added tax can hardly be met. The nature and role of exempt services, small businesses and farmers vary widely from one Member State to another with uneven effects on intra-Community trade. Moreover, invisibles may escape border tax adjustment.

Thus, equal rates among Member States might repair the perceived unfairness of different rates, but they do not really detract at all from Shoup's early warning against applying the equivalence theorem.

## E. Administrative Aspects

One of the great advantages of a destination-principle value-added tax that extends through the retail stage is that in applying border tax adjustments tax administrators do not have to worry about underlying taxable values. The notion of 'taxable value' is irrelevant for export rebate purposes; all prior-stage tax is refunded. But even at the import stage, there is little concern: under a tax-credit type of value-added tax any underpayment of tax due to undervaluation at the border is caught at the first taxable stage inland. Under such a tax, every domestic and imported good is always taxed in full at the rate applicable at the retail level. Thus, the notion 'taxable import value' has little relevance if goods are imported by registered traders. Since the value-added tax extends through the retail stage, only consumers might benefit from under-declaring their imports. But normally, say, in the case of cross-border shopping they would pay the full value-added tax of the exporting country as neither they nor the

72

supplying firm in the foreign country would be entitled to an export rebate. Thus, the advantage, if any, to a consumer would be small. In effect, out-of-State purchases would be taxed on the basis of their origin.

The relative ease with which the tax aspects of internationally traded goods are handled under the destination principle becomes a nightmare when the origin principle is applied in full. Since the country of production then claims the tax on value added up to the time of export, exported goods must be valued for tax purposes. This would be a highly contentious matter. Presumably, in some cases actual selling prices might be taken, but in a large and growing number of interlocking intra-EC transactions recourse would have to be had to some arm's length principle. This would be difficult to administer as anyone familiar with customs operations knows. Similar difficulties would arise on the import side of the ledger. To prevent the import value from being taxed in subsequent stages under the tax credit technique, some notional credit would have to be attached to imports (at the import stage!), by applying the importing country's tax rate to the import value. Again the appropriate underlying value would be an issue on which parties are not likely to agree forthwith.[12]

These administrative problems would be compounded under the restricted origin principle. Imagine goods passing through several Member States before being exported to, say, the United States. First, at each internal border the notional import tax credit, based on the importing country's value-added tax rate (which of course might be the same as or different from the exporting country's tax rate) would have to be established. Next, at the second and further export stages credit would have to be given for the same country's notional import tax. In short, the origin principle requires too much valuation, at each export and import.

### F. Concluding Remarks

In conclusion, on benefit grounds, some may prefer the origin principle, but others would not agree. Purists might make much of the equivalence theorem, but on practical grounds Shoup's early warning remains persuasive. Rate equalization may appear to solve the 'perceived fairness' problem, but it does not leave enough fiscal freedom to the Member States. If any doubt lingers on, administrative considerations weigh heavily against the origin principle. Fortunately, in a recent White Paper, the Commission (1985) has implicitly repudiated its early adherence to this principle.

But if the destination principle is to be retained for intra-Community trade, how then can the early vision of a common market similar to a domestic market

---

12. That the origin principle appears incompatible with the credit method of computing the tax liability has been pointed out by Shoup (1969, p. 264) and Messere (1979, p. 489).

(that is, without border controls and customs posts) be realized? The answer is simple: divorce border tax adjustments from border controls. Border controls are a customs and excise notion associated with physical inspection, but they are unnecessary for effecting border tax adjustments for value-added tax purposes; these can be made just as well through books of account. That solution is to be explored in the next section.

## IV. Removal of Border Controls: Destination-Principle Solutions[13]

This section shows that border controls can be fully eliminated by shifting border tax adjustments to books of account of taxable persons in other Member States. That pragmatic approach, which maintains the destination principle for intra-Community trade, leaves Member States free to set their own value-added tax rates. The approach has two variants. Under the first alternative, the collection of the compensating import tax is shifted to the first taxable person in the importing Member State under what is called a deferred payment scheme. Under the second alternative, the tax on exports is not rebated, but the first taxable person in the importing Member State is permitted a credit for the tax invoiced by the exporter of another Member State. Credits might be settled under an EC-wide clearing mechanism.

### A. Deferred Payment Scheme

The deferred payment scheme was pioneered in the Netherlands and has been in use there ever since the value-added tax was introduced. Under this approach, the compensating import tax, required to put foreign and domestic goods on an equal tax footing, is not levied, nor are imported goods checked physically at the border. Instead, the tax credit mechanism of the value-added tax is relied upon to ensure that the first taxable person in the importing country implicitly pays the compensating tax, because there is no offsetting credit. The method works so satisfactorily that nearly all of the compensating import tax otherwise payable on internationally as well as intra-Community traded goods is shifted inland. Additionally, eligibility for the export rebate may be proven on the basis of documentary evidence (bills of lading, payments from abroad, etc.) rather than physical clearance at the border. To qualify for a rebate, exporters are not required to prove that goods have left the country by a certificate or affidavit signed by the customs authorities.

Under the Dutch deferred payment scheme, therefore, customs clearance methods are set aside by incorporating the compensating import tax in the

13. This section draws heavily on Cnossen (1983a, pp. 153-57).

domestic ambit of the value-added tax. The scheme makes the recipient, not the importer of goods, liable to tax. The former has to compute and report the compensating import tax, but may take credit for that tax in the same return. To illustrate, suppose a manufacturer imports goods worth Df. 10,000 in a month in which his domestic sales are Df. 50,000 and his domestic purchases Df. 30,000. At a value-added tax rate of 19 percent, he has to declare taxable sales and imports totaling Df. 60,000 on which Df. 11,400 gross tax is due. At the same time, he is eligible for a tax credit of Df. 7,600 (Df. 5,700 + Df. 1,900) so that his net tax liability is Df. 3,800 which, of course, exactly equals 19 percent of his own value added of Df. 20,000. The value-added represented by the imported goods will be accounted for when they are incorporated in goods manufactured and sold to the following stage in the production/marketing chain.

The compensating import tax is due at the time the imported goods are received, but at the latest on the eighth day following the day of importation. The day of importation can be verified, because lorry drivers have to drop a copy of the exporter's invoice in a letter box at the border crossing. Similarly, the self-assessment procedure, which in theory is redundant, facilitates compliance control. In most cases, the effect of the scheme is that the import tax is not paid until the underlying goods are resold by the firm that actually receives them. This arrangement prevents a large number of export rebates having to be given in a country heavily engaged in transit trade.

Deferral is compulsory for nearly all registered taxpayers importing goods across the Belgian-Dutch border, as well as for all taxpayers, regardless of the port of entry, importing specified goods that by nature can be used only for taxable activities (in other words, not for personal consumption). Taxpayers importing other goods by sea or across the Dutch-German border may obtain a personal permit enabling them to make use of the deferred payment arrangements (provided they are resident, import regularly, and meet certain book-keeping requirements). Deferral is not permitted with respect to the importation of passenger cars and motor cycles (except by personal permit), goods imported through the postal service (unless a special permit is obtained), excisable goods (except banderolled tobacco products), and for goods imported by individuals, exempt farmers and small businesses, and non-resident taxpayers not having a permanent establishment in the Netherlands. Although nearly all imports are covered, the scheme is not so comprehensive as to make border controls completely redundant.[14]

The philosophy of the deferred payment scheme has also been set down in Article 23 of the Sixth Directive, as amplified in a draft-program of the Commission, as the direction the EC should take initially in an attempt to

14. Recently, the president of Philips, W. Dekker (1984), came out with a deferred payment scheme under which border controls would be abolished by 1992.

abolish border controls for the value-added tax. In 1982 the method became the subject of the Fourteenth Draft Directive. The preamble to the Directive states that experience shows that the scheme meets the requirements of simplicity and effectiveness in combating fraud. The Draft Directive limits the scheme's application to intra-Community trade, to goods used for taxable (i.e. not exempt) activities, and to regular taxpayers. The scheme would be administered through a system of permits. Obviously, like the Dutch scheme, it is not so comprehensively designed as to banish all border controls.[15]

## B. Tax Credit Clearance System

Under the second method, exporters of intra-Community traded goods would pay the value-added tax in their country of registration; export rebates would not be provided. But the first taxable person in an importing Member State would receive a credit for the full foreign value-added tax charged by his supplier. The importer would list that credit, and those of other foreign suppliers, separately on the return that he has to file with the local value-added tax office. Next, the importing State's value-added tax administration would collate and tabulate the various foreign tax credits separately for each exporting Member State. Finally, the foreign tax credits would be presented for payment to the value-added tax administration of exporting Member States. An EC-wide clearing mechanism could be set up to handle the various claims. Net balances would be payable by Member States that are net exporters.[16]

To illustrate this method of removing border controls, assume that exporter A in Member State X is faced with a value-added tax rate of 10 percent, and importer B in Member State Y with a rate of 20 percent. Furthermore, assume that A exports goods worth ECU 200 to B, and that these goods have been

15. As pointed out by Francesco Forte at the time of the conference, Italy has staunchly resisted the Community-wide adoption of the deferred payment scheme if not accompanied by a systematic exchange of information on the volume and kind of goods crossing intra-Community borders. He believed that the scheme would be open to evasion. That these fears are not without ground may be inferred from a study by Pedone (1981, p. 35) who concludes that in Italy: 'under any plausible interpretation . . . evasion is pervasive and large, reducing value-added collections by as much as two-thirds in some broad sectors and by two-fifths overall. Only in the production of energy . . . and in manufacturing, which is dominated by large firms that require modern accounting procedures and complete records to do business is evasion below 40 percent.' Forte saw the compliance with formalities at the border and the attendant congestion as the most important problems calling for a solution. Therefore, he proposed that, similar to excise suspension methods, goods crossing intra-Community borders should be allowed to move to inland clearing points where the goods would be released after payment of value-added tax.

16. For early brief references to this exciting prospect of doing away with border controls, see Jansen (1964, p. 27) and Sullivan (1967, p. 99). For a recent English-language account of the proposal, see Simons (1981, pp. 375-82).

produced with inputs worth ECU 150. Under present border tax adjustments, A receives a rebate of ECU 15 (10 percent of ECU 150) from Member State X; he pays no tax on his own value-added of ECU 50. Furthermore, importer B pays a compensating import tax of ECU 40 to Member State Y. Now, under the proposed method, A would pay ECU 5 (10 percent of ECU 200 minus a tax credit of ECU 15) to his country of registration. Thus, Member State X would receive ECU 20 with respect to the goods sold to B. Following importation, B, who would not be liable to any compensating import tax, would claim a tax credit or refund of ECU 20 from Member State Y, his country of registration. In turn, Y would present a compensation claim for the same amount to X. All tax transactions balance out exactly, because the value-added tax administration in X receives ECU 20 tax from exporter A and those X-country firms that preceded A, which it pays to Y, which in turn extends a credit to importer B for the same amount. And exporter A receives ECU 20 tax invoiced to B, who is reimbursed by the value-added tax administration of Member State Y. Member States X and Y may be said to administer the destination principle jointly.

The tax credit clearance system brings additional administrative obligations in its train (which, it should be noted, can generally be met when it suits the taxpayer), but on the other hand the costs of red tape and delays at the border, in all estimated at 5-7 percent of the value of intra-Community trade, would be eliminated (Commission, 1975). There would be no valuation problems at the time of exportation, because generally the exporter's selling price would be taken as the value for tax. Undervaluation would result in a lower tax credit in the importing country, as well as a lower tax credit clearance payment by the exporting country. An objection might be that the exporter's payment risk is increased by the amount of the value-added tax for which he invoices his foreign client. To meet that problem, the system might be supplemented with a zero-rate notification procedure. Upon his request the exporter would then receive a rebate, the importer would pay tax as if subject to a deferred payment scheme, and the exporting country would not have to compensate the importing country's tax administration. In view of administrative ramifications however, zero-rate notifications should be used sparingly, if at all.

### C. Direct Consumer Purchases and Rate Coverage Alignment

To remove border controls fully, both approaches have to be supplemented by rules exempting or regulating intra-Community imports by non-taxable persons, such as individuals and exempt organizations and institutions, including governments. A good case can be made for the complete elimination of compensating import taxes on internally traded goods bought by individuals. Until recently, individuals were charged the full value-added tax of their country of residence upon importing goods from other Member States with a total value in excess of the personal exemption, even though value-added tax had already been paid in the country of origin. In 1982, however, the European Court of Justice (Case 15/81) issued a prejudicial ruling that an importing country could impose a compensating import tax, but that the residual of the value-added tax paid in the exporting Member State and still incorporated in the value of the product had to be credited against the import tax.[17] Our proposal is that for over-the-counter sales, only the value-added tax of the country of the seller should be payable, i.e. for consumer purchases the tax would be applied on the basis of the origin principle.[18] To minimize abuse, however, mail order firms should be obliged to compute and remit the tax of the customer's Member State.

For current consumer goods the proposed procedure would mean little more than formalizing the *de facto* situation: individual exemptions are so high and cross-border shopping is so difficult to police that nearly all out-of-State purchases are taxed on the basis of their origin. As regards expensive durable consumer goods, such as cars and pleasure yachts, which attract higher rates of value-added tax in some countries, existing registration requirements in residence countries might be used to collect the additional import tax from consumers in the form of an extra registration duty or purchase tax. Of course, durables imported through dealers would be taxed in accordance with the tax credit clearance system. It would seem advisable to apply that system also to governments and other exempt entities. The amounts of tax involved are so large that the destination principle should continue to apply.

Although value-added tax rates do not have to be equalized for the removal of border controls, without question some alignment of the rate structures would facilitate a shift of border tax adjustments to books of account. Credits for foreign tax are easier to check if the coverage of a particular rate is uniform

17. This case, referred to as the Dutch Yacht case, reached the finale on May 21, 1985 (Case 47/84) when the Court of Justice ruled that the credit for foreign value-added tax incorporated in imported used goods should be calculated on their value net of such tax. Furthermore, the Court held that the creditable tax should be equal to: (a) in cases of goods subject to wear and tear: the amount of value-added tax actually paid in the exporting country less a percentage representing the proportion by which the goods had depreciated; and (b) in cases in which the value of the goods had increased: the full amount of the value-added tax actually paid. The Court's decision raises a problem, of course, if the importing Member State's value-added tax rate is lower than that of the exporting Member State. To solve this, the Commission has issued a draft Sixteenth Directive prescribing a special scheme for refund by the exporting Member State of the residual part of value-added tax levied by it on the initial purchase of a product and a scheme for taxing the product on importation on the basis of its second-hand value.
18. During the discussion, Satya Poddar suggested that over-the-counter sales in excess of a specified dollar threshold should also be taxable at the rate applicable in the country of residence of the buyer as evidenced by the address on his driver's license or other identification. But this would require vendors to distinguish between resident and non-resident customers, a task as open to abuse as the application of end-use exemptions.

78

with respect to intra-Community traded goods.[19] Thus, agreement might be sought on a dual rate structure that would comprise a reduced rate for agricultural and food products (simply defined as all items enumerated in the first 21 chapters of the Common Tariff Nomenclature), pharmaceutical and medical supplies, and a standard rate for all other products and services. Although the issue need not block the implementation of the proposed schemes, increased rates might be abolished.[20] Their coverage is mainly confined to motor vehicles and excisable goods. In other words, any revenue loss can be recovered by increasing the rates of corresponding user charges and excises. But apart from these minor adjustments, each Member State would remain free to set its own rate or rates of value-added tax.

### D. Which is the Preferred System?

Under the deferred payment scheme as well as the tax credit clearance system, border controls are removed, but fiscal frontiers, i.e. destination-based border tax adjustments, are maintained. There is nothing against taking this route as long as value-added tax receipts should continue to accrue to the state of consumption. Which scheme is then the best? Deferral has already found its way into the draft Fourteenth Directive. Unfortunately, actions to get the Directive accepted have dwindled in recent months. Possibly, the scheme's revenue implications — its introduction involves a one-time lag in collections — is the greatest obstacle to its adoption. The United Kingdom and Ireland have turned the tables by moving from deferral back to border collection.

The EC Commission (1985) realizes that the deferred payment scheme as set down in the Fourteenth Directive would not result in the complete abolition of border controls since documentation would still have to be provided at customs posts. Eventually, therefore, a tax credit clearance system is envisaged. For the time being, however, such a system is not considered feasible because widely divergent rates and coverage of the various value-added taxes would expose the system to the risk of heavy systematic fraud and evasion. Traders in high-rate Member States might obtain supplies in low-rate States and omit them from their records. According to the Commission, this would be detrimental to revenue and distort trade between low-rate and high-rate Member States.

19. On May 17, 1979 the Finance Committee of the West German Bundestag requested the Federal Government to push for Community harmonization of the coverage of value-added tax rates. See Commission (1980, p. 53).
20. For arguments in favor of a uniform value-added tax rate, see Cnossen (1982, pp. 205-14). Compare also the conclusion in Aaron (1981, p. 6): 'The central technical lesson of European experience is that multiple rates can be used to eliminate the regressivity of the value-added tax, but that the penalties in administrative complexity, increased compliance costs, and distortions in consumption decisions have been high and probably unjustified.'

These arguments deserve to be taken seriously. But fraud and evasion are also possible under the deferred payment scheme, simply by bypassing the letter box at the border crossing and not recording the purchases made abroad. Yet, the Commission (1985, p. 43) notes that deferral is 'a tried and proven system, operated by Belgium, the Netherlands and Luxembourg, and previously by Ireland and the United Kingdom'. More importantly, perhaps, goods shipped from one Member State to another under a deferred payment scheme are tax-free, while goods moved under the tax credit clearance system at least bear the tax of the exporting country; in other words, the 'caution money' feature of the value-added tax is kept intact.[21]

Broadly speaking, both methods are neutral with respect to trade as is the taxation of domestic transactions. Specifically, the value-added tax is not 'prepaid' (in the sense that the tax is due earlier than a retail sales tax would be), as is often believed, provided that tax payment, credit and refund arrangements coincide with commercial payment conditions and bad debts do not arise. To illustrate, assume that A sells taxable goods to B at the end of January on a 30-days payment term and that the relating tax is due at the end of the following tax period, i.e. February. Also assume that A did not purchase any goods with a tax credit attached in January and that B has no taxable sales in that month. The tax implications of this situation are that A invoices tax to B who in turn pays A and that A pays that tax to the tax office which in turn refunds the same amount to B — all at the end of February. The tax office does not receive any revenue until goods and services are sold to consumers. In this respect therefore a value-added tax is again identical to a retail sales tax, the only difference being that under the former the tax office has, as it were, security (caution money) for the tax payable on value added in earlier stages. In practice, tax and commercial terms of payment will not be fully synchronized for each transaction, but on average the result may not be very different from that described above. It can easily be shown that deferral and tax credit clearance systems do not distort this neutrality condition. The import sales tax method, however, under which the value-added tax is collected as if it were an import duty, is not neutral with respect to trade, because the tax must be paid at the border, yet under usual

21. During the discussion of the paper, Satya Poddar suggested that on goods shipped directly by the vendor to another taxable business, tax should be payable at the rate applicable in the country where the goods are being shipped. Such tax collections, identified separately by the vendor on his return, would be transferred to the country of shipment through a tax credit clearance mechanism similar to the one proposed in this paper. In the early 1970s such a system was also proposed in the Dutch professional literature (Tuk, 1971). Although the system might be feasible in a federal country with a centrally administered, if rate-differentiated, value-added tax for all provinces, it might be too complicated for a common market with independent taxing jurisdictions. Firms resident and taxable in one of the Member States would in effect have to become registered and taxable in another Member State for their exports to that State. This seems feasible for direct mail order sales, but would be difficult to police for sales between traders, particularly if various intermediaries, such as agents and freighters, are involved.

procedures it cannot be offset or refunded until the next tax period. Therefore, this method discriminates against imports.

Given the choice between the tax deferral system and the tax credit clearance system, the latter seems to have the edge. As opposed to the deferred payment scheme, the tax is collected 'in advance' from the exporter rather than 'afterwards' from the first inland trader or manufacturer, leaving the security aspect of the tax intact. This might meet British and Irish objections. The tax credit clearance system makes the value-added tax truly an EC affair as it integrates each Member State's value-added tax with the tax of other Member States. Export rebates and compensating import taxes may be said to collapse under a comprehensive clearing mechanism. To be sure, cooperation of the various value-added tax administrations would have to be strengthened in order to match exporters' gross tax liabilities with importers' foreign tax credits. But there is no reason to assume that this cannot be done. An agreement on the exchange of information has already been operational since 1979. The EC Commission is involved in verifying the 1.4 percent contribution to the common fund. And in other tax fields there are bilateral precedents such as the corporate tax imputation credits that France pays into the German Treasury.

## V. Summary and Conclusion

This paper has shown that, under a value-added tax, border tax adjustments, required to put foreign and domestically produced goods on an equal tax footing, can be made unambiguously and expeditiously. Thus, the value-added tax cannot be used to discriminate against goods from other Member States, an important objective of the Treaty of Rome. At present, the tax plays an important but varying role in the tax structure of the various Member States. Although the tax base has nearly been harmonized, rates still differ widely.

When the value-added tax was adopted in the late 1960s, destination-based border tax adjustments were thought to require the maintenance of border controls and these could only be eliminated if the tax were levied in accordance with the origin principle. This paper has argued that although the origin principle may be defended on some grounds, it would be difficult to operate satisfactorily. The conclusion, therefore, is that the various value-added taxes should continue to be based on the destination principle. Fortunately, border controls can be fully eliminated by shifting border tax adjustments to books of account either under a deferred payment scheme (imports taxable at the first inland stage) or a tax credit clearance system (exports taxable but a tax credit for importers payable by the exporting country). Little would change compared to the present situation. Out-of-State purchases by individuals would have to be taxed on an origin basis. Some alignment of the coverage of the various reduced value-added tax rates would be desirable and the increased rates might be abolished. The tax credit clearance system seems the preferred choice.

The most important implication of the proposed arrangements is that every Member State would remain free to set its own value-added tax rate(s) in line with national revenue objectives and social and economic policies. That flexibility is an enormous plus. With national monetary policies eventually being phased out, the weight on fiscal instruments for short-term stabilization and long-term structural adjustments will increase. Harmonization policies should allow maximum freedom in these fields. To be sure, the removal of border controls would cause some diversion of sales in border areas − because individuals might buy in a low-tax-rate State and import for use in a high-tax-rate State − and hence cause some distortion of manufacturing location decisions, but to a large extent those effects are already inherent in present arrangements. In any event, they are a small price to pay for the political and psychological benefits of being able to travel from Sicily to Scotland without having to stop at customs barriers.

Finally, removal of border controls for the value-added tax would not make much sense, if they had to be maintained for the excises. Shifting border tax adjustments to books of account of taxable persons in importing Member States might be possible for the excise on petroleum products, but would be difficult with respect to the excises on tobacco products and alcoholic beverages. It has been proposed, therefore, to shift the adjustments for these products to factory gates and retail outlets, following agreement on uniform bases of assessment (Cnossen, 1983a, pp. 157-62). Besides, a uniform system of in bond transportation of excisable goods should be devised. Furthermore, border taxes in the form of monetary compensatory amounts on farm trade might be done away with. The responsibility for drugs control could be left to the police.

In conclusion, a basic change in emphasis and direction seems to be required. To achieve the elimination of border controls, EC policymakers appear to believe that Member States should first be forced into the strait-jacket of uniform tax systems. Since this throws the baby out with the bathwater, obviously agreement is not forthcoming. This paper has shown that border controls should simply be phased out by shifting border tax adjustments to books of account, leaving national tax systems largely unaffected. In a wider sense, the advantages would be enormous. As Shoup (1969, p. 641) has noted: 'the mere psychological gain from complete absence of border control within a common market can scarcely be overrated; it creates a spirit of unity, an expansiveness of outlook, that is a good, if not close, substitute for political unity.'

Aaron, Henry J. (ed.). *The Value-Added Tax: Lessons from Europe.* Washington DC: The Brookings Institution, 1981.

Berglas, Eitan. 'Harmonization of Commodity Taxes: Destination, Origin and Restricted Origin Principles.' *Journal of Public Economics*, 16, 3, 1981.

Cnossen, Sijbren. 'Dutch Experience with the Value-Added Tax.' *Finanzarchiv*, 39, 2, 1981.

Cnossen, Sijbren. 'What Rate Structure for a Value-Added Tax?' *National Tax Journal*, 35, 2, 1982.

Cnossen, Sijbren. 'Harmonization of Indirect Taxes in the EEC.' In McLure, Charles E. Jr (ed.). *Tax Assignment in Federal Countries.* Canberra: ANU Press, 1983a. Reprinted in *British Tax Review*, 4, 1983a.

Cnossen, Sijbren. 'Sales Taxation in OECD Member Countries.' *Bulletin for International Fiscal Documentation*, 37, 4, 1983b.

Commission of the European Communities. *Simplification Programme.* Com (75) 67, def. *Mimeograph.* Brussels, 1975.

Commission of the European Communities. 'Report on the Scope for Convergence of Tax Systems in the Community.' *Bulletin of the European Communities*, Supplement 1, 1980.

Commission of the European Communities. 'First Report from the Commission to the Council on the Application of the Common System of Value Added Tax.' Document 83/426, September 14, 1983.

Commission of the European Communities. 'Completing the Internal Market.' White Paper from the Commission to the European Council. Brussels, 1985.

Dekker, W. *EC: Five-Year Plan on European Integration.* Brochure. Eindhoven: Philips, 1984.

Dosser, Douglas. 'Economic Analysis of Tax Harmonization.' In Shoup, Carl S. (ed.). *Fiscal Harmonization in Common Markets.* Vols 1, 2. New York: Columbia University Press, 1967.

Dosser, Douglas. 'Introduction to the Theory and Practice of Tax Harmonisation.' In Dosser, Douglas (ed.). *British Taxation and the Common Market.* London: Knight & Co., 1973.

Due, John F. and Friedlaender, Anne F. *Government Finance: Economics of the Public Sector.* 6th edn. Homewood, Ill.: Irwin, 1975.

Georgen, R. 'The Decisions of the Council of Ministers of the Community on the Proposal for a Sixth Directive on VAT.' *European Taxation*, 17, 2, 1977.

Guieu, Pierre. 'EC: Sixth Council Directive on VAT (Uniform Basis of Assessment).' *Intertax*, 7, 1977.

Jansen Committee. 'General Report of the Sub-Groups A, B and C.' In *The EEC Reports on Tax Harmonization.* Amsterdam: International Bureau of Fiscal Documentation, 1963.

Jansen, J.C. *Harmonisatie van de omzetbelasting in de E.E.G.-landen.*

Voordracht gehouden op de Belastingconsulentendag 1964 georganiseerd door de Nederlandse Federatie van Belastingconsulenten. Amsterdam: FED, 1964.

McLure, Charles E. Jr. 'State and Federal Relations in the Taxation of Value Added.' *The Journal of Corporation Law*, 6, 1, 1980.

Messere, Ken. 'A Defence of Present Border Tax Adjustment Practices.' *National Tax Journal*, 32, 4, 1979.

Musgrave, Richard A. *Fiscal Systems*. New Haven: Yale University Press, 1969.

Musgrave, Richard A. and Musgrave, Peggy B. *Public Finance in Theory and Practice*. 3rd edn. New York: McGraw Hill, 1980.

Neumark Committee. 'Report of the Fiscal and Financial Committee.' In *The EEC Reports on Tax Harmonization*. Amsterdam: International Bureau of Fiscal Documentation, 1963.

Organisation for Economic Co-operation and Development (OECD). *Revenue Statistics of OECD Member Countries 1965-1984*. Paris, 1985.

Pedone, Antonio. 'Italy.' In Aaron, Henry J. (ed.). *The Value-Added Tax: Lessons from Europe*. Washington DC: The Brookings Institution, 1981.

Shibata, Hirofumi. 'The Theory of Economic Unions.' In Shoup, Carl S. (ed.). *Fiscal Harmonization in Common Markets*. Vols 1, 2. New York: Columbia University Press, 1967.

Shoup, Carl S. *The Sales Tax in France*. New York: Columbia University Press, 1930.

Shoup, Carl S. 'Taxation Aspects of International Economic Integration.' In Institut International des Finances Publiques. *Aspects Financiérs et Fiscaux de l'Integration Économique*. The Hague: Van Stockum, 1953.

Shoup, Carl S. 'Theory and Background of the Value-Added Tax.' In *Proceedings, Forty-Eighth National Tax Conference*. Sacramento, Cal.: National Tax Association, 1955.

Shoup, Carl S. *Public Finance*. Chicago: Aldine Publishing Company, 1969.

Simons, A.L.C. 'Simplification of VAT Procedures in Intra-Community Trade.' *Intertax*, 10, 1981.

Sullivan, Clara K. 'Indirect Taxation and Goals of the European Economic Community.' In Shoup, Carl S. (ed.). *Fiscal Harmonization in Common Markets*. Vols 1, 2. New York: Columbia University Press, 1967.

Timmermans, Jean-Paul and Joseph, Ghislain T.J. 'Value-Added Tax (V.A.T.): National Modifications to Comply with the Sixth Directive of the Council of the European Communities.' *European Taxation*, 20, 2, 1980.

Tuk, C.P. 'Omzetbelasting. Streven naar opheffing van grenscontrole.' *Weekblad voor Fiscaal Recht*, 5034, 1971.

Whalley, John. 'Uniform Domestic Tax Rates, Trade Distortions and Economic Integration.' *Journal of Public Economics*, 11, 2, 1979.

Whalley, John. 'Border Adjustments and Tax Harmonization: Comment on Berglas.' *Journal of Public Economics*, 16, 1981.

# 3

# Alcohol and tobacco taxes: criteria for harmonisation

*John Kay and Michael Keen**

## I. DEBATES AND ISSUES

This paper is concerned with some of the major issues of economic principle that arise in trying to construct a coherent framework for the taxation of alcoholic drinks and tobacco products. This is not, of course, the enterprise on which the European Community is currently embarked. Instead there has been frequent resort to the simple pragmatism which says that convergence should proceed '. . . by reference to the points of departure rather than to a point of arrival' (Commission, 1980, para. 15). But this position, which attaches significance only to the process and the fact of harmonisation and none to what it is that the Community ultimately harmonises on, is clearly untenable. Nor is it consistently adopted: the discussion of routes to harmonisation is in fact heavily influenced by references to both general principles of taxation and the effects of alternative regimes on producers and consumers. The purpose here is to provide a clearer basis for the articulation of these arguments. We begin by recalling the context and nature of the principal controversies.

Progress on the harmonisation of alcohol and tobacco taxes has been little and slow (for a detailed account see Cnossen (this volume) or Kay and Keen (1985b)). This is hardly surprising. With both alcoholic drinks and tobacco products taxed at exceptionally high rates in many Member States (and, in the case of wine, at particularly low rates in others) apparently minor changes in tax regime can be expected to have substantial repercussions in product markets. Moreover the interest groups most directly affected — farmers, state monopolies, oligopolistic private producers — are formidable lobbyists. In these circumstances it is difficult to find compromises likely to be acceptable under the present constitutional arrangements of the Community.

The major difficulty in making any advance towards a harmonised alcohol tax regime has been the need to secure agreement on the relative rates of tax to be imposed on beer, wine and spirits. The essential problem is clear from Table 3.1: it is not difficult to guess which Member States are wine producers and

* The authors are grateful to Piervincenzo Bondonio, Sijbren Cnossen and other conference participants for their helpful comments; remaining errors are their own.

which wine importers. There can be little doubt that the domestic tax structures of at least some Member States have served as non-tariff protective devices. This was certainly the view of the Court of Justice when in 1983 it required the United Kingdom to lower the tax on wine relative to that on beer (Court of Justice, 1983); it is also striking that − as at the outset of harmonisation twenty years ago − Germany does not tax still wine, Luxembourg taxes only imported wine and Italy does not tax any wine (nor, now, does Greece).

Discussion of tobacco tax harmonisation has been principally concerned with the balance between specific and ad valorem components in the overall tax mix. As is clear from Table 3.2, the main respect in which Member States differ is not the level at which they tax cigarettes but the way in which they do so. The issue here is more than a technicality: once again, protective instincts are aroused. It is not difficult to explain, for instance, why France and Italy advocate predominantly ad valorem taxation. In both countries domestic manufacture is by a state monopoly using home-grown tobacco subsidised under the Common Agricultural Policy (CAP), whereas the principal importers typically use blond tobaccos that are inherently more costly − generally being regarded as of higher quality − and that are in any event (mostly) grown without CAP support; ad valorem taxation serves to widen the absolute price difference between domestic and imported products, to the benefit of the former. Conversely, of course, manufacturers of higher quality cigarettes have exerted pressure for the adoption of predominantly specific taxation. Under the terms of the current (and repeatedly extended) second stage of harmonisation, the ratio of specific to total tax on the most popular price category of cigarettes is required to lie between 5 and 55 per cent; as is evident from the table, positions have now become firmly entrenched, with most countries to be found close to the extremes of that permitted range.

*Table 3.1 Examples of excise duties on alcoholic drinks in the EC, as at March 1985*

| | Excise (ECU per litre) on: | | | National Currency per ECU (15.3.85) | |
|---|---|---|---|---|---|
| | Beer | Wine | Spirits (40% alcohol) | | |
| Belgium | .13 | .33 | 5.04 | BF | 44.69 |
| Denmark | .65 | 1.35 | 12.78[a] | DK | 7.95 |
| France | .03 | .03 | 4.50 | FF | 6.80 |
| Germany | .07 | 0.00 | 4.57 | DM | 2.22 |
| Greece | .22 | 0.00 | .21 | Dr | 93.83 |
| Ireland | 1.14 | 2.74 | 10.45 | IR£ | .71 |
| Italy | .18 | 0.00 | 1.00 | LIt | 1,402.04 |
| Luxembourg | .06 | .13 | 3.39 | LF | 44.69 |
| Netherlands | .23 | .33 | 5.05 | DG | 2.52 |
| United Kingdom | .70 | 1.60 | 10.27 | £ | .61 |

*Note:* a. Estimated average.
*Sources:* Duties: Commission, 1985a; ECU exchange rates: *Official Journal of the European Communities*, C 69/1 of 16.3.85.

*Table 3.2 Cigarette taxes in the EC, as at October 1, 1985[a]*

| | Proportional Taxes (Tax-Inclusive Rates) | | | Specific Excise (Per Thousand Cigarettes) | | Ratio of Specific to Total Tax[b] | Proportion of Tax in Consumer Price[b] |
|---|---|---|---|---|---|---|---|
| | VAT | Excise | Total | | | | |
| Belgium | 5.66 | 60.70 | 66.36 | BF | 107.00 | 6 | 70 |
| Denmark | 18.03 | 21.64 | 39.67 | DK | 538.20 | 54 | 86 |
| France | 25.60 | 45.46 | 71.06 | FF | 7.95 | 5 | 75 |
| Germany | 12.28 | 31.50 | 43.78 | DM | 56.50 | 40 | 73 |
| Greece | 3.85 | 53.58 | 57.43 | Dr | 76.95 | 5 | 61 |
| Ireland | 18.70 | 14.89 | 33.59 | IR£ | 33.20 | 55 | 74 |
| Italy | 15.25 | 53.39 | 68.64 | LIt | 2,348.25 | 5 | 72 |
| Luxembourg | 6.00 | 57.55 | 63.55 | LF | 67.00 | 5 | 67 |
| Netherlands | 15.97 | 37.94 | 53.91 | DG | 29.85 | 25 | 72 |
| United Kingdom | 13.04 | 21.00 | 34.04 | £ | 26.95 | 54 | 74 |

*Notes:* a. In percent unless otherwise indicated.

b. On most popular price category of cigarette.

*Source:* Industry source.

The issues described in the last two paragraphs seem to us the most substantive to have emerged from the harmonisation debate, and are of central concern in what follows. We do not attach similar significance to the links between alcohol and tobacco taxation and the CAP which have also been an important consideration in harmonisation proposals, although often only implicitly. It may be desirable to subsidise agricultural production within the Community, either in general or with particular reference to grapes and tobacco. But as both a practical matter and a point of economic theory these objectives are best achieved by direct action, not by distorting the consumer price of commodities for which agricultural value added is almost always an insignificant proportion of the final selling price. We also consider only briefly the health issues associated with tobacco and alcohol products; this is not because we believe these matters to be unimportant, but because this is a complex area in which we have no particular expertise.[1]

The structure of the paper is as follows. In Section II we consider how the relative tax rates on distinct but closely related commodities should be determined; here we describe and develop the theory relevant to the selection of tax rates to be applied to different alcoholic drinks or tobacco products. In Section III we then consider the appropriate balance between specific and ad valorem taxation for a particular product. These two sets of issues are closely related, and in the final section we draw together the implications of the analysis for both the design of excise tax structures and the policy of harmonisation.

1. See Atkinson (1974), Cnossen (1981), Grant, Plant and Williams (1982), Harris (1980), Maynard and O'Brien (1982) and O'Hagan (1983) for a flavour of the issues.

## II. Relative Tax Rates on Different Commodities

### A. Structures of Commodity Taxation

Although countries tax alcoholic drinks in a wide variety of ways, the British regime illustrates the issues and the possibilities. It distinguishes three principal groups of alcoholic drink: beer, wine and spirits. All are the subject of specific taxation at different rates; for spirits and, in effect, for beer the tax is based on the alcohol content; for wine the tax is based on quantity and is independent of strength. There are special rules for sparkling and fortified wines.

In considering how the relative tax rates on these three commodity groups should be determined, three principles have been advocated. One of these is the application of the inverse elasticity rule which is sometimes proposed for commodity taxation more generally. This implies that there should be relatively high tax rates on goods which display a low own-price elasticity of demand. Since this argument is often used (on flimsy evidence) to justify high rates of tax on tobacco and alcoholic drink in general, it might seem particularly appropriate to go on to apply it to the relative rates of tax on these commodities. Certainly such considerations seem to have influenced recent trends in the UK to reduce the rate of taxation on spirits relative to that on beer.

A second view is that the relative tax rates should simply be whatever is implied by a specific tax on alcohol content applied at the same rate to all beverages. This idea underlies the Commission's most recent draft directive on the taxation of wine and beer,[2] and a structure of this kind has been characterised as the ideal by the Economic and Monetary Affairs Committee.[3]

A view which contrasts with the inverse elasticity rule is the suggestion that in general all commodities should be taxed at the same rate. The high rates of taxation on alcohol and tobacco are, in themselves, clearly an exception to this principle, but one which might be justified by reference to moral or medical aspects of smoking or drinking. The principle would then imply that different kinds of alcoholic drink or tobacco product should be taxed at the same ad valorem rate.

### B. The Ramsey Rule

With these three options in mind, we review the principal results in the theory of

---

2. See Art. 3(1) of Commission (1985b).
3. 'If, therefore, we were considering a system of excise structure de novo, . . . the most obvious system to propose would be a single rate of excise duty per degree of alcohol for all alcoholic beverages. Such a system would avoid both distortion of competition and problems of definition.' (European Parliament, 1983, para. 22.)

optimal commodity taxation. The simplest optimal tax problem is that in which there is just one consumer (so that no distributional issues arise) with no source of income other than commodity endowments (since otherwise a uniform proportional tax would raise positive revenue with no deadweight loss) and in which the only tax tools available are commodity taxes (i.e. lump sum taxation is impossible). The problem is then to choose specific taxes $t_i$ to maximise indirect utility $V(p)$, p denoting the vector of $N + 1$ consumer prices, subject to a revenue constraint

$$\sum_{i=0}^{N} t_i X_i = R \qquad (2.1)$$

where $X_i$ denotes net purchases of commodity i, and R the required revenue. Since the value at consumer prices of net purchases is zero, the scale of p is arbitrary; for this reason the tax on some good, say good 0, is normalised at zero. With either constant producer prices or taxation of pure profits at 100 per cent the necessary conditions for this problem are the familiar Ramsey-Samuelson rule

$$\sum_{i=0}^{N} t_i S_{ki} = - \Theta X_k \qquad k = 0, \ldots, N \qquad (2.2)$$

where $S_{ki}$ denotes $\partial X_k / \partial p_i \big|_u$ and (for $R > 0$) $\Theta > 0$.

The derivation of simple results from (2.2) requires some restriction on the structure of preferences. The rule that the rate of tax on some commodity j should be inversely proportional to its own price elasticity of demand is a result of this kind, emerging from the special case in which there are no compensated cross-price effects with other taxed commodities; for with $S_{jk} = 0$, $j \neq 0$, k (2.2) becomes

$$t_j S_{jj} = - \Theta X_j \qquad (2.3)$$

which on rearrangement gives

$$\frac{t_j}{p_j} = - \Theta \left( \frac{1}{\varepsilon_{jj}} \right) \qquad (2.4)$$

where $\epsilon_{jj}$ is the compensated own price elasticity.[4] However, it is clear that this result is of little relevance in the present context. It is precisely because the cross-price elasticities between different alcoholic drinks are not zero that we group these commodities together for taxation and other purposes.[5]

Very different implications follow if instead of setting cross-price elasticities to zero we let them become infinite. In the three good case, for instance, (2.2) gives

$$\frac{t_1/p_1}{t_2/p_2} = \frac{\epsilon_{20} + \epsilon_{12} + \epsilon_{21}}{\epsilon_{10} + \epsilon_{21} + \epsilon_{12}} \qquad (2.5)$$

where $\epsilon_{ij} = -(p_j/X_i)\partial X_i/\partial p_j\big|_u$; as the compensated cross-price elasticities between the tax goods tend to infinity, the optimal ad valorem rates on the two thus become identical.

## C. Commodity Taxes and Leisure

A somewhat different view of the appropriate structure of commodity taxation emphasises the fact that there is one commodity — leisure — which necessarily escapes taxation. This issue is best explored by making use of the distance function, an approach pioneered by Deaton (1979, 1981); see also Auerbach (1981). The distance function $d(u, X^*)$, defined on utility u and consumption $X^*$ (now to be distinguished from net purchases X), is dual to the expenditure function and implicitly defined by

$$f(X^*/d(u, X^*)) = 1 \qquad (2.6)$$

where f denotes the direct utility function; d thus gives the fraction by which the consumption bundle $X^*$ must be scaled down to bring it into the indifference curve labelled u. The general properties of the distance function are discussed in Deaton (1979) and Deaton and Muellbauer (1980); the most important for present purposes is that its derivative with respect to $X_i^*$ is the compensated inverse demand function for commodity i, normalised by income m

---

4. A similar result involving uncompensated cross-price elasticities emerges if there are no uncompensated cross price effects.
5. The empirical evidence on cross-price effects is limited: for the UK, see McGuinness (1982) and Walsh (1982).

$$\frac{\partial d(u, X^*)}{\partial X_i^*} = a_i(u, X^*) = \frac{p_i}{m} \qquad (2.7)$$

For brevity we refer to $a_i$ as the shadow price of commodity i. In (2.7) m is to be interpreted as the value of any lump-sum income received from sources external to the household (taken here to be zero) plus the money value of its endowments $X^* - X_i$. Assuming that leisure is the only commodity with which the consumer is endowed, and taking this to be the untaxed good, the Ramsey rule (2.2) may be re-expressed as

$$\frac{t_i}{p_i} = \rho \left\{ 1 + \frac{1}{\eta_{00}} \frac{\partial \mathrm{Ln}\; a_i}{\partial \mathrm{Ln}\; X_0^*} \right\} \qquad (2.8)$$

where $\rho = R/m$, and

$$\eta_{00} = - \partial \mathrm{Ln}\; a_0 / \partial \mathrm{Ln}\; X_0^* \qquad (2.9)$$

(Deaton, 1979). Since d is concave in $X^*$, $\eta_{00} > 0$. Thus the Ramsey optimal tax rate on a particular commodity is positively related to the elasticity of the compensated inverse demand function with respect to leisure. Loosely speaking, suitable candidates for heavy taxation are commodities closely complementary with leisure in the sense that willingness to pay increases strongly with a compensated increase in leisure consumed (i.e. strong Hicksian q-complements).

The implications of (2.8) for the tax rates to be imposed on closely related commodities are clear. The rates to be levied on any two commodities are related as

$$\frac{t_i}{p_i} - \frac{t_j}{p_k} = \frac{\rho}{\eta_{00}} \left\{ \frac{\partial \mathrm{Ln}(a_i / a_j)}{\partial \mathrm{Ln} X_0^*} \right\} \qquad (2.10)$$

Thus it is optimal to tax commodities at the same rate if and only if their relative shadow prices are independent of leisure consumed; more precisely, commodities L to N are to be taxed at a uniform rate if and only if the distance function is implicitly separable between these commodities and the rest, meaning that it is of the form

$$d(u, X^*) = d(u, X_1^*, \ldots, X_{L-1}^*, g(u, X_L^*, \ldots, X_N^*)) \qquad (2.11)$$

(Deaton, 1979). It follows that differentiation between varieties of alcoholic drink can only be justified on efficiency grounds in terms of variations in relative shadow prices of this kind. In the absence of any reason to suppose that, for instance, the shadow price of spirits relative to that of wine varies with leisure – and we can think of none – there is some presumption in favour of uniformity.

## D. Taxation and Commodity Characteristics

We noted that the Economic and Monetary Affairs Committee had formulated the proposition that tax rates should reflect alcohol content. Such an argument would require that the alcoholic strength of a beverage be of central importance to its qualities in either production or consumption. Since it is evident that alcohol content is not a significant determinant of the costs of producing alcoholic drinks, such a relationship must be sought on the consumption side. The notion here, presumably, is that such similarities as exist between the demand responses of beer, wine and spirits arise principally from the common feature that all deliver alcohol. The simplest framework within which to develop these ideas is that of the linear characteristics model of Gorman (1980) and Lancaster (1966). Suppose then that preferences are defined not over the $(N+1)$ vector of consumption of marketed goods $X^*$ (the asterisk henceforth being dropped) but over a $(K+1)$ vector of characteristics Z, the latter being derived from the former through a fixed coefficients technology

$$Z = \Delta X \qquad\qquad (2.12)$$

where the element $\delta_{ji}$ of $\Delta$ denotes the quantity of characteristic j embodied in one unit of commodity i.

In general, the authorities cannot tax characteristics directly but only commodities, although they can relate commodity tax rates to the characteristics of these commodities (only if $N \geqslant K$ do commodity taxes imply unique characteristic taxes, and if $N > K$ then in general not all commodities will be bought). The Ramsey problem can readily be reformulated to deal with this; the only consequence is that the demand responses appearing in (2.2) must be seen as deriving from more primitive responses relating to the underlying characteristics. The additional structure that this lends to the tax rules is easily derived. Denoting by D(u, Z) the distance function characterising preferences over characteristics, the corresponding distance function over commodities is defined by

$$D(u, Z) = D(u, \Delta X) = d(u, X) \qquad\qquad (2.13)$$

Differentiating the second equality with respect to X gives

$$a_i(u, X) = \sum_{j=0}^{K} \delta_{ji} A_j(u, Z) \qquad (2.14)$$

where

$$A_j(u, Z) = \frac{\partial D(u, Z)}{\partial Z_j} \qquad (2.15)$$

is to be thought of as the shadow price of characteristic j. Thus the shadow price of any commodity is just the sum of the shadow prices of the characteristics, each weighted by the amount of the characteristic embodied in the commodity. Differentiating (2.14) and assuming, for simplicity, that leisure is itself a distinct characteristic with no other sources or uses, the Ramsey rule can now be expressed as

$$\frac{t_i}{p_i} = \sum_{j=0}^{K} w_{ji} \left( \frac{T_j}{A_j} \right) \qquad (2.16)$$

where

$$\frac{T_j}{A_j} = \rho \left\{ 1 + \frac{1}{\eta_{00}} \frac{\partial \text{Ln} \, A_j}{\partial \text{Ln} \, X_0} \right\} \qquad (2.17)$$

and

$$w_{ji} = \frac{\delta_{ji} A_j}{\sum_{k=0}^{K} \delta_{ik} A_k} \qquad (2.18)$$

By analogy with (2.8), $T_j/A_j$ may be thought of as the constrained optimal tax rate on the jth characteristic; note, however, that it will in general differ from the tax that would optimally be imposed on this characteristic if all characteristics were directly taxable. With this interpretation, (2.16) gives the Ramsey optimal commodity tax rate as a weighted average of the constrained optimal characteristic taxes, the weights being the implicit value share of each characteristic in the final commodity.

93

An immediate implication of these results is that commodities intensive in characteristics that are relatively strong q-complements with leisure are likely, on that score, to attract relatively high tax rates. Perhaps more interesting for present purposes are the implications for the taxation of commodities having some characteristics in common. For alternative forms of drink, for instance, (2.16) does indeed suggest that optimal commodity tax rates will vary systematically with alcohol content, tending to be higher on stronger drinks so long as alcohol is q-complementary with leisure. Note, however, that this will typically not be the only source of variation in tax rates across drinks: unless the shadow prices of non-alcohol characteristics supplied differentially by the alternative forms of drink are independent of leisure the optimal tax rates will, in general, reflect these other features of their characteristic composition. Whilst it is difficult to be sure precisely what these non-alcohol characteristics are — and this reflects a more general difficulty in rendering household production models operational — it is beyond doubt that other aspects of drink are important to consumers.

Indeed it is far from clear that alcohol itself is properly regarded as a characteristic. Even if the alcoholic drink would be preferred by consumers to a non-alcoholic but in all other respects identical beverage, the consumption of alcohol is not an end in itself but a device to achieve euphoria, relaxation and so on. In a richer model than that used here, the optimal tax structure is likely to reflect the relative advantages of the varieties of drink as means towards these ends, rather than just their alcohol content per se. While alcohol content is the most obvious similarity between beer, wine and spirits, it is not necessarily also the most important source of difference.

Given then some doubt as to the desirability of differentiating taxes on drink by alcohol content, one final result may be noted. Suppose that some subset of characteristics $Z^+$ is implicitly separable from leisure, so that the distance function can be written $D(u, X_0, Z^-, g(u, Z^+))$ where $Z^-$ denotes the complement of $Z^+$ and $X_0$. Clearly then the constrained optimal taxes on these characteristics are identical. From (2.16), it follows that the optimal tax rates on commodities containing only elements in $Z^+$ are also identical. In the absence of any reason to suppose the relative shadow prices of the characteristics embodied in the varieties of drink to vary systematically with leisure there is, again, a presumption that they should be taxed at the same rate.


### III. The Choice Between Specific and Ad Valorem Taxation

#### A. Preliminaries

We have noted that the balance between specific and ad valorem taxation has been the principal issue in attempts to harmonise the structure of tobacco taxation. With the relative tax rates on broad commodity groups determined, a similar question arises for the form of alcohol duties. For both wine and spirits, there are very large cost and quality differences between products, and the structure of the tax regime has very different incidence depending on whether it is predominantly specific or predominantly ad valorem.[6] The Commission has tended to favour the ad valorem taxation of tobacco products, and the specific taxation of alcoholic drinks; the economic rationale of this distinction is not apparent.

Both Barzel (1976) and Kay and Keen (1983) have argued that specific and ad valorem taxes, whilst equivalent in perfect competition with homogeneous products, may have significantly different effects when product quality and variety are endogenous. This can readily be seen by considering how the two kinds of tax affect the problem of profit maximisation perceived by the firm. In the absence of taxes, profits are

$$\pi(p, q) = pX(p, q) - c(q)X(p, q) - F \qquad (3.1)$$

where q is some scalar measure of product quality, affecting both demand and production costs, F denotes the fixed costs of production, and the marginal cost of output is, for simplicity, assumed to depend only on q. Introducing a specific tax $t_s$ and an ad valorem tax at tax-inclusive rate $t_v$, net profit becomes

$$\pi = (1-t_v)pX - \{t_s + c(q)\}X - F \qquad (3.2)$$

Note that q is assumed to be such that variations in quality do not affect the specific tax payable, a point to which we shall return. Maximising profit is then equivalent to maximising

$$\frac{\pi}{1-t_v} = pX - \left\{ \frac{t_s + c(q)}{1-t_v} \right\} X - \frac{F}{1-t_v} \qquad (3.3)$$

Comparing (3.1) and (3.3), the specific tax is precisely equivalent to an increase in the marginal cost of output, the extent of this increase being independent of product quality. An ad valorem tax tends to reinforce this effect of specific taxation, but in itself has two distinct features: it increases fixed costs, and it increases the marginal cost of quality at a given output. This latter characteristic of ad valorem taxation – often referred to as the multiplier

---

6. The choice between specific and ad valorem taxation will in general also involve a variety of administrative and political considerations, concerning in particular the ease and nature of indexation. Some of these issues are discussed in Kay and Keen (1982); we concentrate here on underlying questions of general economic principle.

effect – has been central to the tobacco taxation debate.

These simple observations suggest some likely effects of alternative tax structures. Specific taxation will tend to induce the firm to substitute quality for quantity, producing fewer but better goods. The multiplier effect of ad valorem taxation, in contrast, might be expected to induce degradation of quality; and if there are fixed costs (of, say, advertising or re-equipping) associated with the production of particular brands then one would similarly expect product variety to be less under a predominantly ad valorem regime. As a corollary product prices might be expected to be higher under a specific regime than when the same revenue is raised by ad valorem taxation. Effects of this kind may be negligible when the overall level of tax is low; for commodities taxed as heavily as drink and tobacco, however, apparently minor changes in tax structure may have significant implications for both producers and consumers. The rest of this section examines these implications more closely.

### B. When Quality is Endogenous

We begin with the simplest model of products of variable quality. Consumers do not differ in preferences or in incomes, and the product market is taken to be competitive in the sense that, in equilibrium, the net of tax price equals the tax-inclusive marginal cost

$$(1-t_v)p = c(q) + t_s \tag{3.4}$$

(equivalent to a zero profit condition in the absence of fixed costs) and the net marginal willingness to pay for quality equals its marginal cost

$$(1-t_v) \left. \frac{\partial p}{\partial q} \right|_u = \frac{\partial c}{\partial q} \tag{3.5}$$

The implications of (3.5) depend on the form of $\partial p/\partial q|_u$, the consumer's marginal valuation of product quality. Suppose that consumers treat a quality improvement identically to a reduction in price, so that the indirect utility function of the representative consumer is of the 'full price' form $V(p, q) = V(p + H(q))$ for some H. In this case (3.5) becomes

$$h(q) = \frac{-1}{(1-t_v)} \tag{3.6}$$

where $h(q) = \partial H/\partial q$ and we have normalised $c(q) = q + c$ for some constant c.

96

If H is strictly convex (so that the marginal willingness to pay for quality decreases as quality rises), it follows that the equilibrium quality level falls as the rate of ad valorem taxation is increased. Quality is here completely unaffected by the specific component of taxation.

Thus ad valorem taxation reduces product quality; specific taxation does not. The question is then: what form of taxation should be instituted? The answer will of course depend on precisely what it is that one is trying to accomplish. We focus here on the standard efficiency problem: that of raising a fixed amount of revenue at minimum welfare cost to consumers. Governments may in practice have other considerations in mind, perhaps the most plausible in the present context being health concerns and a simple desire to maximise revenue. The former, however, seem to us likely to influence mainly the appropriate level of the tax rather than its structure, and the latter is discussed in detail elsewhere (Kay and Keen, 1985a).

Consider then the problem of maximising $V(p + H(q))$ with respect to $t_v$ and $t_s$, subject to the revenue constraint

$$\{t_s + t_v p\} \, X(p + H(q)) = R \tag{3.7}$$

and subject also to the equilibrium conditions (3.4) and (3.5). The solution turns out to be simple: the optimal rate of ad valorem taxation is zero, the required revenue being raised entirely by specific taxation (Kay and Keen, 1983). A formal proof of this will emerge below, but the essentials of the argument can be developed geometrically. In Figure 3.1 we show in $(p, q)$ space the zero profit locus defined by (3.4); this has slope $(1 - t_v)$, and so (3.6) is tangential in equilibrium to a level curve of V, as shown at point A. Note that, by Roy's identity, indifference curves in $(p, q)$ space coincide with level curves of market demand $X(p + H(q))$. Starting from an initial equilibrium at A, consider a shift from ad valorem to specific taxation of the form

$$dt_s = -p^0 dt_v > 0 \tag{3.8}$$

where $p^0$ is the initial price. The effect is shown in Figure 3.2. Since the perturbation is such that profits at the initial price-quality configuration are unchanged, its effect is to rotate the zero profit locus anticlockwise about A. Clearly the new tangency must lie along AB, and the perturbation must increase price, quality, quantity demanded and consumer welfare. With welfare increased, the perturbation will be desirable so long as tax revenue does not fall. Since demand is increased, revenue from the specific component will certainly increase so long as $t_s > 0$; similarly expenditure rises, and hence so too do ad

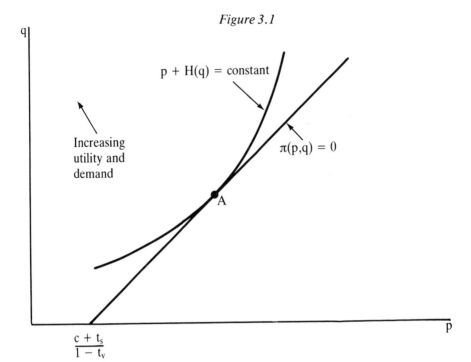

*Figure 3.1*

valorem receipts so long as $t_v > 0$. Proceeding in this way the ad valorem rate is optimally driven to zero.[7]

The result can be rationalised as follows. In order to raise revenue by indirect taxation one must necessarily distort prices, driving a wedge between the prices paid by consumers and received by producers. But the need to tax does not of itself imply a need to distort quality. In the absence of any extraneous reason for wishing to influence quality, the Bhagwati principle that intervention should be targeted as closely as possible to its object suggests that it would be better not to distort quality decisions. Since in this model it is only ad valorem taxation that affects quality, efficiency then points to reliance on specific taxation alone.

## C. When Product Variety is Endogenous

Both alcohol and tobacco are characterised by extensive product differentiation. Some of this differentiation reflects genuine and costly

---

7. Note that this argument cannot be continued to infer an optimally negative ad valorem tax, since the revenue consequences of further reductions in $t_v$ are then adverse.

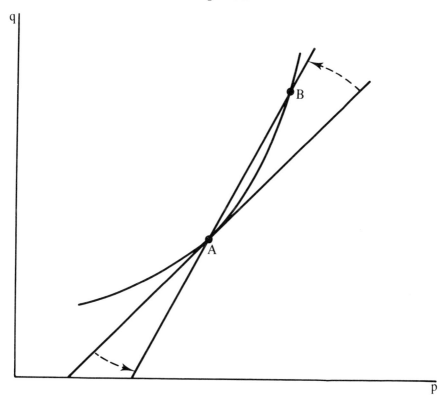

*Figure 3.2*

variations in quality, and it is vertical differentiation of this kind which is considered in subsection B above. Products are also differentiated by their positioning across the spectrum of consumer tastes. We may observe that different brands of beer, or cigarette, or malt whisky, have similar production costs, but some consumers will prefer one and others a different variety. There is also differentiation of the product which is the result of advertising and other promotional activities which create a product image in the mind of consumers without significantly affecting the objective characteristics of the commodity concerned.

Models which reflect these latter two types of horizontal differentiation are typically complex. In Kay and Keen (1983) we consider a Hotelling-Salop model of monopolistic competition in which consumers differ continuously as to their preferred product type, and set-up costs imply that only a finite number of products will be produced in equilibrium. Two main results emerge from the analysis there. First, the number of products available in equilibrium turns out to be decreasing in the ad valorem rate and independent of the specific component; this tends to confirm the earlier intuition that ad valorem taxation discourages product variety, and echoes the result concerning product quality just discussed. Second, minimising the excess burden of taxation in this case calls for a positive ad valorem tax; the optimal ad valorem rate emerges as 75 percent. The social function of this ad valorem tax is not, however, to raise revenue: it is a property of the model that the no-tax outcome involves socially excessive product differentiation, and an ad valorem tax of 75 percent serves to move product variety to its first-best level. On this account we would wish to levy the ad valorem tax even if no revenue were desired from the tobacco tax. The ad valorem tax rate is fixed, and the specific rate rises or falls with desired tax revenue. The tendency towards excessive differentiation is of course model-specific, and it is known that other models generate too little variety in the no-tax equilibrium (see, for instance, Dixit and Stiglitz, 1977); in such cases one might even expect optimality to call for negative ad valorem taxation. The principal conclusion to be drawn from these arguments and those of the preceding subsection is thus a broad association of targets and instruments, ad valorem taxes being used to control product variety and specific taxes to yield government revenue.

### D. When Commodity Units are Variable

In subsection B we showed that when quality is variable it is generally inappropriate for governments to use ad valorem taxation. This result depended, however, on preferences taking a particular form: quality variation was there seen by consumers as equivalent to a variation in price, and this is also true of the model underlying the discussion in subsection C. An alternative possibility is one in which consumers perceive quality variations as substitutable for quantity variations. Clearly this could not sensibly be applied to wine, or to tobacco quality, for example: you do not feel compensated for the inferior quality of a wine, or a cigarette, by being offered an opportunity to drink or smoke more.

But quantity and quality are directly substitutable when the product can be made more or less concentrated. If the quality of a cigarette were measured by its length, for example, then a smaller number of higher quality cigarettes could be seen as similar to a larger number of inferior ones. Spirits can be prepared in more concentrated form, and diluted by consumers to their requirements; and manufacturers have in fact responded to limitations on the quantity of duty-free spirits which may be imported by distributing higher strength bottles for the purpose. Suppose then that both welfare and production costs depend only on the product $qX$: $X$, for instance, might be litres of whisky and $q$ its proof strength, or, to take an example in Barzel (1976), $X$ a number of light bulbs and $q$ their durability. Then $V(p, q) = V(p/q)$ and with constant returns, $C(q, X) =$

100

$cqX$, $c > 0$, so that the equilibrium conditions analogous to (3.4) and (3.5) become

$$(1-t_v)p = t_s + cq \qquad (3.9)$$

and

$$(1-t_v)p/q = c \qquad (3.10)$$

which together imply $t_s/q = 0$.

The implication is clear. If a specific tax is specified as so much per litre of whisky, if manufacturers are able costlessly to concentrate whisky into tiny volumes, and if drinkers can costlessly reconstitute the concentrated product, then together seller and buyer can avoid the tax by dealing in infinitely small volumes of infinite strength which will in due course be taxed at an infinitely high rate. An ad valorem tax however, does not necessarily distort quality in this model; with a wholly ad valorem regime, (3.9) and (3.10) reduce to

$$1 - t_v = cq/p \qquad (3.11)$$

so that adjustment to the tax can come only from p, only from q, or from both.

Doubtless the costs of avoiding specific taxes in this way are often significant, but the underlying issue is an important one: what exactly is it that one is trying to tax when imposing a specific tax on some commodity? This leads back to the view of commodities as bundles of characteristics. If, as was assumed in Section II, it is impossible to alter the characteristic content of a unit of the product then avoidance of specific taxation in the way just described is impossible; it is when characteristic intensity can be varied that potential problems arise. To preclude them, it would be necessary to define specific taxes in terms of units of particular characteristics. The difficulty here is that some characteristics may be unobservable; nevertheless, it may be sensible to relate specific taxes to such attributes as can be monitored. This provides some rationale for relating the taxes on alcoholic drinks to their respective strengths. It also suggests some merit in the old United Kingdom system of taxing cigarettes by the weight of their tobacco content.

For the reasons just described, specific taxes commonly need to be defined relative to some distinctive characteristic of the commodity concerned. Loosely speaking, the principal margin of non-price choice for the firm is then in the unmonitored set of characteristics: the specific tax payable on a cigarette may depend, for instance, only on its tobacco content, but that tobacco can be a cheap or expensive blend, the cigarettes attractively or poorly packaged, and so on. It is in respect of these unmonitored attributes that the analysis of subsection B is most appropriate, and it is for this reason that we earlier specified q to be such that quality variations do not affect liability to specific taxation.

## E. When Income Distribution is of Concern

Ad valorem taxation implies relatively low taxation of relatively low quality products. If these are mainly purchased by low income households, then ad valorem taxation will be more progressive than specific taxation in its distributional effects. This does not itself imply that ad valorem taxation is to be preferred, since efficiency aspects must also be considered. The purpose now is to examine how distributional considerations affect the earlier arguments suggesting a presumptive superiority of specific taxation.

Suppose that the population can be divided into $N_1$ 'poor' households and $N_2$ 'rich'. The former purchase a cheap (and presumably nasty) commodity variant whose quality we take to be fixed; the welfare of a poor household then depends only on its lump-sum income, $m_1$, and on the price of the relevant brand, $p_1$, giving an indirect utility function of the form $V^1(p_1, m_1)$. The rich purchase a more expensive product, $p_2 > p_1$, whose quality q may vary in the way described earlier; we take the preferences of this group to be of the form $V(p_2 + H(q))$. For simplicity, again, we assume that changes in the tax system do not induce any brand switching. Denoting by $x_i$ the per capita consumption of good i by group i, i = 1, 2, and by W the social welfare function, the formal problem is then to maximise the Lagrangean

$$L = W[N_1 V^1(p_1, m_1), N_2 V^2(p_2 + H(q), m_2)]$$

$$+ \lambda \left[ \sum_{i=1}^{2} \{t_s + t_v p_i\} N_i x_i - R \right] \tag{3.12}$$

subject to the maintenance of market equilibrium. Equilibrium in the market for the cheap variant is characterised by a zero profit condition of the form (3.4), while the analogue of (3.5) is also required for variant 2. It is then routine to show that

$$\frac{dp_1}{dt_s} = \frac{dp_2}{dt_s} = \frac{1}{1-t_v} \tag{3.13}$$

(so that the two prices respond by an identical amount to the specific component), while

$$\frac{1}{P_1}\frac{dp_1}{dt_v} = \frac{1}{P_2}\frac{dp_2}{dt_v} - \frac{1}{P_2(1-t_v)}\frac{dq}{dt_v} = \frac{1}{1-t_v} \tag{3.14}$$

where from (3.6)

$$\frac{dq}{dt_v} = \frac{-\{h(q)\}^2}{h'(q)} < 0 \tag{3.15}$$

Thus the proportionate increase in price induced by ad valorem taxation is smaller for the more expensive variant, part of the response coming as a degradation of quality; if the quality of variety 1 were also liable to vary, the effect on the relative price could of course go either way. Performing the maximisation and using (3.11) and (3.12) together with the earlier result that $dq/dt_s = 0$ gives the necessary conditions[8]

$$\sum_{i=1}^{2} p_i n_i x_i (1-b^i) + \sum_{i=1}^{2} \{t_v + t_s p_i\} n_i s_{ii} p_i + \xi t_v n_2 x_2 = 0 \tag{3.16a}$$

$$\sum_{i=1}^{2} n_i x_i (1-b^i) + \sum_{i=1}^{2} \{t_v + t_s p_i\} n_i s_{ii} = 0 \tag{3.16b}$$

where $n_i$ denotes the proportion of the population in group i, $\xi = dq/dt_v$, $s_{ii} = \partial x_i/\partial p_i|_u < 0$ and

$$b^i = \frac{(\partial W)/\partial V_i)(\partial V^i/\partial m_i)}{\lambda} - \{t_s + t_v p_i\}\frac{\partial X_i}{\partial m_i} \tag{3.17}$$

denotes the net social marginal utility of income to group i; we shall take it that $b^1 > b^2$.

To see the implications of these conditions, consider the effects of a shift from specific to ad valorem taxation. An increase in the ad valorem tax imposes a welfare loss on each group proportional to its initial expenditure $p_i n_i x_i$, and (to the first order) raises revenue in an amount also proportional to expenditure; the welfare losses are to be weighted by $b^i$, so that the additional revenue is more than worth its welfare cost if

8. The earlier proposition that efficiency requires $t_v = 0$ can be derived by setting $n_1 = 0$, multiplying (3.16b) by $p_2$ and comparing the result with (3.16a).

$$\sum_{i=1}^{2} p_i n_i x_i (1-b^i) > 0 \qquad (3.18)$$

which is equivalent to the condition

$$cov[b^i, \ p_i x_i] < 0 \qquad (3.19)$$

where cov[·] denotes a population covariance. In the absence of efficiency considerations, ad valorem taxation is thus beneficial if the rich not only purchase a more expensive variant than the poor but also spend more on it. Specific taxation, however, raises revenue and imposes welfare losses in proportion to quantity purchased, and so is attractive in the same sense if

$$\sum_{i=1}^{2} (1-b^i) n_i x_i = - \ cov[b^i, \ x_i] > 0 \qquad (3.20)$$

so that the rich purchase more units of the product than do the poor. There are also efficiency aspects to the comparison between specific and ad valorem taxes. The second terms in (3.16) indicate that both kinds of tax impose a deadweight loss of the usual kind; this is of no special interest here. As we have seen, however, ad valorem taxation involves another inefficiency: quality distortion. Note that this mitigates against the use of ad valorem taxation even if zero weight is given to the welfare of the rich (who are here the only group to be affected by quality variation): for the only reason the authorities are then interested in the rich is as a source of revenue enabling the tax burden on the poor to be reduced, and a high ad valorem tax will have the undesirable effect of eroding the taxable capacity of the rich by degrading the quality of their preferred brand. This consideration is naturally stronger the larger the market share of the more expensive variant.

The appropriate balance between these various considerations becomes clearer if one solves (3.16) to give

$$t_v = \frac{cov[b^i, \ (\bar{p}-p_i)x_i]}{\lceil s.var[p]+\xi n_2 x_2 \rceil} \qquad (3.21)$$

and

$$t_s = \frac{cov[b^i, \ x_i]}{s} - t_v \bar{p} \qquad (3.22)$$

104

where $\bar{p} = \sum\limits_{i=1}^{2} n_i p_i$ denotes the average price paid for the product (in terms of the number of purchases rather than quantities bought), the variance var[p] is defined analogously, and it has been assumed for simplicity that substitution responses are the same in the two groups,[9] so that $s_{ii} = s$, $i = 1, 2$. Since the rich pay a price above the population-wide average, the numerator of (3.21) is unambiguously positive, and hence so too is the optimal rate of ad valorem taxation.[10] Moreover, (3.21) shows clearly how the optimal ad valorem rate depends on the balance between considerations of equity and efficiency. The former are captured in the numerator, which can be rewritten as

$$\bar{p}.\text{cov}[b^i, x_i] - \text{cov}[b^i, p_i x_i] \qquad (3.23)$$

and so, recalling our earlier discussion, can be seen as measuring the extent to which ad valorem taxation has distributional attractions distinct from those offered by specific taxation; intuitively, this is necessarily positive because ad valorem taxation will, like specific taxation, pick up any correlation between $b^i$ and $x_i$, but will also pick up the effects of the difference between the prices paid by the two groups. The denominator reflects efficiency losses through both price and non-price distortions; in particular (3.21) confirms that the optimal ad valorem rate is lower the more sensitive is quality and the greater the volume of affected demand. The sign of the optimal specific tax is in general ambiguous, though if the rich do not purchase the product in greater amounts than the poor — and this is perhaps not implausible for tobacco and alcohol — then it is optimal to provide a specific subsidy. Thus the optimal balance between specific and ad valorem taxation is surprisingly sensitive to the recognition of distribution concerns: while efficiency calls for only specific taxation to be used, the introduction of equity considerations may plausibly point towards the use of ad valorem taxation not only to raise revenue but also to finance a specific subsidy.

Distributional arguments may thus provide some justification for the use of ad valorem taxation. But we attach little importance to such considerations in the European context. For if effects of the kind just described were significant then it would at some point be worth introducing appropriately differentiated specific taxes on the alternative product variants, albeit at some additional

9. The more general solutions are of the same form as (3.21) and (3.22) but with p and var[p] replaced by analogues calculated with weights $n_i s_{ii} / \sum\limits_{i=1}^{2} n_i s_{ii}$

10. This conclusion is conditional on the assumption of identical substitution responses.

administrative cost. Moreover it is clear that excise taxation is an extremely blunt instrument with which to pursue distributional objectives; while it is only in special cases that commodity taxes have been shown to be superfluous (Atkinson and Stiglitz, 1976) one would certainly expect income tax-transfer schemes to be a more powerful device than either alcohol or tobacco taxation, particularly in view of the heterogeneity of consumers' preferences towards these goods. Distributional considerations may be relevant to the choice between specific and ad valorem taxation in some less developed countries with creaky institutions and unsophisticated income taxes; they should be given little weight in the European Community.


## IV. Conclusions

### A. For the Theory of Commodity Taxation

There is an apparent inconsistency between the directions of the arguments in Sections II and III. Section II made a case for taxing different but closely related commodities at the same rate. Section III concluded that individual commodities were often best taxed wholly by means of specific taxation. This implies that higher value products would generally bear lower tax rates than inferior ones, if these tax rates were expressed on an ad valorem basis. How can these two arguments be reconciled?

The answer is that what is meant by 'taxing commodities at the same rate' is by no means as obvious as it appears at first sight. It is natural to assume that this implies a common rate of ad valorem taxation. But this is a considerable oversimplification. Suppose I have the choice between a commodity at £1 and a similar commodity of higher value at £2. The higher value commodity may simply last twice as long or be twice as large. In that case it is effectively two of the inferior commodity, and an ad valorem tax achieves the objective of taxing both at the same rate. Alternatively, I may perceive the £2 commodity as worth £1 more. It saves me £1 in labour to buy it, or use it, or in repair costs. In that case, the £2 commodity is, as far as I am concerned, the same as the £1 commodity plus £1. An ad valorem tax does not tax the two items at the same rate; it taxes the more expensive commodity more heavily.

The point is well illustrated by experience in the UK tobacco market. Prior to Britain's entry into the EC cigarettes were taxed by weight of tobacco content, and many brands were sold with coupons which could be collected and exchanged for valuable gifts. This form of forced saving was apparently popular with many consumers, and the value of the coupons was presumably reflected in the price of the cigarettes; the provision of coupons was an unmonitored quality attribute in the sense of the discussion above, and the 'full price' of the cigarettes was the nominal price less the anticipated value of the gifts. After the introduction of ad valorem taxation, coupons quickly disappeared from the market. For the multiplier effect meant that cigarettes with coupons were effectively taxed more heavily than those without. The social loss from the destruction of this curious institution was probably small but the example is a clear illustration for other, more important, but less obvious issues; cases where the taxed characteristic cannot be readily substituted or achieved in other ways.

Thus the central problem is that uniform taxation requires sensitive interpretation when commodities consist, as they generally do, of characteristics bundled in different ways. As Section II showed, what we should be seeking to tax are those characteristics which ultimately yield utility to consumers; all we can actually tax is commodities. If all commodities (including leisure) were taxed at the same rate, this would be unimportant since all characteristics would also be taxed, implicitly, at the same rate. The issue is relatively minor for commodities which are taxed at low, and broadly similar, rates – although there are still the complications described in subsection II.C arising from differences in the degree of complementarity with leisure. But for commodities such as drink and tobacco where the tax rates are extremely high these issues cannot be avoided.

The answer is that as far as possible the tax structure should be based on characteristics rather than on commodities as such. It is then necessary to spell out which characteristics of drink and tobacco it is that have led to the imposition of high tax rates on these commodities, and this is far from obvious. But it seems unlikely that these undesirable characteristics include tobacco quality, or packaging, or the availability of brands of alcohol or tobacco close to one's personal preference, or the length of time for which a whisky or wine has matured, all of which are implicitly taxed under ad valorem but not specific taxation.

The design of the particular form of such specific taxation requires identification of those product characteristics which have led to the imposition of rates of commodity taxation much in excess of those applied to commodities at large. We can identify two: medical arguments, and the association of both commodities with leisure which yields both efficiency arguments for taxation and a feeling that they are suitable subjects for heavy taxation even at some efficiency cost. The first of these considerations would point to taxation based on alcohol and tobacco content, possibly modified to the extent that there was evidence that particular forms of alcohol or tobacco consumption are more or less than averagely associated with health risks – either because of their innate characteristics or because they are more or less addictive. The second argument suggests uniformity in effective tax rates across product types; but such taxation should not be levied as an ad valorem tax because of the resulting tendency to inefficient product quality degradation, with resulting welfare and revenue loss. This illustrates an important general observation: 'taxing all

107

commodities at the same rate' is not synonymous with a uniform rate of ad valorem taxation.

## B. For Policy Towards Tax Harmonisation

In this paper, we have sought to consider the appropriate structure for an excise tax regime for a single country or group of countries. We believe this is the relevant perspective in the light of the Commission's latest proposals; in Kay and Keen (1982) we gave some consideration to an intermediate stage of harmonisation in which Member States might levy different rates of tax within a structure which minimised trade distortions. We have also treated the choice of regime as primarily a matter of economic efficiency. Thus we reject the view that excise tax harmonisation is essentially a political issue – the theory of convergence by reference to point of departure rather than arrival. Since we have demonstrated that alternative structures are likely to have large differences in their economic effects, this political argument would require that it be demonstrated that the advantages of a common alcohol or tobacco tax regime for the Community were so large as to outweigh any conceivable measurement of those differences. Such a demonstration has not been made and we do not know how one might seek to establish a proposition of that kind.

Indeed it is not apparent to us that there are substantial advantages of any kind from excise duty harmonisation; the view that harmonisation of the excises is required if intra-Community border controls are to be removed has been challenged forcefully (and in our view convincingly) by Cnossen (1983) and Cnossen and Shoup (this volume). The argument that harmonisation is useful as a way of curbing Member States' ability to use internal taxes as non-tariff barriers has some merit (Keen, 1986), but neglects the many other functions that excises perform within domestic budgetary structures.

Two basic propositions to emerge from the discussion are that taxation should, as far as possible, be based on product characteristics rather than on commodities themselves, and that it should principally reflect those characteristics which reflect product quantity rather than product quality. This implies a rather limited role for ad valorem taxation, but such taxes retain two purposes – to ensure that peripheral product characteristics are taxed at a rate similar to that on other commodities and to reduce differentiation and prices in oligopolistic market structures. These considerations would point to ad valorem rates on alcohol and tobacco products at the upper end of the range applied to other commodities, with the balance of required revenue raised from specific taxation.

The tax structures implied are then the following. Drink and tobacco should be subject to VAT at one of the highest general rates applied in any Member State, but there is little case for further elements of ad valorem taxation. For

108

alcoholic drink, revenue should in part be raised by a specific duty on alcohol content, common to all beverages. The balance should be derived from specific taxes on the principal categories of drink − beer, wine, spirits − at rates designed to ensure broad equality of implied ad valorem rates on products of average quality in each of these groups. Similarly, tobacco products should be the subject of a general duty on tobacco itself, supplemented by a specific tax on cigarettes. These proposals are tentative, since any detailed prescription must depend on a quantitative assessment of these general arguments. Our purpose in this paper has been to define the framework of analysis within which such an assessment should take place.

Atkinson, Anthony B. 'Smoking and the Economics of Government Intervention.' In Perlman, Mark (ed.). *The Economics of Health and Medical Care*. London and New York: Macmillan, 1974.

Atkinson, Anthony B. and Stiglitz, Joseph E. 'The Design of Tax Structure: Direct Versus Indirect Taxation.' *Journal of Public Economics*, 6, 1976.

Auerbach, Alan J. 'The Theory of Excess Burden and Optimal Taxation.' National Bureau of Economic Research, *Working Paper* 1025, 1981.

Barzel, Yoram. 'An Alternative Approach to the Analysis of Taxation.' *Journal of Political Economy*, 84, 6, 1976.

Cnossen, Sijbren. 'Issues in Excise Taxation: The Alcohol Problem.' In Roskamp, Karl W. and Forte, Francesco (eds). *Reforms of Tax Systems*. Detroit: Wayne State University Press, 1981.

Cnossen, Sijbren. 'Harmonization of Indirect Taxes in the EEC.' In McLure, Charles E. Jr (ed.). *Tax Assignment in Federal Countries*. Canberra: ANU Press, 1983. Reprinted in *British Tax Review*, 4, 1983.

Cnossen, Sijbren. 'Tax Structure Developments.' Chapter 1, this volume, 1986.

Cnossen, Sijbren and Shoup, Carl S. 'Coordination of Value-Added Taxes.' Chapter 2, this volume, 1986.

Commission of the European Communities. 'Explanatory Memorandum' to 'Proposal for a Council Directive Amending Directive 72/464/EEC on Taxes other than Turnover Taxes which Affect the Consumption of Manufactured Tobacco'. 1980.

Commission of the European Communities. 'Completing the Internal Market.' White Paper from the Commission to the European Council. Brussels, 1985a.

Commission of the European Communities. 'Proposal for a Council Directive Laying Down Certain Rules on Indirect Taxes which Affect the Consumption of Alcoholic Drinks.' *Official Journal of the European Communities*, C 114 of 8.5.85, 1985b.

Court of Justice of the European Communities. 'Commission of the European Communities v United Kingdom of Great Britain and Northern Ireland.' Judgement in Case 170/78. *Reports* 7, 1983.

Deaton, Angus. 'The Distance Function in Consumer Behaviour with Applications to Index Numbers and Optimal Taxation.' *Review of Economic Studies*, 46, 3, 1979.

Deaton, Angus. 'Optimal Taxes and the Structure of Preferences.' *Econometrica*, 49, 5, 1981.

Deaton, Angus and Muellbauer, John. *Economics and Consumer Behaviour*. Cambridge University Press, 1980.

Dixit, Avinash K. and Stiglitz, Joseph E. 'Monopolistic Competition and Optimum Product Diversity.' *American Economic Review*, 67, 3, 1977.

European Parliament. 'Report on the Communication from the Commission to the Council.' Document 1-1121/83, 1983.

Gorman, W.M. 'A Possible Procedure for Analysing Differentials in the Egg Market.' *Review of Economic Studies*, 47, 5, 1980.

Grant, M., Plant, M. and Williams, A. *Economics and Alcohol: Consumption and Control*. London: Croom Helm, 1982.

Harris, Jeffrey E. 'Taxing Tar and Nicotine.' *American Economic Review*, 70, 3, 1980.

Kay, John A. and Keen, Michael J. *The Structure of Tobacco Taxes in the European Community*. London: Institute for Fiscal Studies, 1982.

Kay, John A. and Keen, Michael J. 'How Should Commodities be Taxed?' *European Economic Review*, 23, 1983.

Kay, John A. and Keen, Michael J. 'Commodity Taxation for Maximum Revenue.' *Mimeograph*, 1985a.

Kay, John A. and Keen, Michael J. 'Alcohol and Tobacco Taxes in the European Community: Criteria for Harmonisation.' Institute for Fiscal Studies, *Working Paper* 73, 1985b.

Keen, Michael J. 'Welfare Effects of Commodity Tax Harmonisation.' *Mimeograph*, 1986.

Lancaster, Kelvin J. 'A New Approach to Consumer Theory.' *Journal of Political Economy*, 74, 2, 1966.

Maynard, Alan and O'Brien, Bernard. 'Harmonisation Policies in the European Community and Alcohol Abuse.' *British Journal of Addiction*, 77, 3, 1982.

McGuinness, Tony. 'The Demand for Beer, Spirits and Wine in the UK, 1956-1979.' In Grant, M., Plant, M. and Williams, A. *Economics and Alcohol: Consumption and Control*. London: Croom Helm, 1982.

O'Hagan, John W. 'The Rationale for Special Taxes on Alcohol: A Critique.' *British Tax Review*, 6, 1983.

Walsh, Brendan M. 'The Demand for Alcohol in the UK: A Comment.' *The Journal of Industrial Economics*, 30, 4, 1982.

# 4

# Optimal tax perspective on tax coordination

## *Manfred Rose\**

### I. INTRODUCTION

Why is the theory of optimal taxation (OT) an appropriate framework for dealing with tax harmonization in the European Community (EC)? The answer to this question can be deduced from one of the main objectives laid down in the EC Treaty. The activities of the Community shall include 'the institution of a system ensuring that competition in the common market is not distorted'.[1] Distortions are exactly the phenomena with which OT is primarily concerned.

The special feature of this tax theory is that lump-sum taxes that only create income effects but no substitution effects are not at our disposal for financing public expenditures. If a government can only choose between alternative tax systems that induce substitution effects, the 'first-best social welfare optimum' cannot be reached because of the tax-created wedge between relative consumer and relative producer prices. Taxes themselves are responsible for distortions of relative prices. This is the well-known excess burden of taxation, i.e. the loss of utility that the consumer has to bear in addition to that which arises in the case of lump-sum taxation.

The theory of OT is concerned with rules for fixing disposable tax parameters so as to maximize social welfare, which is equivalent to minimizing the inevitable excess burden. It should be noted that if the consumer can only be taxed in a distortionary way, at least one consumption commodity cannot be taxed. Otherwise, we would have a general consumption tax that is similar in quality to a lump-sum tax.

So, because OT was designed to find tax structures that guarantee a minimum loss of welfare resulting from the distortionary tax system, in fact it should be an appropriate tool for dealing with the problem of distortions which the Commission referred to in its last proposal for harmonizing the various national tax systems in the EC (Commission, 1980). The main aims are closer alignment of tax bases and eventually of tax rates. The question whether the

* The author wishes to thank Maurice Marchand and Jo Ritzen for their comments on his paper.
1. See Article 3(f) of the EC Treaty.

results of OT and the established understanding of their meaning can be used to evaluate such proposals implies asking whether the most recent OT guidelines can cast some light on the features of optimal tax systems for EC Member States. I do not believe that this is a promising way to achieve the desired insights. The very first rule of optimal commodity taxes can be used to support this judgement. The famous Ramsey rule, for example, recommends in one of its interpretations taxing relatively highly those goods that are relative necessities at the optimum. But this rule is immediately changed when, for example, profits and their taxation are to be taken into account or some tax rates are predetermined and cannot be set optimally because of political or practical restrictions.

This means that optimal tax rules are, among other factors, highly sensitive to opening the model to more realistic phenomena, to externally given distortions in any case, and finally to the range of tax instruments assumed to be at the disposal of the government concerned. In view of the manifold trade relations between Member States and the distortions that arise from the EC itself, e.g. the agricultural sector regulations, financing the budget of the Community through its own resources (i.e. taxes), and fixing import tariffs (i.e. rates of trade taxes), we have to expect misleading interpretations if the traditional rules are applied directly to optimal tax problems in the EC.

There is no main theorem that we can immediately apply to problems of tax harmonization in the EC from the point of view of welfare. Taking this into account, there is no way other than the theoretical one, i.e. we have to get some information on optimal tax formulae for countries in the EC from a welfare-maximizing model in which at least some of the actually existing restrictions are incorporated.[2] This, I think, is the only correct way to see how the traditional rules are changed by circumstances that are typical of Members of the EC.

This paper is organized as follows. The second section introduces a model from which we get optimal tax formulae for countries in the EC. The section contains only a brief description of the main economic assumptions that are made to develop a very simple general equilibrium model for the EC-region which is connected with the rest of the world by market interdependence. The mathematical representation of our model is contained and explained in the Appendix. After elaborating the main features of the reference model used to study tax harmonization from the point of view of welfare, some special propositions derived from rules for non-coordinated as well as fully coordinated tax systems in the EC are presented in Section III. The

2. It is remarkable that there are very few papers in which optimal tax problems are analyzed for open economies. This was attempted, for instance, by Boadway, Maital and Prachowny (1973) and Dasgupta and Stiglitz (1974). In the existing literature I could not find any attempt to develop optimal tax formulae for member countries of a community with the characteristics of the EC.

understanding and interpretation of these formulae should cast some light on the direction of welfare-improving tax harmonization efforts in the Community. Some brief final remarks are made in Section IV.

## II. Requirements for Tax Harmonization

The desire for tax harmonization primarily resulted from the objective to remove tax-induced distortions of trade among Member States. But what are trade distortions, and are they eliminated when we have a single market with characteristics similar to those of a domestic market? (Commission, 1980, p. 8). Furthermore, can we hope to reach neutrality of taxation in respect of merchandise trade, as the Commission (1980, p. 7) supposes?

As stated above, we know from the theory of optimal taxation that even if all regular conditions of competition are satisfied there are 'inevitable distortions' as a result of taxation itself. Trying to abolish such distortions we cannot focus on the producer side alone. Since any departure from the equality of the marginal rates of substitution and transformation implies a welfare loss, we have to recognize the imposition of consumer taxes as a welfare-decreasing distortion as well. Without lump-sum taxes being available such distortions cannot be avoided.

Hence, trade distortions exist if one of the countries with which trade takes place establishes an institutional framework so that its consumers have to pay more per unit of the imported goods than the foreign producers receive on the relevant market as revenue per unit. Furthermore, we can conclude that there are as many trade distortions created by taxation as there are traded goods that are taxed. So trade distortions caused by taxes remain, even if free competition works on the supply side and even if there are so-called single markets.

If lump-sum taxes are not available to fulfill the task of financing public expenditures, the imposed commodity taxes necessarily distort economic behaviour and the trade that is being taxed. Usually, the government of each trading country is oblivious to how domestic taxes affect the welfare of consumers in foreign countries. On the other hand, foreign tax systems influence the utility levels of domestic consumers through their influence on market prices for traded goods. This can be interpreted as a situation in which the domestic government cannot completely control all instruments that are relevant for the maximization of national welfare.

From the purposes set out in the EC Treaty it follows that no Member State should improve its welfare at the expense of its trading partners in the integrated area by means of taxation. So if we can deduce from the main objective of the EC the need to eliminate or at least reduce even unintended exploitation of other Member States, there is a definite requirement for the coordination of all national tax systems in the Community. This may have the consequence that some countries lose welfare if the rules for optimal internal taxes are linked to objectives of coordination. Furthermore, trade among Member States may be the reason why not all possible gains from trade, especially with the rest of the world, can be realized. As will be shown below, welfare improvements of some Member States may arise without any welfare losses in the EC by way of coordinating the tax systems.

To get an idea of the requirements for *tax harmonization (coordination)* we use an optimum tax model with a very simple structure. Firstly, with the simplifying assumption of one-consumer economies in the EC, income distribution problems disappear. In each country of the integrated region, conditions of free competition among producers are assumed as given. Furthermore, there are assumed to be no externalities in production or in consumption.[3] In each country, commodities are produced by a representative firm that as a profit-maximizing producer operates under pure competition and decreasing returns to scale. The governments in all countries of the EC are assumed to demand fixed quantities of several goods so that problems of an optimal public provision are ignored. On the tax side we focus on consumer taxes, which may be defined either per unit of the consumption commodities or ad valorem. Taxation of income from labour (which is regarded as a negative consumption good) is not excluded. One commodity that is both consumed in each country of the EC and traded with the rest of the world plays the part of the numéraire and is assumed to be untaxed. The destination principle applies in trade, so that each exported good leaves the representative country free of tax.

In the case of an *autonomous non-coordinated tax policy* we are primarily concerned with the choice of the optimal structure of commodity taxes in a one-consumer economy (or, equivalently, in a many-consumer economy with identical consumers) under the condition of a general equilibrium for the whole region of the EC. Solving its social welfare maximization problem, each government assumes that the other Member States will not change their existing taxes in response to changes in its domestic taxes. Furthermore, each national optimizer has to take into account some special features of the existing institutional framework of the Community.

Firstly, we want to consider one typical characteristic of the very complicated system that was designed to govern the agricultural sector of the EC. An essential feature of this sector is the existence of common producer prices for agricultural products within the EC which are usually higher than the respective world prices. We model this by assuming that producer prices for all agricultural products are fixed at a level that is determined by general politics and cannot be deduced from our model. In this case, an EC authority is obliged to buy every excess supply on agricultural markets that might occur because of

---

3. For a model of an economy with several communities focusing primarily on externalities, see Gordon (1983).

guaranteed producer prices. The bought-up quantities are stored, i.e. we disregard possible influence of these goods on consumer welfare. Hence, to finance the expenditures that arise from the purchases by the EC authority, we assume that own resources are available. They are created by imposing an EC value-added tax at a uniform ad valorem rate. With this charge we have a tax-induced distortion which is caused by the EC following its established objectives. A third kind of distortion, created by the EC itself, is incorporated in the model by assuming that the EC charges tariffs on some goods traded with the rest of the world. Each Member State faces these as well as the Community tax as pre-existing distortions when choosing its national optimal tax system.

Further detailed characteristics of our EC 'general equilibrium model' are elaborated in the first section of the Appendix. The next section there contains the derivation of the relevant first order conditions for a social welfare maximum in the non-coordinated case, which gives us an optimal tax formula. This is compared with an optimal tax formula for the case of full tax coordination, i.e. the most extreme form of tax harmonization. Following the traditional line of welfare economics, this is a situation in which an EC social welfare function containing the utility levels of the consumers of all Member States as arguments is maximized. To simplify, we choose a Benthamite EC welfare function, i.e. the sum over the utility functions of all Member States. This should only be seen as a means of getting a simple representation of the preferences that govern the activities of the Community. We further assume that an EC authority has control over all national tax parameters in all Member States. It is important to point out that our focus on this extreme case does not mean that we recommend giving up national tax sovereignty. It should be noted that in the case of a second-best optimum with full tax coordination it makes no sense to distinguish between national commodity taxes and the EC value-added tax. Budget deficits or surpluses that might occur now are neutralized by appropriate (fictitious) lump-sum transfers among the governments of the Member States.

In the Appendix we derive optimal tax formulae for the two extreme cases of full tax coordination on the one hand and non-coordination on the other. By comparing the two, we identify the requirements for harmonizing the national tax systems in the EC.


III. On the Direction of Excise Tax Harmonization

The excise taxes we actually have, e.g. on tobacco, spirits and mineral oils, are not always consumer or producer taxes in the pure sense of the theoretical taxonomy. Nevertheless, arguing on the basis of general equilibrium models without intermediate stages of production, as we have chosen to treat our problem, one has to adopt one of those two pure theoretical alternatives. So, in

117

the following, we shall focus on excise taxes in the sense of pure consumer taxes.

Although there are only a few specific commodity taxes on domestic consumption in all countries of the EC, the value-added taxes with several rates and their non-uniform tax bases effect a manifold differentiation of taxing commodities in each country. Excise duties are often justified in terms of distributional objectives or merit wants of the national government. The benefit principle of taxation and the internalization of externalities are also invoked. In the following, we are not concerned with such justifications and their implications for tax harmonization in the EC although this would be necessary to arrive at a final solution of the problem under consideration. Commodity taxes in our model are charged only to finance public expenditures.

We are confronted with the task of finding some welfare-oriented arguments for structuring national excise tax systems of EC Member States with respect to the interdependence of the welfare levels of those countries. Tackling this problem by comparing the two optimal tax formulae mentioned above we have to take into account that they at first only represent different structures but not numerically given relationships. Thus, we must state that without empirical information on all components of the general equilibrium model concerned one cannot get a definite answer to whether the tax rates considered are higher or lower in the fully coordinated case than in the non-coordinated case. The best way would be to compute the general equilibrium model with respect to the optima that are to be compared. (See Shoven, 1983.) But this cannot be done here. Therefore, we are forced to interpret the derived tax rules leading us only to first suppositions relating to the definite features of appropriate rules for optimal tax harmonization.

In the following, we present five propositions to get a first impression of how OT could help with the harmonization of consumption taxes. Section IV of the Appendix contains the analytic comparisons between the optimal tax formula in the uncoordinated case and the respective rule for the case of full tax coordination. These analytic studies may help to support some known conclusions that one gets from being concerned with welfare economics and taxes in an international trade context. In part, we think we have found some relations that are not commonly known or obviously deducible from the very little literature on optimal taxation in an international trade context.

## A. Proposition 1

*Fully coordinated rates of tax on commodities that are exported only to (imported only from) Member States of the EC should be higher (lower) than non-coordinated consumption tax rates.*

From the theory of optimal tariffs we know that by imposing trade taxes, one country that has a monopoly power in trade with another country can restrict

118

trade so as to improve its terms of trade and welfare at the expense of its trading partner. And it is well known that imposing appropriate taxes on consumption is a qualitatively similar way to play the nationalistic game (Friedlaender and Vandendorpe, 1968; Vandendorpe, 1972) and circumvent the free-trade orientation of EC or General Agreement on Tariffs and Trade (GATT) rules. If only consumer taxes are available, the exploitation of foreign demand can be realized by subsidizing the domestic consumption of exportables and taxing the domestic consumption of importables. If the exporting country is large with respect to its trading partners the latter have to accept the tax-induced rise of import prices. Therefore, the exporting country is able to improve its terms of trade and, through this, national welfare may be increased at the expense of the foreign countries. Analogously, welfare improvements related to imports can be effected by a tax-induced decline of foreign supply prices.

In the existing literature, these conclusions are mainly derived under the assumption that subsidies can be financed by lump-sum taxes and the revenue from commodity taxes remitted to consumers in a lump-sum fashion. But we have to take into account that only distortionary taxes can be used to finance public expenditures. Nevertheless, we suppose that the general feature of setting taxes with the aim of exploiting one's trading partners would also emerge under such conditions. This means that, other things being equal, exportables (importables) should bear lower (higher) tax rates than non-traded goods. Therefore Germany, for example, by lowering the rate of tax on commodities that are only exported to EC countries, could improve its welfare at the expense of other Member States. Naturally, these can try to play the monopsonistic game by introducing higher rates of taxes on the consumption of the imported goods. So game theory might be the appropriate tool for analyzing the final outcome. All this contravenes the spirit of the EC Treaty.

Tax harmonization seems to imply that optimal taxes on commodities that are traded only among Member States should not be imposed with the aim of improving the terms of trade. Looking at the optimal tax formulae to see whether they could support such a supposition, our first finding is that the optimal tax rates depend not only on the detailed structure of consumer preferences but also on supply-side characteristics, special features concerning the financing of the budget of an EC authority, and some more complex relations. But for any country in the EC, the rule for optimal taxes in the case of full coordination obviously does not contain terms of excess demand coming from other Member States. This confirms the statement given above.

It is considerably more difficult to establish whether the tax rates on exportables are to be raised in changing from a non-coordinated to a fully coordinated tax system. To get some deeper insights, the frequently used assumption that the considered demands are cross-price independent except with relation to the untaxed good may be valid. Under this condition in closed economies we would arrive at the traditional 'inverse elasticity rule' that calls for relatively low rates of taxes on goods with relatively high own-price elasticities of demand. With some further simplifications to focus on the phenomena of exploiting, as elaborated in the Appendix, the necessary conditions for the uncoordinated case tell us that the optimal tax rate is negatively related to the excess demand from other Member States.[4] As a result, exploiting EC Member States by imposing appropriate commodity tax rates seems to be advantageous in the case of an uncoordinated tax policy. Together with the rule for fully coordinated rates treated above, this supports Proposition 1.

Looking at excise taxes actually realized, there seem to be, perhaps unintentionally, some elements of exploitation in the existing tax system. As elaborated above, the improvement of welfare at the expense of other Member States can be effected by levying extraordinarily high taxes on commodities that are mainly imported from Member States of the EC. This may cast some light on the question of how the relatively high tax on wine in the United Kingdom, for example, is to be seen from a harmonization point of view.

## B. Proposition 2

*If goods are traded internationally, a high own-price elasticity of net exports into Member States can be responsible for rates of taxes on exportables (importables) being higher (lower) in the non-coordinated than in the fully coordinated case.*

An intuitive argument for this statement proceeds along the following lines. If goods, produced in one of the Member States only, are traded internationally, we have to consider demands coming from EC Member States and from the rest of the world. To see how Proposition 1 for tax harmonization is to be modified for this case, let us first look at the uncoordinated case of tax policy. Setting optimal commodity tax rates with the effect that national welfare is improved at the expense of the other EC countries and the rest of the world, the government concerned has to take into account that the total foreign demand for one good declines when its producer price increases. If the quantities demanded by foreign countries are very sensitive to price changes, welfare improvements at the expense of the respective trading partners are relatively small. In the extreme case of an infinite elasticity of foreign demand no exploitation is possible at all. Indeed, we would then be considering the position of the small country in trade, where the country in question faces given world prices. From this it follows that the exporting country has to consider the price elasticities of

---

4. To focus on exploitation we concentrate on the exploitation term in the relevant optimal tax formula, ignoring all other terms that arise from modelling EC structures and that determine the optimal tax rate as well.

all its trading partners (i.e. other Member States of the EC and the rest of the world) when determining its tax structure.

In the case of joint welfare maximization for the whole EC, the maximizing authority has to take into account only the price elasticity of the rest of the world. This would be possible because of the ability to compensate undesirable price effects inside the EC by choosing appropriate national tax parameters in the other Member States. Thus, if the price elasticity for the exported commodity is relatively high in the other EC countries and relatively low in the rest of the world, the producer price concerned will be kept lower in the case of autonomous than in the case of coordinated welfare maximization. Hence, such conditions may lead to a lower tax rate at the fully harmonized optimum. This is confirmed by the optimal tax formula for the non-coordinated optimum where the respective tax rate is positively related to the direct price elasticity of exports to Member States. Thus, there may be trade relations that lead to the recommendation given in Proposition 2.[5]

Note that the elasticity term just discussed also determines the direction of the relevant tax harmonization in the case of monopsony power in trade. Exploiting trading partners is here effected by levying higher tax rates on imported goods, which results in lower foreign producer prices. Such considerations can be important for the continuing discussion on appropriate excise taxes on goods that are primarily imported from EC countries. Hence, one should consider the price elasticity of net exports concerned if one examines, for example, the question of whether the United Kingdom should or should not lower the taxation of wine imported from EC countries in relation to the taxation of British beer.


### C. Proposition 3

*If demands and supplies for agricultural products were independent, the optimal tax rates for the fully coordinated EC tax system should be such that the respective own-price elasticity of demand would equal the marginal excess burden of the respective tax system.*

The simplifying assumption of cross-price independent demand and supply functions allows us to point out one of the typical features of harmonized optimal rates of taxes on the consumption of food and other products. Furthermore, to derive Proposition 3 in the Appendix, we have abstracted from some other components that determine the optimal tax rate in the fully

---

5. Proposition 2 is a second result focusing on the exploitation term in the relevant optimal tax formula. We ignore some other terms (as in establishing Proposition 1), except one of course: here we recognize the non-zero rest of the world excess demands.

coordinated case. As elaborated in Section VI of the Appendix, we ignore among other things the exploitation term discussed above.

We are interested in finding out how the essential characteristics of the organization of agricultural markets in the EC influence the rule for the respective optimal tax rate. Unfortunately, we could not find any intuitive reason why establishing 'the equality of income-compensated own-price elasticity of demand for all agricultural products'[6] is necessary for a second-best EC welfare optimum. Thus, we can only refer to those factors that are primarily at work here.

The formula considered here can be interpreted as a modification of the 'inverse elasticity rule'.[7] The fixed producer prices of agricultural products and the problem of financing the purchases of all excess supplies on these markets by an EC authority lead to a reduction of the respective tax rates in relation to the traditional result. The difference between the two rates is equal to the ratio of the producer price to the consumer price.

The idea underlying the necessity of lowering the tax rate compared with that under 'normal' market conditions is the following. The consumers in all countries of the EC have to bear the burden of financing and storing the excess supplies of agricultural products in the period we consider when analyzing our general equilibrium model. Hence, reducing the taxes under consideration would create smaller excess supplies and thus smaller welfare losses. But this interpretation alone does not make it completely plausible that we should equalize all income-compensated own-price elasticities of demand for agricultural products.

### D. Proposition 4

*Tax rates on agricultural products are expected to be higher in the non-coordinated than in the coordinated optimal tax system.*

Imposing consumer taxes on agricultural commodities normally has the effect of decreasing the respective consumption. Taking the EC regulations on agricultural markets into account we have at the same time an increase in excess supplies. Thus, higher tax revenues are needed to finance the purchases of these additional supplies. Hence, the respective EC authority would be forced to raise

---

6. This is an alternative formulation of Proposition 3. Since all elasticities concerned must be equal to the marginal excess burden, they must be equal to each other. Note that, because the marginal excess burden differs among the countries of the EC, Proposition 3 does not imply that the income-compensated own-price elasticity of French consumer demand is equal to that of German consumer demand.

7. One commentator pointed out that the model leads to the traditional inverse elasticity rule with the unit tax replaced by the price itself. This is correct but does not explain why.

the rate of the EC tax. But this would result in higher consumer prices in all EC countries and create additional excess burdens too.

Following the line of an autonomous tax policy, the government concerned would not deal with the welfare losses that occur in other Member States as a consequence of domestic taxation. But in view of tax coordination requirements we have to consider such relationships. To minimize the joint excess burden of all tax systems in the EC, the respective national fiscal authority is to be restricted in setting rates of taxes on agricultural products. This intuitive argument is in line with Proposition 4 and follows also from a comparison of the optimal tax formulae for the non-coordinated and the coordinated case of tax policy as elaborated in the Appendix.

## E. Proposition 5

*A decrease in profits of the French wine industry effected by a higher rate of tax on wine in the United Kingdom gives no clear evidence for the existence of an indirect protection of British beer in view of the competition between the respective goods.*

As stated by the European Court of Justice in the Fink-Frucht case, the second paragraph of Article 95 of the EC Treaty '. . . forbids the imposition on imported products of any form of taxation "of such a nature as to afford indirect protection to other products". Such protection would occur in particular if internal taxation were to impose a heavier burden on an imported product than on a domestic product with which the imported product is . . . in competition' (see Easson, 1980, p. 34). The Commission was arguing along the same lines when it alleged that the British system of taxing wine was discriminatory (*idem*, p. 34) because the relatively lightly taxed British beer is in competition with wine. Competition can be described by substitutability between the goods concerned. And because such phenomena belong to the main factors contained in optimal tax formulae, one might obtain some insight here from an OT point of view.

We believe that the EC problem in connection with taxing imported goods more heavily than their domestically produced substitutes mainly results from the implied discouragement of the producers in other Member States. One might expect a decline of the profits in the wine industries of France, Italy or Germany, for example, from raising the consumer price of wine in the United Kingdom by imposing higher tax rates. So we have to ask whether the substitutability mentioned above and this tax effect together can produce an argument of harmonization leading to a lowering of the tax on French wine consumed in the United Kingdom.

In the case of a non-coordinated tax system the effects that British taxes have on the profits of firms in other Member States are not directly contained in the

123

optimal tax formula. But nevertheless, under our general equilibrium conditions, there are indirect effects of taxes in one country of the EC on profits in other Member States. In the case of full tax coordination the relevant profit terms enter the respective tax formula, of course. This documents once more that in a harmonized tax system each country of the EC has to consider welfare losses in other Member States that might occur from domestic taxation.

In the tax problem considered here we have to bear in mind cuts in foreign producer prices caused by changing domestic taxes. The decline of profits in other countries of the EC simultaneously implies a decline in the income of households there. Thus, the country's partners in the Community are losing welfare. To get a first impression of the solution to the problem we consider cross-price dependency of demand only with respect to three goods, which could be wine, beer and the untaxed numéraire, for example. Furthermore, only the British consumer price of wine shall be negatively related to the profits in the French wine industry. The United Kingdom is assumed to impose a profits tax of 100 percent.

From the rule for optimal tax rates under these simplifying assumptions we obtain the following insights. A high degree of substitutability between beer and wine, in terms of the cross-price elasticity of demand, would lower the rate of tax on wine in relation to the rate of tax on beer. This effect is strengthened by a high sensitivity of French profits to the consumer price of wine in the United Kingdom. But from this context alone we cannot deduce that harmonization requires a lower rate of tax on wine than in the non-coordinated tax system. The optimal tax formula says that the respective profit effect combined with the own-price elasticity of demand for beer works in the opposite direction, i.e. it calls for a relatively higher tax rate on wine. Hence, the problem can only be solved by inserting empirical data for several variables into our optimal tax formulae.


IV. Concluding Remarks

To obtain first insights into the structure of harmonized tax systems in the EC we use a simple model of optimal tax general equilibrium. Some constraints that are typical in view of the existing regulations in the EC give this model its special structure.

Duality theory has been systematically used to obtain formulae with the tax rates themselves as the dependent policy variables on which our interest is focused. This way, we derive optimal tax rates for the case of isolated national welfare maximization and for the case of joint welfare maximization for the whole EC. From the respective formulae we are able to expose the general characteristics of the two kinds of optima. Furthermore, some of the main differences between optimal taxation under conditions of non-coordinated and

124

coordinated tax policy can be explained. Nevertheless, without detailed empirical information on economic conditions in the EC countries it is impossible to derive the explicit structures of optimal tax systems. The same is true for the evaluation of the proposal to come to a closer alignment of excise and value-added tax rates in the EC countries as made by the Commission (1980, p. 64).

Even with rather heroic simplifications related to demand and supply patterns our model produces no support for the proposition that uniform tax rates in all EC countries are optimal. (For a similar result, see Wiegard, 1980.) Thus, the closer alignment of excise and value-added tax rates has no obvious claim to a social welfare optimum in the EC.


## APPENDIX


### I. General Characteristics of an Equilibrium Model for the EC Region

We distinguish between a set N (containing N elements) of countries of the EC, and the rest of the world.

The representative consumer in each country m of the EC maximizes a well-behaved utility function $U^m(x^m)$, where $x^m$ (for factors supplied $x_j^m < 0$) is the vector of consumption commodities bought at markets. The vector of public production, $g^m$, is assumed to be fixed; any public goods entering $g^m$ that are supplied in fixed quantities may be considered as implicitly contained in $U^m(x^m)$.

For a given vector $q^m$ of consumer prices $q_i^m$, $i \in C^m$, $m \in N$, and a given utility level $U^m$, one obtains income-compensated demand functions

$$x_i^m = E_i^m(q^m, U^m) \; ; \qquad i \in C^m, \quad m \in N, \tag{1}$$

where $C^m$ is the set of all consumption commodities (domestically produced or imported) in country m of the EC. From duality theory we know that the $E_i^m$ are the partial derivatives with respect to $q_i^m$ of the expenditure function $E^m(q^m, U^m)$. The second partial derivatives $E_{ik}^m = \partial E_i^m / \partial q_k^m$ are the Slutsky-Hicks substitution terms.

The representative firm in each country m of the EC is a profit-maximizing producer, operating under pure competition and decreasing returns to scale and supplying quantities $y_i^m$ (for factors demanded $y_i^m < 0$) of commodity i according to the supply functions

$$y_i^m = \pi_i^m(p^m) \; ; \; i \in B^m \; , \quad m \in N, \tag{2}$$

where $p^m$ is the vector of producer prices $p_i^m$ of commodity i, and $B^m$ is the set of all commodities produced in m. The functions $\pi_i^m(p^m)$ are the partial derivatives with respect to $p_i^m$ of the profit function $\pi^m(p^m)$. The second partial derivatives $\pi_{ik}^m = \partial \pi_i^m / \partial p_k^m$ indicate substitutability and complementarity in production among all pairs of commodities produced in m.

The rest of the world excess demand functions for the EC region as a whole are

$$e_i = e_i(p^w) \; ; \quad i \in H, \tag{3}$$

where H is the set of all internationally traded goods and $p^w$ the vector of world prices, i.e. the prices that are effective for all trade between the rest of the world and the countries of the EC.

In addition to consumer demands $x_i^m$, $i \in C^m$, and government demands $g_i^m$, $i \in G^m$, we include commodity demands $g_i^{EC}$, $i \in G^{EC}$, of an EC authority. The quantities $g_i^{EC}$ are to be interpreted as market-clearing demands for agricultural products. This means that the EC authority buys any quantities at a given price $p_i^{EC}$, $i \in G^{EC}$, on these markets.

Assuming that the market for each commodity i in the set of all commodities A is in equilibrium, the market-clearing equations generally will be written as

$$\sum_{m \in N} x_i^m + \sum_{m \in N} g_i^m + g_i^{EC} + e_i = \sum_{m \in N} y_i^m \; ; \; i \in A. \tag{4}$$

For the prices in our EC model we have

$$q_i^m = p_i^m + t_i^m + t_{i,m}^{EC} \; ; \quad m \in N, \; i \in C^m \tag{5}$$

$$p_i^m = p_i \; ; \; m \in N, \; i \in B^m \tag{6}$$

$$p_i^w = p_i - z_i^{EC} \; ; \; i \in H, \tag{7}$$

where $p_i$ is the producer price for commodity $i \in A$ in the EC-region, $t_i^m$ the unit excise tax on consumed commodity $i \in T^m$ charged by the government of country m, $t_{i,m}^{EC}$ the unit excise tax on consumed commodity $i \in T^{EC}$ charged

126

by an EC authority, and $z_i^{EC}$ the tariff on imports of commodity $i \in Z^{EC}$ charged by an EC authority. (In the case of a factor tax the relevant tax parameters are negative.)

As a matter of normalization (see Munk (1978) for closed economies and Dixit and Norman (1980, p. 80 ff) for open economies) commodity zero will be used as the universal numéraire so that the prices $p_0^m$, $p_0$ and $q_0^m$, where $m \in N$ and $0 \in H$, are fixed at 1, i.e. there are no producer taxes, tariffs or consumer taxes on commodity 0. It is assumed that the numéraire good 0 is internationally traded and both produced and consumed in every country of the EC.

We now have to complete the general equilibrium model for the EC-region with three budget constraints. The household budget constraint in each country of the EC reads as

$$E^m(q^m, U^m) = [1 - \sigma^m] \pi^m(p^m) ; \quad m \in N, \tag{8}$$

where $\sigma^m$ is the profit tax rate charged by the government of country m of the EC, and the government budget constraint in each country m of the EC is

$$\sum_{i \in T^m} t_i^m [x_i^m + g_i^m] + \sigma^m \pi^m = \sum_{i \in G^m} q_i^m g_i^m ; \quad m \in N. \tag{9}$$

At least one of the tax parameters $t_i^m$ or $\sigma^m$ for each m is to be seen as a system variable in order to satisfy the corresponding government budget constraint.

We assume that the EC imposes a value-added tax at a uniform ad valorem tax rate $\alpha^{EC}$ on consumption goods. Then we have

$$t_{i,m}^{EC} = \alpha^{EC} q_i^m ; \quad i \in T^{EC} , \quad m \in N. \tag{10}$$

The commodity set $T^{EC}$ does not contain labour or other factors supplied by the household sector.

With the EC unit excise taxes defined in (10) the budget constraint for the EC authority reads as

$$\alpha^{EC} \sum_{i \in T^{EC}} \sum_{m \in N} q_i^m [x_i^m + g_i^m] - \sum_{i \in Z^{EC}} z_i^{EC} e_i$$

$$= \sum_{i \in G^{EC}} p_i^{EC} g_i^{EC} , \tag{11}$$

where $\alpha^{EC}$ is to be taken as an endogenous variable.

Our now fully specified EC 'general equilibrium model' consists of as many market-clearing equations as there are commodities in the set A. We also have N (the number of Member States of the EC) income-expenditure constraints (8), N government budget constraints (9) and finally the EC budget constraint (11).

The system must generate solutions for N utility levels $U^m$, $m \in N$, for $N + 1$ tax variables $t_i^m$, $i \in T^m$, and $\alpha^{EC}$, for all relative producer prices $p_i$, $i \in I$ (that is, the set of all commodities the prices of which are endogenous) and for the commodity demands $g_i^{EC}$, $i \in G^{EC}$, of an EC authority to clear agricultural markets. Because of the numéraire, the set A contains one element more than I and $G^{EC}$ combined. Thus, taken together, the number of equations exceeds the number of variables by just one, and any equation can be dropped using Walras's law.

## II. Non-Coordinated Optimal Consumption Tax Formula for Any Country of the EC

To describe the non-coordinated welfare-maximization problem of a single country n, $n \in N$, we choose the so-called expenditure function approach following Munk (1978) or Dixit and Munk (1977). The control variables are the tax-inclusive consumer prices $q^m$ and the utility level $U^m$; producer prices are determined endogenously, and the implied tax rates then follow from comparing consumer and producer prices. Hence, in view of restrictions (8) and (9), the appropriate Lagrangian for the government's maximization problem is

$$L^n(q^n, U^n, \mu^n, \Gamma^n) = U^n + \mu^n[[1-\sigma^n]\pi^n(p^n) - E^n(q^n, U^n)]$$

$$+ \Gamma^n[ \sum_{i \in T^n} [q_i^n[1-\alpha^{EC}] - p_i][E_i^n(q^n, U^n) + g_i^n]$$

$$+ \sigma^n\pi^n(p^n) - \sum_{i \in G^n} q_i^n g_i^n]. \qquad (12)$$

Producer prices $p_i^n$, $i \in B^n$ — hence profit $\pi^n$ — producer prices $p_i$, $i \in I$, and the EC-tax rate $\alpha^{EC}$ change with each $q_i^n$ and $U^n$ because of market interdependence. It is assumed that the general equilibrium model just described defines (at least locally) twice differentiable functions $p_i = p_i(q^n, U^n)$, $p_i^n = p_i^n(q_i^n, U^n)$ and $\alpha^{EC} = \alpha^{EC}(q^n, U^n)$. Here the variables $p_i$ are the producer prices of the commodities no matter in which country they are produced. If commodity i is produced in n we have $p_i = p_i^n$.

The nature of the optimal consumer tax structure is mainly determined by the following first-order conditions:

$$\frac{\partial L^n}{\partial q_k^n} = \mu^n \left[ [1-\sigma^n] \frac{\partial \pi^n}{\partial q_k^n} - x_k^n \right] + \Gamma^n \left[ x_k^n - \alpha^{EC} c_k^n + \sum_{i \in T^n} t_i^n E_{ik}^n \right.$$

$$\left. - \sum_{i \in T^n} c_i^n \frac{\partial p_i}{\partial q_k^n} + \sigma^n \frac{\partial \pi^n}{\partial q_k^n} - \sum_{i \in T^{EC}} q_i^n c_i^n \frac{\partial \alpha^{EC}}{\partial q_k^n} \right]$$

$$= 0 \; ; \; k \in T^n \; , \tag{13}$$

where the domestic demand is defined as

$$c_i^n = x_i^n + g_i^n \; ; \quad i \in C^n \; . \tag{14}$$

From the properties of the profit function one has

$$\frac{\partial \pi^n}{\partial a} = \sum_{i \in B^n} y_i^n \frac{\partial p_i^n}{\partial a} \; ; \quad a = q_k^n \; , \; U^n \; . \tag{15}$$

Define the foreign excess demand with respect to n as

$$e_i^n = e_i + e_i^{nEC} \; ; \quad i \in D^n \; , \tag{16}$$

where $D^n$ is the set of all commodities that are traded between n and foreign countries, and

$$e_i^{nEC} = \sum_{\substack{m \in N \\ m \neq n}} (x_i^m + g_i^m + g_i^{EC} - y_i^m) \; ; \quad i \in F^n \; , \tag{17}$$

is the excess-demand of Member States with respect to n, $F^n$ being the set of all commodities that are traded between n and other Member States.

Focusing only on n, the market-clearing equations (4) can then be abbreviated to

$$c_i^n + e_i^n = y_i^n . \tag{18}$$

Observing that $p_i^n$ is equal to $p_i$ for $i \in B^n$, from (14) to (18) one can then verify that

$$\sum_{i \in T^n} c_i^n \frac{\partial p_i}{\partial a} = \frac{\partial \pi^n}{\partial a} - \sum_{i \in D^n} e_i^n \frac{\partial p_i}{\partial a} \; ; \quad a = q_k^n , \; U^n. \tag{19}$$

Substituting in (13) yields

$$\theta^n x_k^n = - \sum_{i \in T^n} t_i^n E_{ik}^n + \theta^n [1 - \sigma^n] \frac{\partial \pi^n}{\partial q_k^n} - \sum_{i \in D^n} e_i^n \frac{\partial p_i}{\partial q_k^n}$$

$$+ \alpha^{EC} c_k^n + \sum_{i \in T^{EC}} q_i^n c_i^n \frac{\partial \alpha^{EC}}{\partial q_k^n} \; ; \quad k \in T^n \tag{20}$$

where $\theta^n$, usually called the relative marginal excess burden of distortionary consumption taxes, is defined as

$$\theta^n = \frac{\Gamma^n - \mu^n}{\Gamma^n} \geq 0. \tag{21}$$


### III. Fully Coordinated Optimal Consumption Taxes for Any Country of the EC

The restrictions on the relevant maximization problem are now the individual income-expenditure equations (8) and the overall budget constraint which is simply the sum of (9) and (11). To distinguish between $t_i^m$ and $t_{i,m}^{EC}$ now makes no sense, because the EC authority has the tax parameter $t_i^m$ for all $m \in N$ under its control. Thus, forming the Lagrangian,

$$L^{EC}(U, q, \mu, \Gamma^{EC}) = \sum_{m \in N} U^m + \sum_{m \in N} \mu^m[[1-\sigma^m]\pi^m(p^m) - E^m(q^m, U^m)]$$

$$+ \Gamma^{EC}\left\{ \sum_{m \in N} \sum_{i \in T^m} [q_i^m - p_i][E_i^m(q^m, U^m) + g_i^m] + \sum_{m \in N} \sigma^m \pi^m(p^m) \right.$$

$$\left. - \sum_{i \in Z^{EC}} z_i^{EC} e_i(p) - \sum_{m \in N} \sum_{i \in G^m} q_i^m g_i^m - \sum_{i \in G^{EC}} p_i^{EC} g_i^{EC} \right\} \qquad (22)$$

where q is the vector of all consumer prices in the EC-region, $\mu$ is the vector of Lagrange multipliers, and U is the vector of N utility levels in the EC-region. We assume that twice differentiable functions $p_i^m = p_i^m(U, q)$, $p_i = p_i(U, q)$ and $g_i^{EC} = g_i^{EC}(U, q)$ can be obtained from the general equilibrium model.

Setting the partial derivatives of $L^{EC}$ with respect to $q_k^n$ to zero and rearranging the equations thus obtained, using (19), one obtains the first-order conditions

$$\theta^n x_k^n = - \sum_{i \in T^n} t_i^n E_{ik}^n + \sum_{m \in N} \theta^m [1-\sigma^m] \frac{\partial \pi^m}{\partial q_k^n} - \sum_{i \in H} e_i \frac{\partial p_i}{\partial q_k^n}$$

$$+ \sum_{i \in Z^{EC}} z_i^{EC} \frac{\partial e_i}{\partial q_k^n} + \sum_{i \in G^{EC}} p_i^{EC} \frac{\partial g_i^{EC}}{\partial q_k^n} \; ; \quad k \in T^n , \qquad (23)$$

where the marginal excess burden is

$$\theta^n = \frac{\Gamma^{EC} - \mu^n}{\Gamma^{EC}} \geq 0 . \qquad (24)$$

## IV. Explanatory Notes on Proposition 1

To concentrate on monopoly power effects of domestic consumer taxes, we assume that all terms related to profits and financing the EC budget are almost zero. Furthermore, commodity demands and supplies shall be assumed independent except in relation to the numéraire; that is

$$E_{ik}^n = \pi_{ik}^n = e_{ik}^n = 0 \; ; \quad i \neq k , \quad i, k \neq 0 . \qquad (25)$$

131

Hence, the *non-coordinated optimal tax formula* (20) reduces to

$$\theta^n x_k^n = - t_k^n E_{kk}^n - \sum_{i \in T^n} e_i^n \frac{\partial p_i}{\partial q_k^n} + \alpha^{EC} c_k^n \, . \tag{26}$$

Differentiating the market-clearing conditions for non-agricultural products and incorporating (25) we obtain

$$\frac{\partial p_i}{\partial q_k^n} = 0 \; ; \qquad \frac{\partial p_k^n}{\partial q_k^n} = \frac{E_{kk}^n}{\pi_{kk}^n - e_{kk}^n} < 0 \; ; \qquad i, k \in I \, , \quad i \neq k \, , \tag{27}$$

assuming that all demand and supply functions respond normally to price. Substituting (27) in (26), the tax formula becomes

$$\theta^n x_k^n + \frac{e_k^n E_{kk}^n}{\pi_{kk}^n - e_{kk}^n} - \alpha^{EC} c_k^n = - t_k^n E_{kk}^n \, . \tag{28}$$

Dividing by the consumer price $q_k^n$ and the Slutsky-Hicks substitution term $E_{kk}^n$, one obtains

$$x_k^n = \frac{\theta^n}{\tau_{kk}^n} - \frac{\alpha^{EC} c_k^n}{\tau_{kk}^n x_k^n} + \frac{1}{q_k^n} \frac{-e_k^n}{\pi_{kk}^n - e_{kk}^n} \tag{29}$$

where

$$\tau_{kk}^n = \frac{-E_{kk}^n q_k^n}{x_k^n} > 0 \tag{30}$$

is the compensated elasticity of demand for commodity k with respect to its own price, $q_k^n$, and

$$\alpha_k^n = t_k^n / q_k^n \tag{31}$$

is the ad valorem rate of tax on commodity k.

The first term on the right-hand side of (29) represents the traditional 'inverse elasticity rule' for optimal consumer tax rates. The third term is positive (negative) in the case of net imports (net exports). Hence, the government in n chooses lower (higher) consumer tax rates on the exportables (importables) than in the closed economy case.

All variables valued at the fully coordinated optimum shall be labelled by $\hat{\ }$, so that $\hat{\alpha}_k^n$ is the rate of tax on commodity k in this situation. Disregarding all terms in (23) that are related to profits, tariff revenues and buying excess supplies on agricultural markets, one obtains, in the simplified case of independent demand and supply patterns, the *fully coordinated optimal tax rates*

$$\hat{\alpha}_k^n = \frac{\hat{\theta}^n}{\hat{\tau}_{kk}^n} - \frac{\hat{e}_k}{\hat{\pi}_{kk}^n - \hat{e}_{kk}} \frac{1}{\hat{q}_k^n} . \tag{32}$$

In the non-coordinated optimum commodity k bears $\alpha_k^n$ imposed by the government in n and additionally $\alpha^{EC}$, charged by an EC authority. Hence, to establish Proposition 1, one has to ask whether

$$\alpha_k^n + \alpha^{EC} \gtreqless \hat{\alpha}_k^n . \tag{33}$$

From the consumer price equation (5), the EC unit tax formula (10) and the definition of $\alpha_k^n$ in (31) we have

$$\hat{p}_k = [1 - \hat{\alpha}_k^n]\hat{q}_k^n \tag{34}$$

in the fully coordinated case and

$$p_k = [1 - \alpha_k^n - \alpha^{EC}]q_k^n \tag{35}$$

in the non-coordinated case. Substituting for $e_k^n$ from (16), we then have to establish

133

$$\frac{\theta^n}{\tau_{kk}^n} + \alpha^{EC}\left[1 - \frac{c_k^n}{\tau_{kk}^n x_k^n}\right] - \frac{[1 - \alpha_k^n - \alpha^{EC}][e_k + e_k^{nEC}]}{p_k[\pi_{kk}^n - e_{kk} - e_{kk}^{nEC}]}$$

$$\gtreqless \frac{\hat{\theta}^n}{\hat{\tau}_{kk}^n} - \frac{[1-\hat{\alpha}_k^n]\hat{e}_k}{\hat{p}_k[\hat{\pi}_{kk}^n - \hat{e}_{kk}]} \qquad (36)$$

If commodity k is traded only among Member States, i.e. $e_k = \hat{e}_k = 0$, and $e_k^{nEC} > 0 \, (< 0)$, it seems reasonable to suppose that the inequality $< \, (>)$ will hold.

## V. Explanatory Notes on Proposition 2

Rearranging (36), one obtains

$$\frac{\theta^n}{\tau_{kk}^n} + \alpha^{EC}\left[1 - \frac{c_k^n}{\tau_{kk}^n x_k^n}\right] - \frac{[1 - \alpha^{EC} - \alpha_k^n][1 + [e_k^{nEC}/e_k]]}{\dfrac{\pi_{kk}^n}{e_k}p_k + \ae_k + \dfrac{e_k^{nEC}}{e_k}\ae_k^{nEC}}$$

$$\gtreqless \frac{\hat{\theta}^n}{\hat{\tau}_{kk}^n} - \frac{1 - \hat{\alpha}_k^n}{\dfrac{\hat{\pi}_{kk}^n}{\hat{e}_k}\hat{p}_k + \hat{\ae}_k} \qquad (37)$$

where

$$\ae_k^{nEC} = - e_{kk}^{nEC}p_k/e_k^{nEC} \qquad (38)$$

is the direct price elasticity of net exports to EC Member States, and

$$\ae_k = - e_{kk}p_k/e_k \qquad (39)$$

134

is the direct price elasticity of net exports to the rest of the world.

Thus, the comparison under consideration here turns mainly on the trade situation $e_k^{nEC}/e_k$, a term which is positive in our model, and the elasticity $æ_k^{nEC}$ in the third term on the left-hand side of (37). In the case of exportables (importables) we have $æ_k > 0 (< 0)$ and $æ_k^{nEC} > 0 (< 0)$. Hence, for very high values of $|æ_k^{nEC}|$ relative to $|æ_k|$ in (37) we obtain the inequality $> (<)$, i.e. $\alpha_k^n + \alpha^{EC} > (<) \hat{\alpha}_k^n$ in the case of exportables (importables).

## VI. EXPLANATORY NOTES ON PROPOSITION 3

To isolate characteristic features of optimal taxes on agricultural products we disregard the second, third and fourth terms on the right-hand side of (23).

The market-clearing equation that is relevant here gives, after differentiation with respect to $q_k^n$,

$$\frac{\partial g_k^{EC}}{\partial q_k^n} = - E_{kk}^n > 0. \tag{40}$$

It is again assumed that demand and supply patterns are independent. Hence, the optimal rate of tax on agricultural products is characterized by

$$\hat{\alpha}_k^n = \frac{\hat{\theta}^n}{\hat{\tau}_{kk}^n} - \frac{p_k^{EC}}{\hat{q}_k^n} \tag{41}$$

or, substituting for $\hat{q}_k^n$ from (34), by

$$\hat{\theta}^n = \hat{\tau}_{kk}^n , \tag{42}$$

if all tax rates in the EC are fully coordinated.

## VII. EXPLANATORY NOTES ON PROPOSITION 4

In the non-coordinated case, (20) gives

$$\alpha_k^n = \frac{\theta^n}{\tau_{kk}^n} - \frac{\alpha_k^{EC} c_k^n}{\tau_{kk}^n x_k^n} + \frac{1}{E_{kk}^n q_k^n} \sum_{i \in T^{EC}} q_i^n c_i^n \frac{\partial \alpha^{EC}}{\partial q_k^n} . \qquad (43)$$

Differentiating the EC budget constraint (11), using (40), and considering the obtained sum term in (43) we have

$$\alpha_k^n = \frac{\theta^n}{\tau_{kk}^n} - \frac{p_k^{EC}}{q_k^n} - \alpha^{EC} - \frac{1}{E_{kk}^n q_k^n} \sum_{\substack{m \in N \\ m \neq n}} \sum_{i \in T^{EC}} q_i^m c_i^m \frac{\partial \alpha^{EC}}{\partial q_k^n} . \qquad (44)$$

Comparing $\alpha_k^n + \alpha^{EC}$ with $\hat{\alpha}_k^n$ on the basis of (41) and (44), we find that the question of whether agricultural products bear higher or lower consumer taxes in the non-coordinated than in the fully coordinated case depends on, among other factors, how the EC tax rate $\alpha^{EC}$ changes with the consumer price $q_k^n$. Differentiating the EC budget constraint (11) it can be shown that $\partial \alpha^{EC}/\partial q_k^n$ is positive because the tax rate on agricultural products does not exceed 100 percent. Hence, we assume $\alpha_k^n + \alpha^{EC} > \hat{\alpha}_k^n$, i.e. agricultural products bear higher consumer taxes in the non-coordinated than in the fully coordinated case.

### VIII. EXPLANATORY NOTES ON PROPOSITION 5

Let us take commodity 1 to be French wine and commodity 2 to be British beer, and assume that consumer demand patterns in the United Kingdom satisfy

$$E_{ik}^{UK} = 0 ; \quad k = 1, 2 ; \quad i > 2 . \qquad (45)$$

To isolate the effect of changes in French profits on the optimal tax rate on French wine in the United Kingdom, we disregard all other profit terms, the monopoly power term, the tariff revenue effect and the possibility of a change in expenditures of the EC authority for buying excess supplies on agricultural markets.

From (23) our fully coordinated optimal tax formulae are

$$\hat{\theta}^{UK} \hat{x}_r^{UK} = - \sum_{i=1}^{2} \hat{t}_i^{UK} \hat{E}_{ir}^{UK} + \hat{\theta}^F [1-\sigma^F] \frac{\partial \hat{\pi}^F}{\partial q_r^{UK}} , \quad r = 1, 2 . \qquad (46)$$

136

Furthermore, we assume that the changes in the UK consumer price of beer, $q_2^{UK}$, do not affect French profits; that means $\partial \pi^F / \partial q_2^{UK} = 0$.

After some rearrangement we find that the relation between optimal tax rates is characterized by

$$\frac{\hat{\alpha}_1^{UK}}{\hat{\alpha}_2^{UK}} = \frac{\hat{\tau}_{12}^{UK} + \hat{\tau}_{22}^{UK} - \dfrac{\hat{\theta}^F[1-\sigma^F]}{\hat{\theta}^{UK}\hat{x}_1^{UK}} \hat{\tau}_{22}^{UK} \dfrac{\partial \hat{\pi}^F}{\partial q_1^{UK}}}{\hat{\tau}_{21}^{UK} + \hat{\tau}_{11}^{UK} - \dfrac{\hat{\theta}^F[1-\sigma^F]}{\hat{\theta}^{UK}\hat{x}_1^{UK}} \hat{\tau}_{21}^{UK} \dfrac{\partial \hat{\pi}^F}{\partial q_1^{UK}}} , \qquad (47)$$

where the own-price elasticity is defined as in (30) and the cross-price elasticities are

$$\tau_{ik}^{UK} = \frac{E_{ik}^{UK} q_k^{UK}}{x_i^{UK}} \quad ; \quad i, k = 1, 2 ; \quad i \neq k . \qquad (48)$$

We have assumed that the government in the UK does not buy French wine or British beer so that $c_1^{UK} = x_1^{UK}$ and $c_2^{UK} = x_2^{UK}$.

Now, we can expect that a higher consumer price of wine in the United Kingdom would reduce the profits of the French wine industry, i.e. $\partial \pi^F / \partial q_1^{UK} < 0$. But (47) does not give a clear-cut answer to the question of how the relation between tax rates is linked with the effect of $q_1^{UK}$ on the French profit $\pi^F$. $\tau_{21}^{UK}$ indicates how the demand for British beer reacts to changes in the British consumer price of wine. It would not be correct to conclude from high values of this substitution term alone that the reduction of French profits provides an argument for a relatively lower tax rate on wine in the United Kingdom. High values of the own-price elasticity of demand for beer, $\tau_{22}^{UK}$, could point to a relatively higher tax rate on wine.

Boadway, R., Maital, S. and Prachowny, M. 'Optimal Tariffs, Optimal Taxes and Public Goods.' *Journal of Public Economics*, 2, 1973.

Commission of the European Communities. 'Report on the Scope for Convergence of Tax Systems in the Community.' *Bulletin of the European Communities*, Supplement 1, 1980.

Dasgupta, P. and Stiglitz, J.E. 'Benefit-Cost Analysis and Trade Policies.' *Journal of Political Economy*, 82, 1974.

Dixit, A. and Munk, K.J. 'Welfare Effects of Tax and Price Changes. A Correction.' *Journal of Public Economics*, 8, 1977.

Dixit, A. and Norman, V. *Theory of International Trade.* Cambridge University Press, 1980.

Easson, A.J. *Tax Law and Policy in the EEC.* London: Sweet & Maxwell, 1980.

Friedlaender, A. and Vandendorpe, A. 'Excise Taxes and the Gains from Trade.' *Journal of Political Economy*, 76, 1968.

Gordon, R.H. 'An Optimal Taxation Approach to Fiscal Federalism.' *The Quarterly Journal of Economics*, 98, 1983.

Munk, K.J. 'Optimal Taxation and Pure Profit.' *Scandinavian Journal of Economics*, 80, 1978.

Shoven, J.B. 'Applied General Equilibrium Tax Modeling.' *IMF Staff Papers*, 30, 1983.

Vandendorpe, A.L. 'Optimal Tax Structures in a Model with Traded and Non-Traded Goods.' *Journal of International Economics*, 2, 1972.

Wiegard, W. 'Distortionary Taxation in a Federal Economy. *'Zeitschrift für Nationalökonomie*, 40, 1980.

# Part Three

# Taxes on Motoring

# 5

# Motor vehicle tax harmonization

*Roger S. Smith\**

## I. INTRODUCTION

As is true for all significant revenue sources, motor vehicle taxes serve multiple objectives (Walters, 1968; Smith, 1975). Governments require funds for road transport related expenditures and for other purposes. Motor vehicle taxes help to meet revenue needs. These taxes as a share of total tax revenues in nine EC countries are given in Table 5.1 for 1972 and 1982. France, Italy, and Belgium each apply higher value-added tax (VAT) rates to automobiles than to other goods, and since it has not been possible to disaggregate these revenues from other VAT revenues, the share in these countries is understated. There remains substantial variation in the importance of motor vehicle taxes, which in 1982 ranged from 12 percent of total taxes in Ireland to 0.7 percent in Luxembourg and from 5 percent to 0.3 percent of Gross Domestic Product (GDP). In all countries there has been a decline in motor vehicle taxes as a share of total taxes from 1972 to 1982, with the decline being relatively sharp in all except Denmark.[1] Further, they have been an inelastic source of revenue, and did not keep pace with the growth in GDP from 1972 to 1982.

Publicly provided goods, where possible, should be priced to encourage an efficient allocation of resources. Therefore, in addition to raising revenue, motor vehicle taxes are used as prices for the use of publicly provided road systems. Governments may also seek to achieve some post-tax income or wealth distribution through motor vehicle taxes; other objectives may include efficient tax administration, and increased control over foreign trade and foreign reserves. However, EC policy has focussed on revenue adequacy and efficient

\* The author is grateful to Sijbren Cnossen and Brian Bayliss who have been particularly helpful with their comments. Neither, of course, is responsible for any shortcomings resulting from the author's failure to heed their sound advice.
1. Motor vehicle taxes are generally relied upon more heavily as a 'tax handle' by countries with lower incomes. This is due to limited alternatives, income distribution objectives at a point in the development process, and administrative factors. EC evidence supports the generalization, even if it is more questionable for higher income countries. The final column in Table 5.1 gives 1980 per capita income in European Units of Account (EUA). Spearman's rank correlation coefficient for per capita income and motor vehicle tax revenues as a share of total tax revenues indicates that there is an inverse relationship between the two.

pricing for taxes applying to the road haulage industry. EC policy objectives for motor vehicle taxes applied to cars have received less attention.

The state of the art for the efficient pricing of roads has contributed little to EC harmonization of motor vehicle taxes even though there is extensive literature. There is general agreement that road users should be charged the social marginal cost (SMC) of use of the road for each additional kilometer driven (to the extent that this cost can be determined and the charge administered). This will vary with the level of congestion, road surface, vehicle weight, vehicle speed, air conditions, noise level, and a variety of other factors. Hence, determining the cost is extremely difficult even when road replacement,

Table 5.1 Motor vehicle tax revenues as a percentage of total tax revenues, 1972 and 1982

| Country | Year | Fuel Tax | Purchase Tax[a] | Use Tax | Total | Percent of GDP | Per Capita Income[b] |
|---|---|---|---|---|---|---|---|
| | | % | % | % | % | % | EUAs |
| Ireland | 1972 | | | | | | |
| | 1982 | 6.96 | 2.81 | 2.09 | 11.86 | 4.69 | 3,400 |
| Denmark | 1972 | 2.51 | 2.59 | 1.63 | 6.73 | 2.89 | |
| | 1982 | 2.64 | 2.14 | 1.59 | 6.37 | 2.80 | 9,300 |
| France | 1972 | 4.57 | (VAT) | 0.49 | 5.06 | 1.79 | |
| | 1982 | 3.35 | (VAT) | 0.55 | 3.90 | 1.71 | 8,800 |
| United Kingdom | 1972 | 7.06 | – | 2.25 | 9.31 | 3.15 | |
| | 1982 | 4.71 | 0.53 | 1.68 | 6.92 | 2.74 | 6,700 |
| Germany | 1972 | 4.97 | – | 1.65 | 6.62 | 2.30 | |
| | 1982 | 3.83 | – | 1.12 | 4.95 | 1.84 | 9,600 |
| Italy | 1972 | 9.08 | (VAT) | 1.05 | 10.13 | 2.89 | |
| | 1982 | 5.96 | (VAT) | 0.40 | 6.36 | 2.11 | 5,000 |
| Belgium | 1972 | 4.65 | (VAT) | 0.94 | 5.59 | 2.07 | |
| | 1982 | 2.58 | (VAT) | 0.97 | 3.55 | 1.66 | 8,500 |
| Netherlands | 1972 | 3.42 | 0.81 | 1.54 | 5.77 | 2.33 | |
| | 1982 | 1.99 | 0.81 | 1.51 | 4.31 | 1.96 | 8,200 |
| Luxembourg | 1972 | 0.09 | – | 1.00 | 1.09 | 0.35 | |
| | 1982 | 0.07 | – | 0.61 | 0.68 | 0.26 | 11,000 |

Notes:  a. Where value-added tax (VAT) is stated, motor vehicles are subject to a VAT rate higher than the normal rate, but it is not possible to disaggregate the data. Where there are dashes ( – ), the normal VAT rate applies. Where purchase tax figures are given they reflect a special purchase tax and do not include revenues from the normal VAT rate. The table indicates that Ireland, Denmark, the United Kingdom, and the Netherlands apply a special purchase tax, Germany and Luxembourg apply the normal VAT rate, and France, Italy, and Belgium apply a higher than normal VAT rate.

b. Per capita income figures (in European Units of Account) were calculated from data on page 1 of the Statistical Yearbook of the European Communities (1983).

Source: Organisation for Economic Co-operation and Development (1984).

or long-run, costs are ignored. Transportation experts have not yet determined how best to enter long-run costs into a pricing strategy. The complexity is great, and without agreement among the experts, agreement among EC Member States is more difficult.[2]

A second stumbling block in the harmonization of taxes affecting transport services has been the diversity of factors affecting transportation costs. The theory of the second best indicates that tax harmonization may worsen rather than improve results. Diversity in wages, working hours, working conditions, safety standards, weight limits, motor vehicle dimensions, paperwork, emission controls, insurance requirements, government subsidy programs, and the quality of roads and other infrastructure are among the factors contributing to total costs and efficiency of operation. This diversity has caused the EC to move to standardization in areas such as conditions and hours of work, and vehicle safety standards.

Motor vehicle transport is, of course, only one part of the total transportation system. It has, however, been by far the most rapidly growing part, both for internal transport within Member States and for transport between Member States. Long-distance road transport in Germany increased from 30.8 percent of total ton-kilometers of goods transported in that country in 1972 to 42.4 percent in 1982. In Belgium the increase was from 35.3 percent in 1963 to 51.5 percent in 1972 and 59.7 percent in 1982; and in the Netherlands from 55.5 percent in 1971 to 74.0 percent in 1982.[3]

Growth has been even more rapid for transport *between* Member States. From 1965 to 1982, total ton-kilometers of domestic road haulage grew by 59 percent in Belgium while international haulage grew by 356 percent. From 1966 to 1982 in the Netherlands the licensees' capacity of all forms grew by 95 percent

2. The Economic and Social Committee (1983, p. 28) recently stated that 'With the aid of renowned experts, individual Member State Governments and the Commission have been making serious and thorough attempts for many years to come up with a basic solution to this problem.' Unfortunately, no solution has yet been found or accepted. Meyer and Straszheim (1971, p. 29), who have examined transportation pricing issues at great length, conclude that 'in general, the choice of a pricing strategy depends, at least to some extent, on subjective preferences and objectives of public policy. This is true even within a relatively limited and static view of technologies and demand structures. Among the range of issues to be considered are development objectives, administrative questions, and welfare issues. In short, any viable generalization about what constitutes an optimal pricing strategy is likely to be difficult, if not impossible, to obtain.'
3. In Germany rail's share of goods transport fell from 41.7 percent (1972) to 31.3 percent (1982), and inland water's share fell from 27.5 percent (1972) to 26.3 percent (1982). The decrease in rail's share in Belgium was from 25.4 percent (1972) to 23.2 percent (1982), and in the Netherlands from 6.4 percent (1971) to 4.1 percent (1982). Inland water's share in Belgium fell from 23.1 percent (1972) to 17.1 percent (1982), and in the Netherlands from 38.1 percent (1971) to 21.9 percent (1982). (Germany – Statistisches Bundesamt Wiesbaden, 1983, p. 246; Belgium – Nationaal Instituut voor de Statistiek, 1984, and Moore, 1976, p. 71; The Netherlands – Centraal Bureau voor de Statistiek, 1972 and 1983.)

while that for international license holders grew by 241 percent. Table 5.2, providing data for the Netherlands and Belgium, shows a substantial increase in the share of tonnage carried by road to and from various trading partners. The actual tonnage carried by other forms of transport decreased in some cases. Harmonization of motor vehicle taxation, important in the 1960s, is more important in the 1980s, and likely to be even more important in the 1990s.

The substantial difference in transport systems in Member States is a third obstacle on the road to harmonized taxes. Data in Table 5.3 show that roads account for 88 percent of goods transport in Italy, and 52 percent in Germany. Rail accounts for 4 percent in the Netherlands, 32 percent in France and 26 percent in Germany. The Dutch, the British, and the Italians are less concerned than the Germans and the French with protecting state-owned railway systems, and the trucking industry has been subjected to higher taxes and stricter regulation in countries where the railway is protected. One result has been the 'liberalization' view versus the 'harmonization of competition' view (Button, 1982, 1984; Economic and Social Committee, 1983). Countries with the 'liberalization' view have included the United Kingdom, Belgium, and the Netherlands, all with relatively competitive trucking industries, and all wishing to move goods freely by truck to larger EC markets such as France, Germany and Italy.[4] Larger countries have been more interested in harmonizing competition among the various transport modes. In general, it is understandable that countries with smaller internal markets wish to access larger markets through use of efficient transportation.

The focus of the above is on commercial freight transportation. Whereas there may be some general EC agreement on the objectives of road pricing policies for commercial transport, policy objectives on the taxation of cars are less clear. In an article on the European car industry *The Economist* (March 3, 1985) noted: 'Europe, despite the EC, remains divided into a series of national markets. National pride and political realities make it almost inconceivable that any of the big European producers will be allowed to go under'. Murfin (this volume) found that 'the European car market does not appear to be competitive over price and the exercise of monopoly power is leading to welfare losses for European consumers'. Murfin reports that in 1982 net of tax prices in Denmark were 59 percent of the UK level; and prices in Luxembourg, Belgium, the Netherlands and France were all less than 75 percent of the UK level.

A variety of tools can be used to protect and encourage a national car industry. Speed limits are an example. Imposition of strict speed limits in Germany would, over time, be likely to have a substantial impact on the market for the relatively high-powered cars produced in Germany. Likewise,

---

4. Moore (1976) found that the limited regulation and increased competitiveness of trucking in the Netherlands, Belgium, and the United Kingdom, when compared with Germany, had resulted in greater efficiency, lower rates, better service, and greater profits.

*Table 5.2 Growth of international road haulage relative to other means of transport: evidence for the Netherlands and Belgium, 1972 and 1982 or 1983*

| A. Netherlands Share of Tonnage Carried by Road To and From: | 1972 | 1983 | Percentage Change | |
|---|---|---|---|---|
| | | | Road | All Modes |
| | Based on thousands of tons carried | | | |
| France | 23.1 | 33.6 | 101.5 | 38.3 |
| Germany | 14.7 | 22.3 | 53.5 | 1.2 |
| Italy | 11.0 | 37.6 | 180.7 | - 18.0 |
| Denmark | 5.1 | 17.3 | 216.0 | - 6.6 |

| B. Belgium Share of Tonnage Carried by Road To and From: | 1972 | 1982 | Percentage Change | |
|---|---|---|---|---|
| | | | Road | All Modes |
| France | 35.2 | 61.6 | 66.3 | -7.4 |
| Netherlands | 31.2 | 40.2 | 40.4 | 9.1 |
| Germany | 30.0 | 41.5 | 59.1 | 14.9 |
| Italy | 19.1 | 47.0 | 198.8 | 21.8 |

*Sources:* Belgium – Nationaal Instituut voor de Statistiek (1974, pp. 72-75; 1984, pp. 201-203); Netherlands – Centraal Bureau voor de Statistiek (1973, p. 233; 1984, p. 18). The 1983 figures for the Netherlands are projected based on the actual figures for the January-September 1983 period.

*Table 5.3 Inland surface goods transport in EC countries, 1981 or 1982*

| Country (Year) | Mode of Transport | | | Total |
|---|---|---|---|---|
| | Road | Water | Rail | |
| | Percent of Total Tonnage | | | |
| France (1982) | 63.9 | 4.4 | 31.7 | 100 |
| Germany (1982) | 52.5 | 21.7 | 25.8 | 100 |
| United Kingdom (1981) | 84.7 | 0.1 | 15.2 | 100 |
| Italy (1981) | 87.8 | 0.1 | 12.1 | 100 |
| Netherlands (1981) | 68.5 | 27.3 | 4.2 | 100 |
| Belgium (1981) | 56.8 | 18.1 | 25.1 | 100 |

*Source:* International Road Federation (1983, pp. 81 and 83).

substantial relaxation of speed limits in other countries could be expected to alter their markets. The need for, and impact of, emission control regulations differ substantially from country to country. Effective January 1, 1985 German states 'introduced tax incentives under which anybody who buys a car with a (catalytic) converter up to the end of 1986 will be exempted from paying motoring tax for 10 years. At current rates that would mean a total saving of up to DM 3,000 over 10 years. . . . Any manufacturer exporting to Germany is already being forced to respond to what amounts to a fait accompli' (*The Economist*, March 3, 1985). The $ 500 cost of a catalytic converter is much greater proportionately for a small car than for a large car.[5] Smaller engines and speed limits are alternative means for reducing fuel consumption and emissions. As the various non-tariff barriers to trade are reduced, harmonization of car taxes becomes relatively more important in achieving free movement of cars among EC countries (Bayliss, 1985, p. 4).

The use of cars for passenger transportation has also grown. Data in Table 5.4 show that cars per capita increased rapidly in the EC, but the level still remains far below that in the United States, Canada, and Australia. The car population of the EC was 88 million in 1981. If there had been the same level of car ownership as in the United States, the car population would have been 61 million higher.[6] Motor vehicle tax harmonization within the EC may influence the extent to which European industry participates in an expanding market in the EC and elsewhere.

The remainder of the paper is divided into four parts. Section II reviews EC transport policy objectives. Section III considers progress toward harmonization of taxes on commercial road transport over the past 15 years. Section IV examines the harmonization of taxes on cars. Section V briefly summarizes the paper.

## II. EC POLICY OBJECTIVES

'Like the Community's other fundamental objectives, its common policies cannot be brought to fruition without recourse to the instrument of taxation. A typical example is afforded by the common transport policy. One of the prime objectives of this policy is that each mode of transport should bear its fair share of infrastructure costs. In the case of road haulage or road passenger transport the instrument chosen to achieve this objective is taxation: in the final analysis,

---

5. German pressures have resulted in EC agreement to stricter exhaust controls for all new cars over a six year period beginning in 1988, and a decision that lead-free petrol is to be available throughout the Community by 1989 (*The Economist*, March 3, 1985).

6. An in-depth study of the automobile in America projects that the fleet of 120 million cars in America in 1980 will expand to between 145 million and 160 million cars in 1990 (Meyer and Gomez-Ibanez, 1981, p. 90).

*Table 5.4 Number of cars and motor vehicles per 1,000 of population, 1965 and 1981*

| Country | Number of Cars 1965 | 1981 | Number of Motor Vehicles 1981 |
|---|---|---|---|
| Germany | 158 | 385 | 414 |
| France | 197 | 349 | 401 |
| Italy | 105 | 330 | 363 |
| Netherlands | 111 | 324 | 351 |
| Belgium | 139 | 325 | 355 |
| Luxembourg | 186 | 378 | 437 |
| United Kingdom | 166 | 283 | 320 |
| Ireland | 99 | 226 | 249 |
| Denmark | 159 | 267 | 316 |
| Greece | 12 | 94 | 142 |
| EC | *148* | *325* | *357* |
| United States | 387 | 557 (1980) | |
| Canada | 268 | 430 (1980) | |
| Australia | 254 | 403 (1980) | |

*Sources:* Statistical Office of the European Communities (1983, p. 4). Data for non-EC countries are taken from Tanner (1983, p. 59).

taxes on vehicles and on motor fuels will have to be fixed in such a way that their yield in aggregate total corresponds to the share of infrastructure costs to be borne by these vehicles.' (Commission, 1980b, p. 11.)

Articles 74 to 84 of the Treaty of Rome specify that the Community is to introduce a common transport policy. EC objectives in transportation are to eliminate discrimination on the grounds of nationality, through taxation, through regulations, at border crossings, or through state aid. Member States are not to use their motor vehicle tax systems to achieve gains at the expense of other jurisdictions. The Community is to strive to achieve an integrated transport system with a basis for open competition between modes and within modes in order better to ensure use of the most efficient mode. However, differences in existing economic and social conditions and differences in weights given to various objectives logically result in a wide variety of motor vehicle tax systems.

Early action by the EC included Council Directives and Regulations for the harmonization of working conditions (driving and rest periods, breaks, second drivers, minimum ages, and safety requirements), the establishment of community quotas on licenses given to each Member State for international haulage, the establishment of minimum and maximum (bracket) tariffs within which rates must be set for international haulage, and duty-free admission of fuel in fuel tanks — all pertaining to road haulage. There was also considerable discussion on the need to coordinate infrastructure development in the EC and to establish a common pricing system for the use of the infrastructure. Throughout the 1970s and early 1980s the Directives and Regulations of the 1960s have been updated. For example, in 1984 Council removed all restrictions on the duty-free admission of fuel contained in the normal fuel tanks of commercial motor vehicles. Bracket tariffs have been adjusted, legislation on working conditions has been extended through Council Regulations and Decisions, and recording equipment has been introduced to assist in the enforcement of Regulations and Decisions. The quota on EC trucking licenses has also been regularly expanded (Button, 1984, p. 81).[7] There has been recent agreement on emission controls and on maximum weights for vehicles.[8] Still, the achieved level of harmonization has been disappointing to many.[9]

Activities of the 1960s resulted in a major proposal by the Commission to the Council (1968) for the 'Development of National Systems of Taxation on Commercial Vehicles'. The objective was to harmonize the structures of the

7. Following is a partial listing of the various Directives and Regulations pertaining to road transport policy that have been issued over the years. Relating to the need to coordinate infrastructure development and establish a common pricing system are Council Directive 68/297; Council Regulations 1018/68, 1174/68, 543/69; and the proposed 'Directive on the Adjustment of National Taxation Systems Relating to Commercial Vehicles' presented by the Commission to the Council in 1968. Removal of restrictions on the duty-free admission of fuel contained in the normal fuel tanks of commercial motor vehicles is reported in the *Bulletin of European Communities* 17, no. 3, 1984, p. 57. Adjustments in bracket tariffs are found in Regulations 293/70, 2826/72, 3255/74, 3330/75, 3181/76, 2831/77. Updating of the harmonization of social legislation is found in Regulations 514/72, 515/72, 2827/77; and Decisions 72/366, 78/85, 78/86, 82/72. Regulations pertaining to recording equipment include 1463/70, 1787/73, 2828/77. Regulations pertaining to the quota on Community trucking licenses include 2329/72, 2063/74, 3331/75, 3164/76, 3024/77, 3062/78, 2963/79, 2964/79, 663/82.
8. Agreement was finally reached in late 1984 on a 40 ton maximum (38 tons in the United Kingdom and Ireland). In 1979, maximum limits were 32 tons in the United Kingdom, 38 in France and Germany, and 44 in Denmark and Italy. Lack of uniformity meant that trucks efficient in one market could not be used in another. Where the limit has been raised, infrastructure expenditures will be required.
9. Munby (1962, p. 69) was one expert who perceived shortcomings of various EC transportation policy directions in the early years. He argued that there was little about the market for transport which required special controls. He saw as least damaging regulations that place overall limits on the number of lorries that may operate in certain markets. More damaging would be controls on the use of lorries, still more damaging would be controls on charges. In international road transport the EC has not been able to free itself from controls in any of these three areas. The result is failure to use the least-cost form of transport on many occasions.

systems of taxation — the basis for calculation, modes of application, and the relation between the rates applicable to various categories while leaving member countries free to set the level of taxation. The intent was to ensure that the basis of taxation — laden or unladen weight, axle load, axle arrangement — was the same in Member States. The systems of taxation were to be based on the *use* of road infrastructures and costs associated with such use. A general road tax was to depend on the characteristics of the particular vehicle and on the type of fuel used. This tax was to be coupled with taxes on fuel to reach a sum that reflected the marginal costs associated with the use of each vehicle. The marginal costs were to include maintenance costs, renewal costs, and costs associated with the operation and management of road infrastructures caused by additional traffic. Since fuel taxes were unlikely to be varied to reflect adequately the additional costs of use by a particular vehicle, and since even within a State it may not be possible to vary fuel taxes to reflect the marginal cost of use by different vehicle types, a road tax was proposed to reflect use of road infrastructure and the existing level of fuel taxes in any Member State.

The 1968 proposed directive was followed by a Commission memorandum to Council (Commission, 1971) focussing on marginal social cost pricing, and on the need to couple this with adequate financing of infrastructure. Not only were taxes to be set according to marginal social cost, but they were also to generate sufficient revenue (a) to provide the needed road maintenance, repairs, sound barriers, etc., and (b) to provide the needed expansion to the existing system. Fifteen years after these two initiatives, little action has accompanied the continuing discussion.

Lack of action in the 1970s toward the harmonization of motor vehicle taxes created frustration among those interested in a common market. With respect to transport policy generally, the Economic and Social Committee (1983, p. 11) concluded that 'the Community can no longer afford very different national transport systems which do not allow optimum use of resources and which have become so expensive that the costs can no longer be borne without serious damage to the Community in the long-term'. This Committee feels that there is substantial agreement now on the dual objectives of charging no less than marginal social costs for the utilization of infrastructure *and* of achieving overall budgetary balance for the transport network.[10]

10. On January 22, 1983 the President of the European Parliament brought before the Court of Justice action against the Council for failure to act in the field of transport policy (*Bulletin of the European Communities* 16, 1, 1983, p. 34). The decision of the Court of Justice was against the Council (Case 13/83) (Commission of European Communities, 1985, p. 29). The Court held that 'The Council had infringed the Treaty by failing to ensure freedom to provide services in the sphere of international transport and to lay down the conditions under which non-resident carriers may operate in a Member State' (Court of Justice of the European Communities, 1985, p. 13).

Differences in motor vehicle tax levels are, of course, only one factor which has prevented more competition in transportation services. The number of trucks used in international transport continues to be tightly controlled. The number of EC licenses any country has is based on a strict quota system, and movement of truck transport between any two Member States is limited by bilateral agreements (Button, 1984, pp. 68-74). And as earlier noted, maximum vehicle size, emission controls, and other factors varied among Member States.

To overcome these quantitative restrictions requires increased recognition of the benefits to the Community to be gained by a more competitive and open transportation system, and a willingness by government to compensate some of the losers. For example, restricted entry into the German trucking industry has resulted in a substantial market value for long-distance haulage licenses.[11] To realize a reasonable rate of return on this as well as other components of his investment, a German trucker must charge higher freight rates than in countries where easier entry results in little or no market value for licenses. If the German trucking market were wide open, existing trucking firms would experience substantial capital losses as the value of licenses fell to zero.

The *Opinion* offered by the Economic and Social Committee (1983) starkly reflects the nature of the problems to be overcome. First, there may be incompatibility between charging marginal social cost and budgetary balance. Balancing the two objectives may differ substantially from one Member State to another. In countries where motor vehicle use is growing rapidly, and where the road system is currently least developed, the need to expand the network is greatest. This may or may not be adequately reflected in taxes based on marginal social costs of road use. Road expenditures as a percentage of road taxes in 1982 were 24 percent in the Netherlands and 72 percent in Germany, and taxes on cars were substantially higher in the Netherlands.[12]

The Committee (1983, p. 40) also writes that 'The basic principle must be to allow competition as free a rein as possible but to limit it, though only to the degree necessary, in specific instances where overriding public interests require', and 'neither carriers nor workers should suffer from an opening up of the transport markets' (p. 48). These statements reflect the difficulty of the EC in developing a policy in which the costs and benefits of change are shared equally

11. Moore (1976, p. 43) reported a value for a long-distance license in North Rhineland-Westphalia of DM 110,000 and DM 60,000 for one issued in West Berlin. In a separate study, Bayliss (1973, p. 43) reported a value between DM 40,000 and DM 90,000. Similarly, Moore (p. 72) found in Belgium that would-be truckers are often willing to pay a premium in order to avoid having to wait nine years to earn a national license. The going price was US$7,500 to US$8,500 for an unlimited license and the original owner had to be half owner of the new enterprise and participate in the management of the firm.
12. To meet infrastructure needs there was 15 million ECU in the 1983 Community budget. This amount was to grow in future years and reflects the need for Community action to address some infrastructure bottlenecks (*Bulletin of the European Communities* 16, 7/8, 1983, p. 48).

among Member States. As Button (1984, p. 18) points out, Article 75(3) of the Treaty of Rome 'effectively provides for a permanent veto in the Council of Ministers where proposed transport policies "might seriously affect the standard of living and the level of employment in certain regions and also the utilization of transport equipment". Quite clearly any major policy decision would fall within this category.'

EC policy objectives for taxes on cars have received less attention. In a common market there should be the free sale of goods across borders without tariff or non-tariff barriers inhibiting the flow of goods. Large differences in taxes on cars and their use continue to be found in Member States. This may reflect the existence of other important barriers enabling substantial price discrimination (Murfin, this volume).

Car purchase taxes, if varied according to car characteristics (e.g. value or engine size), may discriminate against cars produced in some Member States, whereas a uniform rate applied to all cars presumably would not do so. Even in this case, however, a sufficiently high purchase tax rate applied to all cars may eliminate higher priced cars for the bulk of the market. Rates applying in Denmark may have this effect. Similarly, for a specific excise tax rate applied to gasoline, the higher the rate the greater the incentive for the car buyer to purchase a car that consumes less fuel. Car registration taxes have traditionally been varied in EC and other countries according to car characteristics. Thus, it is possible for Member States to use purchase taxes (even if applied at a uniform rate), fuel taxes, and registration fees to favor the purchase of some cars over others. An objective of a common market is to reduce this type of discrimination. As we shall see in Section IV, limited progress has been made by the EC in this area.


III. HARMONIZATION OF TAXES ON COMMERCIAL ROAD TRANSPORT

With respect to commercial road transportation, tax harmonization has to be considered as it relates to competition between carriers from different Member States competing in the same market, and competition between different modes of transport.


A. Harmonization Between or Within Transport Modes

The Commission surely viewed the policies proposed in 1968 to be steps toward the development of a common transport policy more generally, and not only a step toward tax harmonization. First, charges in each form of transport were to reflect infrastructure costs in comparable fashions and ensure that the least-cost form of transport was used. Second, revenues were to be raised to finance the required infrastructure for the efficient movement of goods between, as well as through and within, Member States. Balancing of these objectives is difficult if not impossible. Charges which keep infrastructure costs in balance between two forms of transport within each of two Member States will in all likelihood result in charges for each form of transport between the two Member States that are out of harmony.

Given the complexities of achieving a fully harmonized transport policy, the Community may be better served by first pursuing harmonization *within* each transport sector and then harmonization *between* sectors. This may evolve naturally as French truckers increasingly see Dutch truckers on their roads and vice versa as international transport grows more rapidly than domestic transport. As French truckers become more concerned with competition from foreign truckers relative to competition with state-owned railways, the focus will shift from internal harmonization to external harmonization.

Tax harmonization goals within the commercial motor vehicle sector must also be more ambitious. Several different forms of motor vehicle taxes exist − fuel excise taxes, annual registration fees, and special purchase taxes. The sum of these taxes for a vehicle may (on average) be equal in two Member States. Yet a serious lack of harmonization may exist even when the tax reflects, on average, the marginal social cost of use in each of the states. Consider the following example:

|  | State A | State B |
|---|---|---|
| Fuel taxes | DM 5,000 | DM 1,000 |
| Registration fees | DM 1,000 | DM 5,000 |
| Sum | DM 6,000 | DM 6,000 |

Fuel taxes in Member State B are substantially lower than in A. In a situation of registration in A, and active operation in B and similar States, vehicles operating out of State A will have a cost advantage over those operating out of State B. Increased internationalization of trucking during the 1970s and 1980s has sharply lessened the adequacy of the type of harmonization (special annual road taxes levied to adjust for fuel tax differences) recommended by the Commission in the late 1960s.

## B. Increased Competition?

Increased harmonization and competition may have occurred to a significant extent without specific Community action. There is evidence of growing competition. In the 1970s Moore (1976, p. 3) found that the 'Dutch are known as the most efficient truckers in Western Europe and dominate the international haulage market there'.[13] From 1956 to 1972 there was a sharp increase in the

13. Moore found that 'The Dutch have a deserved international reputation for being the leading trucking nation in western Europe . . . Dutch trucks carry nearly three-quarters of the traffic →

share of road goods crossing the Dutch border that were transported in Dutch trucks, a rise from 54 to 74 percent. The Dutch were out-competing other EC countries. From 1972 to 1981 the trend was sharply reversed, falling to 53 percent. German, French, Italian, and other European carriers substantially increased their share of goods being carried from the Netherlands to their countries (Centraal Bureau voor de Statistiek, 1973 and 1983; Moore, 1976, p. 96). German trucking, which Moore (1976) found to be heavily regulated and subject to heavy taxation, held its share of the market in road goods being transported across the German border, rising from 63 percent in 1965 to 66 percent in 1980, and then falling to 65 percent in 1983 (Bundesverband des Deutschen Guterfernverkehrs, 1984, p. 49).

If there has been an increase in competition, to what extent has tax harmonization or a fall in the real and relative value of taxes contributed to this end? Or has increased harmonization resulted from the increased competition? Causation probably flows in both directions.

## C. Taxes on Fuel

Data problems are significant in the development of comparisons of fuel and registration taxes over a period of time in the EC. A number of data sources are drawn upon in the following tables. Table 5.5 shows taxes on diesel fuel for the four major EC countries from 1973 through 1984, and states the coefficient of variation (s/x) and the maximum tax relative to the minimum tax in each year. The coefficient of variation dropped substantially from 73 percent in 1973 to 33 percent in 1984, indicating major convergence of taxes on diesel fuel in the four countries. In 1973 the highest tax had been over five times the lowest. In 1984 it was less than two-and-a-half times the lowest. Data in Table 5.6, provided by a German trucking association for seven EC countries, confirm the trend. With Belgium, the Netherlands, and Luxembourg added, the coefficient of variation falls from 62 percent in 1972 to 54 percent in 1984. The maximum tax, which

---

crossing the borders of the Netherlands. They have about 77 per cent of the professional traffic to West Germany and nearly 78 per cent of the return loads. Truckers in the Netherlands have been increasing their share of the international market steadily. . . . The pre-eminence of Dutch trucking suggests that the Dutch truckers offer good service. It has been alleged that it also reflects their disregard of EEC rules on drivers' hours and their relatively low tax rates. No doubt these factors play a role.' (Moore, 1976, pp. 96-97.) However, from 1972 to 1981 the share of goods hauled across the Dutch border, in both directions, that was carried in Dutch trucks dropped substantially. For example, the share going to France dropped from 70.4 percent to 32.2 percent, the share going to Germany from 76.6 percent to 37.8 percent, the share going to Italy from 64.3 to 30.4 percent. Over 50 percent of the goods coming from these countries was in Dutch trucks in each of the two years, but in all cases it was lower in 1981 than in 1972. (Germany – Bundesverband des Deutschen Guterfernverkehrs, 1984, p. 49; Netherlands – Centraal Bureau voor de Statistiek, 1973 and 1983, and Moore, 1976, p. 96).

*Table 5.5 Taxes on petrol (regular) and diesel fuel in four major EC countries,
1973-84*

| Year | France | Italy | United Kingdom | Germany | $x^a$ | $s^b$ | $s/x^c$ | Max/Min |
|------|--------|-------|----------------|---------|-------|-------|---------|---------|
| | | | Tax in US Cents per Gallon | | | | % | |
| *Regular Petrol* | | | | | | | | |
| 1973 | 38 | 29 | 26 | 70 | 40.75 (40.75) | 20.16 | 49.5 | 2.69 |
| 1979 | 78 | 76 | 45 | 74 | 68.25 (41.87) | 15.59 | 22.8 | 1.73 |
| 1980 | 81 | 89 | 62 | 77 | 77.25 (41.98) | 11.32 | 14.7 | 1.44 |
| 1981 | 84 | 115 | 73 | 79 | 87.75 (43.10) | 18.71 | 21.3 | 1.58 |
| 1982 | 96 | 127 | 99 | 92 | 103.50 (47.92) | 15.93 | 15.4 | 1.38 |
| 1983 | 101 | 161 | 108 | 92 | 115.50 (51.79) | 31.03 | 26.9 | 1.75 |
| 1984 | 115 | 185 | 114 | 93 | 126.75 (54.40) | 40.14 | 31.7 | 1.99 |
| *Diesel Fuel* | | | | | | | | |
| 1973 | 23 | 13 | 26 | 66 | 32.00 (32.00) | 23.34 | 72.9 | 5.08 |
| 1979 | 45 | 10 | 48 | 70 | 43.25 (26.53) | 24.81 | 57.4 | 7.00 |
| 1980 | 49 | 13 | 69 | 74 | 51.25 (27.85) | 27.69 | 54.0 | 5.69 |
| 1981 | 49 | 14 | 74 | 75 | 53.00 (25.98) | 28.65 | 54.1 | 5.36 |
| 1982 | 52 | 17 | 88 | 82 | 59.75 (27.66) | 32.56 | 54.5 | 5.18 |
| 1983 | 65 | 33 | 105 | 82 | 71.25 (31.95) | 30.31 | 42.5 | 3.18 |
| 1984 | 73 | 41 | 99 | 84 | 74.25 (31.87) | 24.60 | 33.1 | 2.41 |
| *Diesel Tax as a Percent of Petrol Tax* | | | | | | | | |
| 1973 | 60 | 45 | 100 | 94 | | | | |
| 1984 | 63 | 22 | 87 | 90 | | | | |

*Notes:* a. x is the average for the four countries. The figures in parentheses are the values in 1973 US cents. See the Appendix for price indices. For the fifty U.S. states in 1983 the average tax on a U.S. gallon of gasoline was 19.08 cents (including a nine cent federal tax), the standard deviation was 2.1 cents, and the coefficient of variation was 11 percent (Bowman and Mikesell, 1983). For the ten Canadian provinces, the mean was 9.04 Canadian cents a litre (including the federal tax of 1.5 cents/litre) and the standard deviation was 4.61 cents, with a coefficient of variation of 51 percent. Two Canadian provinces, Alberta and Saskatchewan, do not tax gasoline (Canadian Tax Foundation, 1983, p. 106).

b. s is the standard deviation.

c. s/x is the coefficient of variation.

*Source:* US Directorate of Intelligence (1984, p. 19).

154

had been nearly ten times the minimum in 1972, was only four times the minimum in 1984, again showing convergence in taxes applied to diesel fuel.

Tables 5.7 and 5.8 set forth the prices of diesel fuel in various EC countries. We expect convergence here, as in the case of taxes alone, since diesel fuel is a freely traded commodity. For the four major EC countries, diesel fuel prices converged from 1973 to 1984. The maximum price in 1973 (in Germany) was over four-and-a-half times the minimum (in Italy), and in 1984 the maximum (United Kingdom) was only one-and-a-half that in Italy. The coefficient of variation dropped from 67 percent to 16 percent. Table 5.8, for nine EC countries, provides similar evidence for the period 1970 to 1982. Evidence indicates that there has been substantial convergence in diesel fuel tax rates over at least the past fifteen years.

When adjusted for inflation, the differences in diesel fuel taxes are further reduced. The mean values given in parentheses in Table 5.5 and Table 5.6 indicate a substantial drop in the real value of per unit diesel fuel taxes from the early 1970s to 1980. Since 1980 there has been some increase, but the 1984 real level is still below that in the early 1970s. Over the same period the increase in the real price of diesel fuel was significant (40 to 50 percent).

Cost differences for 40,000 litres of diesel fuel can be calculated for nine EC countries from 1970 to 1981 from the data in Table 5.8. Using the Netherlands (which has been viewed as aggressively competitive in trucking) as a base, we find that in 1970 fuel would have cost 424 EUA less in Denmark and 4,424 EUA more in the United Kingdom, a spread of 4,848 EUA. In 1981 (again with the Netherlands as the base) the range was from − 3,840 EUA in Greece to + 8,272 EUA in the United Kingdom, a spread of 12,112 EUA. When adjusted for inflation the differential fell from 4,848 EUA to 4,101 EUA, a fall of 15 percent.


### D. Registration Taxes

Registration taxes vary substantially for commercial motor vehicles. Taxes for 38- and 32-tonne trucks, as compiled by a German trucking association, are given in Table 5.9. The convergence of registration taxes has not been similar to that for taxes on diesel fuel. The coefficient of variation for both 38- and 32-tonne trucks rose from 1972 to 1984. However, Table 5.9 also shows a sharp drop in the mean real value of the registration fees, by over 35 percent, from 1972 to 1984, and this might be viewed as a step towards increased harmonization.

Table 5.10 combines fuel taxes and registration taxes. There is little evidence of convergence in the combined taxes. The divergence between the country with the highest taxes and that with the lowest increased substantially between 1972 and 1982, and then dropped. Similarly the coefficient of variation increased

| | 1972 | 1976 | 1980 | 1984 |
|---|---|---|---|---|
| | | In German Marks | | |
| Belgium | 15.5 | 18.7 | 17.0 | 26.0 |
| Germany | 37.0 | 42.0 | 41.2 | 44.2 |
| France | 29.6 | 31.6 | 32.0 | 27.6 |
| United Kingdom | 42.8 | 27.3 | 43.0 | 54.6 |
| Italy | 25.5 | 13.8 | 5.0 | 16.0 |
| Luxembourg | 8.3 | 7.6 | 9.0 | 13.7 |
| Netherlands | 4.4 | 18.5 | 17.0 | 17.9 |
| $x^a$ | 23.3 | 22.79 | 23.45 | 28.56 |
| | (23.3) | (18.18) | (15.95) | (16.46) |
| $s^b$ | 14.5 | 11.65 | 15.28 | 15.38 |
| $s/x^c$ (percent) | 62.2 | 51.1 | 65.2 | 53.9 |
| Max/min | 9.73 | 5.53 | 8.6 | 3.98 |

*Notes:*  a. x is the average for the seven countries. The figures in parentheses are the values in 1972 German marks. See Appendix for price indices.

  b. s is the standard deviation.

  c. s/x is the coefficient of variation.

*Sources:* Bundesverband des Deutschen Guterfernverkehrs (1972 to 1984).


from 1972 to 1980 and then fell gradually.[14] For the combined fuel and registration taxes, the mean level of taxes, in real terms, fell by nearly 40 percent from 1972 to 1982, and then increased by 1984 to 68 percent of its 1972 level.

It is, of course, possible that tax differences help to offset other differences, contributing to increased efficiency in the allocation of resources. Thus it must be kept in mind that convergence increases economic efficiency only if it is toward an optimum tax. In fact there has been a substantial convergence since the 1960s in diesel fuel taxes. Registration fees have not shown the same convergence. The combination of diesel fuel taxes and registration fees shows a

14. Evidence from a different source for five countries (Belgium, France, Germany, the United Kingdom, the Netherlands) is more encouraging, but also shows an increase in differences from 1974 to 1978, prior to a substantial convergence from 1978 to 1982. Taxes on public carriers goods vehicles of 16 tonnes laden weight operating at 75 percent capacity, travelling 50,000 kilometers per annum and consuming 40 litres of diesel fuel each 100 kilometers were calculated in SDRs. The coefficient of variation grew from 48.4 percent in 1974 to 63.2 percent in 1978 before falling to 30.7 percent in 1982. The ratio of the highest-tax country to the lowest-tax country rose from 3.03 in 1974 to 3.75 in 1978 before falling to 2.14 in 1982 (International Road Federation, 1970 through 1983).

*Table 5.7 Prices of petrol (regular) and diesel fuel in four major EC countries, 1973, 1979 and 1984*

| Year | France | Italy | United Kingdom | Germany | $x^a$ | $s^b$ | $s/x^c$ | Max/Min |
|------|--------|-------|----------------|---------|-------|-------|---------|---------|
| | | | In US Cents per Gallon | | | | % | |
| *Regular Petrol* | | | | | | | | |
| 1973 (Oct) | 56 | 39 | 41 | 97 | 58.25 (58.25) | 26.92 | 46.2 | 2.49 |
| 1979 (Jan) | 113 | 106 | 92 | 127 | 109.50 (67.32) | 14.57 | 13.3 | 1.38 |
| 1984 (Jul) | 224 | 271 | 213 | 185 | 223.25 (96.01) | 35.82 | 16.0 | 1.46 |
| *Diesel Fuel* | | | | | | | | |
| 1973 (Oct) | 38 | 21 | 42 | 97 | 49.50 (49.50) | 32.95 | 66.6 | 4.62 |
| 1979 (Jan) | 79 | 38 | 99 | 125 | 85.25 (52.41) | 36.70 | 43.0 | 3.29 |
| 1984 (Jul) | 176 | 136 | 203 | 180 | 173.75 (74.72) | 27.84 | 16.0 | 1.49 |

*Notes:* a. x is the average price for the four countries. The figures in parentheses are the values in 1973 US cents. See Appendix for price indices.
  b. s is the standard deviation for the sample of four countries.
  c. s/x is the coefficient of variation.
*Source:* See Table 5.5

growing divergence during much of the 1970s, but the situation in the late 1970s and early 1980s shifted to a situation of relatively rapid convergence. More equal taxes on diesel fuel, and a substantial reduction in the real level of combined fuel and registration taxes, may be the result of increasing competition in trucking. They may also contribute to increased competition.

*Table 5.8 Retail prices of diesel fuel per 100 litres in EC countries, 1970, 1975, 1981 and 1982*

| | 1970 | 1975 | 1981 | 1982 |
|---|---|---|---|---|
| | | In EUAs | | In Dutch Guilders |
| Germany | 15.56 | 28.21 | 50.70 | 150 |
| France | 13.01 | 23.50 | 50.63 | 141 |
| Italy | 12.00 | 17.27 | 35.64 | 106 |
| Netherlands | 5.71 | 16.81 | 40.86 | 117 |
| Belgium | 10.18 | 18.72 | 48.11 | 124 |
| Luxembourg | 7.52 | 13.62 | 36.57 | 98 |
| United Kingdom | 16.77 | 21.62 | 61.54 | 175 |
| Denmark | 4.65 | 13.16 | 41.06 | 120 |
| Greece | 7.33 | 13.25 | 31.26 | 94 |
| $x$[a] | 10.30 | 18.46 | 44.04 | 125 |
| | (10.30) | (11.81) | (14.91) | |
| $s$[b] | 4.32 | 5.16 | 9.48 | 26.27 |
| $s/x$[c] (per cent) | 41.9 | 28.0 | 21.5 | 21.0 |
| Max/min | 3.61 | 2.14 | 1.97 | 1.86 |

*Notes:*    a. $x$ is the average for the nine countries. The figures in parentheses are the values in 1970 EUAs. See Appendix for price indices.

         b. $s$ is the standard deviation.

         c. $s/x$ is the coefficient of variation.

*Sources:* Statistical Office of the European Communities (1983); and van der Meijs (1983, p. 50).

Table 5.9 *Registration taxes levied on trucks with laden weight of 38 (32) tonnes in EC countries*

| | 1972 | 1976 | 1980 | 1984 |
|---|---|---|---|---|
| | In German Marks | | | |
| Belgium | 3,850 | 3,150 | 3,016 | 2,371 |
| | ( 2,985) | ( 2,700) | ( 2,585) | ( 2,032) |
| Germany | 9,365 | 9,365 | 9,365 | 9,365 |
| | ( 6,815) | ( 6,815) | ( 6,815) | ( 6,815) |
| Denmark | 6,650 | 9,432 | 8,777 | 7,500 |
| | ( 6,094) | ( 8,645) | ( 8,261) | ( 7,059) |
| France | 250 | 234 | 516 | 392 |
| | ( 250) | ( 234) | ( 516) | ( 392) |
| United Kingdom | 3,174 | 2,770 | 6,059 | 11,607 |
| | ( 3,174) | ( 2,770) | ( 6,059) | ( 9,041) |
| Italy | 1,548 | 835 | 597 | 840 |
| | ( 1,548) | ( 835) | ( 597) | ( 840) |
| Luxembourg | 1,800 | 1,622 | 1,553 | 1,221 |
| | ( 1,542) | ( 1,395) | ( 1,335) | ( 1,050) |
| Netherlands | 6,735 | 3,355 | 3,760 | 3,638 |
| | ( 5,719) | ( 2,910) | ( 3,246) | ( 3,141) |
| $x$[a] | 4,171.5 | 3,845.4 | 4,205.4 | 4,616.8 |
| (1972 DM) | 4,171.5 | 3,068.4 | 2,360.8 | 2,661.0 |
| $x$[a] | ( 3,515.9) | ( 3,288.0) | ( 3,676.8) | ( 3,796.2) |
| (1972 DM) | ( 3,515.9) | ( 2,624.1) | ( 2,501.4) | ( 2,188.1) |
| $s$[b] | 3,132.1 | 3,597.7 | 3,509.9 | 4,299.0 |
| | ( 2,426.6) | ( 2,947.7) | ( 2,997.0) | ( 3,352.6) |
| $s/x$[c] (per cent) | 75.1 | 93.6 | 83.5 | 93.1 |
| | ( 69.0) | ( 89.7) | ( 81.5) | ( 88.3) |
| Max/min | 37.46 | 40.31 | 18.15 | 29.61 |
| | ( 27.26) | ( 36.94) | ( 16.01) | ( 23.06) |

*Notes:*   a. x is the average for the eight countries.

           b. s is the standard deviation.

           c. s/x is the coefficient of variation.

*Sources:* Bundesverband des Deutschen Guterfernverkehrs (1972 to 1984).

*Table 5.10 Registration taxes and fuel taxes for a 32-tonne truck in seven EC countries, 1972-84*

| | 1972 | 1974 | 1976 | 1978 | 1980 | 1982 | 1984 |
|---|---|---|---|---|---|---|---|
| | | | | In German Marks | | | |
| Belgium | 9,185 | 8,427 | 10,180 | 10,456 | 9,385 | 10,936 | 12,312 |
| Germany | 21,615 | 23,615 | 23,615 | 23,615 | 23,275 | 24,475 | 24,475 |
| France | 12,090 | 9,886 | 12,874 | 12,582 | 13,316 | 12,900 | 11,452 |
| United Kingdom | 20,294 | 14,375 | 13,690 | 12,282 | 23,259 | 22,726 | 30,865 |
| Italy | 11,748 | 8,343 | 6,355 | 5,511 | 2,597 | 2,560 | 7,240 |
| Luxembourg | 4,862 | 4,459 | 4,435 | 4,172 | 4,935 | 3,292 | 6,530 |
| Netherlands | 7,479 | 8,515 | 10,310 | 9,641 | 10,046 | 9,976 | 10,293 |
| $x^a$ | 12,468 | 11,089 | 11,637 | 11,180 | 12,402 | 12,410 | 14,738 |
| | (12,468) | ( 9,787) | (9,287) | ( 8,362) | ( 8,048) | ( 7,572) | ( 8,495) |
| $s^b$ | 6,313 | 6,250 | 6,230 | 6,350 | 8,200 | 8,568 | 9,264 |
| $s/x^c$ (%) | 50.7 | 56.4 | 53.5 | 56.8 | 66.1 | 69.0 | 62.9 |
| Max/min | 4.45 | 5.30 | 5.32 | 5.66 | 8.96 | 9.56 | 4.73 |

*Notes:*  a. x is the average registration and fuel tax for the EC countries listed. The figures in parentheses are the values in 1972 German marks. See Appendix for price indices.

b. s is the standard deviation for the sample.

c. s/x is the coefficient of variation.

Fuel taxes are calculated based on the assumption made by the International Road Federation that 80,000 kilometers are travelled per annum and that 50 litres of fuel are consumed every 100 kilometers.

*Sources:* Bundesverband des Deutschen Guterfernverkehrs (1972 through 1984).

## IV. HARMONIZATION OF TAXES ON CARS

Harmonization of the taxation of car ownership and use would mean that the taxation of this commodity should not inhibit its flow across borders more than is true for other products in the Common Market. Subsequent sections show that this has not been achieved. Taxes levied on owners and users of cars can be, and have been, designed to favor the purchase of domestically produced cars. Likewise, existing national systems of taxation favor the production of cars with certain characteristics − size, weight, power, price, emissions, fuel consumption, and so forth. Even if the taxes are applied in the same fashion to cars produced in other Member States, differing systems result in a fragmentation of the EC market. This is true even when there is complete harmonization of tax bases.

The 1980 report on the convergence of tax systems (Commission, 1980b, p. 56) observed that 'it might likewise be argued that the existence of widely differing systems of *registration taxes* for passenger cars in the Community could form an obstacle to the full establishment of a common market for such cars.' The same report commented on the fact that the absolute variations in the *tax rates on petrol and diesel oil* in the Community were large relative to other excise taxes. The previous section discussed the convergence that has occurred in taxes on diesel fuel. Has a similar change occurred for gasoline? Finally, *purchase taxes* vary substantially from country to country, and can also discriminate against particular types of cars, again producing barriers to trade.

## A. Taxes on Fuel

Table 5.5 provided evidence on the substantial convergence of taxes on diesel fuel. Since 1973 there is some, but lesser, convergence in the taxes on gasoline (Table 5.5). The coefficient of variation dropped sharply from 50 percent in 1973 to 15 percent in 1980, but rose to 32 percent in 1984.[15] No such reversal in trend occurred for taxes on diesel fuel. Table 5.7, in which the retail prices of regular gasoline are given, also indicates that some convergence occurred during the 1970s, but since then the coefficient of variation has increased.[16] Any convergence, or divergence, in gasoline taxes or prices has been slight during the 1970s and early 1980s. In contrast to taxes on diesel fuel, the real value of gasoline taxes per unit increased significantly from 1973 to 1984.

Italy, where smaller cars have predominated (Table 5.11), has shown the least reluctance to raise gasoline taxes over the past decade. The strongest resistance has been in Germany, which has continued the successful production and export of larger and more powerful cars. Table 5.5 shows a gasoline tax increase in Italy of 538 percent compared with 33 percent for Germany over the same 1973 to 1984 period. Taxes in Germany were, however, much higher to begin with. Spearman's rank correlation coefficient for the six countries in Table 5.11 shows a clear relationship between the median engine capacity for new cars and the level of taxes on gasoline.

15. From other sources it was possible to examine petrol taxes for Belgium, Denmark, Germany, France, Italy, Luxembourg, the Netherlands, Ireland, and the United Kingdom for 1980 and 1985. Taxes in EUAs per 100 litres for the nine countries, respectively, in each of the two years were 1980 − 21, 24, 18, 25, 29, 17, 19, 21, 13; 1985 − 25, 28, 23, 36, 49, 20, 28, 36, 29. The coefficient of variation for these taxes in the nine countries increased from 23 percent in 1980 to 29 percent in 1985; and the ratio of the highest tax to the lowest tax increased from 2.23 to 2.45 (Commission, 1980a, p. 30; 1985, p. 50).

16. Evidence for a larger number of countries (Germany, France, Italy, the Netherlands, Belgium, Luxembourg, the United Kingdom, Ireland, Greece) is somewhat different, showing an increase in the coefficient of variation from 1970 to 1972 and then a fall to 1982. In 1970 the retail price of 100 litres of premium petrol ranged from 16.62 EUA in Luxembourg to 23.57 EUA in Italy. The mean was 18.69 EUA, with a standard deviation of 2.28 EUA, a coefficient of variation of 12.2 percent, and the maximum price 1.42 times the minimum. In 1982 the coefficient of variation was 13.3 percent and the maximum price was 1.51 times the minimum for the same nine countries (Statistical Office of the European Communities, 1983, p. 50; van der Meijs, 1983, p. 50).

## B. Purchase Taxes

Car purchase taxes for nine EC countries are found in Table 5.12. Luxembourg and Germany have no special tax on the purchase of cars. In France, Belgium, and Italy a special VAT rate is applied to cars. The French tax all cars at a 33.3 percent rate compared with a normal VAT rate of 18.6 percent. In Italy, the standard rate is 18 percent, but for cars with engine capacity over 2,000cc the rate increases to 38 percent. And in Belgium, where the standard VAT rate is 19 percent, the rate on cars below 3,000cc is 25 percent with an additional 8 percent levied on larger cars. The United Kingdom, Ireland, the Netherlands and Denmark all levy special additional taxes on the purchase of cars, with the taxes being particularly high in Denmark.

Purchase taxes vary with engine capacity in Italy, Belgium and Ireland, and with price in the Netherlands and Denmark. The tax system in Italy favors the purchase of cars in which Italy has specialized, those with small engines. Taxes in most countries discourage the purchase of all cars relative to other goods, with discrimination being particularly severe, and more so for high-priced cars, in Denmark. In the cases of Germany, France, and the United Kingdom, the purchase taxes do not discriminate more severely against cars which are more expensive, heavier, or more powerful.

*Table 5.11 Engine capacity, fuel consumption, and gasoline prices*

A. *Engine Capacity and Fuel Consumption*

| Country | Share of Cars with Engine Capacity of | | | Annual Fuel Consumption |
|---|---|---|---|---|
| | <1,000cc | 1,000 - 1,999cc | >2,000cc | |
| | % (1977) | | | Tonnes per 10,000 km (1980) |
| Germany | 9 | 82 | 9 | .716 |
| Italy (1976) | 57 | 41 | 1 | .588 |
| United Kingdom (1978) | 14 | 77 | 8 | .817 |
| Ireland | 19 | 77[a] | 5[b] | .692 |
| Belgium | 13 | 71 | 16 | .886 |
| France | 32 | 58 | 10 | .694 |

B. *Engine Capacity and Gasoline Prices, 1980*

| Country | Median Engine Size for New Cars | Tax per Litre of Gasoline |
|---|---|---|
| | | In EUAs |
| Italy | 0.98 (1976) | .360 |
| France | 1.21 (1977) | .338 |
| Denmark | 1.27 | .331 |
| Ireland | 1.31 | .253 |
| United Kingdom | 1.47 | .183 |
| Germany | 1.55 | .230 |

*Notes:* a. 1,000 – 1,875 cc.
b. > 1,875 cc.
*Sources:* Commission (1980a, pp. 23 and 30); and Tanner (1983, pp. 62 and 65).

162

*Table 5.12 Car purchase taxes in the EC, 1985*

| Country | Value-Added Tax | | Additional Car Tax[a] | Comments[a] |
|---|---|---|---|---|
| | Standard | On Cars | | |
| | % | % | % | |
| Luxembourg | 12 | 12 | none | |
| Germany | 14 | 14 | none | |
| United Kingdom | 15 | 15 | 10* | *on 5/6ths of recommended retail price |
| Italy | 18 | 18* | none | *cars up to 2000cc |
| | | 38** | | **cars exceeding 2000cc |
| Belgium | 19 | 25 | 8* | *Additional tax levied on cars with engine capacity >3000cc, computed on value excluding tax |
| France | 18.6 | 33.3 | none | |
| Ireland | 23 | 23 | 50* | *on value after importation or manufacture |
| | | | 60** | **on value after importation or manufacture for cars over 16 horsepower |
| Netherlands | 19 | 19 | 16* | *on price including both taxes up to Dfl. 10,000 |
| | | 19 | 19** | **on price between Dfl. 10,000 and Dfl. 22,000 |
| | | 19 | 21.5*** | ***on price exceeding Dfl. 22,000 |
| Denmark | 22 | 22 | 105%* | *on purchase price, including VAT, on first DKr. 18,400 |
| | | 22 | 180%** | **on share of purchase price, including VAT, over DKr. 18,400 |

*Note:*   a. Whereas the VAT rates are for 1985, the additional car tax rates and the comments relating to these pertain to 1982. Some change in these special rates may have occurred since then.

*Sources:* Car tax information is taken from *Bulletin for International Fiscal Documentation* (1982, p. 384). Standard VAT rates for 1985 are taken from Commission (1985, p. 49).


## C. Registration Taxes

The basis for registration taxes, applied in all Member States, varies. The tax in Germany and Luxembourg is based on cylinder capacity, in Belgium, France, Greece, Ireland and Italy on horsepower, in Denmark and the Netherlands on unladen weight, and in the United Kingdom a fixed rate is applied. Higher taxes are generally applied to more powerful and heavier cars, with the United Kingdom being the exception, and with little variation in Ireland.

Table 5.13 presents a compilation of annual registration taxes (in EUAs) applied for eight EC countries for a variety of cars in 1980. The table shows a substantial increase in taxes in most countries as vehicle size increases, and substantial variation from country to country. In general, these taxes are a quarter to half as important as purchase taxes and vary less between countries and between types of cars than do purchase taxes. Failure to harmonize these taxes to a greater extent may cost little. At the same time, given the broad tendency to increase the annual tax with vehicle size, this would seem to be an area where there is already substantial agreement and greater uniformity could be achieved at little cost.

163

## D. Overview

Table 5.14 based on data published by the International Road Federation, indicates that there has been little convergence during the 1970s and early 1980s in the overall level of taxes collected on cars. In the case of cars with engine capacities of 1,000 cc and 1,500 cc there appeared to be increased diversity in the taxes collected by the five EC countries, with some convergence from 1976 to 1982, and with greater coefficients of variation in 1982 than in 1970. For cars with 4,500 cc, although diversity did not increase in the early 1970s, there was an increase between 1970 and 1982. The fall in the real value of the combined annual tax seems to have been of the order of 10 to 20 percent, with the greater fall for the larger cars. This indicates limited convergence in taxes being levied on cars of different size. Overall, the evidence does not indicate much, if any, harmonization of tax bases, and the level of taxes did not converge.

Table 5.15 provides an indication of which of the taxes − fuel, purchase, or registration − contribute to the diversity. The greatest diversity is found in the purchase taxes; the least is in the fuel taxes, with the annual registration taxes in between. Generally, fuel taxes are many times as important as the registration taxes, and purchase taxes also raise several times as much revenue as registration taxes. Whereas the tax base for fuel has been harmonized, this is not true for purchase taxes or registration taxes. Slight increases in the harmonization of fuel tax rates may contribute much more to the general harmonization of motor vehicle taxes than would major changes in annual registration taxes. Harmonization of bases for purchase taxes and registration taxes could be achieved at relatively little cost, but would require compromise by Member States. Although harmonization of tax bases is a step in the right direction, the application of widely differing rates can still result in severe discrimination against cars with certain characteristics.

*Table 5.13 Annual registration taxes on cars in eight EC countries, 1980*

| Type of Car Engine Capacity | Unladen Weight | Bel. | FRG | Den. | Fr. | UK | It. | Ire. | Neth. | $x^a$ | $s^b$ | $s/x^c$ |
|---|---|---|---|---|---|---|---|---|---|---|---|---|
| cc | kg | | | | | EUAs | | | | | | % |
| 602 | 600 | 18 | 35 | 113 | 21 | 77 | 7 | 15 | 86 | 46.5 | 39.8 | 85.5 |
| 1,296 | 885 | 42 | 75 | 188 | 34 | 77 | 27 | 15 | 144 | 75.2 | 61.2 | 81.3 |
| 2,778 | 1,455 | 179 | 161 | 327 | 145 | 77 | 137 | 206 | 293 | 190.6 | 83.0 | 43.5 |

*Notes:* a. x is the mean for the eight countries.
b. s is the standard deviation.
c. s/x is the coefficient of variation.
*Source:* Commission (1980a, p. 67).

*Table 5.14 Taxes collected on three types of private cars traveling 15,000 kilometers per annum for selected EC countries, 1970, 1976 and 1982*

| | Type | 1970 | 1976 | 1982 |
|---|---|---|---|---|
| | | | In SDRs | |
| Belgium | I | 223 | 274 | 428 |
| | II | 303 | 353 | 551 |
| | III | 583 | 1,041 | 1,567 |
| France | I | 204 | 263 | 458 |
| | II | 284 | 520 | 664 |
| | III | 635 | 988 | 1,712 |
| West Germany | I | 144 | 283 | 303 (1981) |
| | II | 189 | 367 | 393 (1981) |
| | III | 405 | 768 | 810 (1981) |
| United Kingdom | I | 203 | 273 | 497 |
| | II | 238 | 320 | 593 |
| | III | 381 | 619 | 967 |
| Netherlands | I | 197 | 487 | 548 |
| | II | 250 | 623 | 750 |
| | III | 670 | 1,185 | 1,417 |
| $x^a$ | I | 194.2 | 316.0 | 446.8 |
| | II | 252.8 | 436.6 | 590.2 |
| | III | 534.8 | 920.2 | 1,294.6 |
| $s^b$ | I | 29.7 | 95.9 | 92.1 |
| | II | 44.1 | 129.5 | 133.6 |
| | III | 133.4 | 225.4 | 389.1 |
| $s/x^c$ (per cent) | I | 15.3 | 30.3 | 20.6 |
| | II | 17.4 | 29.7 | 22.6 |
| | III | 24.9 | 24.5 | 30.1 |
| Max/min | I | 1.55 | 1.85 | 1.80 |
| | II | 1.60 | 1.95 | 1.90 |
| | III | 1.76 | 1.91 | 2.11 |

*Notes:*  a. x is the average tax for the five countries.

b. s is the standard deviation.

c. s/x is the coefficient of variation.

Type I:   1,000 cc consuming 1,200 litres of petrol.

Type II:  1,500 cc consuming 1,500 litres of petrol.

Type III: 4,500 cc consuming 2,700 litres of petrol.

*Sources:* International Road Federation (1970 through 1983).

*Table 5.15. Annual taxes on car use in eight EC countries, 1980*

| Engine Capacity | Type of Tax | Bel. | FRG | Den. | Fr. | UK | It. | Ire. | Neth. | $x^a$ | $s^b$ | S/X$^c$ |
|---|---|---|---|---|---|---|---|---|---|---|---|---|
| | | | | | | In EUAs | | | | | | % |
| 602cc | 1/10 purchase tax | 62 | 39 | 343 | 96 | 70 | 51 | 138 | 118 | 114.6 | 98.3 | 85.8 |
| | annual reg. tax | 18 | 35 | 113 | 21 | 77 | 7 | 15 | 86 | 46.5 | 39.8 | 85.5 |
| | fuel tax | 261 | 211 | 303 | 309 | 167 | 329 | 231 | 247 | 257.3 | 54.8 | 21.3 |
| | sum | 341 | 285 | 759 | 426 | 314 | 387 | 384 | 451 | 418.4 | 148.3 | 35.4 |
| 1,296cc | 1/10 purchase tax | 107 | 57 | 1,106 | 157 | 154 | 84 | 259 | 209 | 266.6 | 345.5 | 129.6 |
| | annual reg. tax | 42 | 75 | 188 | 34 | 77 | 27 | 15 | 144 | 75.2 | 61.2 | 81.3 |
| | fuel tax | 427 | 346 | 497 | 507 | 275 | 539 | 379 | 405 | 421.9 | 89.5 | 21.2 |
| | sum | 576 | 478 | 1,791 | 698 | 506 | 650 | 653 | 758 | 763.8 | 425.6 | 55.7 |
| 2,778cc | 1/10 purchase tax | 270 | 134 | 3,495 | 406 | 375 | 429 | 841 | 669 | 827.4 | 1,100.2 | 133.0 |
| | annual reg. tax | 179 | 161 | 327 | 145 | 77 | 137 | 206 | 293 | 190.6 | 83.0 | 43.5 |
| | fuel tax | 696 | 563 | 810 | 827 | 447 | 879 | 618 | 660 | 687.5 | 146.5 | 21.3 |
| | sum | 1,145 | 858 | 4,632 | 1,378 | 899 | 1,445 | 1,665 | 1,622 | 1,705.3 | 1,220.7 | 71.6 |

*Notes:* a. x is the mean for the eight countries.
b. s is the standard deviation.
c. s/x is the coefficient of variation.
*Source:* Commission (1980a, p. 67).

## V. CONCLUSIONS

An important question is the extent to which differing levels of fuel taxes and other taxes on motor vehicles reflect differing costs of motor vehicle use given the road conditions, congestion, air and noise pollution, wear and tear, and various other factors. This study does not address this issue. For this reason it is not possible to say whether any observed convergence of taxes is a movement towards an optimum tax. However, the author is not aware of evidence that existing differences in motor vehicle taxation are, in any way, related to differing costs. Unless there is such evidence, movement toward a common market in road freight and private passenger transportation services, and in the production and sale of cars, suggests that convergence of motor vehicle taxes is a good thing.

In the area of commercial road haulage there is evidence of convergence of taxes and increased competition. There has been a substantial convergence of taxes on diesel fuel, as well as a fall in their real value. Although registration fees have continued to vary greatly from Member State to Member State, the fall in real value has reduced their importance as a factor inhibiting competition. Whereas the coefficient of variation has not fallen for diesel fuel taxes and registration taxes when combined, their 1984 real value was 30 percent below the 1972 level, again reducing the impact that differences may have on competition. Harmonization has occurred in working conditions,

166

safety standards, maximum weights, and in a variety of other areas. The Dutch, who were rapidly expanding their share of the trucking market up to the early 1970s, have experienced sharply increased competition in the past ten years and have lost market share to other truckers.

Road haulage has rapidly increased its share of total freight haulage between and within Member States. Trade between Member States has grown particularly rapidly. When a larger share of total transport was internal, it was natural for countries to focus more on intermodal competition within the transport sector of a country. With more rapid growth in the movement of goods between States than within States, the focus on intramodal harmonization of competitive conditions between Member States takes on growing importance. It is likely that this has resulted in a greater awareness of differences in motor vehicle taxes, and is probably a factor contributing to the convergence in taxes on diesel fuel and to reductions in the real value of registration and fuel taxes on commercial vehicles. Policymakers may find it easier, and just as effective, to pursue harmonization through a fall in the real value of a tax rather than to develop and adhere to a Community policy. However, if motor vehicle taxes are to reflect marginal costs, this approach has severe limitations. There is already concern that taxes paid by heavier trucks are insufficient (OECD, 1983). Any further convergence of tax rates may be more difficult to achieve if greater emphasis is given to the goal of covering marginal costs of use.

Harmonization of taxes on cars and their use has made less progress. The real value of gasoline taxes has increased, and there has been little, if any, convergence in the level of taxes. Italian taxes on gasoline, relative to other countries, discourage the purchase of large cars. German taxes now do the reverse. Similarly, combined registration taxes and purchase taxes in Italy and France provide a much greater incentive to purchase a small car than is true in Germany or the United Kingdom. Lack of a speed limit creates a market for large and powerful cars and reduces the market for cars that may be under-powered for sustained high speed travel or for acceleration at high speeds. Emission controls, in the form of catalytic converters, increase disproportionately the price of smaller, cheaper models. Not surprisingly, national policies generally support and protect the domestic automobile industry. This inhibits rationalization of EC car production and blurs the focus on larger international markets.

The size and/or diversity of fuel taxes and purchase taxes dictate that the differences in these two forms of taxation are more important than differences in automobile registration taxes. Small differences in fuel taxes can far outweigh what appear to be relatively large differences in car registration fees. Purchase taxes vary greatly, and generally encourage purchase of smaller cars, although this is not the case in Germany, Luxembourg, France, or the United Kingdom. Speed limits and emissions controls are two further areas where harmonization is required if the Community is to be a true common market.

167

# CONSUMER PRICE INDICES USED AS DEFLATORS IN VARIOUS TABLES

|  | Germany | EUR 10 | United States |
|---|---|---|---|
| 1970 |  | 64 |  |
| 1971 |  | 68 |  |
| 1972 | 83 | 72 |  |
| 1973 | 88 | 78 | 83 |
| 1974 | 94 | 88 | 92 |
| 1975 | 100 | 100 | 100 |
| 1976 | 104 | 111 | 106 |
| 1977 | 108 | 123 | 113 |
| 1978 | 111 | 132 | 121 |
| 1979 | 116 | 146 | 135 |
| 1980 | 122 | 167 | 153 |
| 1981 | 129 | 189 | 169 |
| 1982 | 136 | 210 | 179 |
| 1983 | 140 | 225 | 185 |
| 1984 | 144 | 238 | 193 |

*Note:* Due to data available to the author, the EUR 10 index for 1970 and 1971 was projected back from the 1972 figure based on GDP deflator information from the IMF *International Financial Statistics Yearbook, 1984*, p. 125. The CPI indices for all three series were projected forward based on information from IMF data since the *Eurostat Review* data were available only to 1982.

*Sources:* European Economic Community, *Eurostat Review, 1973-82 and 1972-81* (Luxembourg: EEC, 1983 and 1984), p. 100, and IMF, *International Financial Statistics*, May 1985, (Washington DC: IMF, 1985), p. 67.

Bayliss, B.T. 'Licensing and Entry to the Market.' *Transport Planning and Technology*, 2, 1973.

Bayliss, B.T. 'Motor Vehicle Tax Harmonization in the EEC.' Comments presented at the International Seminar on Public Economics. Rotterdam, August, 1985.

Bowman, John H. and Mikesell, John L. 'Recent Changes in State Gasoline Taxation: An Analysis of Structure and Rates.' *National Tax Journal*, 36, 2, 1983.

Bundesverband des Deutschen Guterfernverkehrs. *Verkehrs-wirtschaftliche Zahlen*. Frankfurt/Main: issues 1972 through 1984.

Button, K.J., *Transport Economics*. London: Heinemann, 1982.

Button, K.J. *Road Haulage Licensing and EC Transport Policy*. Hampshire, England: Gower, 1984.

Canadian Tax Foundation. *Provincial and Municipal Finances, 1983*. Toronto: Canadian Tax Foundation, 1983.

Centraal Bureau voor de Statistiek. *Statistiek van het Binnenlands Goederenvervoer*. The Hague: Staatsuitgeverij, annual issues.

Centraal Bureau voor de Statistiek. *Maandstatistiek Verkeer en Vervoer*. The Hague: Staatsuitgeverij, Mei 1973, Juli 1982, Maart 1984.

Commission of the European Communities. *Memorandum of the Commission to the Council on the Pricing for the Use of Infrastructure*. COM(71), 268. 1971.

Commission of the European Communities. *Interim Report. Special Group on the Influence of Taxation on Car Fuel Consumption*. (150-2/VII/80-EN-Rev.2). Brussels: 1980a.

Commission of the European Communities. 'Report on the Scope for Convergence of Tax Systems in the Community.' *Bulletin of the European Communities*. Supplement 1, 1980b.

Commission of the European Communities. 'Completing the Internal Market.' White Paper from the Commission to the European Council. Brussels, 1985.

Council of the European Communities. *Proposal of a First Directive by the Council regarding the Development of National Systems of Taxation on Commercial Vehicles*. Presented by the Commission to the Council. July 17, 1968.

Court of Justice of the European Communities, Information Office. *Proceedings of the Court of Justice of the European Communities: Week of 20 to 24 May 1985*. No. 13/85. Luxembourg, 1985.

Economic and Social Committee of the European Communities. *Transport Policy for the 1980s: Opinion*. Brussels: March 1983.

International Road Federation. *World Road Statistics*. Washington DC and Geneva: Annual issues.

Meyer, J.R. and Gomez-Ibanez, J.A. *Autos, Transit, and Cities.* Cambridge: Harvard University Press, 1981.

Meyer, J.R. and Straszheim, M.R. *Pricing and Project Evaluation: Techniques in Transport Planning.* Vol. I. Washington DC: The Brookings Institution, 1971.

Moore, Thomas G. *Trucking Regulation: Lessons from Europe.* Washington DC: The American Enterprise Institute, 1976.

Munby, D.L. 'Fallacies in the Community's Transport Policy.' *Journal of Common Market Studies*, 1, 1, 1962.

Murfin, Andy. 'Price Discrimination and Tax Differences in the European Motor Industry.' Chapter 6, this volume, 1986.

Nationaal Instituut voor de Statistiek. *Vervoerstatistieken.* Brussels, various years.

Organisation for Economic Co-operation and Development. *Impacts of Heavy Freight Vehicles: A Report Prepared by an OECD Road Research Group.* Paris, 1983.

Organisation for Economic Co-operation and Development. *Revenue Statistics of OECD Member Countries 1965-1983.* Paris, 1984.

Smith, Roger S. 'Highway Pricing and Motor Vehicle Taxation in Developing Countries.' *Finanzarchiv*, 33, 1, 1975.

Statistical Office of the European Communities. *Statistical Yearbook: Transport, Communications, Tourism.* Luxembourg, 1983.

Statistisches Bundesamt Wiesbaden. *Wirtschaft und Statistik.* Stuttgart und Mainz, 1983.

Tanner, J.C. *International Comparisons of Cars and Car Usage.* TRRL Laboratory Report 1070. Crowthorne: Transport and Road Research Laboratory, 1983.

US Directorate of Intelligence. *International Energy Statistical Review.* Washington DC, November 27, 1984.

van der Meijs, A.G.M. *Auto en Overheid.* The Hague: Kluwer for Instituut voor Onderzoek van Overheidsuitgaven, 1983.

Walters, A.A. *The Economics of Road User Charges. Occasional Paper*, 5. Washington DC: World Bank Staff, 1968.

# 6

## Price discrimination and tax differences in the European motor industry

*Andy Murfin**

### I. Introduction

The harmonisation of taxation within the European motor industry is one element in the evolution of a common transport policy, and, more generally, in the elimination of all barriers between the EC's national markets. The slow pace at which such a harmonisation has proceeded is perhaps indicative both of the differences in national economic policies and goals, and of the differential performance and industrial structure of this sector among the Member States. While considerable progress has been made towards free intra-EC trade, this study of the motor industry reveals the extent to which certain markets may still be insulated from significant elements of competitive behaviour. It is demonstrated that the harmonisation of the remaining differences between the national tax systems will not be sufficient to promote a full integration of the Community's car markets. The present tax differences are shown to explain only a small proportion of the variation in price levels between countries. Price discrimination is shown to be both significant and persistent[1] within the European Community. Further sources of this discrimination are shown to lie in differences in price elasticities, in industrial concentration and a lack of price competition and in other features specific to the United Kingdom car market. The principal theme to emerge below is that the welfare gains to European consumers might be better promoted by a furthering of competition within the Community rather than by the harmonisation of taxation *per se*. This will necessarily involve an examination of producer collusion, unwarranted differences in product specification, the control of dealer networks,

* The author is grateful to Keith Cowling, John Cubbin and Denis Leech for the use of their data. John Cubbin made many helpful comments during the preparation of this paper and the author is especially grateful to Richard Bird, Sijbren Cnossen, John Kay, Roger Smith and Dirk Wolfson for their comments during and after the ISPE Conference. The usual disclaimer applies. Financial support from the ESRC is gratefully acknowledged.
1. See, for example, Ashworth *et al.* (1982), and BEUC (1981).

171

discriminatory licensing practices, refusal to supply across national boundaries, etc.

## II. Price Levels and Tax Rates in the EC's Car Markets

For the past five years or so, there has been considerable attention paid to the wide differences in the prices of cars in different European markets by the media, consumer bodies and academics. The Bureau Européen des Unions Consommateurs (BEUC) has been particularly active in pointing out these price differences (BEUC, 1981, 1982, 1983) and the European Commission has responded with the implementation of Article 85 of the Treaty regarding the sale and distribution of automobiles. This, it appears, will allow for free trade in vehicles, by-passing official dealers, once a base price differential between two countries exceeds 12 per cent, for at least six months.

In the context of this volume, the role of tax differences is shown to be important both in affecting base prices directly and in affecting the EC's policy against price discrimination. One defence of the car industry against the charge of discrimination has been that price differences, like tax differences, may reflect the different economic characteristics of national markets. However, while European integration has thus far facilitated a parallel integration of production decisions and the expansion of multinational enterprise, the car industry provides clear evidence of the continued segmentation of national markets. Arguably, the European consumer has yet to gain as much from integration as has the European producer. As such, a study of the car industry provides considerable insight into the problems and potential advantages of advancing towards a more coordinated and integrated Europe.

The objective of this section is merely to report the differences both in price levels and in tax rates between EC countries as they stand in the early 1980s. In Table 6.1, the average basic prices for a range of identical models between 1981-83 in the different countries are presented (on a Unit of Account basis). These are culled from the series of BEUC reports, although these do not take account of certain national pricing characteristics (Ashworth et al., 1982). They do indicate, however, that significant differentials both exist and persist for lengthy periods. The base price shows the firm's price before tax and it is clear that the UK faces the highest prices and Denmark the lowest. Belgium has relatively low prices too, while France and Germany are mid-ranking and broadly comparable. It should be noted that these rankings are consistent with those reported by Mertens and Ginsburgh (1984) using a much larger and more heterogeneous sample for 1983. At the extreme then, UK base prices are approximately 80 per cent higher than those in Denmark. There appears to have been a gradual equalisation of prices over 1981-83, perhaps as a result of the EC's interest.

172

*Table 6.1 Comparison of basic prices (net of tax) as percentage of the highest price*[a]

| Country | June 1981 | June 1982 | October 1983 |
|---|---|---|---|
| Denmark | 55 | 59 | n.a. |
| Luxembourg | 65 | 65 | n.a. |
| Belgium | 66 | 65 | 72 |
| Netherlands | 66 | 74 | n.a. |
| Germany | 70 | 77 | 83 |
| France | 72 | 74 | 81 |
| Ireland | 82 | 93 | n.a. |
| United Kingdom | 100 | 100 | 100 |
| Italy | n.a. | 81 | n.a. |

*Notes:* a. Relative price levels are defined using European Units of Account for conversion to a common currency.

n.a. = not available.

*Sources:* BEUC (1981, 1982, 1983).

That at least some of the differences in base prices can be explained by reference to the differences in product tax rates can be seen intuitively from Table 6.2, where pre- and post-tax prices are compared. Denmark is most notable in that its high tax rate means that its cars are priced lowest pre-tax but highest post-tax. Details of each country's tax schedules are presented in Table 6.3, again drawn from BEUC (1981). There are considerable differences in each country's tax structure despite the broad adherence to value-added taxation (VAT). Supplementary taxes are present in Denmark, Belgium, the Netherlands, Ireland and the UK while Italy has a split-rate VAT schedule.

*Table 6.2 Comparison of car prices, 1981*

| Country | Net of Tax | Tax-Inclusive |
|---|---|---|
| | UK = 100 | |
| Denmark | 55 | 133 |
| Luxembourg | 65 | 57 |
| Belgium | 66 | 66 |
| Netherlands | 66 | 77 |
| Germany | 70 | 63 |
| France | 72 | 78 |
| Ireland | 82 | 86 |

*Source:* BEUC (1981).

This has laid the ground for the next stage which is an investigation of the extent to which tax differences are important in determining price differences. Another factor to be borne in mind during the following discussion is the relative size of Europe's car markets. Table 6.Al in the Appendix presents the basic registration data for 1982-83. France and Germany are the largest markets

173

*Table 6.3 Taxes imposed on the purchase of a new car*

| Country | Value-Added Tax (VAT) | Other | Typical[a] Level of Tax as Percent of Base Price |
|---|---|---|---|
| | % | | |
| Denmark | 22 | Supplementary tax on price including VAT of 105 percent on first 15,000 Dkr and 180 percent beyond. | 190 |
| Belgium | 25 | A luxury tax on vehicles >3,000cc. | 25 |
| Netherlands | 19 | Special tax on base price of between 16 - 21 1/2 percent. | 46 |
| Luxembourg | 12 | | 12 |
| Germany | 14 | | 14 |
| France | 33 1/3 | | 33 1/3 |
| Italy | 18 if <2,000cc 35 if >2,000cc | | 18 |
| Ireland | 10 | An excise duty of 35 percent on the base price. | 45 |
| United Kingdom | 15 | A Special Car Tax of 10 percent of 5/6 of base price. VAT is levied on base price plus Special Car Tax. | 25 |

*Note:* a. For a Ford Escort 1.3L.
*Sources:* Value-added tax rates: Commission (1985); other taxes: BEUC (1981). See also Smith (this volume).

at 2-2.5 million units per annum, followed by Italy and the UK at 1.5-1.8 million. Denmark and Ireland are small markets by comparison. The countries' markets are therefore quite varied; one influence of the size inequality may mean that pressure towards price equalisation might lead to price increases in the smaller markets rather than reductions in the larger ones. At the extreme, this might mean that 'European producers' would withdraw from markets such as Denmark or Belgium and leave them in the hands of Japanese competitors.

### III. Tax Rates and Car Prices: Regression Analysis

It is hypothesised that at least part of the variation in net-of-tax car prices among the EC countries can be explained by the corresponding variation in national product tax rates. However, Mertens and Ginsburgh (1984, p. 8) emphasise that 'tax differentials alone *will not* induce producers to discriminate . . . Producers will discriminate only if price elasticities are different'.

This can be seen from the standard microeconomic textbook analysis of a monopolist's pricing strategy in the face of an *ad valorem* excise tax (Musgrave,

1959). With a linear demand curve, the price elasticity of demand increases in the direction of the price axis. The more elastic is demand, the smaller the proportion of tax borne by the consumer. This applies to movements along a simple linear demand curve and is also recognised in the literature with respect to travel costs and freight absorption (Neven and Phlips, 1984).

For estimation purposes, this inverse relationship between net-of-tax prices and the tax rate can be incorporated within a model of oligopolistic pricing of the form proposed by Cowling and Waterson (1976). Under a simple monopoly, let us define:

P(q) the demand function (price)
C(q) the supply function (cost)
r      the rate of *ad valorem* tax

Total revenue is P(q).q while total net revenue to the monopolist is:

$$N = P(q).(l-r).q$$

Under profit maximisation, the firm sets net marginal revenue equal to marginal cost (MC):

$$P(q).(l-r) + q.(l-r).P'(q) = C(q) + q.C'(q)$$

Then market price may be written as

$$P = \left[\frac{1}{1-r}\right] \left[\frac{1}{1+1/\eta}\right] MC$$

where $\eta$ is the price elasticity of demand. So, the extent to which price is raised by a higher tax rate depends on price elasticity; the more inelastic is demand the greater the proportion of the tax passed on to the consumer.

This formula can be readily adapted to admit oligopolistic behaviour. The Cowling and Waterson model effectively incorporates the Herfindahl index of industrial concentration as an indicator of the probability of oligopolistic collusion, where

$$H = \sum_{1}^{N} S_i^2$$

and $S_i$ is the market share of the $i$th firm in the industry. This index takes the value of unity under monopoly; for values less than unity, a higher value indicates a tighter-knit oligopoly within which as greater coordination and more efficient policing are facilitated collusion is more probable (Stigler, 1964; Hannah and Kay, 1977). This enables us to write the base price $P_B$ in the following way:

175

$$P_B = (1-r) \cdot \left[ \frac{1}{1+H/\eta} \right]$$

For empirical purposes, it is possible to measure base prices, tax rates and the appropriate Herfindahl indexes. However, no full set of price elasticities is yet available and nor are marginal cost data. For the purpose in hand, the relationship is estimated in ratio form. The ratios are defined using Denmark as the denominator and by assuming marginal cost to be constant across countries. The price elasticity of demand is an omitted variable.[2] The estimated equations take the form

$$\frac{P_{ik}}{P_{iD}} = \alpha_0 + \alpha_1 \frac{H_k}{H_D} + \alpha_2 \left[ \frac{(1-r_k)}{(1-R_k)} \bigg/ \frac{(1-r_D)}{(1-R_D)} \right] + \alpha_3 \, UK + U_t$$

where $P_{ik}$ is the price of car i in country k
$P_{iD}$ is the price of car i in Denmark
H is the Herfindahl index of concentration
r is the average tax rate on passenger cars
R is the average tax rate on all goods
UK is a dummy variable taking the value unity for the UK sample.
Tax rates are adjusted to impose homogeneity[3] and a dummy variable is indicated for the UK in view of its position as the highest-priced market. Note that the explanatory variables are defined nationally while the dependent variable covers a range of models in each country. It is not possible to include a full set of national dummies and so test the pooling of the sample because of perfect multicollinearity. Amongst the explanatory variables there is an inter-correlation between the UK dummy and the tax rate term (see Table 6.4).

Furthermore, the correlation matrices show that the relative price ratio (RP) is most strongly positively correlated with the UK dummy variable; the positive association between the price level ratio and the industrial concentration variable (RH) is weak. This variable (RH) is also only weakly correlated with the UK dummy (negatively in 1981); this demonstrates that the UK price premium is not to be explained by reference to simple measures of competition (see Section V).

The sample is derived from the 1981 and 1982 BEUC reports, which provide

2. Experiments were undertaken using advertising intensity but this proved to be insignificant and/or incorrectly signed. See Table 6.A2 for advertising intensities and Section V on price elasticities.
3. Average tax rates on all goods are defined using the ratio of indirect taxes to private final consumption. Source: OECD National Accounts.

*Table 6.4 Correlation Matrix*

| | 1981 | | | | 1982 | | | |
|---|---|---|---|---|---|---|---|---|
| | RP | RH | RT | UK | RP | RH | RT | UK |
| RP | 1.0000 | | | | 1.0000 | | | |
| RH | 0.1130 | 1.0000 | | | 0.2266 | 1.0000 | | |
| RT | 0.4517 | 0.2176 | 1.0000 | | 0.4289 | 0.2379 | 1.0000 | |
| UK | 0.7848 | - 0.0688 | 0.4731 | 1.0000 | 0.7508 | 0.1332 | 0.4731 | 1.0000 |

*Notes:* RP is relative base price.
RH is the relative Herfindahl index.
RT is the relative product tax rate.
UK is a dummy variable, equal to unity for the UK, zero otherwise.

15 models (identical across countries) in the former year and 17 in the latter;[4] some of the sample characteristics have been summarised above. The sample models cover many of the best-selling cars within Europe (see AID Ltd, 1984). The countries in the sample are Denmark, Belgium, the Netherlands, Germany, France, and the UK. The Herfindahl indexes have been calculated from market share data for each year (see Table 6.5). It is noteworthy that the Low Countries and Denmark have *very* low concentration levels and that France and Italy have the highest levels.

*Table 6.5 Herfindahl indexes, 1981-82*

| Country | 1981 | 1982 |
|---|---|---|
| Denmark | 0.0821 | 0.0882 |
| Belgium | 0.0851 | 0.0619 |
| Netherlands | 0.0917 | 0.0813 |
| Germany | 0.1667 | 0.1252 |
| France | 0.3126 | 0.2567 |
| United Kingdom | 0.1499 | 0.1541 |
| Italy | n.a. | 0.2302 |

*Sources:* AID Ltd (1984); *L'Automobile dans le Monde* (various years).

Table 6.6 shows the basic regressions for 1981 and 1982. The coefficients on the explanatory variables emerge with their expected signs, suggesting that the relative base price level increases both as the relative level of industrial concentration rises, and as the average rate of tax falls relative to that in Denmark. There is also an additional effect working to raise UK prices quite substantially. Comparison of equations (1), (2) and (3) for each year suggests an

4. Ten of which are common to both years. See BEUC (1981, 1983).

*Table 6.6 Base prices in the EC relative to those in Denmark (RP), 1981-1982, pooled regressions*

| Equation | Constant | RH | RT | UK | $\bar{R}^2$ | SE | SSR | M |
|---|---|---|---|---|---|---|---|---|
| **1981** | | | | | | | | |
| (1) | 1.0367 (0.2075) | 0.0438 (0.0209) | 0.0745 (0.1156) | 0.5464 (0.0580) | .631 | .174 | 2.139 | 1.374 |
| (2) | 0.1858 (0.2781) | 0.0044 (0.0306) | 0.6202 (0.1490) | | .182 | .258 | 4.809 | 1.374 |
| (3) | | 0.0342 (0.0241) | 0.6379 (0.0296) | 0.4201 (0.0603) | .508 | .200 | 2.891 | 1.374 |
| (4) | | 0.0043 (0.0305) | 0.7169 (0.0351) | | .188 | .258 | 4.838 | 1.374 |
| **1982** | | | | | | | | |
| (1) | 1.0245 (0.1933) | 0.0392 (0.0248) | 0.0876 (0.1059) | 0.4594 (0.0533) | .568 | .173 | 2.421 | 1.344 |
| (2) | 0.3117 (0.2407) | 0.0444 (0.0342) | 0.5067 (0.1296) | | .181 | .238 | 4.648 | 1.344 |
| (3) | | 0.0377 (0.0287) | 0.6354 (0.0264) | 0.3389 (0.0555) | .426 | .199 | 3.260 | 1.344 |
| (4) | | 0.0433 (0.0343) | 0.6697 (0.0309) | | .174 | .239 | 4.743 | 1.344 |

*Notes:* Standard errors in parentheses. SE is standard error of the regression. SSR is sum of squared residuals. M is the mean of the dependent variable. RH, RT and UK are as defined in Table 6.4.

inter-relationship between the constant term, the tax rate and the UK dummy variables. The three explanatory variables are only significant when the constant term is suppressed; its suppression, in particular, raises the coefficient on the tax variable. For 1982, equation (3) implies an elasticity of relative price with respect to relative tax rate for the UK of 0.07, against 0.41 from equation (1) (see Table 6.A3 for full sample means).

Using these parameters, the abolition of the 10 percent Special Car Tax in the UK,[5] *ceteris paribus*, would imply a fall in relative UK base price of between 0.6 percent and 5.2 percent. Thus, firms might not pass on the tax reduction in full to the consumer. It should be noted that if the UK dummy, rather than the constant term, is suppressed, as in equation (2), the tax elasticity is close to our higher estimate. One inference is either that firms price highly in the UK but take no account of the tax rate (equation (1)) or that they do set price in accordance with tax rate (and elasticity) (equation (2)) and so tax reductions in the UK could increase profit margins. From the residual sum of squares, it is the

5. So that RT for the UK rises from 1.411 to 1.595 (i.e. by 13 percent).

exclusion of the UK dummy which most reduces explanatory power, although the exclusion of either the UK dummy or of the constant term would be rejected on statistical grounds. The elasticity of the markup with respect to the Herfindahl index appears to be in the order of 0.05 so that a 10 percent rise in the level of concentration will raise the price level relative to costs, by 5 percent.[6] One implication of these results is that if two, or more, of the principal European car producers were to merge, price levels could be expected to rise with the implied increase in industrial concentration, market by market. Merger is, within this framework, a means to perfect collusion.

It appears then that product tax rate differences in the EC can explain only a limited amount of the price differentials for identical cars between Member States. As the BEUC (1981) suggested, the effect of tax rate differences is mainly to be found in Denmark where a very high tax rate has forced firms to reduce base prices significantly. For the remaining countries, it appears that minor differences between tax rates can explain only a small proportion of inter-country price differences. However, the results do suggest that tax rates are inversely related to base prices; therefore, any reduction in tax rates would not be fully passed on to the purchaser as firms would absorb some of the decrease by an offsetting rise in base price. It would appear, however, that an equalisation of tax rates would indeed lead to a slight movement towards base price equalisation in the European car market. Despite this, there is still considerable evidence that prices would remain unequal for other reasons and it is these that we now turn to discuss.

## IV. Explanations of the Price Differentials

Price discrimination occurs at the most basic level when an identical commodity is sold at different prices to different consumers. With even the smallest amount of non-homogeneity some price dispersion is to be anticipated. Phlips (1983, p. 7) therefore argues that 'what is typical, for discrimination, is that prices reflect the opportunities for larger profits from selling to several submarkets simultaneously, at different prices, while maximising overall profits'. That is, it is the pursuit of profit that will generate price discrimination, although this will require that separate markets can be identified and that the product cannot be resold. Within the European car industry, large price differences can be observed for near-identical products. One obstacle to re-sale is the right-hand-drive requirement of UK cars and in addition there is a myriad of other type approval restrictions.[7] Thus, even if tax rates and tariffs were to be equalised,

---

6. See Murfin (1982, 1983).
7. See Mertens and Ginsburgh (1984) for a full account.

there remain quantitative restrictions on trade which would assist firms wishing to segment EC markets.

Philips' (1983) work also sets a framework in which price discrimination might be judged. The emphasis within his work is that 'price discrimination is not good or bad per se' (*op. cit.*, p. 17). This sees monopoly power as a real world constraint upon welfare maximisation and as such second best 'optima' may require some form of discrimination. Neven and Phlips (1984) pursue this aspect of pricing within a common market where discrimination can arise from differences in the price elasticity of demand.[8] They suggest that total welfare can be higher with non-uniform pricing than with a uniform price structure. However, a basic premise of this paper is that it is the proximity of price to marginal cost that is of most concern to the consumer.

Mertens and Ginsburgh (1984) investigate the nature of price discrimination in the European car markets. They show that product differentiation in terms of technical characteristics is quite extensive but that this can be removed using hedonic regressions. Beyond this, they find that price discrimination is still large relative to this differentiation. Essentially, they show that there are significant national market effects in determining the prices of individual models across markets. In addition, their evidence suggests that while domestically produced cars may on average command a price premium, this premium is in the range of approximately 4 percent. It is thus difficult to attribute price variations to national preferences for domestic cars. Indeed, as Ashworth *et al.* (1982) demonstrated, the prices of *all* cars are higher in the UK than on the continent. Mertens and Ginsburgh do not allow for cooperation between producers but they do suggest that national price levels may reflect in part differences in the degree of industrial concentration, or of competition. This was shown to have a small positive impact on price in Section III.

The Mertens and Ginsburgh study finds no significant inverse relationship between the level of Japanese import penetration and the price level. However, Ashworth *et al.* (1982) argue that Japanese cars are relatively cheaply priced in the UK but that a company purchaser preference for domestically produced cars maintains the high UK price level. Japanese cars are competitively priced in the UK but perhaps only to the extent that different producers are able to command different premia for 'broad loyalty'. Further examination of the role of differences in non-tariff barriers to extra-EC producers in various Member States might still provide a partial explanation of price differences.

The possible effects of collusive behaviour by car firms are considered by Cowling and Sugden (1984). They focus on the impact of exchange rate movements on pricing behaviour in an oligopolistic industry. Following a

---

8. Or from transport cost differences under linear demand curves i.e. the freight absorption problem.

Sweezy (1939) type analysis, price cutting behaviour is considered to be taboo,[9] and so any cut in supply costs may not be passed on as price cuts. Rivalry among oligopolists effectively induces an awareness of the interdependence amongst participants that actions may be responded to. A reduction in price would lead to an expectation of reduced profits. Exchange rate fluctuations since the early 1970s will be important in view of the trans-national production and marketing bases of the European car firms (see United Nations, 1983), which will lead to cost fluctuations for their traded goods. Thus, an appreciating currency reduces the price of imports but this may only raise the price-cost margin if cost reductions are not passed on. As a result, the UK price premium is viewed as 'the incomplete adjustment within this oligopolistic market to the appreciation of sterling and the rise in production costs within the UK relative to the rise elsewhere in the EEC' (Cowling and Sugden, 1984).

Thus far we have seen that price differences may be the result of tax differences, differences in the price elasticity of demand, product differentiation or oligopolistic responses to cost changes. Other factors which may be important include the nature of the dealer structure, where official dealerships may act to maintain price levels through supply restriction (especially between countries). An open dealership system might preclude any cooperation between producers and distributors. Another influence may be the variation in inflation rates, a variation which may take time to be reflected in exchange rates, given the dubiousness of purchasing power parity as an explanation of exchange rate adjustment, particularly in the short run. This may help to segment markets according to the degree to which car prices must move in line with the overall price level. Other factors which will be important are price policies and vehicle road testing procedures, both often adduced as explanations of the low Belgium price level. Discounting from list prices is another factor, one which has emerged in the UK as a result of its high price level. However, the size of the discount is small in relation to the UK price premium (see Ashworth *et al.*, 1982). Country-specific effects can be important, and so we now turn to examine the UK experience, since this market exhibits the highest price levels.

## V. THE UK PRICE PREMIUM

### A. The Emergence of the Premium

It is possible to trace many of the above influences on price-setting behaviour for the UK car industry over the past 25 years. In this time, the market has

9. Under a kinked demand curve analysis price change may be 'sticky'; alternatively, price-cutting behaviour may be 'taboo' in that price wars are known not to be in the best interest of the firms in the industry or are considered destabilising. See Cowling (1982) for a full discussion.

## Table 6.7 Price levels and tax rates in the U.K. car market, 1957-83

| Year | Quality-Adjusted Price, Tax-Inclusive | Quality-Adjusted Price, Tax-Exclusive | Average Tax as a Percent of Tax-Inclusive Price[a] | Index of Price/ Cost Margin[b] |
|------|------|------|------|------|
| 1957 | 14.2 | 11.8 | 33 | 71.5 |
| 1958 | 15.2 | 12.6 | 33 | 82.2 |
| 1959 | 14.8 | 12.6 | 30 | 86.4 |
| 1960 | 13.9 | 12.0 | 29 | 82.8 |
| 1961 | 15.3 | 14.0 | 30 | 78.6 |
| 1962 | 13.9 | 14.4 | 26 | 78.0 |
| 1963 | 14.8 | 15.2 | 17 | 84.9 |
| 1964 | 14.9 | 15.4 | 17 | 87.1 |
| 1965 | 15.6 | 15.9 | 17 | 86.1 |
| 1966 | 15.9 | 16.1 | 18 | 77.4 |
| 1967 | 14.0 | 13.7 | 19 | 70.3 |
| 1968 | 16.6 | 15.8 | 21 | 80.6 |
| 1969 | 17.9 | 17.1 | 23 | 81.2 |
| 1970 | 17.7 | 17.3 | 23 | 76.9 |
| 1971 | 17.3 | 17.6 | 21 | 72.1 |
| 1972 | 20.7 | 21.6 | 18 | 85.4 |
| 1973 | 22.8 | 24.1 | 16 | 91.6 |
| 1974 | 23.9 | 25.6 | 15 | 73.9 |
| 1975 | 41.8 | 44.6 | 14 | 89.9 |
| 1976 | 49.4 | 52.7 | 14 | 91.6 |
| 1977 | 63.0 | 67.2 | 14 | 96.2 |
| 1978 | 74.3 | 79.3 | 14 | 99.0 |
| 1979 | 83.4 | 86.1 | 17 | 100.0 |
| 1980 | 100.0 | 100.0 | 20 | 100.0 |
| 1981 | 103.3 | 103.3 | 20 | 92.3 |
| 1982 | 104.3 | 104.4 | 20 | 90.1 |
| 1983 | 104.9 | 104.9 | 20 | 83.1 |

*Notes:* a. Derived from Purchase Tax Schedules which began the sample period in 1957 at 60 percent and ended in March 1973 at 25 percent, since when VAT and Special Car Tax have been in operation.
b. Defined as (tax-exclusive quality-adjusted price/cost index) where the cost index is defined using Average Census of Production weights, 0.74 for materials and fuel and 0.26 for unit labour cost.

*Sources:* HM Customs & Excise; *What Car?; Motor;* Society of Motor Manufacturers & Traders; Industry Sources; John Cubbin, Keith Cowling, Dennis Leech (personal correspondence); HMSO *Census of Production;* CSO, *Economic Trends; British Labour Statistics Historical Abstract;* Department of Employment, *Employment Gazette.*

evolved from a tight-knit oligopoly essentially domestic in character to a seemingly more open oligopoly characterised by a high level of import penetration. British Leyland has lost its dominant position while Ford has become both the largest seller and the largest importer. Amid these structural changes, there have been changes in conduct and in the nature of competition in the industry.

A quality-adjusted price series for the industry over the period 1957-83 is presented in Table 6.7. The tax rate applying to passenger cars fell over 1957-67 and this influenced the quality-adjusted price in a like manner. This index has been derived following Cowling and Cubbin (1972) and more details are

*Table 6.8 Comparison of UK and Belgian car prices, 1975-81*

| Year | UK Car Price Index[a] | UK Consumer Price Index | Belgian Car Price Index[a] | Belgian Consumer Price Index | £Belgian Price[b]/ UK Price |
|------|------------------------|--------------------------|-----------------------------|-------------------------------|------------------------------|
| 1975 | 100.0 | 100.0 | 100.0 | 100.0 | 1.134 |
| 1976 | 126.4 | 116.5 | 113.9 | 109.2 | 1.169 |
| 1977 | 146.9 | 135.0 | 116.5 | 116.9 | 1.152 |
| 1978 | 176.5 | 146.2 | 123.2 | 122.2 | 1.038 |
| 1979 | 205.7 | 165.8 | 128.9 | 127.6 | 0.912 |
| 1980 | 243.4 | 195.6 | 137.3 | 136.1 | 0.764 |
| 1981 | 262.6 | 220.4 | 144.0 | 147.0 | 0.685 |

*Notes:* a. Based on a sample of 21 models comparable both over time and between countries; see footnote 12. Prices are tax-inclusive.

b. Converted at annual average exchange rate.

*Sources: What Car?; Belgique Auto;* Comaubel, 1981; *International Financial Statistics;* Bank of England, *Quarterly Bulletin.*

reported in Cubbin and Murfin (1985).[10] That this price has risen in real terms can be seen from the last column where a price/cost index is presented.[11] Again set at 1980 = 100, this shows a rising price/cost margin over 1974-80, although the price level has fallen slightly in the early 1980s. Tax changes are not responsible for the rise in prices. The change in the margin over time can also be seen by reference to a report in 1957 that UK prices were higher than those on the continent (Economist Intelligence Unit, 1957).

However, this is not to say that UK prices have always been higher. Table 6.8 presents a comparison of UK and Belgian prices for a sample of 21 identical models over 1975-81.[12] This shows that UK prices only become higher after 1978. Before then the differential was reversed.[13, 14] Car prices also seem to be broadly influenced by national price levels. The rise in the UK price-cost index can be considered alongside other changes in the market (Table 6.9).

10. The index is derived from sales-weighted regressions of model price against the characteristics bhp, fuel economy and length for a sample of 1,260 models. They are calculated using the Fisher ideal index. The implicit quality index shows a rise of 30-40 percent over 1957-83. See also Murfin and Smith (1983).
11. This is a weighted cost index of inputs into UK car production where the weights are 0.74 for materials and fuel and 0.26 for unit labour costs in the industry. Source: HMSO, *Census of Production; British Labour Statistics Historical Abstract;* Department of Employment, *Employment Gazette;* CSO, *Economic Trends.*
12. Where the sample is Ford Escort 1.1, Capri 1.3, Allegro 1100 and 1300, Leyland Maxi 1750, Mini 850 and 1000, Toyota Carina, Honda Civic, Peugeot 104 and 304, Citroen 2CV, Fiat 126 and 128, Renault 4 and 12, Opel Ascona 1.6, Kadett 1.2, Lada 1200, VW Golf, and Audi 80.
13. This may lend some support to Cowling and Sugden's (1984) argument. Less price divergence would be expected if exchange rates adjusted to aggregate price differences.
14. This rise in UK prices is similar to that shown in Ashworth *et al.* (1982) but the relative levels differ through the use of different exchange rate conversion factors.

*Table 6.9 Industrial concentration in the UK car market, 1957-83*

| Year | Herfindahl | CR4 | N |
|------|-----------|------|-----|
| 1957 | .2550 | .848 | 8 |
| 1958 | .2402 | .848 | 8 |
| 1959 | .2162 | .861 | 8 |
| 1960 | .2289 | .842 | 8 |
| 1961 | .2167 | .813 | 8 |
| 1962 | .2194 | .869 | 8 |
| 1963 | .2601 | .875 | 8 |
| 1964 | .2211 | .859 | 8 |
| 1965 | .2176 | .847 | 8 |
| 1966 | .2374 | .978 | 6 |
| 1967 | .2143 | .979 | 6 |
| 1968 | .2749 | .983 | 5 |
| 1969 | .2653 | .896 | 12 |
| 1970 | .2441 | .864 | 19 |
| 1971 | .2314 | .831 | 20 |
| 1972 | .1999 | .794 | 22 |
| 1973 | .1812 | .751 | 22 |
| 1974 | .1863 | .747 | 23 |
| 1975 | .1675 | .693 | 27 |
| 1976 | .1628 | .681 | 27 |
| 1977 | .1508 | .675 | 26 |
| 1978 | .1419 | .649 | 28 |
| 1979 | .1499 | .673 | 27 |
| 1980 | .1561 | .671 | 27 |
| 1981 | .1581 | .663 | 28 |
| 1982 | .1541 | .664 | 29 |
| 1983 | .1536 | .679 | 31 |

*Notes:* Herfindahl index $= \Sigma s_i^2$; N = number of firms; CR4 = four-firm concentration ratio.
Market share data are not comprehensive prior to 1969 and for 1957-68 Volkswagen is the principal importer. The number of firms rises significantly in 1969 as Fiat, Honda, Renault, Skoda, Volvo, Alfa Romeo, and Toyota are separately identified.
Principal mergers: British Motor Holdings-Jaguar; Standard Triumph (Leyland)-Rover 1965; British Leyland established 1968; Peugeot-Citroen 1974; Peugeot-Citroen-Chrysler 1978.

The rise in import penetration since the late 1960s has contributed to a decline in industrial concentration as measured either by the Herfindahl index or by the four-firm concentration ratio (CR4). Table 6.9 charts the changes in these variables over 1957-83 in addition to the number of firms present in the market. Over the full period, the Herfindahl index has fallen by 40 percent and CR4 by 20 percent. The inverse of the Herfindahl index can be interpreted as a number-of-equal-size-firms-equivalent (Hannah and Kay, 1977) and this has risen from 3.9 to 6.5. Note, however, that concentration was relatively stable or rising over 1957-69, in part reflecting the creation of British Leyland (BL) from BMC, Jaguar, Standard Triumph and Leyland (see Dunnett, 1980).[15]

A straightforward interpretation of the structure-conduct-performance

15. Note that the number of firms in the market in the earlier period is understated.

paradigm would see the rise in real prices associated with a fall in concentration as paradoxical. To understand the history of price movement during the 1970s it is necessary to look beyond simple aggregate measures of competition. The period up to 1968 was characterised as one of relatively low inflation, when manufacturers attempted to keep prices constant in nominal terms. When inflation accelerated in the early 1970s, British producers were slow to respond. This is one reason for the financial crisis in BL in 1974 (see Cowling *et al.*, 1980, pp. 188-89). The increase in import penetration over the same period was an obvious cause of the downward pressure on real prices as for a time were the voluntary price controls for 1972 (Dunnett, 1980, p. 124). In 1973, anticipation of statutory controls led all British producers to raise their prices. Prices and incomes policies may have had another unexpected impact on the British price of cars. Incomes policies combined with the British tax system led to the wider spread of company cars as part of the remuneration for managers within the British private sector, as a tax-effective benefit (Kay and King, 1978). It is reckoned that company cars constitute 40-50 percent of new registrations (Armstrong and Odling-Smee, 1979). A recent survey also supports this figure.[16] As the net cost of cars to company buyers is less than for individual purchasers, this sector may exhibit a lower aggregate price elasticity.

Another source of upward pressure on prices (BL's financial crisis in 1974) led to pressure for greater protection. In 1975 the British Prime Minister obtained the first of a series of 'voluntary agreements' to limit imports to Britain. Since then, this has affected Japanese imports much more than those from European countries. The government rescue of BL, and its subsequent sponsorship of protective measures aimed at preserving employment in a major British industry, could have provided the umbrella under which a quasi-collusive pricing policy could emerge. Some commentators have argued that this is a relatively expensive form of subsidy, paid by British car buyers to British and foreign producers alike. Indeed, it appears that the net cost to UK consumers of paying UK rather than Belgian base prices was £1.9 million in 1983.[17]

Metcalf (1985), for example, argues that the UK car industry is subsidised on two counts. First, there is an explicit Exchequer subsidy to BL (£346 million in

16. See Table 6.A4 in the Appendix, source Henley Centre (1984). This shows the class and household structure of car ownership and the distribution of company cars. Given a car stock of 16 million, 1.68 million are company cars and a two-year replacement cycle for new cars implies that company sales are 40-50 percent of new registrations each year.
17. Using 1983 as an example and keeping sales volume constant at 1.79 million: the saving in total consumer expenditure from paying Belgian base prices would have been £2.2 billion, of which £450 million is indirect tax revenue for the government. This sees a reduction in consumer spending on cars from £8.2 billion to £6.0 billion. The net revenue reaching firms and distributors falls from £6.6 billion to £4.7 billion. With 'competitive import/penetration' at 30 percent this implies a loss of £0.5 billion on the balance of payments.

1980). Second, 'there is a hidden subsidy – paid for by British consumers because prices in the British market are kept above prices of the same . . . goods elsewhere in the world'. As much of this second subsidy goes directly to foreign car firms, the cost of this 'jobs subsidy' is less efficient than a larger direct subsidy to BL.

## B. Price Elasticities of Demand

Throughout this paper, the potential effects of differences in the price elasticity of demand for cars have been apparent. Accurate estimates are difficult to obtain; the OECD (1983) reports estimates of $-1$ to $-3$ for the UK and $-0.45$ for France. Here, we are able to provide estimates of own-price and expenditure elasticities of demand for five countries: Belgium, France, Germany, Italy and the UK. The almost ideal demand system approach of Deaton and Muellbauer (1980a, 1980b) has been applied to budget share data for expenditure on passenger cars in each country using annual data 1964-84. This system suggests the following estimating equation:

$$W_i = \alpha_0 + \Sigma \gamma_{ij} \log p_j + b_i \log (X/P)$$

where $W_i$ is the budget share of good i, X is total expenditure, P the price index for all goods, and $p_j$ the prices of commodities j. Table 6.10 presents the resulting elasticities of estimating this equation in first differences with a long-run solution derived by including levels of all variables lagged one period.[18] The same dynamic specification was used for each national market on grounds of comparability although this may omit many country-specific influences.

The own-price elasticities differ significantly across countries. The UK emerges with the most price-inelastic demand; while this estimated elasticity appears low it is consistent with the historical evidence for the UK (see Murfin (1985) for recent estimates using the neoclassical model and Harbour (1985) for an exhaustive survey and analysis of reported price and income elasticities for

18. See Table 6.A5 in the Appendix for results. Elasticities are given by

$$\beta_i = \frac{1}{W_i} b_i + 1$$

for expenditure and by

$$e_{ij} = \frac{1}{W_i} \left[ \gamma_{ij} - b_i W_j + b_i b_j \log \left[ \frac{X}{P} \right] \right] - d_{ij}$$

for uncompensated price elasticities; $d_{ij} = 1$ if i = j, zero otherwise.

186

*Table 6.10 Price and expenditure elasticities evaluated at 1982 observations*

| Country | Budget Share | Uncompensated Own-Price Elasticity [a,b] | Budget Elasticity |
|---|---|---|---|
| Belgium | 0.0346 | – 1.2720 | 1.0549 |
| France | 0.0337 | – 0.6775 | 1.3229 |
| Germany | 0.0329 | – 2.7771 | 1.3495 |
| Italy | 0.0402 | – 1.0468 | 1.2189 |
| United Kingdom | 0.0364 | – 0.4371 | 1.0318 |

*Notes:* a. Long-run values.
b. Imposing homogeneity in the long run.

the United Kingdom). France is also relatively price-inelastic while in Germany demand appears to be highly price-elastic. Budget elasticities are low but greater than unity, confirming the luxury status of passenger cars. If these elasticities are believed, they suggest that much of the UK premium can be explained by price inelasticity of demand, rather than by collusive practices.[19] Further work is necessary to confirm this pattern of results and, additionally, to identify the factors determining such an array of elasticities.


## VI. Summary

This paper has examined the structure of price levels and product taxes in the European car market. It appeared that product tax differences explain some of the differences in pre-tax prices, most notably in the case of Denmark. However, other factors are also of major importance since tax differences are not sufficient to explain price discrimination. Differences in the price elasticity of demand are necessary for firms to discriminate. This may be in terms of linear demand within a country or in terms of cross-country differences which, as the results presented here suggest, may be substantial. A third factor explaining discrimination is variation in the level of industrial concentration

19. Applying the Cowling and Waterson (1976) formula:

$$\frac{p-mc}{p} = \frac{\alpha}{\eta} + (1-\alpha)\,\frac{H}{\eta}$$

where $\alpha$ is the degree of collusion, $\eta$ is the price elasticity of demand and H the Herfindahl index of concentration, to these results, gives $\alpha$ values of 0.036 for Belgium, 0.0299 for the UK, 0.587 for Germany and – 0.163 for France. The UK and Belgium therefore seem close to Cournot conjectures. A further factor which has yet to be examined is the influence of the level of capacity utilisation in the industry. A low level of capacity utilisation might be sought as a means of raising the price/cost margin through entry-deterrence. Alternatively, margins might be shaded in response to lower levels of activity.

and implicitly in the degree of collusion between firms. Oligopolistic influences may also include the response to cost and exchange rate changes, as evinced by the changing structure of the differential over time.

The European car market does not appear to be competitive over price and the exercise of monopoly power is leading to welfare losses for certain European consumers. While tax equalisation may encourage an equalisation of prices, sufficient asymmetries exist elsewhere for price discrimination to continue. Further action may be necessary at a national or European level to curb the exploitation of this monopoly power.

# APPENDIX

## Table 6.A1 Market size and Japanese market share

| Country | Volume of Sales 1982 | Volume of Sales 1983 | Japanese Market Share 1982 |
|---|---|---|---|
| Belgium | 344,690 | 338,993 | 21.5 |
| Denmark | 85,405 | 116,238 | 25.3 |
| Ireland | 72,829 | 59,132 | – |
| France | 2,056,490 | 2,017,617 | 2.9 |
| Germany | 2,155,537 | 2,426,774 | 9.8 |
| Italy | 1,688,414 | 1,582,170 | 0.1 |
| Netherlands | 406,774 | 459,131 | 22.4 |
| United Kingdom | 1,555,027 | 1,791,699 | 11.0 |

*Source:* AID Ltd (1984).

## Table 6.A2 Advertising in the EC car markets, 1982

| Country | Intensity[a] | Expenditure |
|---|---|---|
| | % | $ 000 |
| Denmark | 1.46 | 6,000 |
| Belgium | 2.93 | 39,000 |
| Netherlands | 1.73 | 32,000 |
| Germany | 2.10 | 215,000 |
| France | 1.95 | 158,000 |
| Italy | 0.66 | 63,000 |
| United Kingdom | 1.81 | 154,000 |

*Note:* a. Advertising intensity is defined as $ expenditure over volume sales multiplied by average base price in US$.
*Sources:* Industry sources; Cubbin and Murfin (1985).

## Table 6.A3 Mean and standard deviation of regression variables

| Variable | 1981 Mean | 1981 SD | 1982 Mean | 1982 SD |
|---|---|---|---|---|
| RP | 1.3735 | 0.2858 | 1.3435 | 0.2631 |
| RH | 1.9635 | 1.0067 | 1.5401 | 0.7818 |
| RT | 1.9012 | 0.2066 | 1.9012 | 0.2064 |

*Note:* Variables defined as in Table 6.4.

*Table 6.A4 Car ownership in the UK, 1984*

| Social Class | Percent of Households with | | | | Whether Company Car Owned by Household with | | | |
|---|---|---|---|---|---|---|---|---|
| | 1 | 2 | 3+ | Total | 1 | 2 | 3+ | Total |
| All | 46 | 14 | 3 | 63 | 8 | 29 | 34 | 14 |
| AB | 59 | 30 | 5 | 93 | 15 | 42 | 67 | 26 |
| C1 | 50 | 19 | 5 | 75 | 12 | 35 | 27 | 19 |
| C2 | 50 | 14 | 4 | 68 | 6 | 20 | 25 | 10 |
| DE | 33 | 4 | 1 | 38 | 2 | 9 | 40 | 4 |

*Note:*   a. Standard social classifications: AB, professional and managerial; Cl, skilled non-manual; C2, skilled manual; DE, semi- and unskilled manual and those dependent entirely on state benefits.

*Source:* Henley Centre (1984).

Table 6.A5 Budget shares for personal transport equipment, an 'almost ideal demand system' equation, by country, 1964-82[a]

| Country | Constant | $\Delta \ln Pc_t$ | $\Delta \ln X_t$ | $W_{i-1}$ | $\ln(X/P)_{l-1}$ | $\ln(Pc/P)_{l-1}$ | $R^2$ | DW | SSR |
|---|---|---|---|---|---|---|---|---|---|
| Belgium | 0.0029 (0.0439) | -0.0105 (0.0267) | 0.0360 (0.0306) | -0.4299 (0.2769) | 0.0008 (0.0031) | -0.0040 (0.0182) | .274 | 1.663 | .00008 |
| France | 0.0165 (0.0289) | -0.0055 (0.0085) | 0.0516 (0.0379) | -1.1536 (0.2803) | 0.0006 (0.0027) | 0.0126 (0.0083) | .619 | 1.803 | .00006 |
| Germany | -0.0635 (0.0437) | -0.0782 (0.0546) | 0.1235 (0.0433) | -0.5528 (0.2061) | 0.0064 (0.0034) | -0.0332 (0.0504) | .514 | 1.318 | .00013 |
| Italy | -0.0443 (0.0218) | -0.0235 (0.0193) | 0.0016 (0.0239) | -0.7248 (0.2964) | 0.0064 (0.0034) | -0.0018 (0.0143) | .399 | 1.942 | .00007 |
| United Kingdom | 0.0008 (0.0237) | -0.0084 (0.0377) | 0.0601 (0.0701) | -0.7576 (0.3378) | 0.0009 (0.0026) | 0.0154 (0.0227) | .358 | 1.314 | .00032 |

Notes: a. A simple dynamic AIDS equation has been estimated by single equation OLS for each country. The specification corresponds to a first difference specification of the static equation of Deaton and Muellbauer (1980a, 1980b), using level observations lagged by one period to obtain long-run solutions of the form suggested by Davidson et al. (1978). Long-run homogeneity is imposed. The budget share is defined relative to all other consumer expenditure, a restriction which limits the range of substitution possibilities open to the consumer – a restriction which is often rejected (Dunne et al., 1984).

The consumer expenditure data (total (X) and for personal transport equipment) and the price of personal transport series (Pc) are taken from OECD National Accounts; the consumer price index for each country (P) from International Financial Statistics. Wi denotes the budget share of personal transport equipment in each country.

Standard errors in parentheses. DW is Durbin-Watson statistic. SSR is sum of squared residuals.

Armstrong, A. and Odling-Smee, J. 'The Demand for New Cars II: An Empirical Model for the UK.' *Bulletin of the Oxford University Institute of Statistics and Economics*, 41, 1979.

Ashworth, M.H., Kay, J.A. and Sharpe, T.A.E. *Differentials Between Car Prices in the UK and Belgium*. London: The Institute for Fiscal Studies, 1982.

AID Ltd. *1984 Data Yearbook*. 1984.

Bank of England. *Quarterly Bulletin*. Various issues.

*Belgique Auto*. Various issues.

BEUC. *Report on Car Prices and on the Private Import of Cars in the EEC Countries*. Brussels: Bureau Européen des Unions Consommateurs, 1981.

BEUC. *Report on Car Prices and on the Private Import of Cars in the EEC Countries*. Brussels: Bureau Européen des Unions Consommateurs, 1982.

BEUC. *New Car Prices in Belgium, France, Germany and the UK*. Brussels: Bureau Européen des Unions Consommateurs, 1983.

CSO. *Economic Trends*. London: Central Statistical Office, various issues.

Comaubel. *Périodique Mensuel*. Brussels: Comaubel Fegarbel, 1981.

Commission of the European Communities. 'Completing the Internal Market.' White Paper from the Commission to the European Council. Brussels, 1985.

Cowling, K. *Monopoly Capitalism*. London: Macmillan, 1982.

Cowling, K. and Cubbin, J. 'Hedonic Price Indexes for UK Cars.' *Economic Journal*, 82, 1972.

Cowling, K., Stoneman, P., Cubbin, J. *et al. Mergers and Economic Performance*. Cambridge University Press, 1980.

Cowling, K. and Sugden, R. 'Exchange Rate Adjustment and Oligopoly Pricing Behaviour.' Paper presented to European Association for Research in Industrial Economics Conference. Fontainebleau, 1984.

Cowling, K. and Waterson, M. 'Price-Cost Margins and Market Structure.' *Economica*, 43, 1976.

Cubbin, J. and Murfin, A. 'Hedonic Price Regressions and Quality Change: Identifying the Response to Fuel Price Change in the UK Car Market 1957-83.' *Working Paper* 716. London: Centre for Labour Economics, 1985.

Davidson, J. *et al.* 'Econometric Modelling of the Aggregate Time Series Relationship Between Consumers' Expenditure and Income in the UK.' *Economic Journal*, 88, 1978.

Deaton, Angus and Muellbauer, John. *Economics and Consumer Behaviour*. Cambridge University Press, 1980a.

Deaton, Angus and Muellbauer, John. 'An Almost Ideal Demand System.' *American Economic Review*, 70, 1980b.

Department of Employment, *Employment Gazette*. London: various issues.

Dunne, J.P., Pashardes, P. and Smith, R. 'Needs, Costs and Bureaucracy: The

Allocation of Public Consumption in the UK.' *Economic Journal*, 94, 1984.

Dunnett, P.J.S. *The Decline of the British Motor Industry*. London: Croom Helm, 1980.

Economist Intelligence Unit. *Britain and Europe*. London: EIU, 1957.

Hannah, L. and Kay, J. *Concentration in Modern Industry*. London: Macmillan, 1977.

Harbour, G. 'Overview of Academic Research on Vehicle Demand Modelling.' Paper presented to SMMT Conference. London, 1985.

Henley Centre. *Planning for Social Change*. London: Henley Centre, 1984.

HMSO. *Census of Production*. London, various years.

Kay, J.A. and King, M.A. *The British Tax System*. Oxford University Press, 1978.

Mertens, Y. and Ginsburgh, V. 'Product Differentiation and Price Discrimination in the European Community: The Case of Automobiles.' *Discussion Paper* 8424. CORE, 1984.

Metcalf, D. 'Supporting British Jobs Can Pad Foreign Profits.' *The Guardian*. April 10, 1985.

Murfin, A. 'Monopoly and Competition: A Theoretical Reconsideration and an Empirical Application to the UK Car Industry.' University of London Ph.D. thesis. 1982.

Murfin, A. 'Tax Rates and Price Levels in the European Motor Industry.' *Fiscal Studies*, 4, 1983.

Murfin, A. 'New Car Demand in the UK: A User Cost Approach.' *Working Paper* 771. London: Centre for Labour Economics, 1985.

Murfin, A. and Smith, R.P. 'Depreciation and the Quality Adjustment of Prices: An Investigation of the UK Car Market, 1980-81.' *British Review of Economic Issues*, 5, 1983.

Musgrave, R. *The Theory of Public Finance*. New York: McGraw Hill, 1959.

Neven, D. and Phlips, L. 'Discriminating Oligopolists and Common Markets.' *Discussion Paper* 8422. Louvain: CORE, 1984.

Organisation for Economic Co-operation and Development (OECD). *National Accounts*. Various years.

Organisation for Economic Co-operation and Development (OECD). *Long Term Outlook for the World Automobile Industry*. Paris, 1983.

Phlips, L. *The Economics of Price Discrimination*. Cambridge University Press, 1983.

Smith, Roger S. 'Motor Vehicle Tax Harmonization.' Chapter 5, this volume, 1986.

Society of Motor Manufacturers and Traders. *The Motor Industry of Great Britain*. London, various years.

Stigler, G. 'A Theory of Oligopoly.' *Journal of Political Economy*, 52, 1964.

Sweezy, P. 'Demand Under Conditions of Oligopoly.' *Journal of Political Economy*, 27, 1939.

United Nations. *Transnational Corporations in the International Automobile Industry*. New York: UN Transnational Corporation Centre, 1983.

*What Car?* London: Haymarket Publishing, various years.

# Part Four

# Taxes on Capital Income
# and Corporations

# 7

## Interjurisdictional coordination of taxes on capital income

### *Peggy B. Musgrave*

#### I. INTRODUCTION

Capital mobility across jurisdictional boundaries creates a variety of problems for the taxation of capital income the resolution of which calls for multilateral as well as unilateral coordination measures. This paper seeks to identify the nature of these problems, the circumstances in which they arise, and then a set of principles and rules to resolve them. A normative model of capital income taxation in an interjurisdictional setting is proposed, and difficulties in implementing the norms are discussed. Focus is placed on the broad principles and criteria, and little attention is given to the administrative detail involved in fully implementing them. The political setting is next taken into account, with common markets containing elements of both the 'independent nation state' and the 'federal system' models. Finally, developments in tax harmonization within the European Community (EC) are briefly discussed within the paper's theoretical framework.

The problems considered include those involving shares in income earned by foreign investors (interjurisdictional equity), tax neutrality with respect to the location of investment (locational neutrality) and taxpayer equity. The severity of these problems posed for the coordination of capital income taxation will vary with the degree of capital mobility. They take on particular significance within a federal system such as that of the United States where there are few barriers to capital movement – lack of trade restrictions, a single currency, unified fiscal and monetary policy, not to mention a common language and institutional background. On the other hand, problems will be made more acute the higher are the rates of tax on capital income and the greater are the differentials from one jurisdiction to another. In this respect, the EC poses greater difficulties for taxes on capital income than does a federal system where rates are lower. Yet again, as we shall see, the existence of an overarching central fiscal system can help to mitigate the problem in a federal system, whereas in a common market such centralized finance is a minor feature. Added to this aspect is the fact that there may be less competitiveness among governments of sub-units within a federal system for outside capital or for revenue from that capital than within a common market made up of nation states. Thus there are many dimensions to the question of whether problems arising in the coordination of capital income taxation become more or less urgent as economic and fiscal unification develops.

## II. PRINCIPLES OF TAXATION OF CAPITAL INCOME

To simplify matters, let us begin by considering two jurisdictions, A and B, where the residents of A invest in physical assets located in B and receive income $Y_{BA}$ (where the first subscript denotes the source of income and the second indicates the residence of the investor), and at the same time residents of B invest in assets in A and receive income $Y_{AB}$. The relevant question for our purposes is how A and B tax $Y_{BA}$ and $Y_{AB}$. The answer to this question will depend first of all on whether each jurisdiction bases its entitlement to tax on the *source principle*, the *residence principle*, or a combination of the two.

### A. Source Principle

Under the source principle, a jurisdiction bases its income taxes (on individuals and business entities) on the assertion of its right to tax all income arising within its borders. This territorial concept of entitlement is one which is almost universally recognized both at the national and sub-national levels of government. Under the source principle of taxation, country A would include $Y_{AA}$ and $Y_{AB}$ but not $Y_{BA}$ in its income tax base, while country B would include $Y_{BA}$ along with $Y_{BB}$ but would exclude $Y_{AB}$.

As to implementation, it seems clear that the source principle of taxation, reflecting a territorial concept of entitlement, calls for *in rem* rather than personal taxes, for it is concerned with *where* income arises rather than *to whom* it accrues. For this and other administrative reasons, it follows that not all income taxes are equally suited to the implementation of the source principle. In our example, A and B would find it difficult to tax $Y_{AB}$ and $Y_{BA}$ respectively on the source principle by use of the individual income tax. First, the tax is a personal rather than an *in rem* tax and usually imposed at progressive rates, with deductions and exemptions geared to the personal circumstances of resident taxpayers, all of which would violate the source principle. Secondly, the tax would have to be imposed on and collected from non-resident individuals, thus involving severe administrative difficulties. To some degree, this problem might be alleviated by use of withholding taxes by A and B and applied to $Y_{AB}$ and $Y_{BA}$. However, this will only provide a partial solution, inasmuch as withholding taxes are imposed at a flat rate independent of income and to the extent that they only apply to capital income at time of distribution by a company.

198

The answer to this predicament is the corporation income tax (Musgrave, 1983). The corporation tax is an *in rem* tax which may be applied at an appropriate flat rate and is collected closest to the source of income, namely from the corporation. Furthermore, it applies to capital income in its entirety, whether distributed or retained. While the corporation income tax includes the vast bulk of foreign-owned capital income at its source, it should be supplemented by a business income tax applied to unincorporated businesses at a comparable rate. It is interesting to observe that while an absolute corporation income tax may run afoul of a number of well-founded criticisms on other grounds, as an *in rem*, source-based tax it serves well the territorial-entitlement objective since it applies to the most mobile of factors, i.e. capital. (Perhaps this is why it has survived in the face of criticism by so many economists![1]) It is also to be noted that a fully source-based income tax system would require a combination of business income tax and payroll tax rather than an individual income tax, while a value-added tax of the income-origin type would serve as a substitute for both.

As discussed later on, the implementation of a source-based corporation tax within federal systems and common markets is not without its particular problems. These problems largely arise from the difficulty of assigning business income to its jurisdictional source when operations take on multi-jurisdictional forms.[2]

## B. Residence Principle

Alternatively, each jurisdiction might base its income taxes on the residence principle which is founded on each jurisdiction's entitlement to tax all income received by its residents.[3] According to this principle, country A may tax $Y_{BA}$

1. For a fine discussion of the efficiency and administrative shortcomings of the corporation tax in open economies such as federal systems, see McLure (1983). His criticisms are primarily based on a situation of rate differentials.
2. Another problem with the application of source entitlement, pointed out by Charles E. McLure, Jr in discussing this paper, is the case of natural resource taxation. Exercise of the source principle leaves those jurisdictions having large natural resource endowments with an 'unduly' large amount of revenue. (A case in point is the province of Alberta in Canada.) In this connection, I would make the following two points: (1) interjurisdictional equity requires that *all* income be allocated on a uniformly applied source-based formula, and this should include rents and royalties as well as wages and profits; and (2) the problem of the maldistribution of natural resource rents and royalties reflects an improper definition of 'ownership' of such resources in a federal system. The problem is therefore best addressed by fiscal measures which channel such income to the central authority for the national (or community) benefit, rather than by abandonment of the source principle at the sub-national level.
3. As pointed out by John Kay, one of the discussants of this paper, there is an important question of how 'residence' is to be defined for tax purposes. Conceptually, the jurisdiction of 'residence' should be defined as that jurisdiction to which the taxpayer owes his/her/its primary tax →

as well as $Y_{AA}$ (but not $Y_{AB}$) while country B would be entitled to tax $Y_{AB}$ and $Y_{BB}$ (but not $Y_{BA}$). It is to be noted that the residence principle, unlike the source principle, is compatible with a personal system of income taxation; indeed a comprehensive system of individual income taxation must be residence-based. Administratively, an income tax based on the residence principle is more difficult to implement when applied by sub-units within federal systems. This is due to the high degree of factor mobility, and lack of border controls and record-keeping.[4] This is evident with regard to lower-level income taxes in a federal system, although compliance may be improved and administration facilitated by coordination with the federal taxing authority. In these respects, the residence principle may be at once easier and more difficult to implement within a common market system than within a fully federal system.

While in principle the corporation income tax, seen as an *in rem* tax, does not easily fit into a residence-based form of personal taxation applied to individual residents, in practice it may be convenient to apply a residence-based corporation income tax as a means of reaching the foreign income of domestic-based corporations. Again, though this time for efficiency reasons, the corporation income tax is a useful instrument in a situation of capital mobility. However, the residence principle as applied to corporations is not appropriate for states within a federal system. If residence is defined as place of incorporation, it would concentrate the tax within those jurisdictions where businesses tend to incorporate or be headquartered rather than where their profit-making operations are located, thus leading to an arbitrary distribution of revenue. For this and other administrative reasons, lower-level jurisdictions within a federal system usually confine their corporate income taxes to the source principle or, as in the case of the Canadian provinces, have the central authority impose and collect the tax and return the revenue on an agreed formula to the provinces (Smith, 1976). As economic and institutional integration within the European Common Market proceeds, the same

→
allegiance. For the individual taxpayer, this might suggest the jurisdiction of citizenship or that of primary residence (domicile). For corporations, 'residence' might be the jurisdiction of incorporation or, alternatively, of principal place of management. For purposes of economic efficiency, the choice of definition should be one which leaves the taxpayer less ready to shift his/her/its location of economic activity for tax reasons. Thus, for the corporate income tax at the national level, the place of incorporation appears to be the better choice. This follows the US definition of corporate residence. In the United Kingdom, where place of management may be used as the test of residence, corporations apparently find it easy to shift their location of management under the UK tax laws. As discussed in the text, the difficulties of implementing residence-based taxation for the corporation increase as jurisdictions become more integrated economically and institutionally. In a federal system, corporations are very ready to shift either their place of incorporation or place of management among sub-units; thus neither definition of 'residence' is workable in such a system.
4. For a discussion of these problems, see McLure (1983, 1984).

considerations are likely to apply. However, this will require more uniform effective rates of tax than are applied at the present time.

## C. Source and Residence Principles

Thus there may be good reasons why a national jurisdiction may want to base its system of income taxes on both the source and residence entitlement concepts – indeed, this is very often the case. This poses a problem for those who invest outside their jurisdiction of residence. In our example, $Y_{AB}$ and $Y_{BA}$ would be subject to full double taxation as each is subject to taxation by both the country of residence and the country of source. This problem may be resolved by several forms of tax coordination each with its own advantages and disadvantages, as will be discussed later in this paper. For instance, each country may, while recognizing the paramountcy of source entitlement, mitigate the double taxation by means of a foreign tax credit or deduction for purposes of its own residence-based tax. In the extreme case, each country of residence might exempt or lower its rate of tax on foreign-source income $Y_{AB}$ and $Y_{BA}$, leaving it to be taxed entirely at source. In theory the reverse might hold with A and B as countries of source rebating their taxes on $Y_{AB}$ and $Y_{BA}$ respectively, with the residence countries (B and A respectively) claiming the entire revenue. In practice, the country of residence usually makes the concessions necessary to ameliorate double taxation, with deduction, credit or outright exemption provided. However, there are notable exceptions to this practice. In particular, in the EC, some source countries have extended their imputation credits to investors from abroad. Indeed, France transfers that corporation income tax revenue which is attributable to dividends received by German shareholders in French corporations directly to the German treasury (see Cnossen, 1983b).

## III. Criteria for Taxation of Capital Income

Having considered the alternative bases for entitlement to tax in circumstances of capital mobility, we now specify the various criteria by which tax policy might be evaluated and suggest what entitlement systems and methods of interjurisdictional tax coordination would meet these criteria.

The three major criteria which may be applied to the taxation of capital flows are interjurisdictional equity, locational neutrality and taxpayer equity. While there may be other policy objectives which enter into the design of tax policy from time to time, the more fundamental objectives which have widespread acceptance are these three.

## A. Interjurisdictional Equity

This is a concept which, while playing an important implicit role in unilateral tax policy as well as multilateral tax agreements, has been given scant attention in the tax literature. I use this term to suggest 'fair tax shares' or a fair division of the gains which are generated by factor flows between countries (Musgrave, 1972, 1974, 1984). Since it is universally the practice that the jurisdiction of source has prior claim to tax the income earned by foreign residents within its boundaries, this criterion can clearly only be applied to the jurisdiction of source, for the taxes imposed by the jurisdiction of residence will merely determine the division of gains (remaining *after* the source country's taxes) between the public and private sectors in the residence country. Interjurisdictional shares will therefore be determined by (1) how the jurisdiction of source defines its territorial tax base, and (2) the rate of tax which it imposes thereon. As in all matters of equity, and in the absence of an explicit international welfare function, the economist can only illuminate the choices and explore what appears to be accepted practice.

## Definition of territorial tax base

Since we are considering the application of alternative concepts of interjurisdictional equity in implementing source entitlement, we must begin by defining the territorial source of income for tax purposes. This is a knotty problem which becomes increasingly difficult and complex as jurisdictions become more closely integrated and capital more mobile across borders. It is a problem which the EC Member States do not appear to have fully addressed but which, as in the case of states within the United States, will doubtless engage their attention as economic integration progresses. As corporations extend their operations across jurisdictional borders, division of profits among those jurisdictions by the traditional 'separate accounting' method frequently introduces an arbitrary element. This is due to economies of scale and scope, to shared overheads within the various parts of the firm, as well as the absence of 'arm's-length' prices. Quite apart from these economic reasons which render separate accounting a less than objective procedure, there are extensive opportunities for profit-shifting by the firms by under- or over-invoicing and by overhead allocations which pose immense problems for tax enforcement authorities (McLure, 1984). The latter compliance problem worsens as effective tax-rate differentials widen between jurisdictions and the inducement to shift accounting profits strengthens. However, the former aspect (economic interdependencies within the multi-jurisdictional firm) would exist even were all tax rates to be the same. It is for these reasons that in the United States the tax base for the states' corporation income taxes is usually divided by resort to 'formula apportionment'. The EC countries must be approaching the time when the problem of tax-base division has to be addressed, and perhaps a similar mechanism will be needed, if source-based business income taxes are to be retained.[5]

There has been a great deal of discussion in the tax literature as to the merits of alternative formulas for the apportionment of taxable income among jurisdictions of source. As anyone at all familiar with the problem will agree, exploration of this issue would have to be dealt with in another paper. I therefore offer only a brief comment on this point (for a more extensive discussion, see Musgrave (1984)). The most common formula in use at the present time (the so-called Massachusetts formula) gives equal weight to the location of property, payroll and sales, but others are in use or have been advocated from time to time. One argument that is frequently made is that the formula should give the same results as would obtain under separate accounting. But this seems to me a spurious argument since the very reason that formula apportionment is applied is that separate accounting is inappropriate in carving up company profits along geographic lines. Separate accounting has little normative value as a device for the division of profits in these situations. Thus, when all is said and done, the very nature of the formula itself becomes a matter of interjurisdictional equity, since there is no infallible economic rationale for any particular formula. The 'Massachusetts formula' prevalent among the US states seems as reasonable as any, since it uses two factors of production (capital and labor) on the supply side and sales (if destination-based) on the demand side of the value-creating scissors. One can, however, argue about the definition and measurement of these elements in the formula. If payroll is to be used as a proxy for employment, then it would seem that a similar flow variable, such as depreciation, should be used for capital inputs rather than the stock measure of property value. Whatever formula is agreed upon, it is vitally important that the same formula be uniformly applied by all jurisdictions. This uniformity is needed not only for reasons of interjurisdictional equity but also because without it there will be gaps and overlaps in the taxable base with resulting inequities and inefficiencies in source-based taxation, a matter to which we turn presently (McLure, 1983).

## Rate of tax

The second component which must be agreed upon in setting up a standard of

---

5. However, as Sijbren Cnossen has pointed out to me, there may be special circumstances in the EC (such as absence of a central tax authority) which may call for different solutions from the formula apportionment method as used within the United States. The problem deserves further exploration.

interjurisdictional equity is the share of income claimed by the jurisdiction of source. The two more obvious standards of equity in this context are (1) uniform proportionate shares and (2) a benefit-based standard (Musgrave and Musgrave, 1972).

(1) Uniform proportionate shares. It is clear that all jurisdictions, be they nation states acting independently or within common markets, or lower-level political units within a federal system, assert and accept the entitlement to tax all income arising within their boundaries, that is, their right to tax as jurisdictions of source. There has been little recognition, however, of the need for agreement on what the rules and tax rates governing those tax shares should be. The most obvious standard would require reciprocal uniformity as a matter of interjurisdictional equity.[6] Such a reciprocity rule is indeed often invoked in international tax treaties with respect to withholding taxes imposed on dividends and interest income transmitted to foreign residents, but it has not been applied to the far more important corporation and individual income taxes themselves or the payroll tax as they apply to income earned by non-resident factors of production. This is doubtless due to the fact that the structure and rates of the major broad-based taxes are determined by other overriding considerations of revenue needs and taxpayer equity applicable to residence taxation. This conflict in objectives might be resolved by each jurisdiction assigning certain taxes for the purpose of implementing the source principle at rates consistent with mutually acceptable standards of interjurisdictional equity. As indicated earlier, the payroll tax and the corporation tax are well-suited to this purpose since they are *in rem* taxes on factor income best applied at uniform rates and imposed at the source of income. To be sure, both these taxes could be integrated with the residence income tax, so that for residents this would involve no net addition. This would then leave the individual income tax for purposes of implementation of the residence principle, and would permit rate and structural differentiation. It is to be emphasized that the reciprocally equal rates of business (corporate) income tax, established by interjurisdictional agreement, would solely reflect a standard of interjurisdictional equity and need bear no relation to rates which would otherwise be called for in each jurisdiction on grounds of taxpayer equity or revenue needs.[7] Indeed, were the corporation tax to be used for this purpose,

6. Yet another approach to interjurisdictional equity might call for a progressive rate schedule whereby the rate of tax applied by the jurisdiction of source would be inversely related to its own level of per capita income. Poor countries might be allowed to take a larger tax share of income accruing to foreigners than might rich countries. But since jurisdictions, even within federal systems, have difficulty in reaching agreement on equalizing rates of tax, this model may be too utopian to make more than passing mention of it.

7. This is contrary to the traditional practice in international tax treaties and the models on which they are founded which call for 'non-discrimination' in the tax treatment of domestic and foreign investors in the country of source, with 'reciprocity' of rates confined to withholding taxes. For a critique of this practice, see Musgrave (1975).

a fully integrated income tax system would be called for to meet objectives of the residence jurisdiction, a system which tax economists have long advocated on taxpayer equity and allocative efficiency grounds (McLure, 1979).

(2) Benefit-based standard. A more limited approach to interjurisdictional equity is one founded on the concept of a charge for benefits provided. In this case each jurisdiction of source would tax profits to correspond to the cost-saving benefits provided by government via subsidized services. Were this to be the case, however, there are better ways of imposing such benefit charges than through income taxes. In any case, prevalent practice appears to regard the benefit approach to be but a minor component of the source jurisdiction's entitlement to tax, and the problem of implementing that entitlement in equitable ways remains a major factor.

## B. Locational Neutrality

Another major criterion which may be applied to the taxation of capital income in a situation of capital mobility is that of neutrality with respect to factor flows. This suggests that the tax system should not influence the choice of jurisdiction in which to invest on the part of investors resident in any one jurisdiction. Since, for instance, an investor resident in country A will be taxed according to A's tax system on income arising from investments located in A, this criterion requires that the same rate apply to income from investments made in B and in all other countries. It follows from this requirement, then, that the jurisdiction of residence must be primarily responsible for achieving locational neutrality, or efficiency in interjurisdictional resource allocation. Unless all source-based taxation were applied at equal flat rates, locational neutrality cannot be met in the absence of global residence taxation.[8] Thus the application of the residence principle of entitlement by the imposition of a single income tax to the global income of resident investors is the only feasible way of meeting the locational neutrality criterion.

It may be useful at this point to interrupt my main argument by pointing to a confusion which easily arises between the proposition (1) that an investor resident in country A should not be affected by tax considerations when choosing whether to invest in A, B or C; and (2) that tax systems should leave

---

8. An interesting proposition was made in the general discussion of this paper, by Satya N. Poddar, that source-based taxation, even with unequal rates, would be locationally neutral if a single-factor apportionment formula based on sales were applied. While this may indeed be true, the primary purpose of the formula is to generate a 'fair' and acceptable division of the tax base. It is unlikely that apportionment of business profits according to location of sales alone would be considered reasonable by the jurisdictions concerned since this would hardly conform with the source concept. Indeed, in the US sales have been considered the most questionable element in the three-part formula.

corporations resident in A, B and C but operating together in A or B or C subject to the same tax treatment. Item (1) is a generally accepted efficiency rule, sometimes referred to as 'capital-export neutrality', and calls for a residence-based, global tax system with full foreign tax credit. Concept (2), sometimes referred to as 'capital-import neutrality', is based on the notion that producers operating in the same jurisdiction (and, by implication, selling in the same market) should be subject to the same tax treatment and calls for tax exemption for foreign-source income, i.e. for source-based taxation. However, concept (2) is not meaningful as a standard of efficiency in the allocation of capital owned by the residents of any one country. It is correct that a tax regime which conforms with 'capital-export neutrality' will cause national shares in world markets (defined to include sales from investments made at home or abroad) to be different from what they would be under a regime of 'capital-import neutrality'. The capital stocks of each country, whether invested at home or abroad, may depend on the tax systems of each and this will be reflected in commodity market shares, but this has nothing to do with locational neutrality.

There is a further reason why it might be argued that the jurisdiction of residence should be responsible for the achievement of locational neutrality, though a more controversial one. Most countries prefer to retain some sovereignty over the outflow of their productive resources by way of providing tax incentives or disincentives to those outflows. Indeed, countries may be more interested in maximizing national returns than worldwide welfare and thus resort to a tax treatment of their investments abroad which achieves that purpose rather than meeting the neutrality criterion. To this end they may prefer the deduction, rather than credit treatment for foreign taxes. Or, countries may fear that use of the locationally neutral foreign tax credit will leave their revenue hostage to the taxing policy of the source country. It cannot be said that integration of the world economy has yet reached the millenium when all trade and factor flows are free of tax impediments or incentives and for the time being it is reasonable to assume that control over the degree of neutrality which applies to such flows should rest with the country of residence of investors.

Locational (capital-export) neutrality is achieved when residents of each country are subjected to the same rate of tax on all their investment income from wheresoever it is derived (Musgrave, 1969). If there were no source-principle taxation (each jurisdiction taxes only income accruing to its residents, excluding non-residents), then such neutrality is achieved if each jurisdiction taxes its residents on their comprehensive income, treating all investment income equally. Where source and residence principle taxation coexist, however, there will be double taxation of investment income accruing to non-residents. In our model, it is the jurisdiction of residence which would make the necessary adjustments to alleviate such double taxation. Full neutrality (to

206

promote worldwide efficiency in capital allocation) can be obtained by provision of a foreign tax credit (with tax refunds if the foreign tax exceeds the home tax), or partial neutrality by crediting of part of the foreign tax or by deductibility of foreign taxes from taxable income. National efficiency, on the other hand, would call for deductibility.[9] Thus, the degree of neutrality achieved is in the hands of the jurisdiction of residence. We shall discuss the applicability of the locational neutrality criterion in different political settings in a later section of this paper.

### C. Taxpayer Equity

This is a criterion which is fundamental to a good tax system and needs no further explanation here other than to say that it is embodied in standards of both horizontal and vertical equity. This again is a criterion which is necessarily the responsibility of the jurisdiction of residence and inherent in the residence principle of entitlement. Taxpayer equity requires that income taxes apply to global income and only the country of residence/citizenship of the income recipient is in a position to tax this comprehensive measure of economic position. Furthermore, taxpayer equity requires the use of personal taxes and allowance for individual economic positions, unlike interjurisdictional equity which calls for impersonal, *in rem* type taxes. Again, such personal taxes can only be adequately imposed by the jurisdiction of residence of the taxpayer precisely because different jurisdictions may differ in what pattern of burden distribution they wish to apply. More fundamentally, different jurisdictions may be expected to have different notions regarding the requirements for taxpayer equity and wish to apply those standards to their own residents. This includes equity as it applies to residents who invest at home and those who invest abroad. Thus it is appropriate that the jurisdiction of residence be entirely responsible for implementing taxpayer equity. It is to be noted that, as has been argued above, source taxation should be based on interjurisdictional equity, which means in our model that each source jurisdiction takes the same share of income accruing to non-residents. This does not mean that this share should correspond to the burden placed on resident investors in that jurisdiction.

Having sketched out the broad principles and criteria to be considered in interjurisdictional tax relationships, we now combine them in suggesting an interjurisdictional tax order which might simultaneously serve those objectives. This general normative model is first sketched for a system in which each jurisdiction has a fully integrated income tax system in which corporate profits are imputed to the individual shareholder; it is then modified for the non-

9. For a development of this proposition, see Musgrave (1969).

integrated case in which the corporation tax is applied as an absolute tax on corporate-source income. No assessment is made of the relative merits on economic and equity grounds of integration since the focus here is on interjurisdictional coordination under different domestic tax regimes (see McLure (1983) for an extensive discussion of the former aspects). Furthermore, focus is on the two polar cases of full integration and the 'classical' system, without specific reference to partial integration as under the imputation system practised by a majority of the EC countries (see Cnossen, 1983b; and Bird, 1975). These general models are then followed by a discussion of how the conclusions are modified in a setting in which jurisdictions are in varying forms of political relationships, with independent nation states and federal systems at each extreme and common markets at a stage in between. It will be seen that in each the emphasis on objectives, the feasibility of attaining them, and the division of responsibility for meeting them will differ.


## IV. NORMATIVE MODELS

In meeting the three major criteria of locational neutrality, interjurisdictional equity and taxpayer equity, it was seen that jurisdictions need be assigned these responsibilities in their capacities as jurisdictions both of source and of residence. In a world in which business investments and firms' operations extend across boundaries, jurisdictions become both jurisdictions of source of income for non-residents and jurisdictions of residence for firms and individuals who invest outside. Thus, in a normative set of interjurisdictional tax arrangements, each jurisdiction must apply both the source and residence principles of taxation.

Let us consider our earlier illustrative case of jurisdictions A and B, again in a situation where there are capital flows in both directions, with A's and B's investors receiving capital income from both A and B. In order to achieve inter-nation equity, A and B must impose a source-based tax at a common rate. This is best achieved by the imposition of a corporation income tax imposed at a common, mutually-acceptable flat rate combined with a high degree of uniformity in base definition.[10] This resulting effective rate should represent what is considered to be a 'fair share' of the return to foreign-owned capital. (Similarly, a proportional payroll tax at uniform rates would serve the purpose of a source-based tax on income accruing to non-resident labor.) The rate imposed might be more or less than the traditional rates applied at the national level in most industrial nations, rates which have been chosen for revenue-raising purposes or by having the corporation tax act as a proxy for the

10. This case for equal effective rates, based on considerations of interjurisdictional equity, happily coincides with the requirements for locational neutrality in a system of source-based taxation.

individual income tax on undistributed corporate profits.[11] In this manner A and B would each exercise their entitlement to tax as jurisdiction of source, while observing reciprocity in the rates which they apply to income accruing to non-residents. It might be noted that this application of interjurisdictional equity, i.e. through an equal-rate, source-based corporation income tax, does not require the use of withholding taxes on dividends. Nor should investment income received by corporations from other jurisdictions be included in their taxable income. Since capital income is taxed at its source, it would be inappropriate to tax it again in the jurisdiction of source as it passes from one tier of corporations to another.

## A. Integrated Income Taxes

In a model with integrated income-tax systems, taxpayer equity would be secured through the individual income tax, with the domestic corporation tax serving as a withholding tax and credited against the former. Under the global residence principle this would call for the inclusion of capital income earned on outside investments in a comprehensive income base, including each individual's share in the undistributed profits of foreign corporations or foreign-incorporated subsidiaries of domestic corporations in which they have invested. This requirement in practice would present a difficult problem indeed in a situation of independent nation states without an international tax authority to facilitate enforcement.[12] While interjurisdictional equity required that rates of corporation income tax be equalized across jurisdictions, such is not the case for the individual income tax, rates and structure of which would reflect political preferences and differing interpretations of taxpayer equity by different jurisdictions.

There remains the problem, however, of resolving the treatment of foreign taxes paid on the income received by residents of one jurisdiction who invest in another. In our normative model, the question for taxpayer equity is how A should treat the corporate taxes paid to B on income accruing to A's investors in B, and vice versa. There is no single answer to this question in so far as it applies to taxpayer equity. A 'comprehensive' concept of equity (which looks at *total* domestic plus foreign taxes) would require the external tax to be credited against the individual income tax in the country of residence, corresponding to and extending the treatment given the domestic corporation tax in an integrated income tax system. On the other hand, a 'narrower' concept of equity (which

11. See Cnossen (1984), where the author indicates that EC countries which apply differentiated rates to foreign-owned corporations (e.g. Belgium) do so at higher rates.
12. For a full discussion of the problems of income-tax integration in an interjurisdictional setting, see McLure (1979, chap. 6), Sato and Bird (1975), Bird (1975) and Ault (1978).

disregards foreign taxes) might choose to ignore the foreign tax, applying the residence-based personal income tax to foreign income gross of foreign tax. Yet again, the foreign corporation tax might be permitted as a deduction and foreign income included in taxable income net of the foreign tax. While the choice among these three approaches will have implications for locational neutrality, with only the full credit measuring up to the neutrality test, arguments can be made for all three on equity grounds (Musgrave, 1969). It is reasonable to suggest that the treatment given to foreign taxes might reflect the degree of political integration between A and B, and that the closer this is the more the treatment of the foreign tax will correspond to that given to the domestic tax.

In order to secure locational neutrality, investors resident in each jurisdiction must face the same tax on their capital income whether they choose to invest at home or abroad. A global individual income tax imposed by the country of residence and allowing a full credit for the foreign corporation income tax is required for this purpose. This treatment of the foreign tax is consistent with the 'comprehensive' concept of taxpayer equity discussed above. Full neutrality, of course, would require refunds to the taxpayer should the foreign tax exceed the effective rate of individual income tax on the same income in the country of residence. However, refunds would be limited if the common rate of corporation income tax suggested for inter-nation equity purposes is relatively low.

It is also to be noted that in this normative model, there are no allocative inefficiencies arising from the corporate income tax based on the source principle since rates are equalized across jurisdictions in order to meet interjurisdictional equity. Furthermore, if any variation in the effective rate of corporation income tax from one jurisdiction to another were to exist, such variation would be blocked from influence on investors' locational choices by full integration with the residence-based, global individual income tax. Conflict between individual equity and locational neutrality would arise, however, if the former were implemented by only partial crediting, deductibility or even without allowance for the foreign tax. This is more of a problem for the independent nation case where the full crediting of foreign taxes is not unequivocally called for.

Numerical illustration of this 'full integration' case, shown as Model 1, is given in Table 7.1. Here both jurisdictions, A and B, impose a source-based corporation tax at 25 percent and in each the individual income tax (at 50 percent in A and 30 percent in B) is applied to grossed-up corporate income with credit for corporate tax.

*Table 7.1 Numerical illustration of tax coordination model 1 (normative, general, with integrated income taxes)*

|  | $Y_{AB}$[a] | $Y_{AA}$[a] | $Y_{BA}$[a] | $Y_{BB}$[a] |
|---|---|---|---|---|
| *Income* | 100 | 200 | 100 | 300 |
| *Taxes* | | | | |
| Jurisdiction A | | | | |
| Corporation income tax | 25.0 | 50.0 | 0.0 | 0.0 |
| Individual income tax | 0.0 | 50.0 | 25.0 | 0.0 |
| Total | 25.0 | 100.0 | 25.0 | 0.0 |
| Jurisdiction B | | | | |
| Corporation income tax | 0.0 | 0.0 | 25.0 | 75.0 |
| Individual income tax | 5.0 | 0.0 | 0.0 | 15.0 |
| Total | 5.0 | 0.0 | 25.0 | 90.0 |
| Combined | | | | |
| Combined total | 30.0 | 100.0 | 50.0 | 90.0 |
| Effective tax rate | 0.3 | 0.5 | 0.5 | 0.3 |

*Note:* a. First subscript denotes jurisdiction of source of income and second subscript indicates the jurisdiction of residence of the shareholder. Thus $Y_{AB}$ represents income earned in A but accruing to a shareholder resident in B. For explanations of tax systems and rates, see text.

As shown in the bottom row, an equal-rate, source-based corporation tax combined with a fully integrated income tax in each preserves locational neutrality, with all income accruing to A's residents ($Y_{AA}$ and $Y_{BA}$) bearing the same proportional burden of 50 percent and similarly for B's residents who pay an effective rate of 30 percent on both domestic- and foreign-source income ($Y_{BB}$ and $Y_{AB}$). It is also shown in this model that it is possible, at least conceptually, to have the best of all worlds and to meet our three criteria of locational neutrality, interjurisdictional equity and the 'comprehensive' form of taxpayer equity.

### B. Absolute Corporation Tax (Classical System)

If the residence-based income tax system does not provide for the integration of corporate and individual income taxes, the problem of interjurisdictional tax coordination is rendered somewhat more complex. In this imperfect system, the corporation tax acts as a proxy for the individual income tax on undistributed earnings, while imposing an additional tax on dividends. Now the corporation tax becomes an important ingredient of taxpayer equity and in this role may conflict with the requirements of securing interjurisdictional equity as a source-based tax. Thus, the rate of tax based on interjurisdictional equity

211

considerations may be either too high or too low to meet standards of individual equity in the residence country. Some provisions might be introduced to mitigate these difficulties. For instance, a compensatory surcharge or rebate (as the case may be) might be applied to domestic- and foreign-source corporate income accruing to resident taxpayers. Dividends paid to a domestic parent corporation from a foreign affiliate would not be subject to further tax at the corporate level. But all corporate-source income would be subject to surcharge (or rebate) at the shareholder level, with resulting net corporate-source income included in taxable income of the individual shareholder. However, it would be difficult to avoid the under- or over-taxation of undistributed profits accruing to resident shareholders, particularly so for undistributed foreign income.

There are inefficiencies introduced as corporate investments are disadvantaged relative to other forms of investment, but this applies in a general sense and not specifically to the choice between domestic and foreign investments. There will be a tax bias in favor of retention of earnings (for those investors whose marginal rate of personal income tax, combined with the required surcharge or rebate, exceeds the rate of corporate tax), but again this will apply with equal force to retention of earnings in investments made outside as well as inside the jurisdiction. The same considerations apply to taxpayer equity. While investors in corporate equity may be treated inequitably vis-à-vis other types of investors or non-investors, this will be so for those who choose to invest either inside or outside their jurisdiction of residence. The crucial required surcharge or rebate, exceeds the rate of corporate tax), but again this that effectively all corporate tax rates are equal and each country of residence applies the same tax rules to income arising within and without its borders. On the other hand, if uniformity of effective rates does not prevail, integration of corporate and individual income taxes is helpful to the coordination of income tax systems across jurisdictions just as it is to the achievement of taxpayer equity and investment efficiency in a purely domestic setting.

Numerical illustration is given to tax coordination in a classical system of absolute corporation income tax as Model 2 in Table 7.2. Here both jurisdictions impose source-based corporate taxes of 25 percent and the individual income tax is applied to corporate-source income net of the corporate tax. Again, rates of individual income tax are 50 percent in A and 30 percent in B.

Inspection of the bottom row reveals that locational neutrality is again preserved even in the absence of income-tax integration, provided that the source-based corporation taxes are imposed at equal rates.


*C. Second-Best Modifications*

We now consider more realistic situations in which these normative conditions

212

*Table 7.2 Numerical illustration of tax coordination model 2 (normative, general, with absolute corporation tax)*

|  | $Y_{AB}{}^a$ | $Y_{AA}{}^a$ | $Y_{BA}{}^a$ | $Y_{BB}{}^a$ |
|---|---|---|---|---|
| *Income* | 100 | 200 | 100 | 300 |
| *Taxes* | | | | |
| Jurisdiction A | | | | |
| Corporation income tax | 25.0 | 50.0 | 0.0 | 0.0 |
| Individual income tax | 0.0 | 75.0 | 37.5 | 0.0 |
| Total | 25.0 | 125.0 | 37.5 | 0.0 |
| Jurisdiction B | | | | |
| Corporation income tax | 0.0 | 0.0 | 25.0 | 75.0 |
| Individual income tax | 22.5 | 0.0 | 0.0 | 67.5 |
| Total | 22.5 | 0.0 | 25.0 | 142.5 |
| Combined | | | | |
| Combined total | 47.5 | 125.0 | 62.5 | 142.5 |
| Effective tax rate | 0.475 | 0.625 | 0.625 | 0.475 |

*Note:* a. See note to Table 7.1.

are not met. Suppose first that there is no agreement between countries A and B to equalize their corporation income tax rates at levels reflecting 'fair shares'. Now inter-nation equity will not be met. Locational neutrality will still hold, however, provided that each country has a fully integrated income tax system with a residence-based, global income tax applied to individual investors such that the foreign tax is credited. Even in the absence of the latter, a substantial degree of neutrality can be achieved if the corporation tax is now applied on the residence principle, with worldwide income of the corporation, its subsidiaries and affiliates included in taxable income and a full credit allowed for foreign taxes paid. This system would achieve a 'half-way house' of tax neutrality at the corporate level between the corporation's investments at home and abroad. Absence of income-tax integration would then not adversely affect this locational neutrality, for the combination of corporation and individual income tax would impose the same burden per dollar of domestic or foreign profits. Nevertheless, this global approach to the corporation income tax would require imputation of the profits of foreign-incorporated affiliates to the parent corporation, without deferral of tax on undistributed profits. This requirement does not correspond to prevailing current practice in the EC where such profits are usually excluded altogether or only included as repatriated dividends. This leaves corporate retained earnings exposed to the non-neutrality of tax-rate differentials. Thus, in the absence of full income-tax integration with all corporate profits imputed to the individual shareholder, corporate tax rate differentials are likely to violate not only interjurisdictional equity, but also locational neutrality and individual equity as well.

213

## V. Coordination of Taxes on Capital Income: Nation States, Federal Systems and Common Markets

Having examined the conditions which are necessary to achieve the three criteria and suggested normative models of tax systems which would meet those conditions, we now turn to the political and economic settings which tax systems reflect and which in turn determine the forms which tax coordination can take.

### A. Independent Nation States

An independent nation state must apply both source and residence entitlements if it is to exercise its taxing authority over its residents (citizens) and the income earned within its territory. While it cannot unilaterally secure interjurisdictional equity (for which multilateral agreement on equal rates and source rules is needed), it nevertheless can, via a global income tax applied on the residence principle, obtain locational neutrality with the addition of a full foreign tax credit, and can secure taxpayer equity with the addition of either a credit or deduction for foreign tax, depending on whether the broader or narrower view of equity is taken. Furthermore, it can control the degree of locational neutrality by the choice of those two methods of relief for foreign taxes.

At the present time most western industrial nations apply their income taxes on both the residence and source principles. However, the global approach to residence taxation of corporations is only very imperfectly applied, and since individual and corporate income taxes are not by any means fully integrated and international tax coordination not complete, the result is that considerable locational non-neutralities result. Furthermore, interjurisdictional equity among nation states is only imperfectly observed. National corporation income taxes are applied at differing rates which reflect revenue needs, their role as proxies for the individual income tax on corporate retained earnings or as instruments of macro policy, rather than 'fair' shares of capital income accruing to foreigners. Nor do international tax treaties help very much in this regard. Reciprocity in withholding tax rates which such treaties often provide for disregards the far greater departures from equity implicit in the pattern of corporation income tax rates. In any case, a wide-ranging equalization of rates is needed and this can only be achieved via multilateral rather than bilateral agreements. Source rules also display their deficiencies in a world of the multinational corporation where separate-accounting becomes a less acceptable and enforceable procedure for defining the national source of income, particularly in the absence of international cooperation in tax administration.

214

## B. States within Federal Systems

Now we move from the independent nation state to a federal system consisting of a number of constituent states overlaid by the central, federal government, exemplified by the United States. We now have to consider the principles and rules governing the taxation of capital income on the part of the separate constituent states and their relationship with one another and the central government.

In a federal system, with a single currency, total freedom of trade and factor movements, and a centralized fiscal-monetary policy, the exercise of the residence principle on the part of individual states becomes largely impractical, and particularly so for the taxation of corporate income. For one thing, states in which corporations tend to be heavily headquartered or registered would be able to claim most of the corporation tax base. For another, states are unlikely to have the necessary enforcement apparatus to secure reporting of income arising out-of-state. Furthermore, double taxation would arise for income on which both residence-based and source-based taxation applied, requiring the complexities of arrangements for the alleviation of such double taxation. It is also commonly acknowledged in the theory of fiscal federalism that the responsibility for redistribution policy, including that secured through the tax system, should lie with the central government. Thus, in the United States, most *in rem* forms of taxation reside with the states, while the major part of personal taxation (the individual income tax) is applied at the federal level. All this suggests that state income taxation should largely be founded on the source entitlement principle, and it is interesting for our purpose to note that in the United States the corporation income tax at the state level is very largely a source-based tax and one which has been growing as that at the federal level has declined; whereas at the federal level, both the source and residence principles are applied.

Interjurisdictional equity in a federal system also requires that the corporation income taxes of the constituent states be applied at uniform rates and that the source of income be defined in a uniform way. As United States experience has shown, these forms of tax coordination are not easy to secure. Although the rates of tax are low relative to that of the federal tax, differentials in rates are as high as 13 percentage points. Furthermore, as the experience of California in particular has shown, variations in the definition of the apportionable unit (the unitary business) and the question of whether the apportionable base should incorporate foreign income (or stop at the 'water's edge') has caused a good deal of conflict (Carlson and Galper, 1984). The United States' system therefore is far from conforming with a normative model of a federal system in which source-entitlement as it applies to capital income calls for a uniform, source-based corporation tax at the state level.

State corporate tax coordination in a federal system requires agreement on apportionment formulas and tax rates but it does not require use of the foreign tax credit or deduction on the part of states. Equality of rates will secure locational neutrality among the states, and if foreign nation states carry out their responsibility for securing equity and neutrality for their resident taxpayers, such taxes will not interfere with international neutrality. However, there does remain the question of how this lower-level tax should relate to the central (federal) corporation income tax. If tax rates at the state level are equal, then the source-based state corporation tax will cause no neutrality problem within the federal system. However, if rates are not equal (as they are not in the United States), the larger corporation income tax at the federal level can be used to smooth out the differentials, partially by use of a deduction or wholly by use of a credit for the state tax against the federal. Unfortunately, the credit form of neutralization cannot be used in practice since states will merely raise their tax rates to that at the federal level. Thus in the United States state and local corporation income taxes may be deducted from taxable income for purposes of the federal tax.[13] This deduction in a federal system might also be justified from another point of view − that the states' exercise of their entitlement to tax income at source assigns income to the states which is not available to the taxpayer, and that the federal taxing authority should recognize this entitlement via the deduction. In the absence of the deduction, furthermore, combined federal and state taxes could theoretically exceed 100 percent of income.

Table 7.3 gives numerical illustration to tax coordination in a federal system as Model 3, in which states A and B impose source-based corporation taxes at a rate of 10 percent, but no individual income taxes. The federal government applies a global, residence-based corporation income tax at 40 percent, with state taxes deductible from taxable income. The foreign tax rate is 30 percent and the table shows the federal tax liability on foreign-source income (a) when the foreign tax is credited and (b) when it is deductible. Inspection of the bottom row shows that all residents of the constituent states will be taxed at the same effective rate, provided that those states apply their corporation taxes on the source principle at equal rates. But as the last two columns show, non-neutralities creep in as between domestic and foreign investment. If the federal government applies its own corporation tax on the residence principle and permits a credit for the foreign tax, foreign investment will be given more favorable treatment, since our assumption here is that state taxes are only deductible. On the other hand, if foreign taxes are extended the same treatment

13. This deductibility of state corporation income taxes from the federal corporate tax base is maintained in the recent tax reform proposals of the Reagan Administration, even though similar deductibility for other types of state taxes (including the individual income tax) would be terminated.

*Table 7.3 Numerical illustration of tax coordination model 3 (federal system)*

| | $Y_{AB}{}^a$ | $Y_{AA}{}^a$ | $Y_{BA}{}^a$ | $Y_{BB}{}^a$ | $Y_{C(A,B)}{}^a$ With Credit | $Y_{C(A,B)}{}^a$ With Deduction |
|---|---|---|---|---|---|---|
| *Income* | 100 | 200 | 100 | 300 | 100 | |
| *Taxes* | | | | | | |
| State A | | | | | | |
|   Corporation income tax | 10.0 | 20.0 | 0.0 | 0.0 | 0.0 | |
| State B | | | | | | |
|   Corporation income tax | 0.0 | 0.0 | 10.0 | 30.0 | 0.0 | |
| Foreign country | | | | | | |
|   Corporation income tax | 0.0 | 0.0 | 0.0 | 0.0 | 30.0 | |
| Federal government | | | | | | |
|   Corporation income tax | 36.0 | 72.0 | 36.0 | 108.0 | 10.0 | 28.0 |
|   Individual income tax | 16.2 | 32.4 | 16.2 | 48.6 | 18.0 | 12.6 |
|   Total | 52.2 | 104.4 | 52.2 | 156.6 | 28.0 | 40.6 |
| Combined federal and state | | | | | | |
|   Total, federal and state | 62.2 | 124.4 | 62.2 | 186.6 | 28.0 | 40.6 |
| Combined federal, state, foreign | | | | | | |
|   Combined total | 62.2 | 124.4 | 62.2 | 186.6 | 58.0 | 70.6 |
|   Effective tax rate | 0.622 | 0.622 | 0.622 | 0.622 | 0.58 | 0.706 |

*Note:* a. See note to Table 7.1.

as are state taxes (i.e. deducted for purposes of the federal tax), foreign investment will be more heavily taxed if (as is most likely) the foreign tax exceeds the state rate. Of course, with deferral of the United States' tax on retained earnings of foreign incorporated subsidiaries, these non-neutralities will be greater. It illustrates the fact that in seeking locational neutrality, the federal government must take state taxes into account.

## C. Common Markets

The European Community illustrates the particular problems of capital income-tax coordination which arise in the common market form of political setting. As barriers to capital movements come down, the community develops an increasingly unified capital market in the direction of that which holds within a federal system. Yet the level of 'local' tax rates is higher than in the typical federal system where a large part of the budgetary function is centrally performed. As this happens, taxation of corporations yields a revenue distribution among the member nations which becomes increasingly arbitrary, a result exacerbated by the rate differentials which such a sovereign, uncoordinated tax system applies. Since all member countries exempt from tax the foreign income earned by the foreign-incorporated subsidiaries of their resident corporations, direct investment flows are left open to the non-neutralities of tax-rate differentials in what is effectively a source-based system of corporate income taxation. Yet at the same time it becomes more and more difficult to secure compliance with an arm's-length, separate-accounting method of determining source. As firms expand the scale and scope of their operations under the stimulus of a unified market, the international network of incorporated subsidiaries becomes ever more complex, thus rendering the administration of a global-residence approach to the taxation of corporations more obdurate and therefore less feasible as an answer to the locational neutrality problem. At the same time, members of the Common Market are nation states and not lower-level jurisdictions within a federal system. Thus their corporation income tax rates are higher and there is no overarching fiscal authority to moderate rate differentials.

Thus, common markets begin to experience a need for equal effective rates and uniform source rules to be applied to their source-based corporation income taxes so as to avoid an inequitable distribution of revenue, widespread gaps in the tax base as well as the non-neutralities which accompany source-based taxes at differential rates. Meeting this need might well be a major objective of any new initiatives to harmonize further tax systems within the European Common Market, taking precedence over rate equalization for value-added and other taxes.

This objective of source-based, equal-rate corporation income taxes would be compatible with the objective of locational neutrality. Even though, as we have seen, nation states can neutralize rate differentials by use of global, residence-based taxes with full foreign tax credit, there is apt to be a significant gap between theory and practice in this regard, with the tax on undistributed profits of foreign subsidiaries deferred and many other imperfections in the foreign tax credit system, as the United States experience has demonstrated. Furthermore, in the European case, several countries effectively exempt foreign-source income from tax, thus exposing direct investment to the full locational effects of the tax-rate differentials. With corporate tax rates equalized and common agreement on source rules, the individual income tax systems in each country may be allowed to vary and express the differing views of taxpayer equity, leaving the corporation tax to implement interjurisdictional equity based on source-entitlement.

As in the federal system, there are two aspects to the locational neutrality question. One is the problem of securing neutrality among investments within the common market and the other is to promote neutrality between the common market and the outside world. With equal-rate and source-based corporation taxes applied by the member countries, internal neutrality is met provided each country treats the corporation taxes of other members exactly as

218

*Table 7.4 Numerical illustration of tax coordination model 4 (common market, income taxes not integrated)*

|  | $Y_{AB}{}^a$ | $Y_{AA}{}^a$ | $Y_{BA}{}^a$ | $Y_{BB}{}^a$ | $Y_{CA}{}^a$ | $Y_{CB}{}^a$ |
|---|---|---|---|---|---|---|
| *Income* | 100 | 200 | 100 | 300 | 100 | 100 |
| *Taxes* | | | | | | |
| Member country A | | | | | | |
| Corporation income tax | 25.0 | 50.0 | 0.0 | 0.0 | 0.0 | 0.0 |
| Individual income tax | 0.0 | 75.0 | 37.5 | 0.0 | 15.0 | 0.0 |
| Total | 25.0 | 125.0 | 37.5 | 0.0 | 15.0 | 0.0 |
| Member country B | | | | | | |
| Corporation income tax | 0.0 | 0.0 | 25.0 | 75.0 | 0.0 | 0.0 |
| Individual income tax | 22.5 | 0.0 | 0.0 | 67.5 | 0.0 | 18.0 |
| Total | 22.5 | 0.0 | 25.0 | 142.5 | 0.0 | 18.0 |
| Non-member country C | | | | | | |
| Corporation income tax | 0.0 | 0.0 | 0.0 | 0.0 | 40.0 | 40.0 |
| Combined | | | | | | |
| Combined total | 47.5 | 125.0 | 62.5 | 142.5 | 55.0 | 58.0 |
| Effective tax rate | 0.475 | 0.625 | 0.625 | 0.475 | 0.55 | 0.58 |

*Note:*   a. See note to Table 7.1.


*Table 7.5 Numerical illustration of tax coordination model 5 (common market, income taxes integrated)*

|  | $Y_{AB}{}^a$ | $Y_{AA}{}^a$ | $Y_{BA}{}^a$ | $Y_{BB}{}^a$ | $Y_{CA}{}^a$ | $Y_{CB}{}^a$ |
|---|---|---|---|---|---|---|
| *Income* | 100 | 200 | 100 | 300 | 100 | 100 |
| *Taxes* | | | | | | |
| Member country A | | | | | | |
| Corporation income tax | 25.0 | 50.0 | 0.0 | 0.0 | 0.0 | 0.0 |
| Individual income tax | 0.0 | 50.0 | 25.0 | 0.0 | 10.0 | 0.0 |
| Total | 25.0 | 100.0 | 25.0 | 0.0 | 10.0 | 0.0 |
| Member country B | | | | | | |
| Corporation income tax | 0.0 | 0.0 | 25.0 | 75.0 | 0.0 | 0.0 |
| Individual income tax | 5.0 | 0.0 | 0.0 | 15.0 | 0.0 | −10.0 |
| Total | 5.0 | 0.0 | 25.0 | 90.0 | 0.0 | −10.0 |
| Non-member country C | | | | | | |
| Corporation income tax | 0.0 | 0.0 | 0.0 | 0.0 | 40.0 | 40.0 |
| Combined | | | | | | |
| Combined total | 30.0 | 100.0 | 50.0 | 90.0 | 50.0 | 30.0 |
| Effective tax rate | 0.3 | 0.5 | 0.5 | 0.3 | 0.5 | 0.3 |

*Note:*   a. See note to Table 7.1.

its own, for purposes of its individual income tax. It is immaterial whether or not all countries follow the same degree of income-tax integration.

This is demonstrated in our numerical examples for the common market cases shown as Models 4 and 5 in Tables 7.4 and 7.5 respectively. In these models, each member country A and B applies source-based corporation income taxes at a rate of 25 percent and individual income taxes at rates of 50 percent and 30 percent respectively. In Model 4, the income taxes are not integrated and the individual income tax applies to corporate-source income net of corporate tax, while in Model 5 member countries apply fully integrated tax systems, with individual income tax applied to grossed-up corporate income with credit for corporate tax, both domestic and inside and outside the common market. Effective combined tax rates shown in the bottom line of both models show that with or without an integrated system, internal neutrality is preserved. However, without full integration (i.e. crediting of both domestic and foreign corporation taxes against domestic income tax) neutrality between common market and outside investments is not obtainable, as shown in the last two columns of Model 4. This problem can be avoided by full integration on the part of each member country, such integration to apply not only to the corporation tax of other members but also to that of outside countries, as shown in the bottom row of Model 5.

In summary, it may be said that adoption of a source-based, uniform-rate corporation tax to implement jurisdictional equity among the Member States of the Common Market would also be helpful to the achievement of locational neutrality within the Community. This would leave individual income taxes free to reflect each Member State's preferences with regard to rates and structure, as well as the degree of preferred integration, without interfering with internal neutrality. Such is not the case for the attainment of external neutrality, however, which would require full integration by all Member States, including integration with foreign corporation income taxes. In concluding, we should recall that considerations of neutrality have been related to capital movements only. Obviously, income-tax differentials may result in labor movement and thus raise further efficiency problems which fall outside the scope of this paper.[14]


## VI. DEVELOPMENTS IN THE EUROPEAN COMMUNITY

The stated objective of the EC in the field of direct taxation, affirmed in a report of the Commission in 1980,[15] has been the closer alignment of tax

---

14. For an extensive discussion of the taxation of internationally mobile labor, largely in the framework of optimal tax theory, see *Journal of Public Economics* (1982).
15. See Commission (1975 and 1980).

burdens on company income in order to promote locational neutrality. However, since its inception the Community has given priority to the harmonization of the indirect taxes. This endeavor has achieved a reasonable degree of success with the general adoption of the value-added tax and related border-tax adjustments, although equalization of rates combined with application of the origin principle has not as yet been accomplished, thus retaining the need for fiscal frontiers (Andel, 1983). However, the argument for rate equalization combined with the origin principle has become less compelling with the possibility of applying border tax adjustments without the necessity for border checks (Cnossen, 1983a). The Community appears now to be increasingly concerned with the problem of coordinating taxes on company income and in 1975 a proposed directive to this end was made by the Commission. In this proposal, the major objectives were (1) to reduce differentials in rates of company taxation, the latter to range between 45 and 55 percent; (2) to provide for partial integration of the company and individual income taxes on dividends by universal adoption of the imputation (dividends-received credit) method; and (3) to adopt a repayment system whereby the revenue cost of the credit for company tax would be borne by the country of source of the income. It should also be noted that the 1975 Commission proposal did not require a uniform definition of tax base. Such a requirement, however, has been advocated in a subsequent report of 1980 (Commission, 1975 and 1980). Quite clearly, little would be gained by merely equalizing nominal rates.[16]

The time seems ripe for harmonization of taxes on capital income. The development of administrative procedures for the central clearing of border tax adjustments for the value-added taxes greatly reduces the costs of maintaining fiscal frontiers and therefore the need to turn to the origin principle at equalized rates for those taxes (Cnossen, 1983a). The value-added tax may then be allowed to reflect 'tax sovereignty' of the Member States along with the individual income tax, wage-related social security taxes, and property taxes. With reduced scope for the exercise of independent monetary policy, it is also possible to foresee the use of the value-added tax as a fiscal regulator in the stabilization toolkit of Member States. The clearing mechanism applicable to the value-added tax is not readily transferable to a residence-based company tax. But apart from this, it may well be that there is a stronger rationale for the equalization of company tax rates than for rates of value-added tax. This conclusion follows from considerations of interjurisdictional equity and locational neutrality as discussed in the body of this paper. Thus the proposal to contain rate differentials of company taxation within only a limited range is a

16. See the paper by Julian S. Alworth in this volume for an exploration of the causes of present wide variations in effective rates of corporation tax in the Community, variations which appear to be particularly sensitive to the rate of inflation.

step in the right direction. Nevertheless, full equalization of effective rates (with equalization of both rates and base-definition) remains a desirable goal, given the prevailing application of the tax on the source principle.[17]

As to the proposal for a uniformly applied dividends-received credit, this is consistent with but not necessary to locational neutrality *within* the Community, but may well worsen it as *between* the latter and outside countries if the credit is not made available for non-Member company taxes.[18] If company tax rates were equalized, the gain from the credit provision for Community locational neutrality would disappear, although the measure is desirable on taxpayer equity grounds. In all, generalized income tax integration does not contribute greatly to locational neutrality. Equalization of corporate rates would be more productive in this regard. Indeed, if effective rates of corporation tax were equalized, each country would be free to choose its own degree of integration, whether it be zero, full or partial.

The proposal to allow for repayments of the costs of the company tax credit by source to resident countries is an interesting provision which alleviates the conflict between the need for relatively high rates of company tax on undistributed profits (to reduce tax avoidance by high-income investors and the consequent locking-in effect on company profits) on one side and lower rates to reflect 'fair' revenue shares on the part of source countries on the other. Thus proposals within the Community with respect to the coordination of taxes on capital income are in the right direction, in so far as they promote effective equalization of corporate tax rates. Efforts to attain uniformity in the degree and type of integration between corporate and individual income taxes, however, seem uncalled for in the context of neutrality with respect to location of investment; policies on income tax integration should be left to individual countries to decide. However, for reasons of both administrative capability and equitable application of the source-entitlement principle, more attention should now be given to the implementation of uniform source rules including the possibility of formula apportionment of profits; for common market conditions increasingly call for an equal-rate source-based company tax rather than one of unequal rates based on both residence and source principles requiring harmonization through a foreign tax credit.[19]

In concluding, it may be said that the major remaining problem of tax

17. Since equalization of effective rates should apply across all types of investments with varying forms of finance and asset structure, and should hold under varying rates of inflation, tax systems should not only have equal nominal rates and uniform base definition but be designed to be neutral among investment types under all circumstances.
18. For arguments against general adoption of integrated income tax systems within the Community, see van den Tempel (1970).
19. For an earlier position on behalf of residence-based corporation income taxes with foreign tax credit for Common Market countries under the assumption of unequal rates, see Musgrave (1967).

coordination to be faced by the Community is that of company tax harmonization. Harmonization of the value-added tax is well on its way to solution and new developments regarding potential clearing mechanisms will permit freedom of differentiation with a minimum of administrative cost. The problem of the individual income tax continues to be of concern but is also of more limited difficulty. The real problem, then, lies with the company tax. Here, harmonization is especially important with regard to both efficiency and equity (inter-individual as well as inter-nation) aspects. At the same time, more serious difficulties lie in the way of a satisfactory resolution. While rate equalization would be a good first step, it may not prove very meaningful unless linked to base equalization. Beyond this, and most difficult, there remains the problem of division of base among Member States and the eventual adoption of a genuine source solution. For all these reasons it is encouraging to note that company tax harmonization is moving to the center of the discussion.

Alworth, Julian S. 'Taxation and the Cost of Capital: A Comparison of Six EC Countries.' Chapter 9, this volume, 1986.

Andel, Norbert. 'Directions of Tax Harmonization in the EEC.' In Cnossen, Sijbren (ed.). *Comparative Tax Studies.* Amsterdam: North-Holland, 1983.

Ault, Hugh J. 'International Issues in Corporate Tax Integration.' Georgetown University Law Center. *Law and Policy in International Business*, 10, 2, 1978.

Bird, Richard M. 'International Aspects of Integration.' *National Tax Journal*, 23, 3, 1975.

Carlson, George N. and Galper, Harvey. 'Water's Edge Versus Worldwide Unitary Combination.' In McLure, Charles E. Jr (ed.). *The State Corporation Income Tax.* Stanford: Hoover Institution Press, 1984.

Cnossen, Sijbren. 'The Irrelevance of the Restricted Origin Principle.' *Tax Notes*, August 15, 1983a.

Cnossen, Sijbren. 'The Imputation System in the EEC.' In Cnossen, Sijbren (ed.). *Comparative Tax Studies: Essays in Honor of Richard Goode.* Amsterdam: North-Holland, 1983b.

Cnossen, Sijbren. 'Alternative Forms of Corporate Tax.' *Australian Tax Forum*, 1, September 1984. Reprinted as 'Corporation Taxes in OECD Member Countries.' *Bulletin for International Fiscal Documentation*, 38, 11, 1984.

Commission of the European Communities. 'Proposal for a Directive of the Council concerning the Harmonisation of Systems of Company Taxation and of Withholding Taxes on Dividends.' *Bulletin of the European Communities*, Supplement 10, 1975.

Commission of the European Communities. 'Report on the Scope for Convergence of Tax Systems in the Community.' *Bulletin of the European Communities*, Supplement 1, 1980.

*Journal of Public Economics. Income Taxation in the Presence of International Personal Mobility.* Symposium, August 1982.

McLure, Charles E. Jr. *Must Corporate Income Be Taxed Twice?* Washington DC: The Brookings Institution, 1979.

McLure, Charles E. Jr. 'Assignment of Corporate Income Taxes in a Federal System.' In McLure, Charles E. Jr (ed.). *Tax Assignment in Federal Countries.* Canberra: ANU Press, 1983.

McLure, Charles E. Jr. 'Defining a Unitary Business: An Economist's View.' In McLure, Charles E. Jr (ed.). *The State Corporation Income Tax.* Stanford: Hoover Institution Press, 1984.

Musgrave, Peggy B. 'Harmonization of Direct Business Taxes: A Case Study.' In Shoup, Carl S. (ed.). *Fiscal Harmonization in Common Markets*, Vol. II. New York: Columbia University Press, 1967.

224

Musgrave, Peggy B. *United States Taxation of Foreign Investment Income: Issues and Arguments.* Cambridge, Mass.: International Program in Taxation, Harvard Law School, 1969.

Musgrave, Peggy B. 'International Tax Base Division and the Multinational Corporation.' *Public Finance*, 27, 4, 1972.

Musgrave, Peggy B. 'International Tax Differentials for Multinational Corporations: Equity and Efficiency Considerations.' In United Nations, Department of Economic and Social Affairs. *The Impact of Multinational Corporations on Development and on International Relations; Technical Papers: Taxation.* New York: United Nations, 1974.

Musgrave, Peggy B. 'The OECD Model Tax Treaty: Problems and Prospects.' *The Columbia Journal of World Business*, Summer 1975.

Musgrave, Peggy B. 'Commentary on "Assignment of Corporate Income Taxes in a Federal System".' In McLure, Charles E. Jr (ed.). *Tax Assignment in Federal Countries.* Canberra: ANU Press, 1983.

Musgrave, Peggy B. 'Principles for Dividing the State Corporate Tax Base.' In McLure, Charles E. Jr (ed.). *The State Corporation Income Tax.* Stanford: Hoover Institution Press, 1984.

Musgrave, Richard A. and Musgrave, Peggy B. 'Inter-Nation Equity.' In Bird, Richard M. and Head, John G. (eds). *Modern Fiscal Issues: Essays in Honor of Carl S. Shoup.* University of Toronto Press, 1972.

Sato, Mitsuo and Bird, Richard M. 'International Aspects of the Taxation of Corporations and Shareholders.' *IMF Staff Papers*, 22, 1975.

Smith, E.H. 'Allocating to Provinces the Taxable Income of Corporations: How the Federal-Provincial Allocation Rule Evolved.' *Canadian Tax Journal*, 24, 5, 1976.

van den Tempel, A.J. *Corporation Tax and Individual Income Tax in the European Communities.* Brussels: Commission of the European Communities, 1970.

# 8

## Corporate-personal tax integration

### *Richard M. Bird\**

#### I. Integration and Harmonization in the EC

Article 67 of the Treaty of Rome sets out as an ultimate goal of the European Community (EC) the achievement of a free flow of capital within the Community.[1] While the Treaty of Rome does not explicitly provide for the harmonization of direct taxes (as it does for indirect taxes in Article 99), it does provide for the 'approximation' of legislation which affects the establishment or functioning of the Common Market (Article 100) or which creates distortions in the conditions of competition (Article 101).[2] The harmonization of direct taxes is thus in principle not a goal in itself but simply one measure among many that may be needed to attain the desired degree of economic integration. Nevertheless, almost from the beginning of the EC, considerable importance has been attached to the task of bringing the corporate tax systems in the different countries into basic alignment, not least with respect to their relation to the personal income tax. The EC has not, however, found it easy to decide exactly what form of corporate-personal tax integration is best.

In 1962, for example, the Neumark Committee proposed that all EC countries should harmonize their corporation taxes by adopting a uniform

* I am grateful to Sijbren Cnossen, Peggy Musgrave, David Rosenbloom, and other participants at the ISPE conference for helpful comments which have resulted in substantial changes – and, I trust, improvements – in this paper.

1. Article 67(1) reads as follows:
   'Member States shall, in the course of the transitional period and to the extent necessary for the proper functioning of the Common Market, progressively abolish as between themselves restrictions on the movement of capital belonging to persons resident in Member States and also any discriminatory treatment based on the nationality or place of residence of the parties or on the place in which such capital is invested.'
   Other treaty articles related to the free movement of capital include Article 3(c), which sets out the general objective of removing obstacles to the freedom of movement; Article 52, which provides for non-discriminatory freedom of establishment of firms; and Article 221, which provides for non-discriminatory treatment with respect to participation in the capital of companies and firms.
2. Article 220 also provides that Member States should enter into double taxation agreements with each other.

split-rate system, similar to that then in place in Germany, with a different, lower rate being levied on distributed profits (Neumark, 1963). In 1970, however, the van den Tempel report concluded that the best basis for a harmonized corporate tax system would be a so-called 'classic' (unintegrated) system, similar to that in the Netherlands (van den Tempel, 1970). The principal reason for this conclusion appears to have been the emphasis of this report on the international aspects of alternative systems of taxing corporations and their shareholders.[3] In 1975 the EC Commission itself issued a draft directive proposing the harmonization of corporate tax systems along the lines of a partial imputation system, similar to that in France, providing a partial credit to shareholders against their personal taxes for taxes paid at the corporate level (Commission, 1976). Although the Commission reiterated this proposal in 1980 (Commission, 1980), as yet no formal action has been taken to harmonize corporate-personal tax integration in the EC.

The uncertainty as to what to do evident in the above brief summary in part reflects the confused and changing situation both in Europe and elsewhere with respect to the integration of corporate and personal income taxes. The perceived desirability of such integration, the stated reasons for it, and the preferred way to achieve it have all fluctuated from time to time and from country to country. In this situation, it is not surprising that the EC Commission, in the words of Kay and King (1978, p. 204), '. . . appears to have been swimming with the tide rather than setting the pace' — and the tide keeps going in and out. The harmonization of taxes on corporate-source income clearly continues to be regarded as an important problem in the EC, but the appropriate solution as yet appears unclear in the face of differing national interests and fiscal traditions. These difficulties can only be exacerbated by the recent incorporation into the Community of countries with tax systems as diverse as those of Greece, Spain, and Portugal.

As shown in Table 8.1, three of the 12 countries in the expanded EC, for example, have completely unintegrated (classical) systems — the Netherlands, Luxembourg, and Spain; two have partial integration with respect to dividends at the corporate level — one through dividend deduction (Greece) and one through a split-rate system (Portugal); and the remaining seven provide relief for dividends at the shareholder level under some form of 'imputation' or tax credit system (Cnossen, 1984). Even within this last group, however, as Cnossen (1983, p. 95) has noted '. . . the various imputation systems differ substantially from the model proposed by the Commission. Clearly, domestic considerations rather than community concerns have been of overriding

---

3. A similar conclusion, that the international aspects of the 'classical' system were both simplest to deal with and fit best the assumptions of the OECD model tax treaty, emerged from a subsequent analysis by Sato and Bird (1975) although they argued instead for a revision of the model treaty to accommodate different systems of corporate-personal integration.

significance in shaping each country's corporation tax, as well as its relationship to the personal income tax.' As shown in Table 8.1, similar variations are apparent in the rates and revenue importance of corporation taxes as well as in the treatment of international income flows in the different countries.

In 1985, for example, according to Alworth (this volume) the basic national corporate rate on undistributed profits ranged from 35 percent in Spain to 56 percent in Germany (or 62 percent including local taxes *(Gewerbesteuern)* on corporate income). The imputation credit received by shareholders in the seven countries with this system in 1983 ranged from 25 percent of net dividends in Denmark to 56.2 percent (or 71 percent including local taxes) in Germany (Cnossen, 1983). In the same year, corporation income tax yields ranged from only 1 percent of GDP in a number of EC countries to a high of 7 percent in Luxembourg (OECD, 1985). Almost three decades of discussion have not, it appears, succeeded in producing a very uniform corporate tax system in the EC.

A similarly diverse picture is apparent with respect to the treatment of international income flows in EC countries, as shown in Table 8.1. In the first place, there is certainly no uniformity in terms of the withholding tax rates applied by one country on dividends flowing to another country (Alworth, 1985). When these differences are combined with the different underlying corporation tax rates in the various countries, the combined corporate taxes borne by a particular dividend flow within the EC may be anywhere in the range from 0 percent (in Ireland) to up to 53 percent (in Greece). Moreover, imputation credits provided to domestic shareholders are generally not extended to non-portfolio shareholders in other EC countries, thus further increasing the difference in the treatment of corporate-source income depending on the location of ownership (Cnossen, 1983).

In addition, the treatment of foreign-source income in the recipient country may also differ markedly. Most EC countries defer taxes on foreign-source income earned by subsidiaries until such income is repatriated and then provide a credit against domestic income tax for both withholding taxes and underlying corporate taxes. Several countries (France and the Netherlands), however, as a rule, simply exempt such foreign-source income. Different treatment is often provided for income arising from branch operations, however, as well as for corporate and individual portfolio investment (Alworth, 1985). While it is neither possible nor necessary to set out these complex systems in detail here, even this brief account should make it clear that the present situation with respect to corporate-personal tax integration in the EC is, to say the least, not very consistent with the usual view of fiscal harmonization as implying a basically uniform system.[4]

---

4. For an extended critique of this view, see Bird (1984, 1986).

Table 8.1 Corporate-personal tax integration and harmonization in the EC

| Country | Corporate Taxes as % of GDP 1983 | Corporate Tax Rate, 1983[a] | Relationship to Personal Income Tax | Tax Credit as % of Net Dividend[f] | Credit Extended to Foreign Portfolio Investors[k] | Taxation of Foreign-Source Income[n] | Dividend Withholding Taxes for EC Countries 1985 |
|---|---|---|---|---|---|---|---|
| Belgium | 3 | 45 | Imputation | 46[g,h] | No | Credit with deferral[o] | 15 |
| Denmark | 1 | 40 | Imputation | 25[g] | Yes[l] | Credit with deferral[p] | 15 |
| France | 2 | 50 | Imputation | 50[h] | Yes | Exemption | 0-25[u] |
| Germany | 2 | 63.3/46.7[b,c] | Imputation | 56.2[i] | No | Credit with deferral[q] | 5-25[v] |
| Greece | 1 | 48.5 | Dividend deduction[d] | – | – | Credit with deferral | 25-42[w] |
| Ireland | 1 | 50 | Imputation | 42.9 | Yes[l] | Credit with deferral[r] | 0 |
| Italy | 4 | 40.5[b] | Imputation | 33.3[g] | No | Credit with deferral[q,s] | 0-30[x] |
| Luxembourg | 7 | 46.4[b] | Classical | – | – | Credit without deferral[t] | 0-15[y] |
| Netherlands | 3 | 43 | Classical[e] | – | – | Exemption | 0-25[z] |
| Portugal | n.a. | 52/40[c] | Split rate | – | – | n.a. | 10-15[aa] |
| Spain | 1 | 35 | Classical | – | – | Credit with deferral | 10-18[bb] |
| United Kingdom | 4 | 52 | Imputation | 42.9[j] | Yes[m] | Credit with deferral[r] | 0-15[cc] |

Notes:  a.  Some countries have different rates on companies in specific resource industries (Netherlands, Spain), on non-resident companies (Belgium) and on small corporations (Belgium, Ireland, Luxembourg, Netherlands, Portugal, and the UK).

b.  Includes local corporation taxes.

c.  The first rate applies to undistributed and the second to distributed profits.

d.  At the shareholder's option, dividend income is exempt.

e.  A small amount of dividends is effectively exempted.

f.  The UK and Ireland do not give credits to domestic corporate shareholders but instead exempt intercorporate dividends. Only Germany and Italy extend credits to affiliated domestic corporate shareholders but Denmark, France and Belgium exempt all or most of such dividends. Germany also allows the credit to be deducted from corporation tax.

g.  No compensatory tax is levied on dividends paid out of exempt profits.

h.  No refund is paid to individuals if the credit exceeds income tax.

i.  This figure is for federal taxes only.

j.  Refunds are made to exempt entities also.

k.  In accordance with double taxation agreements only.

l.  Credits extended only in the case of the UK.

230

m.  Under some treaties, the UK also extends credit (at half rates) to direct corporate investors.

n.  For income from foreign subsidiaries.

o.  Income from branches is exempt as is income from subsidiaries under most double tax agreements.

p.  Branch income is creditable without deferral; some double tax agreements provide for exemption of subsidiary income.

q.  Branch income is creditable without deferral although most double tax agreements provide for exemption.

r.  Branch income is creditable without deferral.

s.  Creditable against corporate income tax; branch income is exempt for purposes of local income tax.

t.  Branch income is creditable with deferral although most double tax agreements provide for exemption; foreign taxes in excess of the tax credit are deductible.

u.  0% on direct investment for Denmark and Germany and portfolio investment for Germany; 15% for portfolio investment for other countries except 25% for Greece; for direct investment, 25% for Greece, 15% for Belgium, Italy and Portugal, 10% for Ireland and Spain, and 5% for the rest. Tax credit is granted to Belgium, Denmark, Luxembourg, Netherlands, Spain, and UK portfolio investment.

v.  25% on portfolio investment in all cases except Ireland and UK (20%). 25% on direct investment for Greece, Italy, and Portugal; 5% for Spain; and 15% for the rest. No tax credit is granted.

w.  25% for Belgium, Denmark and Italy and 42% for the rest.

x.  30% for Denmark and portfolio investment for the Netherlands, 5% for UK direct investment; 25% for Greece, 0% for Netherlands direct investment; and 15% for the rest.

y.  0% for Italian direct investment; 2.5% for Netherlands portfolio investment; 5% for Ireland and UK direct investment; 10% for Belgium and Denmark direct investment; and 15% for the rest.

z.  0% for Denmark, Ireland, Italy direct and Italy portfolio investment; 2.5% for Luxembourg direct investment; 10% for German direct investment; 25% for Portugal; and 15% for the rest.

aa. 10% for Denmark, France, Spain and UK direct investment; and 15% for the rest.

bb. 10% for Denmark, France, Netherlands, Portugal and UK direct investment; 15% for Belgium, Germany and Italy direct investment and Belgium and Greece portfolio investment; and 18% for the rest.

cc. 0% for Denmark, Greece, Italy and Portugal; 15% for the rest. No tax credit is granted to the four named countries, however.

*Sources:* Revenue data from OECD (1985); rates and nature of integration system from Cnossen (1984), as updated by Alworth (this volume); amount and nature of tax credit from Cnossen (1983); taxation of foreign-source income from Alworth (1985); withholding taxes on dividends from *European Taxation*, as prepared by Alworth.

In principle, however, two quite different approaches to the problem of coordinating the different systems of taxing corporate-source income in the EC are possible. The first approach, that taken by the Commission (1980), is to urge continued movement towards a more harmonized system of corporate taxation along the lines set out in its 1975 proposal. This proposal envisaged a single corporate tax rate between 45 and 55 percent, with shareholders resident in the EC being allowed to credit between 45 and 55 percent of the tax levied on distributed dividends against their personal tax liabilities. Such credits should be non-discriminatory in the sense that dividends received by residents of any one member country are to be treated similarly by that country regardless of their country of origin. The revenue cost of allowing imputation credits on dividends received from other member countries would be borne, however, by those countries through a so-called 'clearing-house' mechanism under which the source country in effect transfers the credited portion of its corporate tax to the residence country.[5]

The apparent rationale behind this approach may be summarized in the form of three propositions. The first proposition is that a roughly uniform degree of integration of corporate and personal taxes is presumed to be independently desirable in all countries. The most common argument for this position in Europe appears to be the desire to encourage greater dividend payouts and hence wider participation in equity markets (Gourevitch, 1977). Cnossen (1983), for example, concluded in his recent review of the imputation system in Europe that the most important argument for imputation is that it might promote more widespread shareholding.

In contrast, as noted below, most academic writers on corporate-personal tax integration have tended instead to emphasize two other arguments: first, since only people can pay taxes in the end, the only equitable income tax system is a fully integrated one; second, that only a fully integrated tax will avoid distorting such economic decisions as those of the form in which to conduct business. It is difficult to reconcile such arguments with schemes for partial dividend relief like those set forth in Commission (1976). Moreover, the case for even full integration has come to seem more suspect than was once thought, as discussed below.

A second proposition underlying the traditional approach is that the achievement of a true common market is presumed to require that capital income be subject to approximately equal tax systems regardless of where the income arises or where its recipient resides. In the European context, this

---

5. For a description and analysis of this system, see McLure (1980). An earlier 'clearing-house' arrangement under the French-German Treaty (described in Norr, 1982, p. 182) was broadly similar.

argument is often stated in terms of establishing 'conditions of fair competition' so that 'production costs, the location of investment projects and the return on invested capital in the Member States are not influenced to unduly differing degrees by taxation . . .' (Commission, 1980, p. 13).[6] Although it has been suggested by Cnossen (1983) that the system proposed in the EC directive is conducive to capital-export (or locational) neutrality, the objective sought by the EC seems better characterized as capital-import neutrality − as, indeed, is emphasized by the Commission's (1980, p. 63) stated preference for exempting profits earned abroad rather than allowing a foreign tax credit.

The exemption of foreign-source income is in fact compatible with capital-export neutrality only in two extreme instances, as shown in Sato and Bird (1975). The first case is when all taxes on corporations are benefit taxes, precisely matching the cost-reducing services received by corporations, *and* when foreign investors receive such services only from the host country. The second case is when all corporation taxes are fully shifted forward *and* when all such taxes are 'classical' (separate entity) levies. Even with full forward shifting, the combination of imputation and the exemption of foreign-source income is locationally neutral only if corporate decisions are assumed to be affected only by taxes on the corporation itself and not at all by taxes on shareholders. While the introduction of withholding taxes obviously complicates both these arguments, the assumptions needed to make exemption compatible with capital-export neutrality seem so far-fetched as to make it more plausible to conclude that the real objective of the EC with respect to the harmonization of direct business taxes appears to be capital-import neutrality.

Similarly, the emphasis throughout both the Treaty of Rome and the subsequent EC discussion on non-discrimination in the sense of equal treatment of residents and non-residents really amounts to a strong argument for capital-import neutrality as the governing allocative goal. Non-discrimination in this sense clearly favors investment in lower-tax countries and hence fosters allocative inefficiency, thus tending to influence the free flow of capital among Member States − *unless*, of course, the taxes in all Member States are identical. Only in this case will both capital-import *and* capital-export neutrality be attained, at least within the EC.

The third proposition underlying the case for requiring approximately uniform corporate-personal tax systems in all EC countries is based on considerations of jurisdictional equity, in the sense that, as Musgrave (this volume) argues, the division of tax revenues obtained by imposing a uniform source-based corporate tax − perhaps even with the tax base allocated among countries on the basis of some uniform formula − is most likely to be accepted as 'fair' in terms of jurisdictional equity within the EC. Even if taxes are uniform in all Member States, however, when corporate and personal income

6. A similar argument was also important in the earlier Benelux discussion; see Krauss (1969), p. 57.

taxes are integrated to any extent investment flows must also be presumed to be roughly balanced between countries − so that it makes little difference which one provides dividend relief − or else countries must be presumed (for some unclear reason) to set community above national interests.[7]

As in the case of the efficiency argument, what seems to be going on in Europe in this respect to some extent may perhaps be interpreted as a curious inversion of the normal process of argument. Tax uniformity is presented as the prescription to attain the desired state of economic integration, but such uniformity, whether in terms of efficiency or jurisdictional equity, only makes sense, it may be argued, if that state has already been attained − and, if it has, the prescribed medicine may not be needed in any case. In the end, perhaps the basic arguments for more uniform taxation of corporate-source income in the EC are thus not economic at all but political in the sense that greater uniformity in this (and other) respects is apparently presumed to be good simply because it will reduce the differences between the Member States of the EC. The rationalization put forth for particular policy prescriptions may thus be less important than the uniformity prescribed: the harmonization of corporate-personal tax integration in this sense becomes an end in itself, and not simply a means to a further end as at first appears to be the case.

The second possible approach to the problem of coordinating the taxation of corporate-source income in the EC is, as already hinted, simply to call into question all three of the propositions just stated. Integration, it may be argued, is not necessarily a desirable reform; identical tax systems may not be either necessary or desirable in a common market, even with respect to the taxation of capital income; and policies whose implementation depends on such non-existent conditions as the existence of an overriding community welfare function are not likely to succeed. As Andel (1983, p. 312) has observed, tax harmonization in practice always implies tax reform, and 'it is hardly surprising that international tax reform should prove so difficult as it does between six and nine [or twelve] countries, each with different economic and social conditions, divergent objectives and staggered elections!'. If the reform in question may not be particularly desirable anyway, and may also not be needed to achieve the objectives for which it is allegedly intended, the failure to make much progress on this front in Europe to date may be neither as surprising nor as lamentable as some seem to feel.

Section II, which reviews briefly some recent related discussion and developments in several non-EC (federal) countries, both leads into the discussion in Section III of the underlying rationale for integration and brings out more clearly the uncertain link between political and economic union that appears to lie at the heart of much of the discussion of fiscal harmonization.

7. As Krauss (1969), p. 57, noted in a slightly different context, '. . . there must truly be a common will if neighbours are to endure each other's problems and find common remedies in response.'

234

Even if the internal pressure for some degree of integration does not fade away, as Section III suggests may be in the process of happening, the 'need' to do anything about harmonizing this feature of tax systems interjurisdictionally has likely generally been exaggerated, at least in economic terms. In the end, however, as already mentioned, the case for interjurisdictional integration of income taxes, as for most tax reforms, will stand or fall, in both theory and practice, largely on political, not economic, grounds. While the political analysis of corporate-personal tax integration in the context of international economic integration is by no means as advanced as the economic analysis, a few brief and preliminary reflections on this important aspect of the issue are therefore offered by way of conclusion in Section IV.

## II. INTEGRATION AND HARMONIZATION IN FEDERAL STATES

The uncertain approach to integration evident in Europe in recent years — with policy often being determined at least in part by international considerations — has been paralleled in other countries. In Australia, for example, which has long had an unintegrated (classical) system, the 1975 Taxation Review Committee recommended partial imputation, the 1981 Committee on the Financial System recommended full integration, and some limited partial dividend relief was introduced in 1982 and repealed (by a different Government) in 1983 (Swan, 1983). More recently, the 1985 White Paper proposed an imputation system roughly on EC lines, largely on the grounds that the benefit of credits can be confined to resident investors only.[8]

Somewhat similar peregrinations in proposals, if as yet seldom in actions, have been apparent in other countries. In the United States, for example, one option considered in the US Treasury (1977) 'Blueprints' report was full integration, and various proposals for full or partial dividend relief were actively and extensively considered in the following years (McLure, 1979). The recent US Treasury Department (1984) tax reform package proposed to allow corporations to deduct from taxable income a proportion of dividends paid — initially 50 percent but subsequently reduced in *The President's Tax Proposals* (1985) to only 10 percent. In striking contrast to the common emphasis in the EC on encouraging dividend distributions, the recent American discussion has generally emphasized equating the treatment of debt and equity and similar efficiency concerns as the reason for moving towards integration.

8. The proposal set forth in *Reform of the Australian Tax System* (1985) later became official policy (Keating, 1985). The Australian discussion on this point largely paralleled that earlier in the United Kingdom (see Sato and Bird, 1975, pp. 433-36) and the Netherlands (see Cnossen, 1983, p. 96). Actually, of course, the UK subsequently extended credits on portfolio investment and, more uniquely, also on direct investment under a number of its bilateral treaties.

An interesting aspect of the 1984 US proposal is that a compensatory withholding tax would be imposed on dividends paid abroad, except where banned from doing so by the withholding tax limits established in existing treaties. In the case of treaties with countries with imputation systems, however, if the benefits of dividend relief were not extended to US residents on a reciprocal basis, the US would be prepared to impose a compensatory withholding tax anyway (*President's Tax Proposals*, 1985, p. 129). Apparently it does not matter in this view what the relative size of the 'reciprocal' relief – let alone the original tax – may be.[9]

Although it was in the Canadian Royal Commission (1966) report that full integration was first presented as a real policy option, in the end, the proposal for full integration of corporate taxes on both undistributed and distributed profits was no more successful in Canada than it has been in Germany, Australia, the United States, or anywhere else. Instead, what Canada ended up with is a system which provides full dividend relief – indeed, for some years more than full relief! – for small companies[10] and partial dividend relief for others. As in Belgium, Italy and Denmark, the amount of the dividend tax credit is completely independent of whether any tax was paid at the corporate level at all. The alleged rationale for this generosity was to encourage Canadians to invest in Canadian industry much of which, particularly in the resource sector, has traditionally paid few, if any, taxes at the corporate level (Bucovetsky and Bird, 1972).

A good illustration of Canada's approach to the international aspects of integration is the recently concluded treaty with the United States. The US constantly criticized Canada throughout the extended negotiations for discriminating by failing to extend its dividend tax credit to non-resident shareholders (Patrick, 1981).[11] In the end, however, Canada won the day, albeit only at the price of reducing the withholding tax on dividends from its preferred 15 percent rate to 10 percent. In the words of one of Canada's

9. Although *President's Tax Proposals* (1985, p. 128) refers rather cuttingly to the 'purely formalistic' manner in which it alleges most imputation countries have been able to deny credits to direct investors while avoiding direct treaty violations, it proceeds to propose to violate treaties if other countries do not reciprocally extend their credits to US shareholders in a manner satisfactory to the US. Although this extension is referred to as 'reciprocal', this use of the term is surely purely formalistic since no attention is paid to either the relative rate of integration or the basic corporate rate. Obviously, the 'effective reciprocity' approach urged in Sato and Bird (1975), which would take into account the total corporate and withholding tax burden, is still a long way from being accepted!

10. Actually, the benefits apply to Canadian-controlled private companies – which are by no means all small!

11. According to Cnossen (1983), Denmark, which similarly grants a credit even for exempt profits, does extend a credit to foreign portfolio shareholders under treaties with Australia and (reciprocally) with the UK (which also extends a ½ credit to direct investors). Belgium and Italy, however, do not.

negotiators, this was an instance of 'a resolution of a fundamental issue by way of a concession in the rates of tax'. (Short, 1981, p. 412). While one may wonder what else might be given away in response to the new US pressures likely to emerge if the dividend deduction scheme mentioned above ever becomes reality, perhaps the more important lesson from this example is that no single feature of a complex international agreement like a tax treaty, even between two independent countries, can really be understood, or appraised, in isolation (Bird and Brean, 1985). This truth is even more evident with respect to fiscal relations among member states in a common market or a federation.

At the present time, three of the largest Canadian provinces (Ontario, Quebec and Alberta) administer their own corporation taxes, with standard rates varying from 15 percent in Ontario to 11 percent in Alberta. The taxes in the seven other provinces, with rates varying from 10 to 16 percent, are administered by the federal government together with its own tax at a standard rate of 46 percent. The federal government allows a credit against federal tax for a provincial tax rate of up to 10 percent, however, so the combined rate of federal and provincial tax varies from 46 percent to 52 percent, depending on the province.[12] The tax base is identical to the federal tax base in those provinces in which the federal government administers the tax and very close to it even in the other provinces. Moreover, a dividend tax credit (at a rate of approximately 50 percent of net dividends) applies in the same fashion for personal tax purposes in all provinces, even Quebec in which, unlike the other nine provinces, the personal income tax is administered independently by the provincial government. Finally, because all provinces accept the attribution of corporate tax base according to a uniform formula worked out some years ago with the federal government, there has been no need to develop any explicit method of tax coordination with respect to provincial corporate taxes. On the whole, therefore, the present system of income taxation in Canada probably approximates about as closely to the sort of system apparently envisaged by the EC directive as one is likely to find in practice. The base is uniform; it is allocated among jurisdictions by a uniform formula; tax and credit rates do not vary much from province to province; and the system of corporate-personal tax integration is uniform.

It is not surprising, therefore, that the evidence of increasing, though still minor, fragmentation of the federal-provincial corporate income tax system in recent years has not been greeted by acclaim by most analysts (Thirsk, 1980). One strand in the on-going arguments around this issue has been the possibly beneficial effects on investment of providing fuller integration at the provincial

12. The rates also vary by industry and size of business from province to province. In 1984 the highest combined rate of 52 percent applied to large non-manufacturing businesses in Newfoundland, Manitoba, and Saskatchewan and the lowest rate of 10 percent applied to small manufacturing businesses in Ontario and New Brunswick (Canadian Tax Foundation, 1985).

level. The most thorough study to date of this question argued that the probability of such a measure having a favorable effect on investment in Canadian circumstances was extremely small, in part because of the high likelihood that the marginal investor would be a non-Canadian who would not benefit (it was assumed) from integration (Hartle *et al.*, 1983). Although the recent Canadian concern with integration at the provincial level appears to have been motivated by different concerns from either the recent discussion in the US or the EC discussion, this conclusion may not hold for the EC, where the marginal investor may be less likely to be a non-EC resident. If so, the pressures to adopt differential integration systems for such domestic policy reasons as attempting to increase investment may be greater in the EC than in Canada.

## The Case for 'Disharmony'

As Boadway and Bruce (1984) stressed in the context of the Canadian debate, if for any reason any province wants its corporate tax (or its personal income tax with respect to investment income) to differ significantly from that elsewhere, it will also generally have to alter its personal (or corporate) tax system in order to achieve any desired treatment of personal capital income. That is, since the corporate and personal taxes on capital income are inextricably connected in economic terms, no province can tax investment income significantly differently from other provinces *unless* it can also adjust the degree to which its corporate and personal taxes are integrated.[13] Provinces − or member states of a common market − may want to make such adjustments either for such economic reasons as inducing more investment, affecting debt-equity ratios, or encouraging distribution and equity markets or to implement their conception of taxpayer equity.

With respect to this first point, contrary to the apparent view taken by some (Musgrave, this volume), there seems no reason to assume that only the national government in a federation is legitimately concerned with equity issues. Indeed, it may be persuasively argued (Tresch, 1981) that provincial pursuit of different redistributional objectives is an essential element in a federal state − and that the freedom to impose different taxes on corporate-

---

13. The effects on investment and savings of taxes on capital income, whether levied at the corporate or personal level, obviously depend significantly on the openness of the economy. In a closed economy, corporation taxes (in the usual model) shift the investment-demand curve while personal capital taxes shift the supply-of-savings curve and both affect the amount of investment. In an open economy, the same effects occur but only business taxes alter the amount of investment while personal tax changes affect only who owns (supplies the savings for) investment. Most economies are probably somewhere between these extremes so that there is indeed some possibility of affecting investment through manipulating corporate-personal tax integration.

source income is an essential instrument of provincial redistributive policy. If so, the present striking uniformity among Canadian provinces, rather than illustrating how well the EC system might work if it ever attained this degree of perfection, may represent a greater loss of policy autonomy at the provincial level than is really healthy for Canada in the long run (Bird, 1984). The considerably more diverse and 'disharmonized' state corporate tax systems in countries such as Switzerland (Bieri, 1979) and the US (McLure, 1983) may thus represent not a mess that needs to be cleaned up in the interests of increased efficiency, as analysts usually conclude, but rather, when considered in the context of the policy system as a whole, a realistic response to the conflicting pressures for both uniformity and diversity that inherently characterize federal states (Bird, 1986).

In a sense, for example, the inevitable tension in any federal state or, to a varying extent, common market may be expressed in terms of differences between the weight that is attached to the 'community' as opposed to the state view in the constitution and that which is attached to it in practice. Conflict seems especially likely when it comes to issues such as tax structure which lie at the heart of national sovereignty. In the EC context, for example, it is striking how often official publications refer to the need to take more account of 'Community interest' and 'Community spirit' in devising national policies in areas such as fiscal harmonization.[14]

Traditionally, in federal states, negotiations on such matters have taken place primarily with the federal government playing the lead role. Recent events in Canada suggest that there may well in future be an increasing need for more direct province-to-province discussions on tax and other matters, without such discussions being mediated, as in the past, through the agency of the federal government. Canada has also pioneered in developing 'two-track' systems within the federal structure, in which as a result of federal-provincial negotiation non-consenting provinces (usually Quebec) are allowed to 'opt-out' of particular uniform arrangements such as those on personal income taxation. The similar system proposed for the EC (as indeed has always been to some extent the case for Benelux) by Tindemans (1976) may well be worth further exploration.

It is by no means clear whether reliance on horizontal coordination is more or less costly than reliance on vertical coordination — and it is even less clear whether, in any case, the results will be 'better' or 'worse', and from whose point of view. Viewed from this perspective, what seems to be going on in Europe, where up to now most direct tax negotiations have been horizontal, appears almost the reverse of what is going on in Canada, with the negotiations

---

14. See, for example, Commission (1980, p. 65), which correctly states that a *sine qua non* for further progression on tax harmonization is 'a strong political resolve to make substantial headway in the construction of Europe'.

on tax harmonization moving gradually − doubtless more gradually than keen Eurocrats would prefer − up to the supranational (or at least multilateral) level of the Community and away from the purely national (or at most bilateral) level that has heretofore largely prevailed. Exactly the same comments, appropriately reversed, may obviously be made about this development.

Even should the broader political 'Community' context come to prevail, so that in effect Europe moves closer to a federal model, it should clearly be realized that tax harmonization problems will by no means be solved. In some federations, such as Germany and Australia, for example, the result of the workings of the political-constitutional process over time has been to produce a highly centralized tax system. In contrast, in Switzerland, where a much higher premium is put on local autonomy, most taxes, including income taxes, have been assigned to the cantons. The US and Canada occupy an intermediate position in the sense that state taxes are almost as diverse in the US as in Switzerland, but they are much less important, while in Canada such taxes are even more important than in Switzerland but much more uniform.

The general conclusions of most commentators on these issues in federal states were well summed up in a recent Australian discussion. On the one hand, most economic commentators on these matters appear to accept (1) that distribution policy is a matter for central government, (2) that non-benefit taxation should be uniform throughout the country, and (3) that in general tax systems should be as simple, neat, and tidy as possible (Groenewegen, 1981). These premises lead almost inexorably to a highly centralized tax system and certainly militate against very divergent income taxes, whether with respect to integration or anything else.

On the other hand, traditional 'federal' arguments (as well as the recent 'public choice' literature) emphasize (1) the need to encourage fiscal responsibility through expenditure-revenue matching and (2) the desirability of recognizing diversity and local autonomy, both to encourage local experimentation and to afford individuals more choice.[15] This perspective obviously suggests that much greater local fiscal independence may well be considered desirable, even at the cost of higher administrative and compliance costs and possible 'efficiency' losses.

Independent tax systems in an economic union (whether a federation or a common market) will in general require the development of explicit horizontal coordinating mechanisms. A uniform source system with the base allocated by formula (Musgrave, this volume) would give rise to few problems, but it would of course mean giving up a substantial degree of fiscal independence. Different systems of corporate-personal integration could be accommodated by a crediting system (Sato and Bird, 1975) if the residence principle of taxation were fully accepted, and if the credited tax were levied on essentially the same base

15. These points are made by R.C. Gates in a comment on Groenewegen (1981).

and also smaller than the tax liability or else were refunded by the other government as proposed by the Commission (1976). If tax bases diverge significantly, the suitability of this method comes into question. Countries concerned with attaining capital-export neutrality would probably be best advised in these circumstances to stay with the 'classical' system (van den Tempel, 1970) or to negotiate reciprocal arrangements with relevant countries along the 'effective reciprocity' lines set out by Sato and Bird (1975) so that foreign and domestic taxes are treated similarly. If countries are concerned more with capital-import neutrality, as was suggested earlier appears to be the case in the EC, some problems would still exist in attaining complete neutrality in the face of different integration systems in different countries unless again foreign and domestic taxes were treated similarly for integration purposes, perhaps through something like the 'clearing-house' system proposed by the Commission (1976).

The costs of the convoluted process of negotiation needed to resolve such interjurisdictional problems through bilateral (horizontal) negotiations could easily be so high as to render a move to more 'federal' (supranational) coordination attractive. Reasonable people may even decide to obviate the necessity for this interim costly stage by moving directly to more explicit agreement between all member units and higher-level governing units on new methods of horizontal coordination. This is presumably what the European Commission has been trying to do, off and on, for almost thirty years with respect to direct tax harmonization.

Even if future discussions bring more success in this endeavour, however, two points should be borne in mind with respect to the particular issue of corporate-personal tax integration. First, as shown in Section III below, the present state of knowledge on this subject is not really such that the practices of any particular country can or should be condemned out of hand. Secondly, as stressed above, such practices should also not be considered in isolation. Many of the measures customarily prescribed to deal with these problems (Musgrave, this volume), for instance, do not seem to recognize sufficiently the need to respect a country's sovereign right to do something stupid in the tax field. If what is done is economically disadvantageous to the country itself, in time the message will presumably be received through the market.[16] If it harms other countries, or is thought to do so, the political message will doubtless also be delivered; whether it will be heeded or not depends, of course, on the general political context. To sum up this line of argument, there thus seems very little case for *requiring* all member states to adhere to a particular corporate-personal tax structure whether within a federal state or a common market. The

---

16. As the interminable debate on protectionism shows, this is doubtless an overly facile comment: it may take a long, long time for the market's message to be heeded − in part for reasons touched on in Section IV below.

benefits to be obtained from integration are primarily a domestic, not an international, issue and there seems no overriding reason why countries cannot to a large extent be left to do what they want in this area. Since, as shown in the next section, the arguments for integration – full or partial – have themselves increasingly been called into question in recent years, it may well be in the future that more countries will in fact choose to do less in this respect than seemed likely when the Commission's (1976) proposal was drafted.

### III. INTEGRATION: A FADING STAR?

The ideal tax system of many public finance economists, at least until recently, would probably have been one with no absolute corporate tax. This view has persisted principally for two reasons, neither of which in the end seems very persuasive (Bird, 1980). The first reason is that, because in the final analysis only people can pay taxes, the best taxes are those that are levied on people openly and directly, so that they can know what is going on, and make their decisions about taxes and expenditures accordingly. As the Canadian Royal Commission on Taxation (1966) put it, corporations in themselves have no independent reality: they are merely a 'conduit' through which money is channelled from some persons – the buyers of corporate products – to others – the owners of the factors of production combined in the corporate form (workers, managers, shareholders).

If corporations pay taxes over to the government, some physical person's income is clearly reduced by this act. It may be that of consumers who, as a result of either administered prices or reduced output, will pay higher prices for corporate goods; or workers, who get lower wages either immediately or in the long run because they have less capital with which to work; or shareholders, who get fewer dividends and capital gains; or all capitalists, to the extent that the tax lowers the rate of return on capital in general; or it may be some mixture of all these groups, depending on the precise nature of the tax, the state of the economy, its degree of openness, the nature of other accompanying policy measures, the time period considered, and so on. As this very condensed summary of several decades of theoretical and empirical literature suggests, the question of precisely whose income is reduced by taxes on corporations is far from simple and perhaps ultimately unanswerable.[17] Economists may feel uncomfortable about this fact, but it hardly follows that the corporation taxes now existing in almost every country should be abolished in whole or part (or

---

17. Shoup (1969) has argued persuasively, for example, that one can say nothing useful about the incidence of the corporate tax as such, in the important sense that only the combined effects of a corporate tax change and the other accompanying measures needed to hold other things equal can ever be observed.

integrated with personal income taxes, which amounts to the same thing) for reasons of intellectual tidiness.

The second, and economically more important, indictment of an absolute corporate tax is that it distorts the market allocation of resources. There are at least five potential distortions in resource allocation arising from the wholly or partially unintegrated corporate tax systems presently existing in most countries, with respect to (1) the choice of business organization, (2) the pay-out ratio, (3) the level of private savings, (4) the choice of financial structure, and (5) real investment decisions. The workings of capital markets are affected because retentions are favored over dividends. Not only the form but also the level of savings may be affected by this distortion in pay-out policy, though the direction of the resulting bias is by no means as clear as seems to have been assumed in most European discussion (Byrne and Sato, 1976; King, 1977). As stressed recently in the US tax reform discussion, there is also a further bias against equity financing, since interest paid on borrowed money is deductible for purposes of corporate tax while dividends are not. Finally, as a rule the taxation of corporate-source income introduces some bias into both savings and investment decision, as indicated above with respect to the recent Canadian discussion.

Furthermore, if one assumes that corporate taxes are 'really' paid by shareholders, the present system, in which unrealized capital gains are not subject to personal taxes and realized gains are taxed, if at all, at favorable rates, means that personal taxes can be avoided by retaining income in a corporation and subsequently, through various devices, taking out the income in the form of capital gains. Moreover, the final tax burden on corporate-source income, whether distributed or not, varies from shareholder to shareholder in a fashion that depends upon the pay-out ratio of the corporation and the relation between the relevant corporate and personal tax rates. There are thus reasons of both horizontal and vertical equity (especially if one assumes the corporate tax is borne by shareholders) as well as of economic efficiency (regardless of what one thinks of the incidence of the tax) for wishing to reform the corporate tax (Mieszkowski, 1972).

The most comprehensive solution that has been put forth to many of the problems noted above is the proposal for 'full integration' of the corporate personal income taxes.[18] What Elysium would be like once attained is always an interesting question; so, however, is the cost of the journey. The relevant policy question is whether the presumed potential benefits of full integration − less distortion in private economic decisions and presumably a somewhat more equitable tax system − are sufficient to be worth incurring such costs as (1)

18. Even full integration of the corporate and personal income taxes would not in itself remove the financial structure and investment biases mentioned above. For that result to ensue, the tax at the corporate level would also have to be made 'neutral' as discussed in this section.

perceived and actual transitional inequities, (2) increased administrative and compliance costs, and (3) the possibly offsetting effects on equity and the efficiency of resource allocation arising from the need to make up the revenue loss with other, possibly even less desirable, taxes.

In view of the uncertainty of knowledge on most of the critical parameters in this problem — the incidence of the corporate tax, the response of the pay-out ratio to changes in corporate and personal taxes, the impact of pay-out changes on savings and investment, and so on — no clear answers can be given to this question at the present time. Moreover, the underlying rationale of integration — that corporate profits *as such* are not a suitable object of taxation — has recently been subject to increasing doubts for a number of reasons.

In particular, this rationale has been called into question by the advocates of a quite different solution to the problems with the corporation income tax under the name of a 'cash-flow' or 'flow-of-funds' corporate tax (Institute for Fiscal Studies, 1978). The background of this latest corporate tax reform proposal lies in the advocacy of a more fundamental reform in the personal tax system from an income to an expenditure base. In the past, it has generally been assumed that, as part of such a reform, the corporate tax should simply be abolished. The two 'ideal' proposals usually contrasted in the literature are thus those for a fully 'integrated' corporate and personal income tax system on the one hand and, on the other, a personal expenditure tax alone, with no corporation tax at all (Head and Bird, 1983).

More recently, however, it has been argued that whether the personal tax system is based on income or consumption, there is a strong case for a continued corporate tax — not just to act as a withholding tax on personal income but to tap economic rents, to reach the income of non-residents, and to provide an appropriate division of revenues between source and residence countries.[19] Many of those who hold these views argue that the efficiency merits of a cash-flow corporate tax make it a leading candidate to play such a role.

The usual textbook model of the investment decision of a firm suggests, for example, that the corporation income tax will discriminate against investment unless one of two conditions is satisfied. Either investment expenditures are deducted as expenses as soon as they occur and interest is not a deductible expense for tax purposes; or interest is deductible (on the full value of the existing capital stock, not just the actual financial interest payments in a period) and depreciation is allowed at the 'true' economic rate (that is, the rate at which the real value of capital deteriorates over time). In either case, for neutrality towards investment to be achieved, losses must be treated exactly symmetrically to profits, that is, there must be full loss-offset provisions. The 'ideal' (operational) corporate tax from this point of view thus appears to be one

19. See Boadway, Bruce and Mintz (1982); Musgrave (this volume) makes the last of these points.

permitting full expensing of investment, no interest deductibility, and full loss offset – in other words, the so-called 'cash flow' tax.

A change to any version of a cash-flow corporate tax, however, would involve an even more substantial upheaval in the present corporate tax than would full integration. The question, as always, is thus whether the result of the game is worth the transitional costs. The alleged full 'neutrality' of this tax once in full operation, for example, depends on perfect loss offset, perfectly functioning capital markets, and the applicability in the real world of the underlying (neoclassical) investment theory. None of these assumptions seems likely to hold completely in practice.

The world analyzed in the investment model underlying the conventional analysis, for example, is far from the real world, and it is difficult to apply conclusions based on the one to the other. The prevalence of uncertainty, the existence of personal taxes, and the interdependence of the economy as a whole, not least its openness, all make the policy relevance of the ideally 'neutral' tax system hard to fathom. The inference some have drawn from conventional analysis is that a major task of corporate tax reform is to move any absolute corporate tax as close as possible to the 'efficient' pure profits base, through such structural changes as a cash-flow tax. One might equally well conclude, however, as was done above with respect to integration, that the present state of economic theory offers no very clear guide as to what can, or should, be done with the corporation income tax.

The current state of professional thought on the role of corporation tax in an 'ideal' tax system may perhaps be summed up, with some trepidation, as follows. If there is a comprehensive personal income tax with full accrual capital gains taxation, there is no apparent need in terms of the comprehensive income tax approach for any tax at the corporate level at all, except for the taxation of non-residents. On the other hand, if capital gains are subject to full personal income tax rates only when realized, even an *unintegrated* corporate tax will be neutral with respect to the payout decision, provided its rate is equal to the marginal personal rate of shareholders.[20] To achieve full neutrality with respect to new shareholders, full integration may still be needed, however.[21]

The general professional consensus thus appears to be either that the corporate tax should in effect be abolished (at least for domestic firms) or that it should be reduced to a 'neutral' tax on 'pure' economic profits. As noted above, however, these arguments rest on a number of strong and suspect assumptions. Moreover, it is far from clear either in theory or in the real world,

---

20. See Bossons (1985); the argument is based on Auerbach (1979), who observed that shareholders face the same tax in present value terms whether earnings are distributed or not.
21. Alternatively, Bossons (1985) argues that allowing the deduction of new share purchases from taxable income will achieve neutrality in this case – with the added benefit of reducing the pressure to extend the benefits of integration to foreigners.

that the 'unneutrality' of the present corporate income tax is as out-and-out bad as it is usually made to appear.[22] Indeed, to the extent it is a tax on old wealth, as has recently been suggested, it may even constitute a particularly efficient and equitable part of the tax system (Auerbach, 1985).

On the whole, reforming corporate taxes, whether in the direction of partial integration or some other, to conform to textbook analysis requires more faith in the direct applicability of undiluted standard theory than seems warranted. Major changes should probably be made in existing tax systems only when their overall social and economic effects can be assumed with some degree of certainty to warrant the undeniable costs of such change. When viewed in this light, the case for abolishing, or even substantially reducing, the present absolute corporate tax burden by a move towards integration seems to be not only 'not proven' but not getting any stronger as time goes by. The case for integration underlying the EC's stated policy in this area thus seems considerably weaker than seems generally to be realized. The likelihood that every member country will voluntarily coalesce on a uniform system of corporate-personal tax integration thus seems little higher than the likelihood, discussed in the previous section, that mandatory adherence to a uniform community policy on this matter is either desirable or necessary.


## IV. The Political Economy of Integration and Harmonization

Shoup (1980) recently suggested that many of the interactions between tax systems in different countries might be characterized as either reaction effects or emulation effects. An example of a reaction effect is the introduction by Canada of the manufacturing and processing tax credit in reaction to the US DISC system – which was itself, of course, a reaction to the benefits US authorities perceived to be received by some European countries from their territorial income tax systems. An example of an 'emulation effect' is the spread of the imputation system in the EC. It is undoubtedly true that the increased international flow of tax information accompanying increased trade and factor flows has clearly influenced the nature of tax discussion in many countries. In no field has this been more true than in the area of international taxation.

It seems high time, however, that the discussion of international tax relations put aside the implicit notion underlying most of the literature in this field to the effect that tax policies are designed and implemented by unified central bureaucracies attempting to satisfy clearly identified national (or community) social welfare functions. In the real world, there are always conflicting interests

---

22. For arguments along these lines see Stiglitz (1973), Auerbach (1979), and Boadway and Wildasin (1984).

within each country, and the resolution of these conflicts domestically must be taken into account in shaping the international dimension of policy. The various international tax subsidies (and disincentives) which have been created in many countries in recent years, for instance, constitute a subset of the general protectionist trend of current policy, which is itself a sub-species of government intervention in general.

Indeed, from one perspective, the principal role of government in modern politics is as an instrument of cross-subsidization and price discrimination (Migue, 1982). There is no reason to exclude international tax policies from the ambit of this statement. When a barrier to international factor or trade flows is erected, it is inevitably attributable at least in part to the domestic political pressures exerted by those who expect to gain in terms of increased rents from the erection of that barrier. Similarly, when such a barrier is demolished or reduced, that fact in itself can be read as an indication of either the diminished influence of the group which originally had that barrier imposed, or the rise to power of some new group which gains from its reduction. From this perspective, the most useful way to approach the analysis of international tax relations may be not with the normative tool of economic efficiency, which dominates the economic literature, but rather with the tool of the new economic theory of politics.

Economists tend often to take economic efficiency to be the over-riding criterion in terms of which policy is to be assessed. The virtues of economic efficiency are indeed often grossly underrated these days by the advocates of protection, subsidy, and special interest whose voice is now heard so loudly throughout most lands. In the international arena, however, as in most spheres of life, focusing on 'world efficiency' (or even 'community efficiency') alone affords little help in understanding what is done, or not done, in the real world of the politics of economic policy. From this perspective, international tax relations may probably best be analyzed within the framework of general theory of government regulation as the outcome of conflicting private interests. This approach has sometimes been disparagingly labelled 'pocketbook politics'. But since taxation is, after all, in the end about whose pocket is picked for how much, it seems likely that the answers to be found by pursuing this approach in the tax field will prove to be more illuminating than yet another exposition of the virtues of capital-export neutrality from the point of view of worldwide allocative efficiency.

When considered in this light what is perhaps most surprising is not that there are so many complex, contradictory and unresolved issues in the field of international taxation, but rather that there is still such an apparently high degree of economic rationality underlying at least some key characteristics of the international tax system. Perhaps, however, this happy state of affairs reflects not so much the triumph of rationality over interest as the relative unimportance of international taxation in the period during which current policies were formulated. If so, both the greater salience of international fiscal relations in recent years and the apparently increasing acerbity of international economic relations in general suggest that the future may be quite different from the present as both domestic and international tax systems are more and more shaped to accommodate the clamour for protectionist policies of one sort or another.

In any event, the future of fiscal harmonization with respect to corporate-personal tax integration in the EC clearly hinges primarily on such broad matters as the political factors determining national policies toward integration and harmonization − and how those political factors affect tax relations will depend largely on the perceptions different groups have on their interests and their power to induce action in accordance with their beliefs. Indeed, it may not be too far-fetched to conclude that the real significance of any future progress towards interjurisdictional integration of corporate and personal income taxes in the EC may be its political symbolism rather than its economic effect. That is, such integration may not be a condition precedent to 'a more perfect union', as the conventional wisdom set out in the first paragraph of this paper suggests, but rather one of the results of closer political approximation to that state.

Alworth, Julian. 'A Cost of Capital Approach to the Taxation of Foreign Direct Investment Income.' June 1985.

Alworth, Julian. 'Taxation and the Cost of Capital: A Comparison of Six EC Countries.' Chapter 9, this volume, 1986.

Andel, Norbert. 'Directions of Tax Harmonization in the EEC.' In Cnossen, Sijbren (ed.). *Comparative Tax Studies*. Amsterdam: North-Holland, 1983.

Auerbach, Alan. 'Share Valuation and Corporate Equity Policy.' *Journal of Public Economics*, 11, 1979.

Auerbach, Alan. 'Integration with Corporate Tax.' In Mintz, Jack. *Report of the Policy Forum on Tax Reform and the Consumption Tax*. Kingston: John Deutsch Institute for the Study of Economic Policy, 1985.

Bieri, S. *Fiscal Federalism in Switzerland*. Canberra: Centre for Research on Federal Financial Relations, Australian National University, 1979.

Bird, Richard M. *Taxing Corporations*. Montreal: Institute for Research on Public Policy, 1980.

Bird, Richard M. 'Tax Harmonization and Federal Finance: A Perspective on Recent Canadian Discussion.' *Canadian Public Policy*, 10, 3, 1984.

Bird, Richard M. *Federal Finance in Comparative Perspective*. Toronto: Canadian Tax Foundation, 1986.

Bird, Richard M. and Brean, D.J.S. 'Canada-US Tax Relations: Issues and Perspectives.' In Fretz, Deborah, Stern, Robert and Whalley, John (eds). *Canada/United States Trade and Investment Issues*. Toronto: Ontario Economic Council, 1985.

Boadway, Robin and Bruce, Neil. 'The Personal Income Tax: Implications for Investments.' In Conklin, D.W. (ed.). *A Separate Personal Income Tax for Ontario: Background Studies*. Toronto: Ontario Economic Council, 1984.

Boadway, R. and Wildasin, D.E. *Public Sector Economics*, 2nd edn. Boston: Little, Brown and Company, 1984.

Boadway, Robin, Bruce, Neil and Mintz, Jack. 'Corporate Taxation in Canada: Toward an Efficient System.' In Thirsk, W. and Whalley, J. (eds). *Tax Policy Options in the 1980s*. Toronto: Canadian Tax Foundation, 1982.

Bossons, John. 'Inflation, Indexation, and the Capital Gains Tax.' Institute for Policy Analysis, University of Toronto, 1985.

Bucovetsky, Meyer and Bird, Richard M. 'Tax Reform in Canada: A Progress Report.' *National Tax Journal*, 25, March 1972.

Byrne, William J. and Sato, Mitsuo. 'The Domestic Consequences of Alternative Systems of Corporate Taxation.' *Public Finance Quarterly*, 4, July 1976.

Canadian Tax Foundation. *The National Finances 1984-85*. Toronto, 1985.

Cnossen, Sijbren. 'The Imputation System in the EEC.' In Cnossen, Sijbren (ed.). *Comparative Tax Studies: Essays in Honor of Richard Goode*. Amsterdam: North-Holland, 1983.

Cnossen, Sijbren. 'Alternative Forms of Corporate Tax.' *Australian Tax Forum*, 1, September 1984. Reprinted as 'Corporation Taxes in OECD Member Countries.' *Bulletin for International Fiscal Documentation*, 38, 11, 1984.

Commission of the European Communities. 'Proposal for a Directive of the Council concerning the Harmonization of Company Taxation and of Withholding Taxes on Dividends.' *European Taxation*, Nos. 2-4, 1976.

Commission of the European Communities. 'Report on the Scope for Convergence of Tax Systems in the Community.' *Bulletin of the European Communities*, Supplement 1, 1980.

Gourevitch, Harry G. 'Corporate Tax Integration: The European Experience.' *The Tax Lawyer*, 3, Fall 1977.

Groenewegen, Peter. 'Apportioning Taxation Powers in a Federation.' In Mathews, R.L. (ed.). *State Taxation in Theory and Practice*. Canberra: Centre for Research on Federal Financial Relations, Australian National University, 1981.

Hartle, Douglas G. *et al. A Separate Personal Income Tax for Ontario: An Economic Analysis*. Toronto: Ontario Economic Council, 1983.

Head, J.G. and Bird, R.M. 'Tax Policy Options in the 1980s.' In Cnossen, Sijbren (ed.). *Comparative Tax Studies*. Amsterdam: North-Holland, 1983.

Institute for Fiscal Studies. *The Structure and Reform of Direct Taxation*. London: George Allen and Unwin, 1978.

Kay, J.A. and King, M.A. *The British Tax System*. Oxford University Press, 1978.

Keating, Hon. Paul. *Reform of the Australian Taxation System*. Canberra: Australian Government Publishing Service, 1985.

King, Mervyn A. *Public Policy and the Corporation*. London: Chapman Hall, 1977.

Krauss, Mel. *Fiscal Harmonization in the Benelux Economic Union*. Amsterdam: International Bureau of Fiscal Documentation, 1969.

McLure, Charles E. Jr. *Must Corporate Income Be Taxed Twice?*. Washington DC: The Brookings Institution, 1979.

McLure, Charles E. Jr. 'International Aspects of Dividend Relief.' *Journal of Corporate Taxation*, 7, Summer, 1980.

McLure, Charles E. Jr. 'Assignment of Corporate Income Taxes in a Federal System.' In McLure, Charles E. Jr (ed.). *Tax Assignment in Federal Countries*. Canberra: ANU Press, 1983.

Mieszkowski, Peter. 'Integration of the Corporate and Personal Income Taxes: The Bogus Issue of Shifting.' *Finanzarchiv*, 31, 2, 1972.

Migue, Jean-Luc. 'Trade Barriers, Regulation and Bureaucratic Supply as Alternative Instruments of Wealth Transfers.' In Quinn, John, and Slayton, Philip (ed.). *Non-Tariff Barriers after the Tokyo Round*. Montreal: The Institute for Research on Public Policy, 1982.

Musgrave, Peggy B. 'Interjurisdictional Coordination of Taxes on Capital Income.' Chapter 7, this volume, 1986.

Neumark Report. *Tax Harmonization in the Common Market*. New York: Commerce Clearing House, Inc., 1963.

Norr, Martin. *The Taxation of Corporations and Shareholders*. Deventer: Kluwer Law and Taxation Publishers, 1982.

Organization for Economic Co-operation and Development (OECD). *Revenue Statistics of OECD Member Countries*. Paris, 1985.

Patrick, R.J. 'The Proposed Canada-United States Income Tax Treaty: Nondiscrimination, Mutual Agreement, and Exchange of Information.' *Report of Proceedings of the 32nd Tax Conference*. Toronto: Canadian Tax Foundation, 1981.

*Reform of the Australian Tax System*. Canberra: Australian Government Publishing Service, 1985.

Royal Commission on Taxation. *Report*. Ottawa, 1966.

Sato, Mitsuo, and Bird, Richard M. 'International Aspects of the Taxation of Corporations and Shareholders.' *IMF Staff Papers*, 22, 1975.

Short, R.A. 'Comment.' In *Report of Proceedings of the 32nd Tax Conference*. Toronto: Canadian Tax Foundation, 1981.

Shoup, Carl S. *Public Finance*. Chicago: Aldine Publishing Company, 1969.

Shoup, Carl S. 'Effects of U.S. Tax Laws on Tax Systems of Developing Countries.' In Hellawell, Robert (ed.). *United States Taxation and Developing Countries*. New York: Columbia University Press, 1980.

Stiglitz, Joseph. 'Taxation, Corporate Financial Policy, and the Cost of Capital.' *Journal of Public Economics*, 2, 1973.

Swan, Peter L. 'An Australian View on Tax Integration.' In Head, J.G. (ed.). *Taxation Issues of the 1980s*. Sydney: Australian Taxation Research Foundation, 1983.

*The President's Tax Proposals to the Congress for Fairness, Growth and Simplicity*. Washington DC: US Government Printing Office, 1985.

Thirsk, Wayne R. 'Tax Harmonization and its Importance in the Canadian Federation.' In Bird, R.M. (ed.). *Fiscal Dimensions of Canadian Federalism*. Toronto: Canadian Tax Foundation, 1980.

Tindemans, Leo. 'European Union.' *Bulletin of the European Communities*, Supplement 1/76, 1976.

Tresch, R.W. *Public Finance*. Plano, Texas: Business Publications, 1981.

US Department of the Treasury. *Blueprints for Basic Tax Reform*. Washington DC: US Government Printing Office, 1977.

US Department of the Treasury. *Tax Reform for Fairness, Simplicity, and Economic Growth*, 3 vols. Washington DC: 1984.

van den Tempel, A.J. *Corporation Tax and Individual Income Tax in the European Communities*. Brussels: Commission of the European Communities, 1970.

# 9

# Taxation and the cost of capital: a comparison of six EC countries

*Julian S. Alworth**

## I. Introduction

Differences in company tax systems across jurisdictions may have various effects on the allocation of resources over time and space. They may affect the decision on where to undertake capital outlays and the form which these should take. Companies may decide to construct and assemble various components of a particular final product in different jurisdictions in response to specific tax incentives. Moreover, tax considerations may play an important role in the financial decision of firms operating simultaneously in several tax jurisdictions. These factors are of greatest importance for large multinational companies, but in a world of increasingly unimpeded capital movements these considerations are likely to affect even smaller firms which have the freedom to decide on an investment and financing strategy which might straddle tax jurisdictions.

Another set of possible effects which can be attributed to differences in tax systems across countries concerns the relative ability of firms located in different jurisdictions to compete with one another. In the 1960s it was often argued that the reliance of most EC countries on destination-based product taxes provided a competitive advantage to firms from these countries over US firms. More recently, it has been argued that Japanese companies have a relative cost of capital advantage over their US competitors because of a more favorable tax system.[1]

Although this paper can be taken as a starting point for addressing some of these issues its focus is somewhat different from these highly charged issues. Its principal objective is to provide a cross-country comparison of the extent to

* This study is an extension of work presented in Alworth (1986). I wish to thank my discussants, Karl Häuser and Charles McLure, for their helpful comments. I am also very grateful to Sijbren Cnossen for his numerous suggestions which did much to improve a previous version of this paper. The views expressed in the paper are my own and not necessarily those of the Bank for International Settlements.
1. This view has been recently challenged by Ando and Auerbach (1985).

which the taxation of savings and investment continues to differ amongst EC countries despite various proposals and actual changes undertaken to harmonise the company tax system. Indeed this paper attempts to show that even if some of these proposed harmonisations were to be adopted wide differences amongst the various countries would continue to persist.

A major problem in undertaking such comparative studies is that the structure of the tax system can differ markedly between countries so that nominal tax rates cannot provide a guide to the actual incidence. A common way of circumventing this problem is to construct effective tax rates based on tax revenues from different sources of income.[2] Such values, however, suffer from two major drawbacks. The first is that tax rates derived in this manner are average rather than marginal rates and hence cannot be used for evaluating the incentive effects of the tax system. In addition, current tax receipts are less likely to reflect present tax laws than to be the result of the long history of past investments and tax provisions. The second major problem with using tax revenues to compute effective tax rates on investment and savings is that very little information is available concerning the distribution of the tax burden amongst individual projects, shareholders and companies. This is a serious drawback, since a peculiarity of most systems is the wide dispersion of effective tax rates found for different types of investment even when the most elementary type of disaggregation is undertaken.

This study is based on the recent work of King and Fullerton (1984) examining the tax laws in four countries (Germany, Sweden, the United Kingdom and the United States) in terms of simulated 'average marginal tax rates'. These effective rates of tax are derived as weighted averages from the 'tax wedge' between the pre-tax rate of return on investment (p) and the post-tax rate of return on savings (s) for a series of hypothetical projects. The strength of this approach does not lie only in its ability to make comparisons across countries, although this is probably one of the principal objectives which King and Fullerton initially set themselves. Rather, it leads to a reasoned dissection of various components affecting the ultimate tax burden on capital − the rates, the tax base, the integration between different taxes − and provides summary measures at a very disaggregated level of how these different provisions interact. This type of disaggregation had not been undertaken in previous studies on company tax harmonisation in the EC (see Musgrave, 1967; and Snoy, 1975). One of the most important implications resulting from the wide dispersion of effective tax rates which is found for different types of investment in each country is that tax harmonisation is a domestic as well as a Community issue.

The rest of this paper is divided into four sections. The first examines the tax

2. Two excellent studies of average tax rates on capital income and company profits are Feldstein, Dicks-Mireaux and Poterba (1983) and Kay and Sen (1984).

systems in the six major EC countries, viz. Belgium, France, Germany, Italy, the Netherlands and the United Kingdom. Its objective is to give an overview of different forms of capital taxation, highlighting the similarities and differences amongst these countries. This section also summarises these provisions in terms of simple tax parameters which can allow for a straightforward numerical computation of effective tax rates. The following section develops briefly the conceptual framework developed by King and Fullerton and explains further the measure of effective tax rates based on the tax parameters developed in Section II. Section IV describes the results of the simulations for these six countries and the implications for the objective of tax harmonisation amongst these six countries. The final section provides some short conclusions.

## II. The Taxation of Capital Income in the EC

### A. Company Tax Systems

The existence of different company tax systems and methods of tax integration means that nominal tax rates are not easily comparable across countries. This section looks at those elements of the system of company taxation which continue to differentiate the nominal tax rates of the six major countries in the EC.

### Systems of company tax integration

Much has been written about the different possible systems of integrating the personal and company tax systems (Cnossen, 1984). At one extreme, the tax liability of the company is entirely independent of that of its shareholders (classical system). At the other extreme, the company is viewed as being completely integrated with its shareholders and corporation tax serves solely as a prepayment of income tax. In between these two extreme cases lie a number of possible systems which partly integrate the taxes on companies and their shareholders. Broadly speaking, such integration can be achieved by a lower company tax on dividends (two-rate system), by regarding company tax as a prepayment of personal income taxes on dividends and allowing a credit against personal income tax up to a certain amount (imputation system), or by a mixture of these two methods.

With the exception of perfect integration, all of these systems have been adopted by some EC countries at one time or another. Over the years, however, there has been a considerable degree of convergence, and in some respects of harmonisation, in the company tax systems adopted by the EC countries although the proposals on harmonisation by various committees have varied considerably (Easson, 1980). At present, with the exception of the Netherlands and Luxembourg, all Member States have adopted some form of dividend integration along the lines of the imputation system proposed in a 1975 EC draft directive.

Although the systems of company taxation have been loosely harmonised, significant differences remain in the way in which the imputation systems work in practice, the rate at which profits are taxed, and the size of credit granted against personal tax. Some of the differences are brought out in Table 9.1, which compares the corporate tax systems of the EC countries in terms of two tax parameters. The first is the basic corporate tax rate $\tau$ – the rate of tax paid if no profits have been distributed. The second variable, $\theta$, is a measure of the degree of discrimination between retentions and gross dividends (G) before deduction of personal taxes. Its value equals the additional dividends which shareholders would receive if one unit of after (corporate) tax profits were distributed (gross of the tax credit). The total revenue (T) on taxable company profits (Y) and gross dividends before payment of personal tax is therefore given by

$$T = \tau Y + [(1 - \theta)/\theta]G$$

Under a classical system (such as in the Netherlands) the value of $\theta$ is unity, since no corporate tax is refunded to shareholders. Under the imputation system the value of $\theta$ exceeds unity by the extent of the tax credit which is granted ($\theta$-1). If the rate of imputation, known also as 'avoir fiscal', is s, the shareholder receives a gross dividend before personal tax equal to the cash dividend distributed times $[1 + s/(1-s)]$. When full imputation of the corporate tax is granted, as in Germany and Italy, dividends are fully deductible against profits and $\theta = 1/(1 - \tau)$.

As can be seen from Table 9.1, the values taken by $\tau$ and $\theta$ differ markedly between countries. The rate of tax on undistributed profits varies from 35 percent for the United Kingdom (as of 1987) to 56 percent (or 62 percent allowing for an estimate of local taxes) in the case of Germany. The value of $\theta$ ranges from 1 in the cases of Greece, Luxembourg and the Netherlands to 2.2727 in the case of Germany. The last column of the table illustrates the extent to which integration between the company tax and personal tax systems is achieved, i.e. the proportion of pre-tax profits earned which is ultimately received by a shareholder before payment of personal tax.

These variables can also be employed to assess the nominal tax burden on distributed equity income before personal tax, i.e. $1 - (1 - \tau)\theta$. According to this criterion, there appear to be three broad groups of countries: (a) those countries which follow a classical system and which have the highest nominal tax burden;[3] (b) those countries which follow an imputation system but where the

3. In Luxembourg, a much more favorable tax system applies to holding companies.

*Table 9.1 Corporate tax variables in the major EC countries, 1985*

| Country | $\tau$ | $\theta$ | $(1-\tau)\theta$ |
|---|---|---|---|
| Belgium[a] | 0.45[b] | 1.40875 | 0.7748 |
| France | 0.50 | 1.5 | 0.75 |
| Denmark | 0.40 | 1.25 | 0.75 |
| Germany | 0.56/0.62[c] | 2.2727 | 1.0/0.8636 |
| Greece | 0.485[d] | 1.0 | 0.515 |
| Ireland | 0.50[e] | 1.4286 | 0.7143 |
| Italy | 0.36/0.4637[c] | 1.5625 | 1.0/0.8380 |
| Luxembourg | 0.40/0.473[c,f] | 1.0 | 0.6/0.527 |
| Netherlands | 0.43[g] | 1.0 | 0.57 |
| United Kingdom | 0.35[h] | 1.4286 | 0.9286 |
| *United States* | 0.46/0.4950[c] | 1.0 | 0.54/0.505 |

*Notes:*
a. As of 1985, the Belgian authorities allow the 'précompte mobilier' withholding tax as a final payment of tax if individuals choose not to declare dividend income. In these cases the value of $\theta$ should equal unity and the marginal personal tax rate is 0.25. Individuals with marginal tax rates exceeding 46.8 percent would prefer this final form of payment.
b. This rate applies to taxable income in excess of B.fr. 1.44 million.
c. Including local income taxes levied on corporate income. Germany and Luxembourg: Gewerbesteuer; Italy: I.L.O.R.; United States: average rate of state income tax.
d. Including 15 percent deductible surcharge. $\theta$ excludes the withholding tax on dividends.
e. This rate applies to taxable income in excess of Ir.L. 35,000.
f. These rates apply to taxable income in excess of L.fr. 1.312 million.
g. This rate applies to taxable income in excess of Fl. 40,000.
h. Tax rate effective from fiscal year ending March 31, 1986 as proposed in the 1984 Budget. Until that date the rates are to be reduced by five percent a year during a phasing-in period. The rate for fiscal year ending March 31, 1985 is 45 percent.

*Sources:* Cnossen (1984) and *European Taxation.*

integration of personal and company tax is not fully achieved for all income tax brackets (Belgium, France, Denmark and Ireland); (c) finally, those countries with a high degree of integration (Germany and Italy).

These tax parameters in isolation cannot, however, be employed to assess the nominal tax burden on firms. In practice, three additional factors need to be borne in mind in determining the nominal tax burden from the summary rates of tax shown in Table 9.1.

Personal taxes

The first factor is the existence of personal taxes. The amount of dividends after tax received by individual or institutional shareholders depends on the marginal tax paid by these investors. This has the effect of, *ceteris paribus*, raising the cost of funds to firms, the precise manner of which is discussed in Section III. Furthermore, the structure of personal tax rates may affect the composition of finance and the types of investment projects which are chosen by firms (Auerbach, 1983). In addition, since marginal rates vary considerably across shareholders, they are likely to give rise to different views as to desirable financial policy and in other cases to tax arbitrages across financial instruments.

## Tax losses

The second factor which needs to be considered for evaluating the effects of different values of $\tau$ and $\theta$ on company decisions is the treatment of tax losses. All tax systems in the EC display considerable asymmetries with regard to the treatment of gains and losses. If the firm is making tax losses ('tax exhausted'), no outright refunds are generally available, and only in Germany, the Netherlands and the United Kingdom can losses be carried backwards against profits from previous years. Carry-forward provisions exist in almost all countries, but they are incomplete to the extent that losses cannot be carried forward with interest and, with the exception of the United Kingdom, cannot be carried forward indefinitely. These limitations on loss offset may have a significant impact on the actual capital costs of firms by reducing the advantages of various tax incentives and by raising the cost of debt finance. The principal effect of losses, however, is to change the effective value of $\tau$ and to render it a complicated function of the timing of taxable income (see Mayer, 1986).

Another important consequence of tax losses is that in many countries the value of $\theta$ is set equal to unity, as is the case for franked investment (or tax-exempt) income. This is particularly true under the imputation system, where company tax is viewed as a partial prepayment of personal tax and the credit is granted only to the extent that the underlying company tax has actually been paid. Whilst the treatment of franked investment income varies, most EC countries (including France, Germany, Italy and the United Kingdom) have adjusted the tax credit under the imputation system to take account of the problems arising from this particular source of income.[4]

---

4. Although $\theta$ equals unity for preference income in all countries adopting the imputation system, the precise manner in which this value is achieved varies significantly. In France a compensatory tax ('précompte mobilier') is levied at the corporate level on any income distributed to shareholders that has not borne the full rate of company tax. In terms of the parameters described in the text this supplementary tax is given by

$$s[G - \frac{(1 - \tau)}{(1 - s)}y]$$

where s is the rate at which gross dividends are deemed to have been taxed.

As of end-1983, a similar system has been adopted in Italy. In the United Kingdom this rôle is assigned to the 'advance corporation tax'. Under the German system all distributed dividends →

The values of $\tau$ and $\theta$ shown in Table 9.1 apply only to the taxation of domestic investments. Portfolio and direct foreign investment are taxed differently and there is no uniform rule within the EC. Furthermore, double taxation agreements – especially the articles covering branches – often result in a non-uniform treatment of income across capital-importing and capital-exporting countries (see Alworth, 1986).

Foreign branches are often subject to special tax rates in the capital-importing countries, and in the home country their profits are in many cases consolidated with those of the parent. In the case of inward investments, subsidiaries are treated like domestic companies in the capital-importing country for corporation taxes, but the value of $\theta$ on distributions to the parent company may differ from those to domestic shareholders (and foreign portfolio investors). Again this issue is particularly relevant for the imputation system, because the tax credit cannot be recovered by the host country's tax authorities. For both direct and portfolio investment, the effective value of $\theta$ is generally set to unity or less because tax credit is not extended to foreign shareholders or because a high compensatory withholding tax is levied.[5]

In the case of outward direct investment through subsidiaries the value of $\tau$ does not correspond to that for domestic investment in the home country, since the system of double taxation relief practised in most countries allows for deferral of tax until earnings are repatriated or exemption from tax applies (see Bird, this volume). In both cases $\tau$ takes the value of the tax rate on profits in the host country. The value of $\theta$, however, depends on the interaction between the tax systems in the host and home countries. Under the deferral system which allows for a credit against underlying company taxes paid abroad (including the withholding tax on dividend repatriations), the value of $\theta$ depends in a complex way on the interaction between the company tax systems in the two countries. In the case of the exemption system only the taxes on repatriated earnings are on the ultimate dividend redistributions to shareholders in the parent country (see Table 9.2). Finally, in the home country, dividend distributions deemed to

---

→
are taxed at a lower rate, but the value of $\theta$ is no longer 2.27 since these dividend payments do not reduce company taxable income. A thorough discussion of the implications of franked investment income for the imputation system is given in McLure (1979) and Cnossen (1984). For some of the issues raised recently by preference income in the Italian case, see Paladini (1985).

5. An important exception is the French-German double tax agreement where for portfolio investment the tax credit is passed on to the final shareholder. The EC directive envisages that such a system be established by all Member States.

come from foreign income are often treated differently if there is a system of dividend integration.[6]


## B. Depreciation Allowances and Investment Incentives

Provisions for depreciation and investment incentives granted on both fixed investment and investment in inventories play a major role in the determination of the actual burden of company taxes and the way companies are affected by taxes in making their investment decisions. This is probably the area in which the differences amongst countries are most marked and in which it is most difficult to make comparisons across countries. Significant further distortions not captured in this study may arise because different assets depreciate at many different rates while tax codes tend to simplify by grouping assets into few categories.

Most countries operate various systems of allowances concurrently and allow wide discretion over which one is employed. It is, however, difficult to distinguish between standard and accelerated depreciation practices, since similar systems of depreciation are regarded differently in each country. In addition, within each country geographical and sectoral incentives, some of which do not go through the tax system, further magnify the differences in tax provisions across asset types. As a result of statistical deficiencies, most of these differences examined in this section relate to the computation of depreciation allowances, to tax lives and to general investment incentives.[7] The additional complexities arising from regional and sectoral incentives are only treated in some specific cases.

The measurement of the value of tax depreciation allowances is complex because it must inevitably involve the discounting of future cash flows. One way of deriving a comparative measure of the tax allowances across countries is to take the present value (A) of all forms of allowances and tax incentives granted over the lifetime of an asset. Following King and Fullerton (1984) such an expression can be decomposed into three parts: (1) $A_d$, the present value of depreciation allowances after the period in which the initial investment is made. These allowances can take various forms, such as straightline, declining balance, etc.; (2) immediate expensing or free depreciation granted at a rate $\tau$;

---

6. The value of $\theta$ generally corresponds to that applicable on franked investment income.
7. A number of other provisions which might affect specific types of investment are also not examined. These comprise amongst others such sectors as mineral exploration and R&D. Furthermore a number of specific differences amongst countries in the manner in which depreciation allowances can be taken, such as the definition of initial period for which depreciation allowances are granted and the provisions for liquidation and sale, are not described.

Table 9.2 Systems of double tax relief: values of $\theta$, $\tau$ and $\theta(1-\tau)$

| General Tax Parameters | Credit, No Deferral | Credit with Deferral | Exemption[a] |
|---|---|---|---|
| $\theta$ | $\theta_h$ | $\theta_h \dfrac{(1-\tau_h)}{1-\tau_a}$ | $\theta_h\theta_a$ |
| $\tau$ | $\tau_h$ | $\tau_a$ | $\tau_a$ |
| $\theta(1-\tau)$[b] | $\theta_h(1-\tau_h)$ | $\theta_h(1-\tau_h)$ | $\theta_h\theta_a(1-\tau_a)$ |

*Notes:* Profits in the host country are taxed at a rate $\tau_a$; the opportunity cost of retaining in the host country in terms of net (of withholding tax) dividends is equal to $\theta_a$. Hence $\theta_a$ equals the additional dividends shareholders could receive if one unit of post-corporate tax earnings were distributed to the parent company. In the home country double taxation relief can be given on taxes paid in the host country in three ways:

(1) Credit no deferral: the tax rate on foreign income is $\tau_h$ but all foreign taxes can be credited. Profits are, therefore, taxed at a rate $\tau_h$. Gross dividends on the foreign income received by the shareholders in the parent country depend in turn on $\theta_h$.

(2) Credit with deferral: taxation is deferred until repatriation of dividends. Hence, $\tau = \tau_a$. When dividends are repatriated they are grossed-up by the underlying taxes borne abroad; domestic profits tax is levied on this amount and credit granted on foreign taxes paid. If dividends are distributed from these earnings $\theta_h$ applies as in the previous case.

(3) Exemption: if foreign taxes are exempt from domestic taxes, $\tau = \tau_a$. Dividend distributions are only subject to tax if they are redistributed to shareholders in the home country.

If $\tau_h < \tau_a$ most countries limit the credit to the domestic tax and operate like an exemption system ('overspill')

a. Also for 'excess credits' or 'overspill' under the credit system with or without deferral.
b. Assuming full repatriation and redistribution of dividends.

(3) cash grants (equivalent to tax credits given at a rate g). If we denote the proportions of a project qualifying for the different forms of incentives as respectively $f_1$, $f_2$, and $f_3$, then

$$A = f_1 A_d + f_2\tau + f_3 g$$

This equation can allow for the whole range of tax allowances and investment incentives relating to the manner in which expenditure on assets can be deducted throughout their useful lives.

# Depreciation allowances and tax lives

Tables 9.3 and 9.4 examine the systems of standard and accelerated depreciation in the six major EC countries. With the exception of buildings, for which most countries require straightline depreciation, the tax laws set guidelines rather than strict norms as to the useful lives and method of depreciation to be followed. In some cases, such as France and Italy, the tax authorities also allow a shortening of the normal tax useful lives if physical or technical obsolescence can be proved. As can be seen from Table 9.3, the useful lives for most assets are generally the same in all countries. The only two countries where useful lives tend to differ are Italy, particularly for buildings, and the United Kingdom where in theory equipment has an infinite life.

As shown in Table 9.4, standard depreciation allowances and systems of accelerated depreciation tend to vary. In most countries, straightline depreciation is the most common benchmark, providing for a yearly constant deduction on the initial value of the assets at a rate given by the inverse of the tax lifetime (L) of the specified asset. The present value of this deduction of $1/L$ per year discounted at a rate $\rho$ is given by (in continuous time u)

$$A_d = {}_0\!\int^L \tau(1/L)e^{-\rho u}du$$

$$= \tau(1-e^{-\rho L})\rho L$$

*Table 9.3 Indicative tax lifetimes of assets in the major EC countries, 1985*

| Country | Industrial Buildings | Furniture and Fixings | Office Machinery | Vehicles | Plant and Equipment |
|---|---|---|---|---|---|
| Belgium[a] | 20 | 10 | 5 | 4 - 5 | 10 |
| France[b] | 20 | 10 | 5 - 10 | 4 - 5 | 5 - 10 |
| Germany[c] | 25 - 50 | 10 | 5 | 4 | 10 |
| Italy | 14 | 8.3 | 8.3 | 3.3 - 5 | 8.3 |
| Netherlands[d] | 25 - 50 | 10 | 10 | 3.3 - 5 | 10 |
| United Kingdom | 25 | _[e] | _[e] | _[e] | _[e] |

*Notes:* a. Under straightline depreciation method. The lifetimes are agreed between the taxpayer and the authorities. For commercial buildings lifetimes are generally set at 33 years.
b. No official lifetimes. These lifetimes are those generally adopted, although shorter ones are allowed if a higher rate of use of the asset can be proved.
c. With the exception of buildings these lifetimes are not compulsory.
d. Lifetimes generally followed.
e. With the exception of buildings, depreciation is on a declining balance at 25 percent on the pool of depreciable assets. This amounts to an infinite lifetime, although in practice almost 90 percent of an individual asset is in fact depreciated by the end of the sixth year.

*Source: European Taxation.*

*Table 9.4 Systems of depreciation allowances in the major EC countries, 1985*

| Country | System |
|---|---|
| Belgium | Straightline at rate 1/L; or double - declining balance at rate $\alpha=2/L$ with switchover at time T to straightline when $T=L(1-\alpha)/\alpha$. |
| France[a] | Straightline[b] at rate 1/L; or declining balance at different rates $(\alpha)$ and switchover to straightline at time T depending on tax lifetimes of assets as follows:<br>$\alpha = 1.5/L$ for asset with useful life of 3-4 years<br>$\alpha = 2.0/L$ for asset with useful life of 5-6 years<br>$\alpha = 2.5/L$ for asset with useful life of >6 years<br>switchover to straightline when $T=L(1-\alpha)/\alpha$. |
| Germany | Straightline[c] at rate 1/L; or accelerated depreciation declining balance at a maximum rate $\alpha=3/L$ with switchover at time T to straightline when $T=L(1-\alpha)/\alpha$. |
| Italy | Straightline. Accelerated depreciation may be claimed on up to 45 percent of cost spread over three years after the date of purchase subject to a maximum of 15 percent each year. |
| Netherlands | A number of methods are permissible amongst which are straightline and declining balance. For all industrial buildings (excepting hotels) only straightline is permissible. Double-declining balance is assumed in simulations for all other assets. |
| United Kingdom | For buildings straightline at a rate (1/L); for other assets declining balance at a rate $\alpha=0.25$. |

*Notes:* See text for explanation of symbols. Starting time of depreciation may differ amongst countries. In most cases the system of depreciation is agreed between the taxpayer and the authorities. There is no system of inflation accounting for depreciation allowances in any of these countries. In the Netherlands, however, companies can deduct a percentage of net worth from taxable income as compensation for price increases. Revaluations of depreciable assets, however, have been allowed twice in Italy during the recent past (in 1975 and 1983, by the 'Visentini' decrees).

    a. Special allowances are available for investments in capital assets made during the period January 1, 1983 - December 1, 1985. The first two years of depreciation allowances are increased by a cumulative figure equal to 40-42 percent of a first full year of depreciation.

    b. With few exceptions, compulsory for buildings and all assets with useful lives under three years.

    c. Compulsory for buildings. All other assets may be depreciated under either method.

*Source: European Taxation.*

In practice most countries allow firms to depreciate equipment at higher rates than those dictated by the straightline method. The most common method permitted is generally a variant of declining balance depreciation, whereby assets are depreciated at a constant rate on their remaining value. The operation of the declining balance system and the rates granted vary from country to country. In most countries, declining balance is computed as a multiple of the straightline useful life with a switchover to straightline at some point of the asset's useful life. In Belgium this multiple is two, in Germany it is three and in France the value of this parameter differs according to the useful life of the asset. The United Kingdom is unique in that all assets excepting buildings are pooled together and depreciated on a declining balance at a rate of 25 percent per annum. Finally, in Italy a maximum rate of 15 percent is granted for the first three years of life of the asset with a switchover to straightline for the remaining life of the asset. The actual formulas for declining balance employed in the simulations reported in Section IV are described in greater detail in King and Fullerton (1984) and have been adjusted to account for the specific country provisions described in Table 9.4.

A feature common to all tax systems in EC countries is that depreciation has to be calculated on the historical cost of the asset. Replacement cost is not allowed by any of the countries, although in some, revaluations can be made on certain special occasions, such as mergers. In Italy, however, general asset revaluations have recently been allowed on two separate occasions. In the Netherlands there is a system of compensating for the loss in the real value of assets whereby a percentage of a company's net wealth is deductible from taxable income.[8]

In conclusion it appears that whilst there is a broad consensus with regard to the allowable type of depreciation methods there is a wide variation in practice. This variation is particularly marked for equipment for which a wide range of depreciation rates are applicable.


Investment incentives

An area in which EC countries differ markedly is that of investment incentives over and above those discussed in the previous section (see Table 9.5). These differences concern the type of incentive given, the eligibility requirements (the sectoral and regional qualifications), the size of the benefits and, finally, whether these incentives are given as a reduction of tax or as cash grants. The most important national incentives are given in Belgium, France and the Netherlands. France and Belgium allow a percentage of the value of investments to be deducted from the tax base. In the Netherlands there is a system analogous to a tax credit. In all three countries the rates at which these incentives are given vary according to the size of the company.

Most of the incentives, however, are specific to particular sectors and geographical areas. With the exception of the United Kingdom and Germany, where the quantification of such incentives has been provided by King and Fullerton (1984), and Italy, where figures have been estimated from information reported in Marotta and Schiantarelli (1983), it was not possible to collect information on the value of these specific incentives. The value of the existing incentives as shown in Table 9.5 is therefore somewhat understated.

---

8. In 1985 this deduction (vermogensaftrek) amounted to 4 percent of a company's net wealth measured at book value for tax purposes. This deduction is not considered in the simulations reported in Section IV.

*Table 9.5 Incentives for investment in machinery and buildings in the major EC countries, 1985*

| Country | System |
|---|---|
| Belgium | Investment deduction of 13 percent of acquisition cost.<br>Additional regional and sectoral incentives not quantified.<br>$f_3=0; f_2=0.13$. |
| France | Investment deduction of 10 percent of investment.<br>Additional regional and sectoral incentives not quantified.<br>$f_3=0; f_2=0.1$. |
| Germany | For a description of the system of grants and other incentives see King and Fullerton (1984). The value of the incentive is given by $g=0.021$ for manufacturing and 0.007 for the other industries.<br>$f_2=0; f_3=1$. |
| Italy | No generalised incentives other than those mentioned in the text.<br>Regional and some sectoral incentives very generous but not quantified.<br>$f_2=0; f_3=1; g=0.1$. |
| Netherlands[a] | The grants have the character of an investment tax credit at a rate of 12.5 percent. $(g=0.125; f_3=1)$. |
| United Kingdom | For a description of the system of grants and regional incentives in manufacturing and other industry see King and Fullerton (1984).<br>In these two sectors $g=0.1946$ for machinery and $g=0.1476$ for buildings.<br>The value of $f_3$ is as follows: |

|  | Manufacturing | Other industry |
|---|---|---|
| Machinery | 0.323 | 0.004 |
| Buildings | 0.831 | 0.007 |

*Note:* a. Law on Investment Incentives (WIR). A general basic premium and a number of special bonuses are granted for qualifying investments. The basic values shown in the table are increased for small companies. There are also special sectoral incentives.

*Source: European Taxation.*

## Inventories

The effective tax burden on firms also depends on the rules governing the valuation of inventories. During each accounting period, the book value of inventories can vary because of changes in volume or price. To the extent that changes in price reflect changes in the general level of prices, such gains and losses are fictitious and not part of the real profits. If the tax authorities follow historical cost or traditional fifo (first-in-first-out) valuation methods, these nominal gains are taxed as they accrue. At present only the United Kingdom operates on a fifo valuation basis. This is somewhat paradoxical, given that prior to 1984 relief for price increases had been at times extremely generous and, in certain years, relief was granted for the entire increase in the book value of inventories.[9]

9. See King and Fullerton (1984, p. 44) for a short description of the history of stock relief in the United Kingdom. The present system is described in detail in Edwards (1984).

In contrast to fifo, the lifo (last-in-first-out) method allows price increases to be deferred almost indefinitely. This system is adopted at the discretion of the company in Belgium, Italy and the Netherlands. Consequently, for these countries the proportion (v) of inventories taxed according to historical cost is nil.

Between the United Kingdom and these three countries are France and Germany where partial compensation for price increases is allowed according to complex formulae. Recourse is had to these types of partial adjustments because lifo is not permitted by law. In Germany the system adopted results in roughly 50 percent of price increases being taxable.[10] The French system allows for deferral of tax for price increases exceeding 10 percent over a two-year period.

The above discussion suggests that much needs to be done in this area to harmonise practices and that during periods of moderate or high inflation there will be marked differences in the way in which companies are taxed on the changes in the value of their inventories.

## C. Personal Income Tax

### Households

As shown in Table 9.6, an important feature of some EC countries is the use of schedular taxes for different forms of capital income to exclude these sources of income from the base for the computation of the progressive income tax. In Italy, for example, a withholding tax is accepted as final payment of tax for interest received on bank deposits (25 percent), bonds issued by special credit institutions (12.5 percent) and convertible bonds (12.5 percent). To some extent this system is a remnant of the pre-1974 tax system, and there are indications that the multiplicity of rates is slowly being eliminated (see Paladini, 1985). In other countries the differences in rates according to the source of capital income reflect an attempt on the part of governments to channel savings into particular sectors and especially to help raise funds to finance large public-sector deficits. In Belgium the recent introduction of the 'précompte liberatoire' at a rate of 25 percent on dividend distributions and on most forms of interest income is more surprising, since Belgium was the first EC country to introduce the imputation system in the recent past.[11] For dividend income this withholding tax effectively

10. The system entails an averaging of opening and closing prices over the accounting period. A description of this method is given in King and Fullerton (1984).
11. The United Kingdom had a system analogous to the imputation system before the introduction of Corporation Tax in 1965.

places a ceiling on the marginal tax rates significantly below the highest rates on personal income taxes.

The estimates of personal marginal tax rates on all forms of capital income not subject to such withholding taxes were rather problematic, since in most cases it was not possible to obtain reliable information on the distribution of taxable income. It is for this reason that many of the estimates reported in Section IV assume a zero marginal tax rate in order to allow a better comparability of the company tax systems across countries.

## Tax-exempt institutions

Tax-exempt institutions do not represent a uniform grouping.[12] The Netherlands and the United Kingdom are notable for the important role played by pension funds as a channel of tax-exempt savings. This status of the pension funds has resulted in a substantial and growing portion of savings in these two countries being virtually exempt of tax.

In most other countries the tax-exempt status of pension funds and other institutions such as religious organisations, foundations, and trade unions is less extensive. In several countries the benefits of the tax credit under the imputation system are not available although no additional taxes are levied. This is the case in Italy, France and to some extent in Germany. Moreover, in Germany some of the tax-exempt institutions (such as trade unions) must pay an additional flat-rate withholding tax.

## Insurance companies

Different branches of the insurance industry are taxed in different manners. For ordinary 'nonlife' insurance the company tax rates generally apply. Income of life insurance companies, however, is in most instances subject to a somewhat different regime since it comes close to having the status of earnings on pension funds. With the exception of the United Kingdom and Germany (see King and Fullerton, 1984) specific information on the tax treatment of insurance companies was, however, not obtainable. Accordingly personal savings through this medium have been treated as being tax-exempt.

---

12. See Tanzi (1984, chap. 1, annex 1) for a description of the various types of institutions treated as tax exempt in various countries.

## Table 9.6 Average marginal tax rates (m) on different types of investors and financial instruments in the major EC countries, 1985

| Country and Investor | Type of finance | | |
| --- | --- | --- | --- |
| | Debt | New Shares | Retained Earnings |
| Belgium[a] | | | |
| Households | 0.25 | 0.226/0.514 | 0.226/0.514 |
| Tax-exempt | 0.25 | 0/0.29 | 0/0.29 |
| Insurance companies[f] | 0.225 | 0/0.225 | 0/0.225 |
| France[b] | | | |
| Households | 0.503 | 0.503 | 0.503 |
| Tax-exempt | 0 | 0.33 | 0.33 |
| Insurance companies[f] | 0.25 | 0.25 | 0.25 |
| Germany[c] | | | |
| Households | 0.398 | 0.480 | 0.480 |
| Tax-exempt | 0 | 0.400 | 0.400 |
| Insurance companies | 0.028 | 0.028 | 0.028 |
| Italy[d] | | | |
| Households | 0.25 | 0.50 | 0.50 |
| Tax-exempt | 0.25 | 0.36 | 0.36 |
| Insurance companies[f] | 0.18 | 0.18 | 0.18 |
| Netherlands[e] | | | |
| Households | 0.40 | 0.40 | 0.40 |
| Tax-exempt | 0 | 0 | 0 |
| Insurance companies[f] | 0.215 | 0.215 | 0.215 |
| United Kingdom[c] | | | |
| Households | 0.3055 | 0.4500 | 0.4500 |
| Tax-exempt | 0 | 0 | 0 |
| Insurance companies | 0.2328 | 0.1765 | 0.1765 |

Notes:  a. The estimates of average marginal tax rates for households are based on the official tax schedule for 1984 and the shares of capital income for each income class in 1982 (appropriately revalued) as reported in *Statistiques Financières* No. 34 (Institut National de Statistique, 1984). The lower of the two values for new share issues and retained earnings assumes that households with marginal tax rates above 46.8 percent choose to pay the 'précompte liberatoire'. In the simulations reported below, the value of $\theta$ in these cases is assumed to be unity. Interest income for households and tax-exempt institutions is taxed at the rate of the précompte liberatoire.

b. The value of the average marginal tax rates for households is based on the official tax schedules for 1984; the shares of capital income for each income class are those for 1982 as reported in 'Impôt sur le revenu en 1981 et 1982', *Statistiques et Études Financières* No. 394. The value of m for tax-exempt institutions assumes that no refunds are available.

c. Estimates as given in King and Fullerton (1984).

d. No statistics available on distribution of dividend income in Italy. Log-normal distribution with a mean income of Lit. 20 million and a standard deviation of .1 was assumed in order to compute the average marginal tax rate. Interest income is assumed to bear only the 'imposta sostitutiva' at a rate of 25 percent.

e. Estimates for marginal tax rates on households computed as for Italy. Mean income was assumed to be Fl. 38,000.

f. In the absence of more detailed information it is assumed that insurance companies can set aside a tax-free reserve for up to 50 percent of their taxable income. Rates shown in the table assume that the earnings of insurance companies are taxed at a rate equal to $.5\tau$.

## D. Capital Gains Taxes

Many EC countries levy taxes on the capital gains accruing to firms at rates close to those on other profits. Such taxes can be particularly important for certain firms and in some countries have been at the centre of much discussion, especially as regards the taxation of foreign exchange gains and losses. The simulations reported in Section IV do not make allowance for these taxes.

In the case of capital gains taxes on individuals, whilst several countries levy capital gains taxes on the sale of substantial holdings in companies, only two countries levy capital gains taxes on smaller holdings of shares. In both France and the United Kingdom these taxes are levied on realisation (respectively at rates of 15 and 30 percent), so that the actual rate on an accrual basis is much lower. In order to allow for this deferral benefit in the simulations reported in Section IV the statutory rate ($z_s$) is transformed to an effective tax rate ($z$). For this purpose we use a simple model of investor behaviour which assumes that a fixed proportion ($\lambda$) of an investor's portfolio is realised in every time period. The present value of the stream of tax payments ($z$) resulting from a unit of accrued gains is given by

$$z = \lambda z_s / (\lambda + \rho)$$

where $\rho$ is the investor's nominal discount rate.

## E. Wealth Taxes

### Wealth taxes on companies

Only Germany levies national taxes on the net wealth of companies.[13] Local taxes on company wealth or on immovable fixed assets are, however, quite common. Within each country the rates of tax differ, often widely, between local authorities. In Germany, for example, a basic parameter is established at the national level but within limits the local authorities can set coefficients to adjust this national rate. Valuations and assessments also vary, and only in rare cases are market values reasonably approximated. In the Netherlands, for example, some property assessments are based on market values whilst others are based on area. In Germany, revaluations are rare and adjustments to approximate market values are made at irregular intervals. Under these circumstances cross-country comparisons become arduous, and of necessity very rough estimates of the wealth tax rates actually charged have been

---

13. Net wealth is computed net of outstanding debt. This provides an incentive to debt finance for German companies in addition to the deductibility of interest expense from corporation tax.

269

employed in the simulations. The rates vary from 0.29 percent in Germany to 2.46 percent in the United Kingdom for buildings. Inventories and equipment are taxed only in Germany and at a rate of 0.96 percent.

In assessing the relative effect of these taxes it is important to realise that in many instances they are likely to reflect differences in the expenditure patterns of the local authorities. It is also important to note that no substantial harmonisation of local taxation appears likely amongst EC countries in the future.

## Stamp duties and registration taxes

New issues of shares or other forms of increase in the capital of firms are generally subject to stamp duty or registration tax at a rate of 1 percent (excepting Italy where the rate is 1.5 percent). Whilst these taxes are generally considered as payment for a service undertaken by the state (benefit taxes), their effect on company financial policy is to lower the attractiveness of new share issues relative to other means of finance. In terms of the parameters developed in previous sections these duties have the effect of reducing the value of $\theta$.[14]

## Personal wealth taxes

The final tax considered in this paper is the net wealth tax on individuals. In Germany and the Netherlands such taxes have been a prominent feature of the tax system for a long time, whilst in France the tax was introduced by the Socialist government in 1982. The latter country is also alone in levying the tax at progressive rates. On the other hand, the exemption limits in Germany and the Netherlands are rather low in comparison with those applying in France. In the Netherlands wealth taxes cannot exceed 80 percent of total taxes levied on an individual. The estimated rates of wealth tax have accordingly been taken as follows: France (1 percent), Germany (0.5-0.7 percent), Netherlands (0.8 percent).

---

14. Taxes on the purchase of securities are not considered in this paper since they affect transactions on outstanding instruments rather than the raising of capital for new investments. The ease with which marketable securities can be issued, however, depends to a large extent on the depth and liquidity of secondary markets. The existence of these taxes and other costs with sharply increasing returns to scale for the size of the transaction explains some of the differences in the structure of securities' markets in different countries. This would appear to be an area in which a closer convergence of practices and a general lowering of costs would be likely to give rise to appreciable benefits. See Jackson and O'Donnell (1985) for a study of the effects of stamp duty on the prices of British shares.

# III. The Theoretical Framework

## A. Effective Tax Rates

The incentive effects of taxation on investment and saving decisions examined in this study take into account the interaction between the personal and company taxes on both income and wealth, the effects of inflation on the tax base and the influence of other tax provisions affecting saving and investment decisions. The summary measure used to capture the effect of all these provisions taken together is the difference between the pre-tax rate of return on a hypothetical marginal investment project denoted by p and the after-tax real rate of return s to the ultimate investor (whether a household or institution). The 'distortion' induced by the tax system is the extent to which the return on the project differs from the real return on the investment. The effective tax rate which is employed to assess this distortion is given by

$$t = (p - s)/p$$

The value of t varies according to the type of project considered because of differences in tax incentives, tax rates and definitions of tax base for different types of assets used in different industries. It also varies because the tax system discriminates amongst alternative types of finance as regards both corporate and personal taxes. This study attempts to capture the range of variation which continues to exist both within and across the major EC countries. The characteristics according to which individual projects are allowed to vary in this study are as follows: (a) type of asset (machinery, buildings, inventories); (b) industry (manufacturing, other industry, commerce); (c) source of finance (debt, new share issues, retentions); ownership category (households, tax-exempt institutions, insurance companies).

## B. The Return on Saving

The link between the saver and the company that carries out the investment is the return on the financial instrument used to finance the investment. In the simplest case where the saver lends to the firm at a nominal interest rate i, the real return ($r = s$) received in the absence of taxes is given by

$$s = r = i - \pi$$

where $\pi$ denotes the rate of inflation.

The relationship between the market rate of interest and the return to the saver is affected by taxes in a number of ways. Firstly, nominal interest rates are

271

taxed at a rate m. As a result the net real return after tax is affected by the interaction between the rate of inflation and the rate of personal tax. Secondly, in some countries there are taxes on certain forms of personal wealth ($w_p$). Hence the post-tax rate of return to the saver is given by

$$s = (1 - m)i - \pi - w_p$$

## C. The Cost of Capital Function

The value of p net of depreciation is given by

$$p = MRR - \delta \tag{1}$$

where MRR denotes the gross marginal (social) rate of return on a specific investment project and $\delta$ is the rate of economic depreciation, assumed to be exponential. If we define $\rho$ to be the rate at which a company discounts cash flows in nominal terms, the acquisition cost of an asset (q) must equal the present discounted value of the return on a project. In the absence of taxes this value is given by

$$q = \int_0^\infty MRR \ e^{-(\rho+\delta-\pi)u} \ du$$

$$= MRR/(\rho+\delta-\pi) \tag{2}$$

Company income and wealth taxes affect cash flows in two ways. Firstly, they reduce the returns received by the amount of tax collected on economic income. If the firm has sufficient taxable income, the corporate profits tax, $\tau$, reduces the value of MRR to $(1 - \tau)$ MRR, whilst the corporate wealth tax $w_c$ reduces the marginal return to MRR - $w_c$. The second effect of the profits tax is to reduce the cost of the asset purchase by the amount of tax allowances and grants (A). Setting q = 1 - A and substituting this value into (1) and (2), and taking account of wealth taxes, the pre-tax real rate of return net of depreciation is found to be given by

$$p = (1-A)(\rho+\delta+w_c-\pi)/(1-\tau) - \delta$$

## D. The Cost of Finance

The final effect of taxation is to influence the firm's discount rate $\rho$ and the market rate of interest. In the absence of taxation $\rho$ and i would be equal.

Company and personal taxes distort this equality as well as making the value of $\rho$ dependent on the source of finance. Three types of finance are considered in this paper: debt finance, new share issues and retained earnings.[15] For debt finance, since nominal interest rate payments are deductible from corporation tax,

$$\rho = i(1-\tau).$$

For other sources of finance the discount rate depends on the interaction between the personal and corporate tax systems. In the case of investment through new share issues, the required yield needed by potential investors must take account of the taxes on distributed profits. In the presence of integrated company tax systems, the measurement of the additional taxes can be divided into two parts. The first, denoted by $\theta$, equals the additional dividends which shareholders could receive if one unit of post-corporate tax earnings were distributed. The second is simply the marginal personal tax rate on this grossed-up yield. In equilibrium assuming certainty, the return on investment in new shares $(1-m)\theta\rho$ must equal the return on debt-financed investment $(1-m)i$. This means that the discount rate for new share issues is given by

$$\rho = i/\theta.\text{[16]}$$

The use of retained earnings enables investors to accumulate at a rate of return that is taxed at a capital gains tax rate $z$. A similar arbitrage argument to that used for new share issues results in the discount rate for retained earnings being given by

$$\rho = i(1-m)/(1-z)$$

### E. The Values of p and r

The value $r$ plays a key role in our comparative analysis of different projects, since it is assumed to be a constant and to take a value of 3 percent per annum. This assumption of a fixed value of $r$ is equivalent to assuming that the rate of return on all types of saving before personal taxes is the same, i.e. that for any

15. Two important sources of finance not considered in this paper are government subsidised loans and intra-company loans of multinational companies. The former have been employed extensively in certain countries (e.g. Italy) and should be included in any more extensive study of transfer payments from the public sector to companies. Intra-company loans can be included in a more extended model of foreign direct investment (see Alworth, 1986).
16. If stamp duties and registration taxes at a rate n for new share issues are included the value of $\rho = i / \theta(1 - n)$.

given saver all projects yield the same value of r but that the value of s varies from one type of saving to another. This arbitrage assumption also implies that the interaction of the tax system with inflation yields a particular form of Fisher effect, namely that

$$i = r + \pi/(1-m^*)$$

where m* is the average marginal personal tax rate on capital income.

An alternative to assuming a fixed value for r would be to take the value of the pre-tax rate of return p as fixed, e.g. the returns across alternative projects are the same. There is no conceptual difference between these alternative assumptions and in the absence of non-linearities in the tax system the effective tax rates derived in the 'fixed-p' or 'fixed-r' case would be the same.

## IV. Estimates of Effective Marginal Tax Rates

### A. Effective Tax Rates on Investment

This section reports the estimates of effective tax rates on investment in each of the six EC countries for 81 possible permutations of assets/industry/source of finance/final ownership. The most satisfactory way of comparing the results on the effective tax rates would be to examine each of the individual projects across countries. This quantity of information is difficult to absorb and, following King and Fullerton, we choose instead to examine a particular subset consisting of weighted averages across investments. This approach has several drawbacks. First, in order to derive average marginal tax rates it is assumed that the marginal increase in investment and saving occurs in the same proportion across all assets and all countries. This is not likely to be the case in practice since investments will be attracted to the more lightly taxed sectors. In particular for the set of simulations reported below which examine the effects of different degrees of tax harmonisation, fixing weights on the various shares of investment obscures any likely resource allocation effects. Second, the weights shown in Table 9.7 have been imposed arbitrarily rather than computed from existing patterns of investment, financing and ownership. Similarly, identical rates of economic depreciation are assumed to exist across countries. Both of these assumptions may bias the reported results to the extent that serious differences exist with respect to these standard parameters and possibly overestimate the effective marginal tax rates to the extent that investment patterns have adjusted to the structure of the tax system. Finally, aggregation partly conceals the degree of variation in tax rates across investments. In this respect perhaps the most important finding of the King-Fullerton study has been the degree to which effective tax rates vary widely even within countries.

274

*Table 9.7 Weights employed for simulation of effective tax rates*

|  | Manufacture | Other Industry | Commerce |
|---|---|---|---|
| **Asset Composition by Type and by Industry** | | | |
| Machinery | 0.3 | 0.05 | 0.05 |
| Building | 0.2 | 0.05 | 0.075 |
| Inventories | 0.2 | 0.25 | 0.05 |
| **Source of Finance Proportions for each Industry** | | | |
| Debt | 0.36 | 0.36 | 0.36 |
| New share issues | 0.04 | 0.04 | 0.04 |
| Retained earnings | 0.60 | 0.60 | 0.60 |
| **Ownership Shares in each Industry** | | | |
| Debt | | | |
| Households | 0.7 | 0.7 | 0.7 |
| Tax-exempt | 0.15 | 0.15 | 0.15 |
| Insurance | 0.15 | 0.15 | 0.15 |
| New shares | | | |
| Households | 0.5 | 0.5 | 0.5 |
| Tax-exempt | 0.4 | 0.4 | 0.4 |
| Insurance | 0.1 | 0.1 | 0.1 |
| Retained earnings | | | |
| Households | 0.5 | 0.5 | 0.5 |
| Tax-exempt | 0.4 | 0.4 | 0.4 |
| Insurance | 0.1 | 0.1 | 0.1 |

Four sets of simulation have been undertaken for each of the EC countries. The first are based on the existing tax laws and inflation rates of zero and 10 percent. These two rates are used to examine the sensitivity to inflation of the company tax systems in each of the countries and the extent to which harmonisation would be made more difficult by inflation. The remaining simulations look at the effects of different degrees of tax harmonisation. The second set of simulations assumes that tax rates on company profits and dividends are harmonised across EC countries. The third set looks at how effective tax rates would be changed if in addition the corporate tax base were harmonised but regional tax incentives and grants as well as personal and wealth taxes which are outside of the corporate tax were left in place. The final set of estimates looks at the effects of doing away with all investment incentives and of indexing the corporate tax system.

## B. The Present Tax System

Table 9.8 summarises the effective tax rates on capital income in the six major countries under the assumption that there is no inflation. From the final row of this table we see that the overall effective marginal tax rate calculated by

*Table 9.8 Effective tax rates for each country with zero inflation under the existing tax system*

| | Belgium | France | Germany | Italy | Netherlands | United Kingdom |
|---|---|---|---|---|---|---|
| *Asset* | | | | | | |
| 1. Machinery | 6.46 | 26.48 | 56.57 | −122.02 | −95.10 | 5.09 |
| 2. Buildings | 16.81 | 55.10 | 57.35 | − 26.41 | 26.75 | 48.12 |
| 3. Inventories | 37.79 | 57.36 | 67.46 | 36.39 | 46.19 | 37.99 |
| *Industry* | | | | | | |
| 1. Manufacturing | 19.96 | 47.07 | 59.99 | − 15.18 | 12.33 | 26.92 |
| 2. Other industry | 17.61 | 47.48 | 61.04 | − 23.30 | 10.93 | 43.03 |
| 3. Commerce | 25.25 | 50.33 | 61.76 | − 9.06 | 20.79 | 44.30 |
| *Source of finance* | | | | | | |
| 1. Debt | − 2.12 | 32.71 | 25.54 | −65.25 | − 7.45 | 5.32 |
| 2. New share issues | 41.07 | 54.91 | 59.93 | 5.08 | 44.91 | 30.09 |
| 3. Retained earnings | 27.25 | 53.22 | 70.28 | 5.89 | 18.66 | 43.00 |
| *Owner* | | | | | | |
| 1. Households | 24.96 | 68.11 | 66.41 | −10.52 | 39.79 | 47.19 |
| 2. Tax-exempt institutions | 16.85 | 21.05 | 58.26 | −10.63 | −21.42 | 7.82 |
| 3. Insurance companies | 11.08 | 17.54 | 38.02 | −49.29 | − 8.30 | 24.86 |
| *Overall* | *20.66* | *47.72* | *60.44* | *−15.00* | *13.77* | *32.95* |

weighting the effective rates on each 81 possible combinations of investment is highest for investment in Germany (60 percent), followed by France (48 percent), the United Kingdom (33 percent), Belgium (21 percent), the Netherlands (14 percent) and, finally, by Italy, where there is actually a subsidy (-15 percent).

Each of the remaining rows in Table 9.8 shows the average marginal tax rate over a particular subset of investments. For example, figures in the first row are an average of tax rates over all (27) combinations of investments involving machinery. As for the overall rate, present tax laws are most favorable in Italy, but there are subsidies also in the Netherlands (-95 percent). Furthermore, low rates of tax are also found in the United Kingdom and Belgium. Only France and Germany appear to have high effective rates of tax. The reason for the low rate of tax in Italy and the United Kingdom is to be found in the very generous systems of depreciation allowances. Indeed the Italian system of declining balance and 10-year tax life is almost equivalent in present value terms to the generous 25 percent yearly exponential depreciation allowances found in the United Kingdom. Moreover, in both countries investments in machinery benefit from generous incentives. The principal reason for the subsidy found in the Netherlands is attributable to the very generous tax credit at 12.5 percent and to a lesser degree to the system of double declining balance which has been assumed in these simulations. Despite the existence of generous depreciation allowances, several factors may contribute to the high effective tax rate on German investments in machinery. In particular, company and wealth tax rates

276

are higher than in other countries, and grants are much lower.

The effective tax rates on investment in buildings depend on whether straightline is the only permissible method of depreciation and, in the specific case of Italy, on the length of the useful lives of assets. If only straightline is allowed and there are no special credits or grants, as in the Netherlands, the effective tax rate approximates the value of the corporation tax rate (France and Germany).

The industry breakdown shows that in all the countries commerce is taxed more heavily than the other sectors. This is explained by the relatively higher weighting of buildings in total investment as well as the less generous depreciation allowances and investment incentives.

The breakdown by source of finance reveals that, with the exception of France and Germany, debt-financed investments are very lightly taxed or subsidised. Nevertheless in the case of the United Kingdom there is a striking increase in the effective tax on debt-financed investments in comparison to the generous subsidy which existed before 1984. In contrast to debt finance, new share issues do not receive a subsidy even in those countries such as Germany and Italy in which integration is virtually complete. The imputation system does, however, mean that investments financed by new share issues are taxed at lower rates than those financed by retained earnings. This is seen most visibly by contrasting the United Kingdom, where in addition there is a tax on capital gains, with the Netherlands in which there is a classical system and as a result retained earnings are taxed at a relatively lower rate.

Finally, Table 9.8 shows effective tax rates by ownership category. These rates reflect the differences in personal rates on interest and dividends as well as differences in the taxation of savings by institution. Marginal tax rates on personal incomes and wealth are highest in France and Germany. The treatment of tax-exempt institutions is relatively favorable in Italy, the Netherlands and the United Kingdom.

The effects of inflation on the effective tax rate are reported in Table 9.9. These figures suggest two sets of considerations. Firstly, as a result of inflation overall marginal tax rates rise in all countries. This is most noticeable in Italy where the overall subsidy becomes a tax though well below the nominal rate on company income. France now has in most instances the highest tax rates although these are not significantly different from those in Germany. The overall tax rate for investment in the Netherlands is probably overstated since the deduction allowed to firms on price increase is not taken into account.

The differences reported across countries stem, to a large extent, from the combination of the tax deductibility of interest and the tax treatment of inventories. This effect is particularly important in France, Germany and the United Kingdom. The French inventory valuation method offers very little protection against moderate price increases and this, together with the higher corporate tax rate, explains why the tax on inventories in France exceeds that in

277

*Table 9.9 Effective tax rates for each country with 10 percent inflation under the existing tax system*

|  | Belgium | France | Germany | Italy | Netherlands | United Kingdom |
|---|---|---|---|---|---|---|
| *Asset* | | | | | | |
| 1. Machinery | 38.80 | 66.71 | 72.95 | 33.01 | 33.96 | 38.90 |
| 2. Buildings | 21.65 | 69.10 | 65.28 | 10.87 | 39.49 | 56.97 |
| 3. Inventories | 9.54 | 80.35 | 77.67 | 19.71 | 32.40 | 66.57 |
| *Industry* | | | | | | |
| 1. Manufacturing | 27.07 | 72.72 | 72.65 | 24.02 | 35.22 | 52.97 |
| 2. Other industry | 27.10 | 71.54 | 72.29 | 22.78 | 36.00 | 58.68 |
| 3. Commerce | 27.41 | 72.97 | 72.49 | 20.83 | 36.04 | 60.37 |
| *Source of finance* | | | | | | |
| 1. Debt | −331.74 | 53.44 | −115.53 | −164.78 | −35.76 | 26.31 |
| 2. New share issues | 61.53 | 81.05 | 69.22 | 62.92 | 71.91 | 49.10 |
| 3. Retained earnings | 40.01 | 77.92 | 87.22 | 63.66 | 40.34 | 63.77 |
| *Owner* | | | | | | |
| 1. Households | 42.97 | 102.36 | 89.61 | 38.60 | 94.71 | 86.44 |
| 2. Tax-exempt institutions | 14.66 | 35.59 | 70.15 | 29.42 | −38.01 | −3.01 |
| 3. Insurance companies | −4.02 | 25.86 | −3.03 | −71.72 | 1.81 | 41.00 |
| *Overall* | *27.14* | *72.62* | *72.48* | *23.32* | *35.47* | *55.21* |

the United Kingdom where no allowance is made for inflation. In contrast to these countries as a result of inflation the taxation of inventories falls markedly in Belgium, Italy and to a lesser extent the Netherlands.

Tax deductibility of interest is also important for the general results in those cases where personal income taxes on interest income are low. This is particularly so in Italy and Belgium where the low withholding taxes on this form of saving and the deductibility of debt from taxable income give rise to a significant subsidy.

The second set of considerations arising from the comparison of Tables 9.8 and 9.9 concerns the effects of inflation on the variance of tax rates. The high negative marginal tax rates on debt finance and the relatively high positive taxes on industry suggest that one of the effects of inflation is to increase the variance of tax rates. The actual dispersion of the 81 tax rates is indeed more pronounced than that appearing in the tables. With no inflation most countries tend to have a rather uniform distribution across the spectrum of rates. The effect of inflation is to widen the range of effective tax rates and cluster the shares of investments more markedly around extreme tax values. This is most noticeable in the case of France and Germany.

*Table 9.10 Effective tax rates on savings and investment under different assumptions regarding tax harmonisation*
(Overall Effective Tax Rates, in Percentages)

| Country | No Harmonisation | Harmonisation with $\tau=.5$ and $\theta=2$ | Harmonisation of the Tax Base | Harmonisation with Indexation and Abolition of Investment Incentives |
|---|---|---|---|---|
| *Zero Inflation* | | | | |
| Belgium | 20.7 | 23.6 | 20.6 | 44.7 |
| France | 47.7 | 47.1 | 45.2 | 61.8 |
| Germany | 60.4 | 52.5 | 53.2 | 55.6 |
| Italy | −15.0 | −15.3 | 2.3 | 44.9 |
| Netherlands | 13.8 | 15.7 | 11.1 | 51.3 |
| United Kingdom | 33.0 | 41.6 | 44.9 | 54.6 |
| *10 Percent Inflation* | | | | |
| Belgium | 27.1 | 40.5 | 40.9 | 54.3 |
| France | 72.6 | 72.0 | 61.3 | 71.6 |
| Germany | 72.5 | 66.7 | 62.4 | 63.9 |
| Italy | 23.3 | 20.8 | 33.2 | 55.1 |
| Netherlands | 35.5 | 31.8 | 29.1 | 55.2 |
| United Kingdom | 55.2 | 60.6 | 54.2 | 60.9 |

## C. Harmonising Company Tax Rates

In order to evaluate to what extent the differences amongst the EC countries could be attributed to differences in company tax system, a series of simulations were undertaken assuming that tax rates on returned earnings were equal with $\tau = .5$ and that a full imputation system was adopted with $\theta = 2$. The results of these simulations for the overall weighted effective tax rates are shown in the third column of Table 9.10. The results are not surprising. As expected, overall effective tax rates in Germany and France fall because the harmonised rates are lower than those presently found in both countries. At zero inflation, the overall effective tax rates rise in all other countries excepting Italy. The most interesting country is the Netherlands for which the effective rate of tax on new share issues results in a subsidy (not shown in the table). In practice, the precise effect of introducing the imputation system in the Netherlands would depend on the treatment given to tax exempt institutions.

The harmonisation of tax rates has practically no impact on the responsiveness of the tax system to changes in the rate of inflation and the effects continue to be widely different by types of investment and across countries.

In summary, the effects of harmonising company *tax rates* on the harmonisation of the effective rates of tax on capital income appear to be very small.

## D. Harmonising the Tax Base

A more radical harmonisation of the tax system would consist in having identical depreciation allowances for fixed assets and inventory valuation methods in addition to identical tax rates. In the simulations reported in the fourth column of Table 9.10 it is assumed that in addition to tax rate harmonisation, the EC countries would adopt the following depreciation practices: double-declining balance for machinery, straightline for buildings, and lifo for inventories. On the other hand, individual countries would still be permitted to choose useful lives and provide national and regional investment incentives. Such reforms would be in line with allowing a certain degree of discretion to each country according to differences in income levels, capital utilisation rates, and regional investment patterns. These remaining distinctions in the company tax system can also be interpreted as a *'quid pro quo'* which the politics of individual countries would require in order to permit tax harmonisation to go ahead.[17]

The results for overall marginal tax rates in Table 9.10 suggest that harmonising the tax base in the limited sense which we have suggested does lead to some degree of convergence amongst the tax systems of the various countries. In comparison to the case where only the tax rates are harmonised, tax rates rise significantly in Italy and somewhat less in the United Kingdom, and fall in the Netherlands, Belgium and France. The effect of greater harmonisation of effective tax rates, however, is somewhat surprising at higher rates of inflation since it narrows considerably the range of variation of overall effective tax rates. This effect is due largely to the introduction of lifo in France, Germany and the United Kingdom.

## E. Total Harmonisation of the Company Tax System

Short of total indexation, the most thorough harmonisation of the company system could be accomplished by setting depreciation allowances equal to (unindexed) economic depreciation and to abolish any form of investment incentives.

Not surprisingly, the results for such a standardisation shown in the last column of Table 9.10 reveal a marked convergence in the effective rates of tax. In the absence of inflation within each country tax rates across assets are identical unless there are local property or wealth taxes. Hence differences in effective taxes across sources of finance and ownership remain to some extent

---

17. In practice any form of harmonisation would probably be arbitrary and limited in scope. It is likely that at least in the first stages of harmonisation many tax incentives would continue to be operative especially at local levels.

as a reflection of differences in personal income and wealth taxes.

Inflation, however, disturbs this picture. The effective tax rates in the countries with high marginal personal tax rates rise significantly. A further result of not having indexation of personal taxes is to maintain to a certain degree the dispersion of effective rates amongst different types of investment.

## V. CONCLUSIONS

This paper has examined the effective taxation of capital income in six EC countries and the effects of various possible harmonisation proposals on the structure of rates. Whilst the effective tax rates cannot be considered point estimates of actual burdens, they are suggestive of probable differences in magnitude existing both across sectors and across countries. As a result, and in view of the numerous simplifying assumptions which have been made, the following broad set of conclusions can be derived:

– effective tax rates on capital income vary widely within each country across sectors and the range of differences is extremely sensitive to the rate of underlying inflation;

– despite some degree of harmonisation in company tax systems across EC countries, there are still wide disparities in effective tax rates. These divergences are attributable in order of importance to the following three sets of factors:

(1) differences in the definition of the tax base;

(2) differences in tax and other fiscal incentives; and

(3) differences in personal income and wealth taxes;

– as a result, unless harmonisation is applied internally across sectors and extended beyond nominal tax rates, it is unlikely that tax harmonisation will be effectively achieved within EC countries.

Alworth, Julian S. *Finance and Investment Decisions of Multinationals: The Tax Aspects.* Oxford: Blackwells, 1986 (forthcoming).

Ando, Albert K. and Auerbach, Alan J. 'The Corporate Cost of Capital in Japan and the US: A Comparison.' *Working Paper,* 1762. Boston: National Bureau of Economic Research, 1985.

Auerbach, Alan J. 'Taxation, Corporate Financial Policy and the Cost of Capital.' *Journal of Economic Literature,* 31, 1983.

Bird, Richard M. 'Corporate-Personal Tax Integration.' Chapter 8, this volume, 1986.

Cnossen, Sijbren. 'Alternative Forms of Corporate Tax.' *Australian Tax Forum,* 1, September 1984. Reprinted as 'Corporation Taxes in OECD Member Countries.' *Bulletin for International Fiscal Documentation,* 38, 11, 1984.

De Clercq, W. 'Allégements fiscaux en faveur des particuliers et indépendants: 1981-1984.' *Bulletin de Documentation.* Belgium Ministry of Finance, Jan.-Feb., 1984.

Di Majo, A. 'Incentivi fiscali, decisioni d'investimento, e riforma tributaria.' *Rivista Internazionale di Scienze Sociali,* 44, 1973.

Easson, A.J. *Tax Law and Policy in the EEC.* London: Sweet & Maxwell, 1980.

Edwards, Jeremy. 'The 1984 Corporation Tax Reform.' *Fiscal Studies,* 5, 2, 1984.

Feldstein, Martin S., Dicks-Mireaux, Louis and Poterba, James. 'The Effective Tax Rate and the Pretax Rate of Return.' *Journal of Public Economics,* 21, 1983.

Jackson, P.M. and O'Donnell, A. 'The Effects of Stamp Duty on Equity Transactions and Prices in the UK Stock Exchange.' *Discussion Paper,* 25. London: Bank of England, 1985.

Kay, J. and Sen, J. 'The Comparative Burden of Business Taxation.' *Working Paper,* 45. London: Institute for Fiscal Studies, 1984.

King, Mervyn A. *Public Policy and the Corporation.* London: Chapman Hall, 1977.

King, Mervyn A. 'Tax Reform in the UK and the US.' *Economic Policy,* 1, 1985.

King, Mervyn A. and Fullerton, Don (eds). *The Taxation of Income from Capital: A Comparative Study of the United States, the United Kingdom, Sweden, and West Germany.* University of Chicago Press, 1984.

Marotta, G. and Schiantarelli, F. 'Nota sulla stima del prezzo "effettivo" dei beni capitali per il settore della trasformazione industriale in Italia, 1960-76.' In Rossi, N. and Rovelli, R. (eds). *Ricerche di Economia Applicata: il Caso Italiano.* Milan: Franco Angeli, 1983.

Mayer, Colin P. 'Corporation Tax, Finance and the Cost of Capital.' *Review of Economic Studies,* 53, 1986.

McLure, Charles E. Jr. *Must Corporate Income be Taxed Twice?* Washington DC: The Brookings Institution, 1979.

Musgrave, Peggy B. 'Harmonization of Direct Business Taxes: A Case Study.' In Shoup, Carl S. (ed.). *Tax Harmonization in Common Markets,* Vol. II. New York: Columbia University Press, 1967.

Organisation for Economic Co-operation and Development. *Taxes on Immovable Property.* Paris: OECD, 1983.

Paladini, R. 'La tassazione delle attività finanziarie: una vicenda non conclusa.' *Centro Europa Ricerche,* 4, 1, 1985.

Snoy, Bernard. *Taxes on Direct Investment in the EEC: A Legal and Economic Analysis.* New York: Praeger, 1975.

Tanzi, Vito (ed.). *Taxation, Inflation and Interest Rates.* Washington DC: International Monetary Fund, 1984.

# Part Five

# Other Issues in Income Taxation

# 10

## Determination of company profits

### *Norbert Andel**

### I. INTRODUCTION

If it is assumed
- that the economic advantage of using capital is usually adequately reflected in profits before tax,
- that investors allocate capital to maximize profits after tax,
- that international differences in the burden of direct taxes may lead to situations where, from the investor's point of view, the ranking of projects according to profits after tax diverges from the ranking according to profits before tax,
- that capital is mobile,

differences in direct-tax burdens, compensating or even overcompensating differences in profits before tax, can be expected to induce factor movements that reduce efficiency or prevent those that enhance it.

Since the Common Market is conceived of not only as a common product market but also as a common factor market, and given the goal to increase efficiency by factor movements within the Common Market, in principle the case for harmonisation of direct taxes is of no less importance than that for harmonisation of indirect taxes.

The questions are:
(1) whether capital is really mobile among the Member States;
(2) whether there are differences in effective tax burden; and
(3) whether the disadvantage of reduced national tax autonomy counts for less than the advantage of more intra-Community neutrality of direct taxes.

ad (1) Of course, when the EC was founded, owing to restrictive national measures, capital was much less mobile among Member States than were products or capital within a national market. But the goal of the EC being to create a Common Market with 'conditions similar to those of an

---

* The author is indebted to J. van Hoorn, Jr, Helmut Krabbe and Gerd Sass for supplying information and giving their opinion, and to Sijbren Cnossen, Jan Christiaanse, Albert Rädler and other participants of the Conference for helpful comments. Susanne Gerecht, Jan Kmenta, Norbert Solomonson and in particular Sijbren Cnossen did much to improve the style of this paper.

internal market where economic relations between the Six are concerned' (Neumark Committee, 1963, p. 16), the need for harmonisation should be evaluated from the very beginning in view of the situation aimed for.

ad (2) Differences in taxation of company profits were, and still are, large. This has been shown by several studies using different approaches, such as the pioneering contribution by Peggy B. Musgrave (1967), the dissertation of Bernard Snoy (1975), several reports of the Commission on the computation of business profits for tax purposes (e.g. Kommission, 1972; Commission, 1980b), Fischer's analysis of normal depreciation (1980), and the studies edited by King and Fullerton (1984).

As far as differences in the tax burden on company profits are compensated by different advantages to the corporate sector through budget expenditure, the need for harmonisation may be reduced or even non-existent. So far, however, that aspect has been of theoretical interest only. Relevant studies of the incidence of public expenditure are not available. Besides, company profits can hardly be conceived of as a satisfactory basis for the benefit principle.

ad (3) In contrast to tariffs, tax differences usually spring not so much from differing protective aims as from differing general national goals and national economic and social conditions. To improve the achievement of national goals by national tax measures is, in principle, not less important than to improve efficiency by international economic integration. It would be unreasonable to demand the reduction of tax differences even if the reduction of tax distortions is felt to be of less significance than the cost of reduced national fiscal flexibility.

Of course, opinions differ as to where to draw the line.


## II. Starting Points for Tax Harmonisation

Once the decision has been made to harmonise taxes on company profits, the question arises of how to proceed. With respect to the turnover taxes, the Commission has developed a strategy of harmonisation in three stages:
- harmonisation of tax type;
- harmonisation of tax base; and
- harmonisation of tax rates.

This sequence has obvious advantages in the field of indirect taxes. By the destination principle, differences in tax rates can be prevented − more or less perfectly − from distorting competition. Therefore, harmonisation need not necessarily imply budgetary problems from the very beginning. With respect to revenue, for example, a change of tax base may be compensated by a change of tax rates. In terms of political feasibility, postponing the unavoidable reduction of budgetary flexibility with respect to the overall revenue to a later stage of harmonisation is, of course, advantageous.

The situation is different for taxes on corporate profits. On the one hand, there is no device such as the destination principle available to make differences in tax burden compatible with production efficiency. On the other hand, harmonising the tax base may be started even if the type of corporation income tax is not yet agreed upon. By harmonising the type of corporation income tax, the tax rates and the imputation system, it is also possible to reduce immediately the segmentation effects associated with the present system. The tax credit could be extended to all residents of the EC without waiting for the tedious, time-consuming work of harmonising the tax base to be accomplished. (This aspect seemed to have been disregarded when the European Parliament discussed the proposal for a Directive of the Council concerning the harmonisation of systems of company taxation.)

### III. DIRECT-TAX HARMONISATION: A REVIEW

From a review of the Commission's harmonisation activities, especially those related to corporation income tax in general and to the corporation income tax base in particular, the following picture emerges:

(1) The harmonisation of direct taxes was considered much less urgent than the harmonisation of indirect taxes, especially turnover taxes.

(2) While in the case of value-added tax a harmonisation programme was agreed upon within a few years, to accomplish the same for corporation income taxes took much longer. Priorities and preferred solutions have changed considerably through time.

(3) The question of which type of corporation income tax was preferable was faced and decided at a rather late stage. However, preparatory activities concerning the analysis of the influence of direct taxes on capital movements were already mentioned in the Second General Report of the Activities of the European Economic Community (Kommission, 1959).

(4) These preparatory investigations concentrated on an inventory of the relevant regulations of the Member States, subdivided according to their concern with depreciation, capital gains and losses, and valuation of stock-in-trade and loss-carry-over. Apparently, a rather intensive phase of work came to an end in 1964 without inducing effective measures.

(5) Thereafter, the interest seemed to shift towards those tax aspects which impede the cooperation of enterprises located in different Member States or prevent the creation of an integrated Community-wide capital market free of tax-induced distortions.

(6) In June 1979, Parliament decided to suspend its opinion on the proposed Directive of the Council concerning the harmonisation of company taxation systems and of withholding taxes on dividends until the Commission submits recommendations for the computation and control of

taxable profits. In response, the Commission reactivated Working Group IV (Direct Taxes), which concentrated its discussions on the harmonisation of depreciation rules.

(7) Until the end of 1983, none of the central problems of the harmonisation of the profit-tax base had been put forward as a proposal for a Council Directive, despite all the activities in the area of direct taxes. They were only marginally or indirectly touched upon, e.g. in the proposed Merger Directive, in the Mutual Assistance Directive and in (proposed or adopted) directives on company law.

(8) Only in 1984 did the Commission submit its first proposal for a directive directly related to the computation of profits for tax purposes. However, it did not concern depreciation but the carry-over of losses.

I will now review the endeavours to harmonise the rules of computation of profits for tax purposes in more detail. Section IV refers to activities directly and comprehensively related to tax-base harmonisation. Section V deals with activities which concern special aspects only or activities where the influence on the tax base is more of a by-product.

## IV. DIRECT-TAX HARMONISATION: DETERMINATION OF TAXABLE PROFITS

### A. The Period Before 1979

Already the Second General Report of the Activities of the EC states: 'Es zeigte sich alsbald, daß das Problem der Harmonisierung der Umsatzsteuern und der indirekten Steuern unverzüglich in Angriff genommen werden muß' (Kommission, 1959, p. 89). No similar unequivocal statement can be found for direct taxes. Admittedly, in the same Report we find the sentence: 'Auch über die wirtschaftlichen Auswirkungen der direkten Steuern wurden verschiedene Untersuchungen eingeleitet' (p. 90). But then as well as later on it was only a matter of 'auch'. Besides, these studies do not seem to have been directed towards specific problems, as is testified by the topics mentioned as 'examples' in the Third General Report of the Activities of the EC: 'the influence of taxation on capital movements, agriculture, public enterprises, depreciation and energy sources' (Kommission, 1960, p. 138).

The initiative to take a closer look at the problems of profit computation for tax purposes came from the Ministers of Finance. In October 1961, Working Group IV (Direct Taxes), comprising delegations of the Member States, was formed. Its investigations resulted in a report 'Conclusions of Working Group IV' which is not available to the author. They are summarized in the Commission's Seventh General Report (Kommission, 1964, pp. 95-96):

− As to depreciation, a distinction is made between measures considered to be neutral and measures with an incentive character.

290

- Some sort of coordination of incentive schemes is envisaged, at least as far as future measures are concerned.
- While the same suggestion is made for capital gains and capital losses, rules for the valuation of stock-in-trade or the carry-over of losses are, for the time being, not considered a problem.

A second result of the investigations of Working Group IV was a compilation of the rules of the Member States concerning the computation of business profits for tax purposes, later updated in the 'Report on the Base of Taxes on Business Profits' (Kommission, 1972).

These activities of the early 1960s did not lead to specific measures. The interest in problems of profit-tax base seems to have soon vanished. For many years they were not even mentioned in the Commission's General Reports. Activities shifted toward those tax aspects which impede the cooperation of firms located in different Member States and prevent the creation of an integrated capital market free of tax-induced distortions.

Things changed when Parliament decided in June 1979 to suspend its opinion on the proposed Directive on Company Taxation and invited the Commission 'to draw up a proposal for a Council decision laying down the guidelines for the future harmonisation of company taxation and, as soon as possible, proposals for coordinating Member States' systems of assessing and controlling companies' taxable profits' (Parliament, 1979, p. 20).

### B. The Period 1979-83: Depreciation for Tax Purposes

In 1979 the Commission, intent on reactivating the investigation into the computation of business profits for tax purposes by Working Group IV, submitted working documents reviewing the problems and trying to relate the discussion to earlier studies referred to in Subsection A. The Working Group decided to start with the analyses of depreciation and to restrict, for the time being, the field of analysis further by excluding incentive schemes, special measures to take account of inflation, and problems resulting from the relationship between tax law and company law.

As a matter of fact, Member States' rules of normal depreciation diverge considerably, as shown, for example, by Fischer (1980). In a more recent study, based on the tax law in force at the beginning of 1984, Fischer calculated the increase in cost due to the difference between writing off investment expenditure at once and the relevant national depreciation rules, expressing it as a percentage of investment expenditure. The underlying assumption was that less favourable depreciation schemes result in more debt finance. At a supposed interest rate of 10 percent and a tax rate of 50 percent, the percentage of cost increase ranges:
- for buildings, from 4.8 in Ireland to 53.2 in Luxembourg; and

*Table 10.1 Cost increase due to the difference between national depreciation rules in force and 100 percent depreciation in the first year (interest rate 10 percent, tax rate 50 percent)*

| Member State | Buildings | Machinery[a] |
|---|---|---|
| Ireland | 4.8 | 4.8 |
| United Kingdom | 15.8 | 8.7 |
| Italy | 17.6 | 12.1 |
| Greece | 30.1 | 16.7 |
| Belgium | 36.3 | 18.3 |
| France | 37.7 | 15.7 |
| Denmark | 38.4 | 14.3 |
| Germany | 48.7 | 14.0 |
| Netherlands | 48.8 | 22.8 |
| Luxembourg | 53.2 | 14.0 |

*Note:* a. Cost-recovery period − 10 years.
*Source:* Fischer (1984, Anlage IV and V).

− for machinery with a cost-recovery period of 10 years, from 4.8 in Ireland to 22.8 in the Netherlands (see Table 10.1).

In other words: on the assumptions made, less favourable depreciation rules than those in Ireland lead to an increase in cost of 48.4 percent of investment expenditure for buildings in Luxembourg and 18 percent of investment expenditure for machinery with a cost-recovery period of 10 years in the Netherlands.

Working Group IV met several times in 1979, finally discussing sketches for a draft directive on depreciation for tax purposes. Suddenly, the work was interrupted, and left for more than two years. When it was resumed in spring 1983, the discussions were based on a Commission's draft proposal for a directive on depreciation rules for tax purposes which envisaged the following:

(1) The directive applies to all undertakings subject to corporation income tax, income tax or a comparable tax, and which draw up annual accounts consisting of a balance sheet and a profit-and-loss account.

(2) Depreciable assets comprise all fixed tangible assets as defined by Article 15 (2) of the Fourth Council Directive (on the annual accounts of certain types of companies) which necessarily suffer depreciation.

(3) The basis for depreciation is equal to purchase price or production cost minus tax-exempt subsidies.

(4) Acquisition and production costs are to be allocated systematically over the period of probable useful life.

(5) With respect to tangible assets, the undertaking has a choice between the straight-line and the declining-balance method. In the latter case the rate of depreciation is subject to an upper limit of 2.5 times the percentage applied under the straight-line method.

292

(6) For other assets, either the straight-line method or the depletion allowance can be applied.

(7) Exceptional depreciation is possible if its justification is proved.

(8) Acquisition and production cost of low-value items (value limit 500 ECU) can be deducted at once.

(9) Formation expenses may be deducted at once or distributed over a period of five years.

(10) The same holds for expenditure incurred in creating the trade name, the clientele or a trade mark.

(11) Where the trade name, the clientele or a trade mark has been acquired for a valuable consideration, the cost of acquisition shall be written off in equal amounts over a period of five (ten) years.

(12) Costs of research and development, as far as they are not regarded as part of fixed assets pursuant to national law in a Member State, may be deducted at once or written off in equal amounts over a period of no more than five years.

The Commission's suggestions seem reasonable to me. Not surprisingly, however, Working Group IV criticized the proposals. Several delegations required a closer connection with the Fourth Directive and the possibility of retaining the pool system.[1] They objected to granting several options to firms only, not to the national legislators, and they criticized the Commission's change of position with respect to inflation: whereas in 1979 the Commission intended the Member States to retain full freedom, since 1983 it has wanted to exclude depreciation according to replacement cost, preferring subsidies or tax-exempt reserves instead.

If the Council adopted such a directive, it would be an important first step towards tax-base harmonisation. Nevertheless, there would still remain some severe problems. They are primarily connected with what is not included in the preliminary draft proposal referred to.

(1) First of all: so far, the problems of taking inflation into account, e.g. by switching from depreciation according to historical cost to depreciation according to replacement cost, have been excluded. This may be considered deplorable, for obviously even uniform depreciation rates, uniform depreciation periods and uniform tax rates imply divergent tax burden if in periods of diverging rates of inflation depreciation is based on historical cost.

Nevertheless, the Commission was well advised not to tackle the treatment of inflation for depreciation purposes in such a way. Several Member States, as a matter of principle, would never accept switching to replacement cost or similar devices.

---

1. In a pool system depreciation allowances are not granted for each asset separately, but on the aggregate book value of all qualifying assets.

As a consequence, the possibility cannot be excluded that harmonisation according to the Commission's proposal increases the difference of tax burdens, for instance, when Member States which at present have more generous depreciation rules also have higher rates of inflation.

(2) So far, the Commission has also avoided systematic consideration of the problems resulting from the relationship between company law and tax law. That aspect is important for Member States (in particular, Germany and Luxembourg) applying the 'principle of linkage' ('Maßgeblichkeitsprinzip') by which (with certain exceptions) the tax balance sheet is derived from the commercial balance sheet.

(3) Even within the restricted harmonisation goal of the Commission's draft proposal, much depends on the correct estimation of the period of useful life of assets, to which the period of depreciation should be related, and on the avoidance of any considerable and systematic divergences among Member States.


## C. The Period 1983-84: Carry-Over of Losses

Given the main subject of the discussions of Working Group IV, the Commission was expected to start tackling the problem of tax-base harmonisation by proposing a directive concerning depreciation. But things turned out quite different.

The problems of the carry-over of losses did not play a prominent role during the investigations of the early 1960s. After resuming its activities in 1979, Working Group IV at first discussed these problems rather casually in connection with the question of whether depreciation should be mandatory or might be suspended in periods of losses.

As Table 10.2 shows, the rules concerning carry-over of losses diverge considerably within the Common Market.

In the spring of 1983, the Commission sent a Working Document, surveying problems of carry-over of losses and indicating possible solutions, to the delegations of Working Group IV. The Group discussed it only once. Therefore, it came as a surprise when in September 1984 the Commission submitted to the Council a 'Proposal for a Directive of the Council on the harmonisation of the laws of the Member States relating to tax arrangements for the carry-over of losses of undertakings' (Commission, 1984). For all Member States, its provisions are more liberal than the rules now in force, albeit, of course, to very different degrees. In particular, the proposal envisages the following:

(1) The Directive is binding on all undertakings which draw up, for tax purposes, annual accounts consisting of a balance sheet and a profit-and-

294

*Table 10.2 Carry-over of losses in EC Member States*

| Member State | Carry-Back | Carry-Forward |
|---|---|---|
| Belgium | – | 5 years<br>(unlimited for losses resulting from force majeure or depreciation; also for starting-up losses) |
| Denmark | – | 5 years |
| Germany | 2 years<br>(limited to DM 10,000,000) | 5 years |
| France | – | 5 years<br>(unlimited for losses resulting from depreciation) |
| Greece | – | 5 years<br>(3 years for undertakings having a commercial activity) |
| Ireland | 1 year<br>(3 years in the case of cessation of trading) | Unlimited |
| Italy | – | 5 years |
| Luxembourg | – | 5 years<br>(unlimited up to a level of 50 percent of losses resulting from depreciation in sectors experiencing a crisis) |
| Netherlands | 3 years | 8 years<br>(unlimited for start-up losses) |
| United Kingdom | 1 year<br>(3 years in case of cessation and for losses attributable to first year depreciation allowance) | Unlimited |

*Source:* Commission (1984, Annex).

loss account and which are subject to income tax, corporation income tax, capital gains tax or any other identical or substantially similar taxes (Article 1).

(2) For the purpose of the proposed directive, profit or loss is defined as the positive or negative result of an undertaking, after any possible set-off against other income; results recorded abroad by permanent establishments or subsidiaries of the undertaking are not taken into account.

(3) An undertaking showing a loss for a given financial year has a choice between:
  – loss carry-back up to two years followed, if need be, by unlimited loss carry-forward; and
  – unlimited loss carry-forward (Article 3 (1)).

(4) The undertaking may choose not to set off losses against profits which have not been taxed in the State where it is subject to tax or which have been taxed at a reduced rate (Article 3 (1)).

(5) Where a loss has been set off against distributed profits which carried entitlements to tax credit, the resulting tax repayment shall be reduced by the amount of that tax credit to the extent to which it has not been covered by a compensating tax (Article 3 (2)).

(6) Member States applying different tax rates to different categories of profit and requiring losses to be set off category by category, shall refrain from applying this restriction where a loss could not be set off against profits of the same category after five years (Article 3 (3)).

As a whole, this proposal is to be welcomed. It would bring about some harmonisation of the tax base, it would increase tax neutrality, for example by decreasing discrimination against small, undiversified undertakings or against those engaged in risky activities, and it would improve the 'investment climate'. Over the last few years, several Member States have adopted or at least considered measures pointing in the same direction.

The Commission, too, seems satisfied with its proposal: 'the Commission considers that its proposal is at the same time simple, useful and efficient and that for these reasons it should be welcomed without reserve and rapidly adopted by the Council' (Commission, 1984, p. 2). However, whether such optimism is justified is doubtful. Despite the advantages of a more liberal carry-over of losses, many Member States will probably oppose the proposal because of the implied (uncertain) budgetary consequences.

Before turning to capital gains and capital losses, let me add one remark: when a Member State taxes different categories of profits differently, understandably it will try to prevent the indirect extension of tax advantages by setting off losses of low-tax categories against profits of high-tax categories. The Commission's proposal includes a compromise between that aim on the one hand and a liberal loss-offset on the other hand: according to Article 3 (3), the restriction is not applied if during a period of five years a loss cannot be set off. An alternative possibly more acceptable to the Member States, resembling the solution chosen in Article 3 (2), is to allow a set-off not in the ratio 1:1 but in inverse proportion to the tax rates applied. Of course, such a procedure cannot be used for tax-exempt categories.

## D. Capital Gains and Capital Losses

As far as capital gains and capital losses are concerned, Member States predominantly tax realized capital gains only but allow unrealized losses to be deducted. Most Member States treat capital gains as normal profits but allow the tax liability to be deferred by reducing the book value of replacement assets (Germany, Greece, Italy, Luxembourg, the Netherlands, the United Kingdom, Belgium (involuntary disposals only)).

In the United Kingdom and similarly in Denmark, realized capital gains are deducted from the depreciable base of the pool, thereby increasing future profits. In case of individual depreciation, capital gains corresponding to depreciation are taxed as normal profits, whereas capital gains exceeding procurement or production costs are liable to the (reduced) capital gains tax only.

296

In France, 'short-term' capital gains (gains realized on the disposal of fixed assets held for less than two years and that portion of gains from fixed assets held for more than two years that corresponds to depreciation deducted) are taxed as normal profits, whereas long-term capital gains are subject to reduced rates.

Working Group IV only once (in 1984) discussed capital gains and capital losses. In that context the Commission endeavoured to reduce the field of investigation by concentrating on realized ordinary capital gains and excluding non-realized gains as well as gains realized in connection with the closing down or sale of an undertaking. The Commission seems to prefer the tax-deferral system already practiced by most Member States and to favour not restricting the choice of replacement asset.

Of course, for supporters of the Schanz-Haig-Simons-concept of income, that is not easy to swallow. However, from a political point of view, the Commission's concept has at least three advantages:
− it corresponds to what has already been practiced by most Member States;
− it corresponds more or less to what has already been suggested in the proposed Merger Directive and found acceptable by Member States; and
− it does not deal explicitly with inflation.
Probably, the main points for future discussion will be:
− Should the deferral be conditioned on the acquisition of assets after realization of capital gains? At present, this is not required by the pool system of depreciation: the value of assets acquired earlier may be reduced. Some Member States consider this a superfluous *ex-post* form of subsidy.
− Should it be made possible to reduce replacement cost of non-depreciable assets by capital gains realized on depreciable assets?

### E. Valuation of Stock-in-Trade

As far as I know, the fourth aspect of tax base harmonisation taken into consideration since the discussions of 1961-64 − valuation of stock-in-trade − has not been the subject of discussion in the context of Working Group IV since 1979. Neither am I aware of a Working Document indicating the Commission's position. Obviously, that aspect is not considered of great importance.

Not surprisingly, rules of Member States concerning valuation of stock-in-trade differ, too (Commission, 1980b). In six Member States, the principle of 'the lower of cost or market value' is either prescribed or practiced voluntarily (Germany, France, the United Kingdom, Ireland, Italy, Luxembourg). In Denmark and the Netherlands valuation at market value at balance sheet date is permitted, too.

First-in-first-out (fifo), last-in-first-out (lifo) and average cost may be used in Belgium, Denmark, Germany and Luxembourg − fifo and lifo in Germany

297

and Luxembourg only if it is proved to correspond to the taxpayer's actual practice. In France, the United Kingdom and Ireland, fifo — in contrast to lifo — is admissible; in France also weighted average cost. In the Netherlands, in addition to lifo and fifo, a base stock system is permitted. Italy allows a system which comes close to lifo; other methods are in practice allowed by the tax administration.

### F. Summary

Of the four main aspects of computing business profits for tax purposes — depreciation, carry-over of losses, capital gains and losses, valuation of stock-in-trade — valuation of stock-in-trade has not been the subject of the investigations reactivated in 1979. Capital gains and losses have been discussed once by Working Group IV. The problems most intensively treated since 1979 have been those connected with depreciation; there exists a draft proposal for a Council Directive on that matter.

So far, no measures have been taken effectively to harmonise the base of taxes on company profits. A Commission proposal for a Council Directive concerning the carry-over of losses (Commission, 1984), which is at present being discussed by the Group 'Financial Matters' of the Council, represents the most advanced stage.

### V. OTHER ACTIVITIES

Finally, let me turn to activities which, though not focusing on the general problems of determining company profits, are nevertheless of some marginal or indirect influence. In this context I would like to mention:
— measures harmonising company law;
— the proposed Merger Directive;
— measures to avoid international double taxation; and
— the Mutual Assistance Directive.

### A. Harmonisation of Company Law

Measures to harmonise company law, for example the Fourth Council Directive on the annual account of certain types of companies (Council, 1978) or the (amended) 'Proposal for a Council regulation on the Statute for European companies' (Commission, 1975), are not primarily related to tax matters. Nevertheless, their provisions[2] may have fiscal implications,

2. Compare the valuation rules contained in Articles 179-89 of the proposed Council regulation on the Statute for European companies.

particularly in those Member States practising the principle of linkage, that is to say, deriving the tax balance sheet from the commercial balance sheet.

### B. Proposal for a Directive on the Tax Treatment of Mergers

As early as 1967, when submitting a 'Programme for the harmonisation of Direct Taxes', the Commission analysed in a rather detailed manner the problems of transnational cooperation and combination of undertakings (Kommission, 1967). Two years later, the Commission proposed a 'Council Directive on the common tax arrangements applicable to mergers, scission and contribution of assets involving companies in different Member States' (Kommission, 1969a). It aims at providing the same tax treatment national laws usually provide for domestic undertakings only, for mergers and similar acts involving companies in different Member States, in particular avoiding any tax to be levied at the time of merger. On the other hand, it is recognized that the fiscal interest of the absorbed company's State has to be safeguarded. Therefore, no tax should be due, for instance, on capital gains from contributed assets provided these assets are allocated to the permanent establishment which the receiving company maintains in the country of the contributing company (Article 4). In addition, provisions and reserves of the contributing company constituted under partial or total tax exemption may be transferred free of tax to the books of the permanent establishment of the receiving company which thereby takes over the rights and obligations of the contributing company (Article 5).

The adoption of the proposed Merger Directive was opposed by Germany and the Netherlands. Both were afraid that their companies might use the new provisions to merge out: outside Germany to escape the Codetermination Law, outside the Netherlands (with the classical corporation income tax system) to Member States applying an imputation system. I understand these apprehensions have been dispelled in the meantime.

However, even if the proposed Merger Directive should be adopted soon, it would be of limited influence only, for transnational mergers are hindered not only by fiscal provisions but also by company law.

### C. Proposed Measures to Avoid International Double Taxation

International double taxation is another source of problems, even if national tax rules concerning transactions by nationals were uniform throughout the EC. In this context, two Council Directives should be mentioned, both proposed by the Commission, but so far not adopted by the Council.

The proposed 'Council Directive on the common tax arrangements

299

applicable to parent and subsidiary companies in different Member States' (Kommission, 1969b) aims to avoid double taxation of dividends paid from a subsidiary in one Member State to a parent company in another. For that purpose, it is proposed that dividend payments should be exempted from withholding tax at the subsidiary level (Article 5), and from corporation tax at the parent company level (Article 4). Moreover, Article 7 envisages for a later stage the possibility of opting for taxation according to a system of consolidated profits: profits and losses of the subsidiary are included in the profits and losses of the parent company and taxes already paid by the subsidiary are taken into consideration.

In 1976, the Commission submitted the 'Proposal for a Council Directive on the elimination of double taxation in connection with the adjustment of transfers of profits between associated enterprises (arbitration procedure)' (Commission, 1976), not adopted so far by the Council. To prevent double taxation due to unilateral increases of taxable profits on the grounds that they have been reduced as a result of conditions agreed upon with an associated enterprise in another Member State and which differ from those that would have been agreed upon between independent enterprises, an arbitration procedure is proposed ranging from appeals to the competent tax authorities (Article 1 (1)), mutual agreements between the tax authorities concerned (Article 2) to binding decisions of a commission consisting both of representatives of the tax authorities concerned and of independent persons of standing (Article 3). Since both proposed Directives encounter the criticism of several Member States, adoption by the Council cannot be expected in the near future. Different opinions exist as to the legal form to be used (directive or multinational convention), the character of the arbitration procedure (voluntary or obligatory), whether the participants can appeal to national courts, and whether the decisions of the arbitration commission are subject to the control of the European Court of Justice.


### D. Mutual Assistance Directive

In 1977 the Council adopted a 'Directive on the mutual assistance by the competent authorities of the Member States in the field of direct taxation' (Council, 1977).[3] It aims at preventing tax evasion and tax fraud, and thus helps to make rules concerning the computation of company profits for tax purposes – whether harmonised or not – effective. You may call it the only harmonising measure so far taken in the field of direct taxes.

Article 1 stipulates that the competent authorities of the Member States should exchange in accordance with the provisions of this Directive any

3. Its field of application was subsequently extended to value-added tax.

information that may enable them to assess taxes on income and capital correctly. The information may be given upon request in a particular case (Article 2), automatically without prior request for categories of cases to be determined (Article 3) or spontaneously without prior request in certain circumstances specified in Article 4.

All information received by a Member State under this Directive is to be kept secret in that State in the same manner as information received under its domestic legislation. It shall in no circumstances be used for other than taxation purposes (Article 7 (1)).

The Directive does not oblige Member States to carry out enquiries for or to provide information to other States which by their own law or administrative practices cannot do so themselves. Information may be withheld if business secrets or public policy are at stake, or if the State requesting the information is, for practical or legal reasons, unable to reciprocate (Article 8).

So far, the Mutual Assistance Directive has not been transformed into national law by all Member States. I am not informed about how far it has really changed the mutual assistance as provided for in double-taxation treaties.


## VI. Concluding Remarks

Why has harmonisation policy, in 25 years of endeavour, so far achieved no success – in the form of binding agreements – with respect to the determination of company profits (or, for that matter, direct taxes in general)?

Of course, there is a general tendency among Member States to retain as many tax parameters as possible, to have to change as little as possible. To many national delegates, nothing seems to be more satisfying on their return from Brussels than being able to announce: 'For us, nothing will have to be changed!'

This is true of the whole field of tax harmonisation, even of harmonisation of legislative provisions in general. More specifically related to direct taxes is the fact that for quite some time the Common Market was primarily seen as a common product market rather than a common factor market. The first stages were dominated by pre-programmed measures to build up the customs union. In addition, no direct-tax problem was considered so urgent and so much calling for reform as the cascade-type of turnover tax in the field of indirect taxes. Given the capital mobility achieved, the obvious differences in burden of direct taxes, and the segmentation effects of partial imputation systems, one wonders whether such indifference is still justified.

Bundesministerium der Finanzen. *Die Steuerharmonisierung. Mimeograph.* Bonn, 1984.

Commission of the European Communities. 'Proposal for a Council Regulation on the Statute for European Companies.' Amended proposal presented by the Commission to the Council on May 13, 1975, pursuant to the second paragraph of Article 149 of the EC Treaty. *Bulletin of the European Communities*, Supplement 4/75, 1975.

Commission of the European Communities. 'Proposal for a Council Directive on the Elimination of Double Taxation in connection with the Adjustment of Transfers of Profits Between Associated Enterprises (Arbitration Procedure).' Submitted by the Commission to the Council. *Official Journal.* C 301, 21.12.76, 1976.

Commission of the European Communities. 'Report on the Scope for Convergence of Tax Systems in the Community.' *Bulletin of the European Communities*, Supplement 1, 1980a.

Commission of the European Communities. *Report on the Computation of Business Profits for Tax Purposes.* Doc. XV/271/80. *Mimeograph.* Brussels, 1980b.

Commission of the European Communities. *Proposal for a Directive of the Council on the Harmonization of the Laws of the Member States relating to Tax Arrangements for the Carry-Over of Losses of Undertakings.* Submitted to the Council by the Commission. COM (84) 404 final. *Mimeograph.* Brussels, 1984.

Council of the European Communities. 'Council Directive of 19 December 1977 concerning Mutual Assistance by the Competent Authorities of the Member States in the Field of Direct Taxation (77/799/EEC).' *Official Journal*, L 336, 27.12.77, 1977.

Council of the European Communities. 'Fourth Council Directive of 25 July 1978 based on Article 54 (3) (g) of the Treaty on the Annual Accounts of Certain Types of Companies (78/660/EEC).' *Official Journal*, L 222, 14.8.78. 1978.

Council of the European Communities. 'Council Directive of 6 December 1979 Amending Directive 77/799/EEC concerning Mutual Assistance by the Competent Authorities of the Member States in the Field of Direct Taxation (79/1070/EEC).' *Official Journal*, L 331, 27.12.79, 1979.

Fischer, Lutz. *Die Wettbewerbswirkungen unterschiedlicher Normalabschreibungen in den Ertragsteuergesetzen der EG-Staaten.* Baden-Baden: Nomos Verlagsgesellschaft, 1980.

Fischer, Lutz. 'Steuerliche Abschreibungen in der Bundesrepublik Deutschland vor dem Hintergrund der Bemühungen der EG-Kommission um die Harmonisierung der Abschreibungen.' Lecture given before the

German, Luxembourg, and Austrian Section of the International Fiscal Association. Mimeograph. Regensburg, 19.5.84, 1984.

King, Mervyn A. and Fullerton, Don (eds). *The Taxation of Income from Capital: A Comparative Study of the United States, the United Kingdom, Sweden, and West Germany.* University of Chicago Press, 1984.

Kommission der Europäischen Gemeinschaften. *Zweiter Gesamtbericht über die Tätigkeit der Gemeinschaft (18. Sept. 1958 - 20. März 1959).* Brussels, 1959.

Kommission der Europäischen Gemeinschaften. *Dritter Gesamtbericht über die Tätigkeit der Gemeinschaft (21. März 1959 - 15. Mai 1960).* Brussels, 1960.

Kommission der Europäischen Gemeinschaften. *Siebenter Gesamtbericht über die Tätigkeit der Gemeinschaft (1. April 1963 - 31. März 1964).* Brussels, 1964.

Kommission der Europäischen Gemeinschaften. 'Programm für die Harmonisierung der direkten Steuern.' Mitteilung der Kommission an den Rat vom 26.6.1967. *Bulletin der Europäischen Gemeinschaften,* Sonderbeilage 8/1967.

Kommission der Europäischen Gemeinschaften. 'Vorschlag einer Richtlinie des Rates über das gemeinsame Steuersystem für Fusionen, Spaltungen und die Einbringung von Unternehmensteilen, die Gesellschaften verschiedener Mitgliedstaaten betreffen.' Von der Kommission dem Rat vorgelegt. *Amtsblatt,* C 39, 22.3.69, 1969a.

Kommission der Europäischen Gemeinschaften. 'Vorschlag einer Richtlinie des Rates über das gemeinsame Steuersystem für Mutter- und Tochtergesellschaften verschiedener Mitgliedstaaten.' Von der Kommission dem Rat vorgelegt. *Amtsblatt,* C 39, 22.3.69, 1969b.

Kommission der Europäischen Gemeinschaften. *Bericht über die Bemessungsgrundlage der Steuern auf Unternehmergewinne.* Dok. XIV/90/72. *Mimeograph,* Brussels, 1972.

Musgrave, Peggy B. 'Harmonization of Direct Business Taxes: A Case Study.' In Shoup, Carl S. (ed.). *Fiscal Harmonization in Common Markets,* Vol. II. New York: Columbia University Press, 1967.

Neumark Committee. 'Report of the Fiscal and Financial Committee.' In *Tax Harmonization in the Common Market.* Chicago: Commerce Clearing House, 1963.

Parliament of the European Communities. 'Resolution on the Harmonization of Systems of Company Taxation and of Withholding Taxes on Dividends.' *Official Journal of the European Communities,* C 140, 5.6.79, 1979.

Rädler, Albert J. *Die direkten Steuern der Kapitalgesellschaften und die Probleme der Steueranpassung in den sechs Staaten der Europäischen Wirtschaftsgemeinschaft.* Amsterdam: Internationales Steuerdokumentationsbüro, 1960.

Snoy, Bernard. *Taxes on Direct Investment Income in the EEC: A Legal and Economic Analysis.* New York: Praeger, 1975.

# 11

## Tax harmonisation and labour mobility

### David Ulph*

#### I. INTRODUCTION

To date, a great deal of concern with tax harmonisation in the European Community has focussed on the harmonisation of commodity (product) taxes. Largely, no doubt, as a result of the progress that has been made in this area, attention is now shifting to the harmonisation (coordination) of factor taxes, so that progress can be made towards one of the fundamental objectives of the EC Treaty which was the establishment of a common market in which there is a free movement of goods and services, as well as labour and capital.

The purpose of this paper is to explore the implications of tax harmonisation, and, in particular, the proposals put forward by the Commission (1979) for labour mobility. While in many ways the considerations affecting labour mobility are similar to those affecting capital mobility, as discussed by Musgrave (this volume) there are crucial features of labour, such as individuals having preferences about where they live and work and their forming family units, which introduce vital differences that not only limit the scope for tax harmonisation to affect mobility, but also how we appraise the desirability of such harmonisation.

Moreover, as the Commission (1985) recognises, there are many other factors affecting labour mobility to do with mutual recognition of qualifications amongst Member States which may be as critical as tax harmonisation. A discussion of these measures lies outside the scope of this paper, and indeed in the discussion I shall proceed on the assumption that the Commission has been largely successful in achieving its objectives of removing these other obstacles to mobility. Without such an assumption it is almost impossible to say anything about the efficiency impact of tax harmonisation. This caveat should be borne in mind throughout the paper.

The plan of the paper is as follows. In the next section I shall outline some general principles that bear on the positive and normative analysis of the impact

* The author is grateful to Maurice Marchand and Jo Ritzen for their comments as discussants at the conference.

of tax harmonisation on labour mobility. Subsequently, I shall briefly summarise the proposals made by the Commission, and then, in Section IV, bring the principles of Section II to bear on the proposals.

## II. TAXATION AND MOBILITY OF LABOUR

In this section I shall discuss three separate sets of issues that will be relevant to the later discussion. The first concerns the different principles that may apply to the taxation of labour income. The second set involves the principles of appraising labour income taxation, while the third examines the implications of these two sets of principles in the context of some explicit models of mobility.

### A. Principles of Taxation of Labour Income

There are three principles of taxation that can be considered.

### Taxation at source

Under this principle each country is entitled to tax all labour income generated within that country, whether this accrues to a resident or a non-resident. This is simply a way of ensuring that some of the rewards from the pursuit of economic activity within the country accrue to the government. Ideally, this principle calls for *in rem* taxation, which, in the context of labour income, would correspond to a payroll tax.

One obvious question to ask is whether the source principle gives rise to a sufficiently well defined basis of taxation that there is no significant amount of distortion and loss of revenue as individuals arrange their affairs to avoid paying tax.

One way to understand the issues here is to consider the underlying structure of production. In describing production, commodities are typically distinguished by physical characteristics, location and date of delivery. For some types of labour input, however, it may be the case that the location of labour is either meaningless or irrelevant so that production is best described by omitting any location label for that labour or perhaps by assuming that there is perfect substitutability between all (or at least some) locations of the labour. An example of the former case would be of an individual resident in country A who writes a consultancy report for a firm in country B on the basis of research done while visiting country C, the report being written on a plane flying the individual from country D to country E. An example of the latter would be of a

306

company transporting goods from country A to country B which can employ labour in either country to undertake delivery.

In the first example it would appear to be conceptually impossible to apply the same principle, while in the latter any attempt to do so in one country but not the other could lead to arbitrary distortions.

The conclusion that emerges from this discussion is that for the same principle to be valid it must be the case that labour from a particular country is essential to the production of a particular firm. Whether or not this is true is an empirical matter which depends a great deal on the type of labour and the type of production. It is certainly not a universally coherent principle, and, one suspects, with the growth of information technology, may become increasingly difficult to apply.

## Taxation on residence

Under this principle taxes are imposed (usually at a progressive rate) on the entire income of each resident irrespective of source. This accords well with the ability-to-pay principle of taxation and is embodied in the almost universal use of income taxation.

In practice all countries in the European Community appear to employ both these principles to the extent that they tax all income of residents irrespective of source and all income of non-residents arising in the Member State (see Platt, 1985). In addition, all states operate some form of payroll tax or employer social security contribution. Many deduct personal income tax from employment at source, this, for residents, being credited against the total amount of tax they have to pay on all sources of income.

While countries appear to apply both principles there are elaborate double taxation agreements designed to ensure that at least some of the tax withheld from non-residents is credited against the tax to be paid by residents. However, since countries have different definitions of residency these provisions only operate imperfectly giving rise to some residual double taxation which is the cause of concern to the Commission.

## Taxation on the basis of citizenship

Under this principle states are entitled to tax the income of their citizens or nationals irrespective of source or residency. This is the principle that is widely discussed in the context of developing countries trying to recoup some return on the resources they invest in the training and education of their citizens who then live and work abroad, often, though not always, commanding much higher salaries than they could earn within their country of origin. This was the subject

307

of the recent symposium on taxation and labour migration edited by Bhagwati (1982).[1]

This is a principle which has no analogue in the case of capital, and though it will not figure much in the subsequent discussion of labour mobility within the European Community, it is worth recognising that it can play an important role in the wider discussion of general labour movements between states.

## B. Principles of Evaluating Labour Income Taxation

There are three different criteria that can be applied when appraising schemes of labour income taxation.

### Efficiency

In the context of labour mobility, this reduces to the more special requirement of locational neutrality − namely that the tax system should not introduce arbitrary distortions into individual choices as to where to work. The exact conditions that are required to achieve such efficiency, and therefore the tax systems that will produce these conditions, will depend crucially on the types of mobility that are being considered (see subsection C of this section), but roughly speaking, what this principle requires is a correspondence between each individual's marginal rate of substitution between work in different areas, and their marginal rate of transformation (rate of marginal products).

### Taxpayer equity

Although the concepts of vertical and horizontal equity are familiar, as are the attendant difficulties in defining and applying them, there are some features of this particular context (labour mobility) which give rise to additional complexities.

If we take the concept of vertical equity, then this can be applied at two levels, that of the individual Member State and that of the European Community at large. At the level of the individual state there is the difficulty of deciding just

1. The problem of migration is one of concern to the European Community, and has been widely discussed (see, e.g., Salt and Clout, 1976; Klaassen and Drewe, 1973; Bourguignon and Gallois-Hamanno, 1977). While some of this migration, particularly with the accession of Greece, is internal to the Community and could therefore come within the scope of this paper, I have taken the view that the problem is essentially one involving the relations between the Community and other countries outside the Community, and have not dealt with it in this paper.

what is the population about whom the state is or should be concerned (see, for example, the discussion in Mirrlees, 1982) — is it to be employees, residents or citizens? If we are concerned solely with mobility within the Community then this poses no problem since presumably we are concerned with all community residents.

Even if a Member State and the Community as a whole had a shared concern over a given sub-group of the population, it is possible that they would take a different view about the desirability of a given reform. Consider, for example, a proposal to eliminate double taxation which benefited some individuals who were amongst the richest in a particular state, though poor within the Community overall, while at the same time, the scheme reduced the tax revenue and hence the funds available for redistribution to even poorer individuals in the Member State. If, for example, a scheme of rank-order weights were used to capture concern with vertical equity then it is quite possible that the overall desirability of such a proposal would appear very different when viewed at the level of the Member State and of the Community overall.

As this example perhaps makes clear the fundamental source of the conflict between the different levels is the fact that the European Community has no overarching authority for distribution within its area. It has only a limited budget for redistribution between states leaving redistribution amongst individuals to be pursued by those Member States. If the Community had general powers of redistribution it could step in and correct any adverse distributional consequences it perceived to be arising from tax harmonisation.

In what follows I shall take it that in discussing the consequences of tax harmonisation on vertical equity it is the Community's judgements that are to be employed, though recognising that the individual Member States' views will play a role since they determine what redistribution responses these Member States may make to the tax harmonisation.

Turning to horizontal equity, we have, in addition to the usual problems of deciding who are the equals who are to be treated equally, the problem of determining whether it is to be all employees, residents or citizens of a state who are to be treated equally. In other words, should we, for example, take the view that all residents of a particular country be treated equally, irrespective of citizenship. If so, then any attempt by a country to tax its citizens when living abroad in addition to any tax they pay as residents would violate this principle of horizontal equity.


Inter-state equity

As pointed out above, the European Community has neither the power nor the authority to undertake any significant redistribution of income between Member States. This implies that in general the marginal value of government revenue to different states will be different where these marginal values are to be understood to be calculated with reference to some overall community welfare function of the type referred to in the previous section. The principle of inter-state equity will therefore be violated to the extent that any tax reforms cause tax revenue to rise in states with low marginal values and fall in states with higher marginal values.

## C. Types of Mobility

As should be clear the type of mobility with which we are concerned in this paper is inter-state mobility rather than occupational or regional mobility. In thinking about this problem it is helpful to distinguish between two different models or views of such mobility. I do not claim that these areas are in any sense exhaustive.

### Frontier workers

This is a group about which the Community is particularly concerned. They are defined as workers who live in one Member State but work in another, returning home across the frontier every night, or, more precisely, for at least two-thirds of the total number of days for which they work outside their state of residence.

This group of workers could be characterised in the following way:
(1) to all intents and purposes their consumption takes place entirely in their country of residence;
(2) since they are effectively working in the same region they are locationally indifferent about where they work, except to the extent that working outside the country of residence may impose some additional travel costs.

In thinking about this category of workers I shall employ the following stylised model. The worker has a utility function which depends on $c_1$, his total consumption in the country of residence, and on $H_1 + H_2$, where $H_1$ is the number of hours of work in the country of residence and $H_2$ the number of hours of work outside the country of residence. The fact that utility depends on the sum of these reflects locational indifference. If $W_1$ and $W_2$ are the wages the worker receives in the two countries, and if k is the amount of additional travel costs, per hour, incurred by the worker, then efficiency would require that these wages equal the worker's marginal product in the two countries, and that he works outside his country of residence if and only if

$$W_2 \geqslant W_1 + k$$

310

Combining these conditions, efficiency requires the individual to work outside his resident state if and only if

$$MP_2 \geqslant MP_1 + k \tag{1}$$

where $MP_i$ is the marginal product in state i.

To see what kind of tax systems are capable of efficiency let us suppose two states operate payroll taxes whereby

$$W_i = \tau_i MP_i \quad i = 1, 2 \tag{2}$$

and proportional income taxes at rates $t_i$, $i = 1, 2$. Transport costs are allowed against tax, and a proportion $\phi$ of the tax paid in state 2 is credited against tax to be paid in state 1. Then the individual will work abroad if and only if

$$[1 - \frac{(1 - \phi)t_2}{(1 - t_1)}](\tau_2 MP_2 - k) \geqslant \tau_1 MP_1 \tag{3}$$

Now since we are dealing with a discrete decision where the optimum is characterised by an inequality condition it is possible that if the inequality in (1) is sufficiently large, then the inequality will also hold in (3) even though the relative payoffs have been altered by taxes. The way to think about distortion in this case, therefore, is to consider the marginal person for whom (1) holds as an equality. In a non-distorting system (3) should then hold as an equality as well. Substituting (1) in (3) produces the following condition for efficiency:

$$[1 - \frac{(1 - \phi)t_2}{(1 - t_1)}](\tau_2 MP_2 - k) = \tau_1(MP - k) \tag{4}$$

For an arbitrary $MP_2$ and k there will be a number of configurations of tax regimes which satisfy this condition. However, if (4) has to hold for all workers and hence for all $MP_2$ and k, then this implies

$$\tau_1 = \left[1 - \frac{(1-\phi)t_2}{(1-t_1)}\right] \tag{5}$$

$$\tau_1 = \tau_2\left[1 - \frac{(1-\phi)t_2}{(1-t_1)}\right] \tag{6}$$

Hence a necessary condition for efficiency is $\tau_2 = 1$.

Applying a similar argument to workers who live in country 2 and consider working in 1 will imply $\tau_1 = 1$, so there should be no payroll taxes.

If $\tau_1 = \tau_2 = 1$ then (5) implies $\phi = 1$ (assuming $t_2 > 0$) and so efficiency implies full tax credit.

The condition that there should be no payroll taxes is clearly unpalatable and arises because of the presence of the transport costs k. If we regard these as small relative to wages and are prepared to discount any efficiency loss associated with them, then setting $k = 0$ in (4) yields (6) as the sole efficiency condition.

If we accept that (6) has to apply whichever country is the home country, and also for any values of $t_1$ and $t_2$ (since countries are free to set their own redistribution policies) then the only way to guarantee this is to have $\tau_1 = \tau_2$ and $\phi = 1$, so countries have equal payroll taxes and full credit for taxes paid in other countries.

This class of workers comes closest in its characteristics to capital where, as Musgrave (this volume) shows, efficiency can be guaranteed by having either personal taxation of capital income with full tax credit, or equal yield *in rem* taxation. Even though there is a great deal of similarity, the presence of location costs affects the discussion to some extent.

### Other non-resident

Here the worker, though officially resident in one state, lives and works in two different states throughout the year. A certain amount of consumption will take place in each of the states, though just how much of his income the worker chooses to spend in each of the states is something he can freely choose. There is no presumption now of locational indifference.

Since the individual is optimally allocating his consumption between the two states, we can take utility to depend on total disposable income in units of resident country currency, c, and the proportion of the year spent in the resident country, x, i.e. u(c, x).

Measuring everything appropriately the condition for efficiency is

$$\text{MRS} \equiv \frac{u_c}{u_x} = (MP_2 - k - MP_1)$$

Assuming the individual prefers, at the margin, to work in his country of residence ($u_x > 0$), then this condition says the individual will only work abroad if his marginal product net of additional costs of working abroad exceeds his marginal product in the country of residence, and the exact amount of time spent in the country of residence will be determined by equality between the marginal rate of substitution and the difference in marginal products, net of additional transport costs.

To see how this condition might be affected by various tax systems, let us consider the type of tax system looked at for frontier workers above. With these taxes in operation the consumer will now choose that value of x for which

$$MRS = (1-t_1)(\tau_2 MP_2 - \tau_1 MP_1 - k) - t_2(1-\phi)(\tau_2 MP_2 - k)$$

Notice that even if there were full tax credit ($\phi = 1$) and if either there were no payroll taxes ($\tau_1 = \tau_2 = 1$) or there were equal payroll tax rates ($\tau_2 = \tau_2 = \tau$) but no additional travel costs ($k = 0$) there would still be a distortion induced by the tax system, since the financial gain from working abroad is reduced, in this latter case, from $MP_2 - MP_1$ to $(1-t_1) \tau (MP_2 - MP_1)$. This result simply reflects the fact that there is no way in which the tax system can give exemption to the 'psychic costs' of working in a different country.

These two categories by no means exhaust all the possible types of mobility, but they provide a useful framework within which some other types can be put. For example, it may be more realistic to think of non-frontier workers having a choice between residing and working in one country and residing and working in another. We could think of this decision being made on a year-by-year basis in which case the above analysis of other non-residents applies, but with the choice of x being restricted to 0 or 1, and with the individual being taxed wholly in state 1 or state 2 (and so tax credit being irrelevant). The above analysis will still show that even if the tax rates are the same in the two countries, there will be a distortion in the mobility decision caused by the reduction in the financial rewards of living abroad.

### III. The Commission's Proposals

The Commission (1980) has put forward three proposals.

#### A. Treatment of Frontier Workers

The only taxes that can be levied on the income of frontier workers by the country of employment are those that are withheld from their employed income. These are to be levied at rates no less favourable than those that apply to that country's own residents. Any tax so levied should be credited in full against the tax due on all income in the country of residence. Where the credit exceeds tax due, full re-imbursement of the difference is to be made.

## B. Treatment of Other Non-Resident Workers

These are to be taxed in the country of employment on terms no less favourable than those applied to that country's own resident workers. Tax reliefs to be applied *pro rata* of the proportion of time spent working in the Member State. The income to be taxed here includes income from personal dependent services and pensions, including social security pensions.

## C. Treatment of Tax Reliefs

If a country grants tax relief on payments such as mortgages, insurance premiums etc. to its residents, it should do so for all taxpayers irrespective of whether that taxpayer is a resident, or whether the payment is made to an institution within that country. Correspondingly, non-resident taxpayers should not get special exemptions from taxes.

## IV. ASSESSMENT OF THE PROPOSALS

I shall take the three proposals in turn, though most of what I have to say concerns the first proposal, which is the one to which the Commission seems to attach most importance.

## A. Treatment of Frontier Workers

If we take our three criteria in turn then we can see from the discussion in Section II that this proposal is an attempt to remove any distortion caused by residual double taxation of personal incomes. However, it will not completely eliminate distortions since it does not cover payroll taxes (employer social security contributions) which are levied at different rates within the Community.

Turning to vertical taxpayer equity, the direct effect of the proposals seems to involve no equity considerations since they effectively reduce the tax rates faced by various frontier workers leading to a Pareto improvement. To the extent that different groups face different opportunities for exploiting this reduction in taxes the gains may be spread unevenly across the population.

There are, however, two important indirect effects which may need to be taken into account. The first is that if the changes do succeed in inducing a significant increase in mobility then there could be complex general equilibrium effects on wages which could potentially induce adverse distributional effects. The second indirect effect involves considerations of inter-country equity.

314

Since the onus is on the resident country to remove the distortion caused by any double taxation, then the immediate effect is that countries will lose tax revenue from those of their resident frontier workers whose tax bills are reduced. To the extent that the proposal induces greater mobility, there will be workers who are currently paying all their tax to the home country who will now pay some tax to the country of employment. If the tax the resident country has to credit is greater than the additional tax generated from the higher income of the new foreign worker then the resident state will again suffer a loss of tax revenue.

How significant all this is will depend on the extent to which there are flows of workers across frontiers in both directions. It will also depend on how states agree to split these flows of tax and credit between themselves — which the Commission's proposal allows them to do. If we take it that any payroll tax levied by the country of employment captures all the tax to which it is entitled by virtue of offering the employment (the taxation at source principle) then the sole consideration that should affect the division of revenue should be inter-state equity. How this issue is resolved will determine not just the inter-country equity effects of the proposal, but also the taxpayer equity effects, since significant changes in tax revenue will affect a Member State's ability to redistribute income among its residents.

Finally, the proposal is in line with the principle of treating all residents of a country on an equal basis.

## B. Treatment of Other Non-Resident Workers

I found it hard to understand the rationale for this proposal. It is certainly true that from the point of view of eliminating distortion it does not matter much whether place of residency or place of employment is taken as the basis of taxation provided all income is treated in a uniform way and full credit is given for taxes paid in another country. However, it is hard to see why frontier workers should be taxed on the basis of residency and others on the basis of employment.

Although, as we saw in Section II, giving full tax credit is not sufficient to remove distortion when dealing with other non-resident workers, it does go some way towards reducing the distortion, and it is puzzling that this recommendation did not incorporate the provisions for full tax credit such as those of the first proposal. If full tax credits are allowed then it does not matter whether exemptions are *pro rata* since the country responsible for giving credit can take full account of all tax paid or not paid.

## C. *Treatment of Tax Reliefs*

These proposals have much in common with those for eliminating double taxation. If, for example, we think of an individual deciding whether to reside (temporarily) in one country or another for a full year, then, ignoring relocation costs and payroll taxes, but taking account of exemption levels $e_1$ and $e_2$ in the two countries, the individual will be comparing

$$W_1 (1 - t_1) + t_1 e_1$$

with

$$W_2 (1 - t_2) + t_2 e_2$$

Then even if the tax rates are the same in the two countries, if the exemption levels are not the same (because, for example, a payment allowable in one country is disallowed in the other) then this will generate additional distortions in exactly the same way as any resident double taxation. A harmonisation of the exemption levels will therefore reduce, though not eliminate, the overall distortion of location decision.

This harmonisation of exemption levels could of course have revenue effects which are adverse in terms of inter-country equity.

## V. Conclusion

In this paper, I have examined the impact of tax harmonisation on labour mobility within the European Community. I have argued that, because of the special features of labour, the analysis of tax harmonisation is more complex, and its scope for improving mobility more limited. This is not simply because there are many factors other than taxes that generate distortions which limit mobility, but also because it is not always the lack of harmony between taxes but simply their presence which, as in many other aspects of labour supply, generates the distortion. Nevertheless, the Commission's proposals, particularly those for frontier workers, do go some way to eliminating distortion though they may have complex distributional consequences, and it would require a detailed investigation to come to an overall assessment of their merits.

Bhagwati, J. (ed.). 'Income Taxation in the Presence of International Personal Mobility: A Symposium.' *Journal of Public Economics,* 12, 1982.

Bourguignon, F. and Gallois-Hamanno, P. *International Labour Migration and Economic Choices: The European Case.* Paris: Organisation for Economic Co-operation and Development (OECD), 1977.

Commission of the European Communities. *Bulletin of the European Communities,* 12, 12, 1979.

Commission of the European Communities. 'Report on the Scope for Convergence of Tax Systems in the Community.' *Bulletin of the European Communities,* Supplement 1, 1980.

Commission of the European Communities. 'Completing the Internal Market.' White Paper from the Commission to the European Council. Brussels, 1985.

Klaassen, L.H. and Drewe, P. *Migration Policy in Europe: A Competitive Study.* New York: Saxon House, 1973.

Mirrlees, J.A. 'Optimal Taxation and Induced Migration.' In Bhagwati, J. (ed.). 'Income Taxation in the Presence of International Personal Mobility: A Symposium.' *Journal of Public Economics,* 12, 1982.

Musgrave, Peggy B. 'Interjurisdictional Coordination of Taxes on Capital Income.' Chapter 7, this volume, 1986.

Platt, C.J. *Tax Systems of Western Europe.* Hampshire, England: Gower, 1985.

Salt, J. and Clout, H. *Migration in Post-War Europe.* Milton Keynes: Open University Press, 1976.

# 12

## Personal income taxes: the treatment of tax expenditures

### *Paul R. McDaniel**

#### I. INTRODUCTION

Harmonization or coordination of personal income taxes (PIT) has not been given a high priority by the EC. Indeed, it has been stated that, except for proposals to abolish tax disadvantages suffered by migrant workers, the Commission (1984, p. 8) 'has no plans for harmonizing personal income taxes which are regarded as instruments of national economic policy.' Even more strongly, it was earlier asserted that there is 'no need' to take any steps with respect to personal income taxes as they are the 'most politically sensitive ones' (Commission, 1980, p. 7). Such views have rather consistently been reflected in official and unofficial statements since the Treaty of Rome.[1]

The Treaty of Rome itself makes no direct reference to the harmonization of PIT in the Community. Nonetheless Article 3(c) calls for 'the abolition, as between Member States, of obstacles to freedom of movement for persons, services and capital.' Potentially, at least, variances in the PIT of Member States can produce the proscribed obstacles and need therefore to be considered in light of the broad Treaty objectives. Article 100 may provide some basis for harmonization efforts insofar as it calls for the approximation of legislative and administrative provisions which have an impact on the establishment or functioning of the Common Market. Article 101 is directed to laws, statutory provisions or administrative actions which distort the conditions of competition. Article 92 likewise prohibits 'state aids' which distort competition by favoring 'certain undertakings or the production of certain goods.'

Moreover, as the EC moves toward increasing economic, political and social union, consideration of the issues involved in harmonization of personal

---

* The author wishes to thank Richard Goode and Flip de Kam for their perceptive comments as discussants at the conference.

1. The Commission (1967, par. 258-60) did, however envision ultimate harmonization of personal income taxes within the Community, although differences among the Member States would continue to exist for a considerable period of time. Likewise, the Neumark Committee (1963, pp. 97ff.) believed that some harmonization of personal income taxes would be necessary, although this was a lower priority than harmonization of indirect taxes and corporate taxation. A White Paper (Commission, 1985) did not even mention harmonization of personal income taxes as part of its agenda for completing the Internal Market.

*Table 12.1 Personal income taxes in the EC, 1983*

| | As Percent of Total Tax Revenue | As Percent of Gross Domestic Product |
|---|---|---|
| Belgium | 34.96 | 15.85 |
| Denmark | 52.01 | 24.03 |
| France | 13.41 | 5.98 |
| Germany | 28.26 | 10.56 |
| Greece | 13.08 | 4.31 |
| Ireland | 29.47 | 11.55 |
| Italy | 27.91 | 11.33 |
| Luxembourg | 27.24 | 11.56 |
| Netherlands | 21.34 | 10.09 |
| United Kingdom | 27.70 | 10.47 |
| *Unweighted Average* | *27.54* | *11.57* |

*Source:* Organisation for Economic Co-Operation and Development (1985b), p. 87, Tables 10-11.

income taxes is timely. A personal income tax has consistently been viewed as one of the major revenue sources for the Member States. And the degree of reliance by EC countries on PIT does not permit the subject to be ignored in harmonization discussions. (See Table 12.1.)

## II. Objectives of Coordination of Personal Income Taxes

The first and obvious question to be asked of any effort to coordinate the PITs of EC countries is what it might achieve in light of the objectives of the Common Market. The fundamental theme of the Treaty of Rome is the removal of national law provisions which distort competition within the Market. Could harmonization help achieve this objective or, conversely, are there ways in which a nation's PIT can distort competition? The PIT of a country typically covers the business profits of unincorporated enterprises. Thus, provisions in national PIT legislation that subsidize or penalize particular types of economic activity could have the proscribed effect on competition. Similarly, special tax provisions could affect labor costs, with resulting distortions in competition. Article 92 of the Treaty proscribes certain 'state aids' that distort competition. State aids can be provided as readily (perhaps more readily) through the tax system as through direct government expenditure programs. It is thus important that the state aids of EC countries be identified so that they can be analyzed under the competitive distortion criterion mandated by the Treaty.

More broadly, Article 3(c) of the Treaty appears to prescribe a standard of allocative efficiency when it speaks of the removal of barriers to freedom of movement for persons, services and capital. It is just as possible to create barriers to capital or labor movements through tax provisions as through direct regulatory measures. Moreover, allocative efficiency also requires that we look

320

at the subsidy side and all EC countries use their tax systems to provide subsidies or impose penalties that potentially could affect competition, capital investment and labor movement decisions. The optimal operation of a common market would appear necessarily to involve allocative efficiency issues beyond the narrower one of competition. And here coordination of PIT could be relevant (Dosser, 1967, ch. 1; Easson, 1980, para. 255 ff.).

Article 220 of the Treaty encourages Member States to conclude agreements for the avoidance of double taxation. That process has proceeded on a bilateral rather than a multilateral basis. It is important to examine particular Treaty provisions as well as each Member State's domestic legislation affecting international transactions in light of the Treaty standards.

It is beyond the scope of this paper to attempt to demonstrate that differing levels of taxation, differing tax rates, differing tax bases, differing reliance on direct versus indirect taxes have adverse effects on competition or allocative efficiency within the EC. The purpose is to explore whether tax expenditure analysis can be employed to identify provisions in the PIT systems employed by Member States that are the equivalents of direct government subsidy programs, to examine the PIT bases of three EC countries in light of that analysis, and finally to examine whether the coordination of PIT systems can be achieved even if EC countries desire to continue to use the PIT to encourage or subsidize particular economic activities.

The analysis in this paper will focus primarily on special PIT provisions which are granted to unincorporated enterprises. This focus is justified because of the dominance of the anti-competitive theme in the Treaty of Rome. Although tax preferences provided to individuals to achieve social welfare objectives may affect the free movement of labor, it is probable that such provisions are less likely to affect adversely the purposes of the Treaty in light of the relative immobility of labor. It should also be noted that the approach suggested in this paper is equally applicable to the coordination of corporate income taxes in the EC.


### III. A TAX EXPENDITURE APPROACH TO COORDINATION EFFORTS

Coordination of EC PIT systems neither implies nor requires a single PIT, uniform in all respects throughout the Community. A multinational study ('Study') of the tax systems employed by selected countries that are members of the Organization for Economic Co-Operation and Development (OECD) identified six elements that constitute the structural building blocks for a PIT.[2]

---

2. McDaniel and Surrey (1985, p. 9). The Study was undertaken by fiscal scholars from Canada, France, the Netherlands, Sweden, the United Kingdom and the United States. The purpose of the Study was to provide comparative data on the use of tax expenditures by the respective →

Those elements are (1) a normative definition of income; (2) determination of the general rate structure; (3) definition of the taxable unit(s) liable for the tax; (4) determination of generally applicable rules to assure that the taxes are determined within the time period selected for imposition of the tax; (5) selection of the fundamental rule to implement the tax in international transactions; and (6) determination of provisions necessary to administer the tax. Provisions in a country's tax legislation necessary to implement the policy decisions with respect to each of the six elements constitute part of the 'normal structure' of a PIT. Provisions that deviate from or are not necessary to implement the fundamental policy decisions with respect to each of the six items are classified as 'tax expenditures', i.e. provisions in the PIT which are the functional equivalents of direct spending programs. The Study found that in the PIT systems of each of the six countries, provisions are present which are not necessary or responsive to the decisions made by the country with respect to the structural component of the tax legislation.

*A. The Tax Base*

The first structural element required in the implementation of a PIT is a normative definition of income. After extensive discussion, the Study participants concluded that the only feasible definition that could be employed for comparative analysis of PIT systems was the Schanz-Haig-Simons (S-H-S) formulation.[3] This conclusion was reached despite the fact that none of the countries represented in the Study completely employed the definition in its national tax legislation. But a common definition and agreed-upon application of the definition to particular items were required if provisions actually in each country's legislation were to be classified as necessary to define 'income' or as provisions to achieve non-tax objectives.

The Study experience, I believe, has important implications for EC coordination efforts. As will be discussed below, *effective tax coordination within the EC does not require that each country legislatively adopt an identical tax base*, at least in the sense in which the term 'tax base' is generally employed. What is essential to coordination efforts is that the Commission direct its fiscal experts to employ a sufficiently comprehensive definition of income so that statutory provisions in Member State legislation that are not necessary to that

---

countries. Necessarily that task required that the Study participants agree on common standards to be employed to classify statutory provisions as part of the basic structure of the tax or as tax expenditures. The following discussion relies heavily on the methodology developed by the Study.

3. The definition is the familiar algebraic equation that personal income equals a taxable unit's increase in net worth plus consumption for a given taxable period. See Goode (1976, pp. 11-36) for a discussion of the development and implications of the definition.

definition can be identified and dealt with in a manner consistent with Community coordination objectives. That definition need not be one which is viewed as theoretically pure in every respect by fiscal scholars. Utilization of a widely employed definition is required; agreement on what is an ideal definition of income is not.

Given its broad acceptance in the international fiscal literature, it seems likely that the S-H-S definition should form the basis for identification of tax expenditures in the PIT legislation of Member States. As individual items are considered, some deviations from the pure S-H-S treatment may not be classified as tax expenditures.[4] In this respect, the PIT Guidelines agreed to by the Study participants should prove useful.[5] But, if the approach suggested in this paper is to be employed, those deviations must be relatively few in number.

The practical significance of adopting a single income definition to identify PIT tax expenditures employed by Member States is not that country legislation must conform to the definition. The significance rather lies in how individual country legislation should treat provisions that are classified as tax expenditures, an issue to which we shall turn below.

## B. The Taxable Period

There are two issues involved in the use of a period of time within which to measure a tax. The first is the selection of the time period itself. In the case of the PIT, that time period is generally one year, with either a calendar or fiscal year employed. This aspect of the taxable period element appears to present few practical problems for PIT coordination.

The second issue involves the rules necessary to assign items of income and deduction to the appropriate taxable period. In this respect, country legislation generally seems to allow the cash method of accounting to be used by those whose income is derived from wages and salaries. PIT coordination efforts can accept this rule as normative. For individuals whose income is derived from unincorporated business enterprises, the accrual method of accounting is required to determine accurately the income for a given taxable period. Under the approach to PIT coordination suggested in this paper, it would be necessary to agree in principle on the application of accounting rules to particular types of transactions in order to identify tax expenditures provided through the

---

4. For example, the Study definition deviated from the ideal S-H-S by accepting the realization principle in the taxation of gains from dealings in property and in concluding that gifts need only be included in the tax base of the donor or donee, but not both. See McDaniel and Surrey (1985, pp. 41-42 and 25-27, respectively) for the Study reasoning on these issues.
5. *Idem.* at pp. 21-61. See also the discussion of conceptual issues involved in the classification of legislative provisions under the S-H-S definition in Surrey and McDaniel (1985, pp. 184-226).

accounting provisions in the PIT legislation of Member States. The Study Guidelines again should be helpful in this task (McDaniel and Surrey, 1985, pp. 55-58).

## C. International Aspects

In adopting a PIT, a country must determine how its system will be applied to nationals who invest, do business and perform services in other countries. The principal objective is to mitigate international double taxation. One of two methods generally is employed to achieve this objective: worldwide taxation coupled with a foreign tax credit, or residence taxation with exemption for foreign income. Either method, consistently applied, is acceptable under international tax norms (McDaniel and Surrey, 1985, pp. 58-61), and each appears consistent with Treaty objectives. Bilateral treaties likewise are employed to carry out the Treaty injunction to Member States to take steps to avoid international double taxation.

A country must also apply its tax system to non-nationals who invest, do business and perform services within its borders. The Study concluded that practices in this respect differed so widely among countries that it was not possible at this stage to identify norms for taxation of such transactions (McDaniel and Surrey, 1985, p. 59).

## D. Other Structural Elements

The other structural elements necessary to implement a PIT involve selection of a generally applicable rate structure, determination of the taxable unit, and adoption of administrative procedures to implement the tax. Each of these elements can raise complex coordination issues but, in order to keep this paper to manageable proportions, the discussion will center on the definition of the PIT base, the accounting rules, and international aspects of a PIT. Until agreement can be reached on these matters, it is unlikely that it will be profitable to pursue the coordination issues raised by the other three structural elements.

## E. The Tax Expenditure Component of a PIT

It is now widely accepted that a PIT system can serve as a mechanism for spending national revenues in addition to its traditional function of raising revenues (OECD, 1985a). This recognition came about because as one analyzes the PIT systems of various countries, it is obvious that there are numerous provisions that are not responsive to the question how shall the tax base be normatively defined? The PIT systems also reveal a number of deviations from generally applicable and accepted accounting principles. There likewise are special provisions within each country's system of taxation of its nationals' international transactions which are inconsistent with its basic international taxation system and which are intended to favor domestic over foreign enterprises. The existence of these provisions in national tax legislation cannot be accounted for on pure tax policy grounds. They instead provide incentives to engage in certain activities or share the costs incurred for particular economic activities. The provisions thus are the functional equivalents of direct expenditure programs and have been given the name 'tax expenditures'.

Country tax legislation can thus be divided into two components: one consists of the provisions necessary to implement the fundamental structure of the PIT (the structural component); the other consists of the provisions by which government spending objectives are carried out through the tax system (the tax expenditure component).

Conceptually, tax expenditure analysis posits that a taxpayer computes PIT on income as normatively defined by the country. The taxpayer pays the amount of tax so determined by applying the rate schedule to that tax base and remits a check to the government in that amount. We may call this check the taxpayer's 'economic tax check'. The government in turn then remits to the taxpayer a check which is equal in amount to the subsidies granted through the tax system by means of special deductions, exclusions from income, deferrals of tax, and credits for which the taxpayer has qualified. We may call this check the taxpayer's 'tax subsidy check'. Of course, in practice, the taxpayer and the government do not exchange the two checks. Instead, in the calculation of 'tax' liability, the two imputed checks are netted and the taxpayer remits a check to the government if the taxpayer's economic tax check exceeds his tax subsidy check; conversely, the taxpayer may receive a check from the government if his tax subsidy check exceeds his economic tax check. In the former case, it is traditional to refer to the net check remitted to the government as the taxpayer's 'tax liability'. But, under tax expenditure analysis, that check is not the 'tax'; it is simply a figure which represents the result of the arithmetical process previously described (McDaniel, 1985, pp. 273-74).

The recognition that government expenditures may be made through the tax system just as through the direct spending mechanism has a number of important implications. The most obvious one is budgetary and (within the EC) France, Germany and Spain are required by national legislation to submit annual budgets of tax expenditures. In the United Kingdom, Ireland and Portugal, while there is no legislative requirement that tax expenditure budgets be submitted, in fact the Parliaments receive information on the revenue cost of tax expenditures in each year's annual budget. The Netherlands has conducted a six-year study concerning the feasibility of implementing a tax expenditure budget which should be completed soon. Canada and the United States, major

325

trading partners of EC countries, likewise require the submission of tax expenditure budgets each year. (OECD, 1985a).

As one looks at the tax expenditure budgets and listings of the EC countries and those prepared by scholars from the Netherlands, France and the United Kingdom who participated in the Study, it is apparent that EC countries employ tax expenditures both in large numbers and in large revenue amounts. It also seems likely that EC countries for the foreseeable future will continue to use the tax expenditure mechanism to a significant extent.

Tax expenditures may be provided through special provisions that deviate from the normative rules established for any of the six elements of a PIT. In the context of this paper, we are concerned with tax expenditures granted to business enterprises through special provisions that deviate from a normative definition of income, from generally established accounting rules and from an accepted technique for the relief of international double taxation. In the case of the income definition, amounts may be excluded from the tax base by special exclusions from income, by special deductions or by tax credits. In the case of accounting provisions, deviations may result in deferral of tax, by acceleration of deductions or deferral of income from the period in which they should be reported under the general accounting principles. In the case of international double taxation rules, special provisions may be provided in a worldwide taxation/foreign-tax-credit system, for example, by exemption or deferring tax on foreign source income derived by a country's nationals; in a residence taxation-exemption method, special provisions, for example, may allow foreign losses to offset domestic income even though foreign earnings are exempt. Where the subsidy is given in the form of a special exclusion from income, deduction, or tax credit that eliminates all or part of an item from the tax base, the tax expenditure program is the equivalent of a direct government grant. Where the tax expenditure is provided in the form of a deferral of tax on a particular item through deferrals of income or acceleration of deductions, the tax expenditure is the equivalent of a loan from the government and, typically, that loan will be interest-free and unsecured. The loan is given out in years in which tax liabilities are lower than those that would be called for if the taxpayer were required to pay his economic tax, and is repaid in later years in which his tax liability is higher than would be required if he were to pay his economic tax. EC countries use both types of tax expenditures extensively.

Coordination of the PIT base of EC countries could take one of several different forms. Each country could be required to adopt a commonly agreed-upon definition of income in its country's legislation. If this common definition of income were the S-H-S definition, in effect all tax expenditures would be repealed automatically and, by definition, the tax bases would be coordinated. This approach is a traditional 'tax reform' approach. It seems highly unlikely that any Member State will ever adopt it; agreement to adopt it on a Community-wide basis seems even more unlikely. A second approach would accept the proposition that countries can use their tax systems to provide incentives or relief from hardship and the Community could agree to harmonize those subsidies. Given the wide variety of purposes for which tax expenditures are employed and the fact that those purposes differ from country to country, it likewise seems unlikely that this approach to coordination would ever be successful. The question then becomes whether there is a method of coordination available which can accept the proposition that countries will continue to use tax expenditures and yet insure that the tax systems of the countries are in fact coordinated, regardless of the nature and extent of the tax expenditures employed. After reviewing the use of PIT tax expenditures for unincorporated enterprises in three EC countries in the following section, we shall return to that question in Section V.

## IV. The Use of Tax Expenditures by Three EC Countries

The magnitude of the problem of coordinating PIT systems that employ tax expenditures can be discerned by examining the tax expenditure list compiled for three EC countries – the United Kingdom, the Netherlands, and France – by fiscal scholars from those countries who participated in the Study (McDaniel and Surrey, 1985, pp. 228, 318, 354). The Study revealed that the United Kingdom provides some seventy tax expenditures to individuals, unincorporated enterprises, and corporations through its personal and corporate income taxes, the Netherlands forty-five, and France over one hundred.

The lists include a number of tax expenditures that are provided to unincorporated enterprises (and typically to corporations as well). For example, the Netherlands and France provide tax credits for investment in specific assets; the United Kingdom does not provide an investment credit. An investment credit is, of course, the financial equivalent of a direct grant from government. As will be discussed below, the question under Article 92 of the Treaty is whether the French and Dutch investment tax credits constitute state aids which result in possible distortions in competition, especially as compared with the United Kingdom which does not provide an investment tax credit.

All three countries provide accelerated depreciation for investments by enterprises in specified types of tangible assets such as machinery and equipment. The Study classified such provisions as tax expenditures to the extent that the resulting depreciation allowances were in excess of declining balance depreciation over the useful life of the asset (i.e. generally corresponding to economic depreciation). The tax deferrals resulting from the accelerated depreciation allowances are interest-free loans from the government. Again, the question for consideration under the Treaty is whether the three governments could grant direct interest-free loans for investment in

327

machinery and equipment without violating Article 92 and perhaps other Articles as well.

The United Kingdom, France and the Netherlands also provide a variety of tax expenditures to agriculture. The tax expenditures are equivalent in some instances to direct grants and in others to interest-free loans. Examples of other tax expenditures for unincorporated enterprises (and corporations) include the following. United Kingdom: special rate reduction for foreign traders; exemption for gain on the disposal of a family business on retirement of the owner. Netherlands: rollovers of gains on dispositions (voluntary and involuntary) of certain business assets; unlimited carryover of losses of new enterprises; exemption for income for travel expenses and the use of a business car. France: accelerated depreciation for film makers; special reserves for newspaper and periodical publishers; a special tax regime for small businesses.

As can be seen from the above highly selected examples from the tax expenditure lists prepared for the Netherlands, France and the United Kingdom, each of these EC countries utilizes tax expenditures for business enterprises to a significant extent. The official tax expenditure lists prepared for Germany and Spain reveal a similar pattern. As noted above, an approach to coordination in the EC that required adoption of a uniform and comprehensive tax base by all Member States would in effect require a repeal of all their spending programs run through the tax system. The Study data show that the economic effects of such a step would be very significant. And the political problems of trying to effect such a proposal would appear insurmountable. Moreover, as will be discussed below, all subsidies by government do not need to be repealed in order to satisfy the objectives of the Community.

## V. PIT Base and Expenditure Coordination

We return now to the question posed earlier in the paper, i.e. whether it is possible to achieve *tax coordination* in the EC under circumstances in which all Member States do, and can be expected to continue to, utilize tax expenditures. Based on the work by the multinational Study, the following describes an approach which appears to offer the possibility that the dual objectives of tax coordination and the use of tax expenditures by Member States can be accommodated. The discussion is put forward in the hope of stimulating thought and debate as to the feasibility of the approach.

### A. Expenditure Coordination

First, given the tax expenditure concept and its utilization in the budget processes in several EC countries, it must be recognized that tax expenditures do not involve an issue of *tax coordination*, they involve the issue of *expenditure coordination*. That is to say, these provisions must be tested under the Treaty and overall Community objectives not as if the provisions are merely tax provisions but as spending programs of government which could be run through the direct spending mechanism. (Indeed, in most countries, one finds tax spending and direct spending programs in the same budget function and often for the same budgetary purposes.)

With this recognition, the first task with respect to tax expenditures, therefore, is to test them out as expenditure programs under the Treaty provisions. Thus, one question is whether a given tax expenditure constitutes a prohibited 'state aid' under Article 92 of the Treaty.[6] A second question is whether, viewed as an expenditure program, each tax expenditure is permitted under the harmonization provisions of Articles 100 and following. Finally, each tax expenditure may also be tested under Article 3(c) concerning freedom of movement for persons, services and capital, depending upon the scope given to that provision.

Where a given tax expenditure would be violative of the Treaty if it were a direct spending program, then repeal of that tax expenditure should be required. If a given tax expenditure is not violative of the objectives or specific provisions of the Treaty, then the country should be permitted to retain it just as it would be permitted to retain a direct spending program. By this process, the notion of expenditure harmonization can be applied to spending programs run through the tax system just as it is applied to direct spending programs.[7]

## B. Tax Base Coordination

The process of identifying tax expenditures for each country as suggested in the preceding discussion involves the acceptance by the Commission's fiscal experts of a common definition of income *in principle*. It does not, however, require each country to adopt the S-H-S definition of income in its country legislation. The definition of the tax base (and accompanying accounting rules) instead is used solely for the purpose of classifying provisions in Member States' legislation as belonging to the tax expenditure component of its PIT legislation or to the normal structure of the PIT. The process of classification does require the use of a single base definition, but the practical effect of use of

6. It has been held that special tax provisions may constitute 'state aids' under Article 92. See, e.g. *Commission* v. *Federal Republic of Germany*. Reports of Cases Before the Court of Justice, vol. 1973-6, p. 813 (1973); *Italian Government* v. *Commission*, Reports of Cases Before the Court of Justice, vol. 1974-5, p. 709 (1974); Commission Decision of 25 July 1973. *Official Journal* no. L253, Sept. 10, 1973, p. 10.
7. See Andel (1967, pp. 311-52) for a discussion of the principles and problems of expenditure harmonization in common markets.

the definition lies in the classification of items as tax expenditures and in the subsequent testing of those tax expenditures against the rules governing direct expenditures by Member States under the Treaty.

Coordination of the PIT tax bases of Member States can also be achieved under a similar process, again without requiring Member States to repeal tax expenditures. The process by which this can be accomplished is a three-step one:

(1) convert analytically (but not actually) each tax expenditure program into an equivalent direct expenditure program, i.e. a direct grant or a loan;
(2) as so converted, determine the tax treatment of the item under the normative definition of income adopted for classification of provisions as tax expenditures or as structural provisions to determine how the item should be treated for PIT purposes;
(3) require the Member State to treat the tax expenditure provision within the PIT the same as the item would have been treated normatively had it been provided through a direct spending program.

The suggested approach can be illustrated by applying it to the different methods by which tax expenditures are provided.

## Tax credits

A tax credit, such as the investment tax credits employed by France and the Netherlands, is the clearest example of a tax expenditure provision that is the equivalent of a direct government grant. Under the approach suggested above, the question should first be posed whether the amount of the credit, if it had been payable as a direct government grant, would have been required to be included in income under the S-H-S definition. If so, then the amount of the credit itself should constitute taxable income, either through immediate inclusion or through the reduction in basis of assets to which the subsidy relates (thus including the amount of the credit in income over time). Inclusion of a tax credit in income, if it should be included in income under normative base definition principles, means that the treatment of the item will be coordinated throughout the Community for tax purposes and there is no problem of expenditure coordination if the credit has passed the tests under the Treaty that are applicable to direct expenditure programs. The important point is that this approach permits a country to use the tax expenditure mechanism but in a way which is consistent with a coordinated Community definition of income.

## Special exclusions and deductions

A similar procedure should be applied with respect to tax expenditures provided through special deductions or exclusions from income which are the equivalent of direct grants. The matter is somewhat more complex where the tax expenditure is provided through these mechanisms rather than through a tax credit. Nonetheless, as has been frequently noted, the financial benefit of any special exclusion or deduction is the top marginal rate of the taxpayer. In effect, this benefit can be converted to a tax credit, i.e. a $ 100 deduction granted to a 50 percent marginal bracket taxpayer equals a $ 50 tax credit. Thus, the approach to tax credits described above could be applied to special exclusions and deductions. Ordering rules would be required where a taxpayer uses multiple deductions or exclusions which move him or her down through lower tax brackets.

## Deferral of tax

In the case of tax expenditures which are the equivalents of loans provided through a direct expenditure mechanism, a different approach is required. Under normative income definition principles, the amount of a loan is not included in income because of the offsetting liability to repay. As discussed above, exactly this same phenomenon occurs where a taxpayer is permitted to defer tax by means of deferred income inclusion or accelerated deductions. Thus, when special tax provisions provide loans to taxpayers, no adjustment to income is required just as there would be no adjustment to income if the loan were provided directly by the government. Again, of course, this assumes that the loan has passed the tests for direct loan programs under the Treaty provisions applicable to direct loans granted by government.

The problem in the case of loans granted through the tax system is that they are almost interest-free. This fact does raise an income measurement problem. The solution, however, is relatively straightforward. Tax coordination (and expenditure coordination) can be achieved if an annual interest charge is imposed on the amount of the outstanding loan granted through the tax deferral mechanism.[8] Alternatively, original issue discount rules could be applied to the interest-free loan, thus resulting in a treatment of a portion of the benefit received in the year of the deferral as ordinary income to the taxpayer, with a portion of the resulting repayments of the loan being treated as interest rather than non-deductible principal. The direct interest charge approach appears the more simple one to administer and should therefore be preferable. The interest charge actually paid by the taxpayer, of course, should be deductible if the loan is associated with income-producing activities and it

8. In the United States, just such an approach is taken with respect to so-called 'interest charge DISCs'. That is, tax is deferred on a portion of DISC income, but an annual interest charge is imposed on the tax deferred.

should be non-deductible if the loan is granted for personal consumption purposes.

With the above steps, the spending programs made through the tax system can be coordinated for *tax* purposes in a manner consistent with a Community-wide definition of income adopted in principle, although again it is to be emphasized that adoption of that definition in principle has not required that it be implemented in such a way as to prevent expenditure programs from being run through the tax system.


## VI. Conclusion

The study of tax expenditures by the multinational Study Group has appeared to open a new approach to analyzing the problems of tax coordination within the EC. The somewhat startling and distinctly non-traditional view of tax preferences that emerges from the above discussion is that under the tax expenditure concept, tax preferences in fact do not erode the tax base. This conclusion derives from the tax expenditure construct described above: a taxpayer in fact pays the tax based upon economic income (normatively defined) and then receives back a tax subsidy check for the amount of the tax expenditures for which the taxpayer is qualified. Given this construct, all that is required for *tax coordination* is that the tax expenditures themselves be treated properly according to the normative income definition principle adopted. It does not prevent the use of expenditure programs run through the tax system, at least not on the ground that such provisions violate the principles of tax coordination. It is a quite separate question whether such provisions violate the rules or principles of the Treaty of Rome with respect to expenditure coordination and the prohibition against subsidies which distort competition. But it would appear that the objectives of the Treaty in terms of tax coordination and expenditure coordination can be better achieved by taking the approach outlined in this paper rather than by a Utopian call for harmonization of all countries under a uniformly agreed-upon tax base which is required to be implemented in individual country legislation. The history and the extent of the use of tax expenditures by Member States does not offer hope that such an approach can ever be implemented.

Andel, Norbert. 'Problems of Government Expenditure Harmonization in a Common Market.' In Shoup, Carl S. (ed.). *Fiscal Harmonization in Common Markets*. Vol. 1. New York: Columbia University Press, 1967.

Commission of the European Communities. 'Programme for the Harmonisation of Direct Taxes.' *Bulletin of the European Economic Community*, Supplement 8, 1967.

Commission of the European Communities. 'Report on the Scope for Convergence of Tax Systems in the Community.' *Bulletin of the European Communities*, Supplement 1, 1980.

Commission of the European Communities. 'Tax Harmonization in the Community.' *European File*, 10/84, May 1984.

Commission of the European Communities. 'Completing the Internal Market.' White Paper from the Commission to the European Council. Brussels, 1985.

Dosser, Douglas. 'Economic Analysis of Tax Harmonization.' In Shoup, Carl S. (ed.). *Fiscal Harmonization in Common Markets*. Vol. 1. New York: Columbia University Press, 1967.

Easson, A.J. *Tax Law and Policy in the EEC*. London: Sweet & Maxwell, 1980.

Goode, Richard. *The Individual Income Tax*. Rev. edn. Washington DC: The Brookings Institution, 1976.

McDaniel, Paul R. 'Identification of the "Tax" in "Effective Tax Rates", "Tax Reform" and "Tax Equity".' *National Tax Journal*, 38, 3, 1985.

McDaniel, Paul R. and Surrey, Stanley S. (eds). *International Aspects of Tax Expenditures: A Comparative Study*. Deventer: Kluwer Law and Taxation Publishers, 1985.

Neumark Committee. 'Report of the Fiscal and Financial Committee.' In *The EEC Reports on Tax Harmonization*. Amsterdam: International Bureau of Fiscal Documentation, 1963.

Organisation for Economic Co-operation and Development (OECD). *Revenue Statistics of OECD Member Countries 1965-1984*. Paris, 1985a.

Organisation for Economic Co-operation and Development (OECD). *Tax Expenditures, A Review of the Issues and Country Practices*. Paris: OECD, 1985b.

Surrey, Stanley S. and McDaniel, Paul R. *Tax Expenditures*. Cambridge: Harvard University Press, 1985.

# Part Six

# European Monetary System

# 13

## The European Monetary System and fiscal policies

### *Vito Tanzi and Teresa Ter-Minassian* [*]

#### I. INTRODUCTION

At its meeting in Bremen on July 6 and 7, 1978, the European Council, composed of the Heads of State or Government of the Member States of the European Community (EC), agreed that closer monetary cooperation between EC countries should be promoted through the creation of the European Monetary System (EMS). The main features of the EMS were set out in a Resolution adopted by the European Council at its meeting in Brussels on December 4 and 5, 1978. The relevant legal texts, in particular the Agreement between the central banks of the Member States of the EC on the operating procedures for the EMS, were subsequently adopted. The system went into operation as of March 13, 1979, with the participation of Germany, France, Italy, Belgium, Luxembourg, the Netherlands, Denmark and Ireland. [1]

At the heart of the EMS is a system of fixed but adjustable exchange rates. Each currency has a central rate expressed in terms of the European Currency Unit (ECU). These central rates determine a grid of bilateral central rates, around which fluctuation margins of ± 2.25 percent (6 percent for the Italian lira) were established. At these margins, intervention by the participating central banks is obligatory and unlimited in amount. The grid of bilateral central rates and intervention limits is supplemented by the 'divergence indicator', which shows the movement of the exchange rate of each EMS currency against the (weighted) average movement of the other EMS currencies. The criterion used is the divergence of the actual daily rate of the EMS currency, expressed in ECUs, from its ECU central rate. When a currency crosses a 'threshold of divergence', set at 75 percent of the maximum divergence spread, there is a presumption that the authorities concerned will

[*] The views expressed are strictly personal. They do not necessarily reflect official views of the International Monetary Fund where the authors are employed. The authors would like to thank Albert Dierick, Owen Evans, Alessandro Leipold, Alessandro Penati, Massimo Russo, Pieter Stek, and Horst Ungerer for helpful comments on earlier drafts, and Shahpassand Sheybani for statistical assistance.
1. For a more detailed description of the history and main features of the EMS, see: Ungerer with Evans and Nyberg (1983); van Ypersele with Koeune (1985); and Ludlow (1982). See also Commission (1982).

correct the situation by adequate measures, such as diversified intervention, measures of domestic monetary policy, changes in central rates, or other measures of economic policy. The ECU plays a central role in the EMS. It serves as the numeraire for the exchange rate mechanism, as the denominator for operations in both the intervention and the credit mechanisms, as a reference point for the divergence indicator, and as a means of settlement and a reserve asset of EMS central banks.

In the words of the Presidency of the December 1978 meeting: 'The purpose of the European Monetary System is to establish a greater measure of monetary stability in the Community. It should be seen as a fundamental component of a more comprehensive strategy aimed at lasting growth with stability, a progressive return to full employment, the harmonization of living standards and the lessening of regional disparities in the Community. The European Monetary System will facilitate the convergence of economic development and give fresh impetus to the process of European Union. The Council expects the European Monetary System to have a stabilizing effect on international economic and monetary relations.'

Thus a full evaluation of the EMS would have to look at its political and not just economic objectives. Van Ypersele and Koeune (1985, p. 16 have emphasized that 'The creation of the EMS was not just the work of economic "technicians" but also, to a great extent, *a political act*'. Thus its political significance could far exceed its purely economic significance. It is not the purpose of this paper even to attempt an assessment of the extent to which the experience of the EMS to date has approached the realization of these objectives. Rather, the paper will be focused on two much more limited questions: (a) to what extent has participation in the EMS contributed to promoting mutually consistent monetary and fiscal policies among member countries; and (b) what would be the consequences of differences in the mix of those policies among the countries. The problem in attempting this type of analysis is that almost invariably one relies on a 'before and after' criterion of evaluation rather than on the more correct 'with and without' criterion. Our paper will suffer from this shortcoming as we shall not be able to provide a description of what would have happened from 1979 to the present without the EMS. We shall rely more on the 'with and without' criterion in the theoretical description and in the concluding section.

One may wonder why a Conference on Tax Coordination in the EC should include a paper on the 'European Monetary System and Fiscal Policies'. The inclusion of such a paper is easily explained when two factors are kept in mind. First, the tax systems of the EC countries are not indexed for inflation (Tanzi, 1980). Therefore, assuming that the EC countries succeeded in coordinating their tax systems at a given moment in time, these systems would soon become uncoordinated if different monetary policies led to different inflation rates. Second, given the absence of indexation, and given that very little has been done

338

towards coordinating direct taxes (Tanzi, 1984b), the distortions in the income taxes that would be brought about by different rates of inflation would promote tax-induced capital movements. These capital movements would be encouraged by the differential tax treatment of interest incomes, business incomes, capital gains, and foreign exchange gains (Tanzi, 1984a). These aspects have not received so far the attention that they deserve.

## II. The Theoretical Framework

In this section we explore, on a theoretical level, the implications of the acceptance of the constraints of a fixed exchange rate regime for countries with initially different rates of inflation and fiscal positions. The framework utilized is a two-country model, with substantial if not perfect capital mobility. For the exchange rate arrangement to be viable *over the medium term*, inflation performances must eventually converge. It is assumed that the burden of this adjustment falls primarily on the higher inflation country (B), which therefore has to gear its monetary policy to promoting a sustained reduction of inflation to the other country (A)'s level over a given time horizon.[2] This implies that the monetary targets of the two countries will tend to converge over time, after allowance for differences in real growth and in structural trends of velocity.

Fiscal positions are assumed to differ significantly between the two countries. Specifically, in country A the public sector deficit is taken to be 'small' in relation to Gross Domestic Product (GDP) and to savings, and its public debt/GDP ratio to be stable or falling. Furthermore, that ratio is not high. The bulk of the deficit is easily financed through sales of bonds to the non-bank public, thus allowing adequate expansion of credit to the private sector, within the constraints set by the authorities' monetary target. In country B, however, the fiscal deficit is assumed to be a substantially larger proportion of GDP and of domestic savings, leading to a rising trend in its already high public debt/GDP ratio.

In the circumstances described above, the authorities in country B, if they wish to keep their monetary target, are confronted with a choice between either curtailing bank credit to the private sector or financing the budget deficit primarily through issues of bonds to the non-bank public. In either instance real interest rates in B will tend to rise above their level in A. In accepting this conclusion we reject two theoretical propositions now fashionable with some theorists, namely, the Ricardian Equivalence Hypothesis and the hypothesis that the supply of funds to the government is perfectly elastic. We shall not discuss the reasons for the rejection of the first of these hypotheses as there is

---

2. The length of the horizon depends, inter alia, on the size of country B's reserves, its borrowing ability, the relative role of absorption and price factors in its trade performance, etc.

ample literature on this issue.[3] We shall, however, briefly discuss the second of these hypotheses as it has received far less attention.

Some economists (for example, Phelps, 1985) have pointed out that in any one year the size of the fiscal deficit (which generally amounts to a few percentage points of GDP) is a small fraction of the total wealth of a country (which is normally at least three times the size of its GDP). Thus, it is argued, a small reallocation in the portfolios of the households should be able to accommodate the increase in the public debt. In a perfect capital market, such reallocation could be induced by a very small increase in the rate of return to bonds. The main weakness of this argument is that it does not recognize that there are significant costs for individuals when they try to convert one type of asset (say, shares in companies, or land, or buildings) into another (e.g. government bonds). Some of these costs may be associated with tax liabilities that result from these shifts (income taxes on realized capital gains, transfer taxes, etc.). Others may involve commissions to be paid to brokers or real estate agents. Others still may involve relocation costs if, for example, the individual would buy more bonds by selling his residence to move into a smaller house. The existence of these costs implies that the supply curve of funds faced by the government or by any other group is upward sloping and the slope increases as the government attempts to borrow more. People will be willing to substitute some of the assets in their portfolios with more government bonds only if the increase in the rate of interest is large enough to make these shifts worthwhile.[4] The above discussion points to the importance of household saving. When bonds are purchased out of current household income, the income saved can go into bonds without any need to convert illiquid assets into money, and then money into bonds. In other words the transaction costs are minimal when bonds are bought with savings out of current income.

The increase in interest rates in country B that can be expected from the persistence of a larger deficit is likely to have several effects on both the demand and the supply of loanable funds. On the demand side, it will adversely affect the interest-sensitive components of domestic spending, primarily fixed investment and stockbuilding. On the supply side, it may, over time, contribute to an increase in the rate of domestic saving in country B as compared to country A. The strength of this effect or even its direction is, however, debatable.[5] As economic theory has long taught us, it is conceivable that an

3. For the modern version of the Ricardian Equivalence Hypothesis, see Barro (1974). For two recent papers that reject Barro's Ricardian Equivalence Proposition, see Modigliani, Japelli and Pagano (1985), and Boskin and Kotlikoff (1984). Several studies claim to have found support for that hypothesis.

4. Several papers have shown that higher deficits (and higher public debts) are significantly correlated with higher real interest rates. See, inter alia, Muller and Price (1984), and Tanzi (1985).

5. For two studies that have found a positive relationship between the level of interest rates and the saving rate, see Boskin (1978) and Gylfason (1981). For two studies that have found a *negative*
→

increase in interest rates could even reduce the saving rate if the income effect prevails over the substitution effect. This could happen if a large proportion of financial assets was held by older, retired individuals who, because of their age, could be expected to have a higher propensity to consume out of their total available resources than those currently of working age.[6] Even if the increase in interest rates does not affect significantly the rate of saving, it is likely, however, to cause a shift in the allocation of savings as between financial and other assets, thereby increasing the supply of loanable funds in the economy, which in turn may tend to dampen the rise in the rates, until a new equilibrium is found.

If, as is assumed here, there is substantial capital mobility between countries A and B, the rise in interest rates in B will induce a capital inflow from A. This may take the form of increased portfolio investments, by residents of country A in securities issued by B, or of financial loans to residents of B by residents of A, or of larger trade credits by suppliers in A to importers in B, etc. These capital movements would tend to reduce the initial differential in interest rates between the two countries but they are unlikely to eliminate them. Of course the greater the obstacles to the free flow of capital, the less tendency there will be toward equalization over time of the interest rates. As a matter of fact, capital controls can in a way reduce the need for adjusting the exchange rates or for coordinating the monetary policies of the two countries. They thus provide an additional though far less desirable instrument to the authorities. But capital controls are not likely to be effective over longer periods.

Depending on their size, capital inflows may pose more or less severe problems of monetary control to the authorities of country B. If the latter want both to keep to their monetary target *and* to avoid an appreciation of the exchange rate, they will try to sterilize the injection of liquidity through the balance of payments by open market operations, increases in reserve requirements, changes in the rediscount policy, etc. In the process, however, interest rates will tend to rise further, possibly leading to additional capital inflows. If capital is sufficiently interest-sensitive and mobile across the two countries, it may be impossible for the authorities of country B to hold to both the monetary target and the exchange rate. In either case the real exchange rate would tend to appreciate in the short run (though not in the long run) leading to

---

→
relationship between the level of interest rates and the rate of saving, see Japan's Economic Planning Agency (1983), and Tanzi and Sheshinski (1984). For a study that has not found any relationship, see Friend and Hasbrouch (1983).
6. See Tanzi and Sheshinski (1984). These authors have used this argument to explain why the rate of saving of the United States did not respond as expected to the extraordinary increase in real interest rates. The aging of the population of industrial countries, which increases the share of retirees as compared to the working population, and their increased affluence are likely to make this possibility progressively more realistic.

a deterioration in the balance of payments of country B and to eventual downward pressure on the nominal exchange rate.

The costs of maintaining divergent mixes of monetary and fiscal policies for countries with fixed exchange rates will tend to increase over time. Real interest rates in the country with a relatively large deficit will tend to rise as the public debt to GDP ratio increases. And, of course, the public debt/GDP ratio will increase faster when real rates rise. There are several reasons for this. If there is an absolute limit to the ratio of *total* (i.e. public and private) debt in the economy (or correspondingly to the total stock of financial non-equity assets) in relation to GDP,[7] then there will be an ultimate limit to the size of the *public* debt as well, when the public debt reaches 100 percent of total debt. This limit may be even lower if there is an absolute maximum size of the *public* debt relative to GDP that individuals want to hold. Once this limit is reached, monetization of the debt becomes likely (Sargent and Wallace, 1981). As the ratio of public debt to GDP rises, long-run inflationary expectations come to exceed short-run inflationary expectations thus raising even more the rate of return on long-term bonds. The spread between the rate of return on long-term bonds and that on short-term treasury bills is thus likely to depend, over the longer run, on the debt/GDP ratio and on its trend.[8]

In any event, the rate of return on the government debt will have to rise, as the debt increases, in order to induce a progressive increase of government paper in the portfolio of the public.[9] This is especially so as individuals' expectations of an eventual monetization of the debt and of a consequent acceleration of inflation are likely to increase as the debt to GDP ratio rises. As a consequence, preferences of economic agents tend to shift toward financial investments with shorter maturities or toward real assets or foreign assets.[10] The return on longer-term bonds must rise relatively to that on short-term securities. This change in the term structure of interest rates may be aided by capital inflows as foreign capital is more likely to be channeled into shorter-term financial assets.

If the government begins to encounter increasing difficulty in placing long-term bonds at reasonable rates, or if it aims at reducing the cost of servicing the public debt (and consequently the size of the deficit), it will rely more and more on the sale of securities with lower maturity and lower interest rates.

---

7. This hypothesis has been put forward for the United States by Friedman (1982). Friedman has shown that in the United States total debt has hovered around 1.45 times GNP over an 80-year period. The evidence for other countries is not as clear-cut. See Goldsmith (1984).
8. In the short run, short-term interest rates are likely to be affected by monetary policy and other short-run factors.
9. The increase in the return on treasury paper would have to be even higher if savers came to expect the imposition of a wealth tax on the holders of public debt or higher income taxes on interest incomes.
10. The phenomenon of currency substitution will be part of these shifts. See Padoa-Schioppa and Papadia (1984).

Alternatively, the government may make bonds of longer maturity more attractive by indexing their rate of return to short-term rates. These measures will undoubtedly reduce the interest cost to the government and, by reducing the current deficit, will make the country's fiscal stance look less expansionary. However, these changes will increase the liquidity of the economy as these indexed longer-term bonds, or the shorter-term instruments, are more liquid and marketable than the bonds they come to replace.

The increasing liquidity of the public debt will reduce the demand for narrow money and will thus reduce the revenue from the inflation tax on the monetary base. Or looking at this from a different angle, the government will have to pay an increasingly higher price in terms of inflation for the same real revenue (expressed as a share of GDP) that it derives from the inflation tax on money balances. This change will also reduce the possibility of cutting the real value of the public debt by inflating. As much of the debt may eventually come to be held in the form of shorter-term securities or indexed longer-term bonds, the government will not gain as much by inflating as it had in past experiences.[11] Thus the government will have less room for maneuver; or, putting it differently, the rate of inflation required to reduce the real value of the debt by a given amount will become much higher. Furthermore, the cost of servicing the debt, and thus the size of the inflation-adjusted deficit, will be much more exposed to shocks coming from changes in real rates abroad.

Finally, as short-term or highly liquid debt is much more mobile than long-term and illiquid debt, an economy in which the public debt is highly liquid becomes more exposed to the vagaries of market sentiment than an economy in which the debt is illiquid. Thus, the lower interest bill has been bought at the cost of higher potential instability. In such an economy bad news can lead to sudden and sizable capital flights making the pursuit of prudent economic policy much more difficult.

In conclusion, if the two closely associated countries have coordinated their monetary policies but pursue widely divergent fiscal policies, the following effects are likely to occur in the country with the more expansionary fiscal policy: (a) the likelihood of a rise in real interest rates especially for longer-term instruments; (b) a reduction in the growth of private investment; (c) a shift in its composition toward projects with shorter maturities and shorter financing, possibly with adverse implications for the medium-term growth potential of the economy; (d) the likelihood that the level of real interest rates will come to exceed the medium-term real rate of growth of the economy, leading to a spiraling escalation of the public debt, interest payments and the deficit, thus requiring sharper fiscal correction (tax increases or non-interest expenditure

---

11. Masera (1984) has provided some empirical estimates of the size of the inflation tax in Italy from 1960 to 1982. He shows that as inflation came to be anticipated the size of the inflation tax was much reduced.

reduction) over time; (e) an increasing expectation that the stance of monetary policy would have to be eased, leading over time to an acceleration of inflation; and, finally, (f) greater instability in the economy.

Over time these factors are bound to have substantial effects on the exchange rate, ultimately undermining the viability of the fixed rate arrangement. In the short run, the exchange rate may be subject to upward pressures in reflection of interest rate differentials. However, over the longer term, as expectations about the prospects for convergence in inflation between the two countries deteriorate, so will expectations about the exchange rate. Foreigners will come to demand higher and higher premiums to bring (or keep) their capital into (or in) country B. Ultimately, capital inflows are likely to be reversed and pressures on the exchange rate will mount. Before the devaluation, interest rates in country B are likely to be pushed up above their equilibrium level. After the exchange rate is devalued, however, and until expectations of a new devaluation set in, capital inflows may resume at a pace which, once again, creates problems for monetary control. These changes in real rates will come to be expected and individuals and companies will try to exploit them for profits. These speculations will complicate even more the task of the monetary authorities and will bring some inefficiencies in the economy. For example, if enterprises come to expect a devaluation, they will increase their holdings of inventories that are imported beyond their optimal level. They may at the same time delay the repatriation of funds until after the devaluation.

### III. The Experience with Monetary-Fiscal Mixes in EMS Countries

#### A. Convergence in the Monetary Area

The previous section has theorized about the consequences of different fiscal and monetary policy mixes when countries are linked by fixed exchange rate arrangements in conditions of capital mobility. In this section we explore the extent to which the experience of individual countries participating in the EMS is broadly consistent with the theoretical framework outlined above. However, some qualifications must be mentioned.

The first important one relates to the two-country nature of the framework presented above. Although intra-EMS trade accounts for a large share of the total trade of its members,[12] their economic performances, and especially their balances of payments, are likely to be substantially affected by their relations

---

12. The shares of exports to other EMS countries in total exports have ranged from over 60 percent for Belgium and the Netherlands to around 40 percent for Germany, France and Italy and to around 30 percent for Denmark and Ireland at the outset of the EMS. They have tended to decline slightly in the last couple of years, mainly reflecting a redirection of trade toward the United States.

with the rest of the world and in particular with the United States. It is difficult to deal adequately with this issue here. In what follows we shall allude to some of the ways in which intra-EMS relations have been affected by factors outside the system.

A second qualification relates to the adjustable nature of the exchange rate arrangement. A limited degree of flexibility within the EMS arrangement is provided by the existence of margins which for Italy are quite significant. More importantly, however, the exchange rates between the EMS countries have not remained fixed. There have been so far eight realignments within the EMS (Table 13.1) resulting in a 27 percent cumulative appreciation of the DM vis-à-vis a weighted average of its EMS partners, and a 24 percent cumulative depreciation of the Italian lira vis-à-vis the rest of the EMS. Thus, these adjustments could accommodate widely divergent monetary and fiscal policies over the period. The last *general* realignment took place on March 21, 1983. The July 20, 1985 realignment affected only the bilateral central rates of the Italian lira vis-à-vis other EMS currencies. Between 1978 and March 1983 the adjustments had become progressively more frequent and more widespread. Only in the last 3 years or so has the system effectively operated as a nearly fixed exchange rate regime. Between the second quarter of 1983 and the fourth quarter of 1985 the bilateral exchange rates between the deutsche mark and other EMS currencies changed by less than 2 percent with the exception of the Italian lira which depreciated by about 12½ percent.

During the period between the inception of the EMS and the last general realignment, however, exchange rate movements between EMS currencies only partially offset inflation differentials. Over that period some countries experienced an appreciation of their real exchange rates against the deutsche mark (Ireland, Italy). These countries had higher rates of inflation than their partners. Others experienced a depreciation in their real exchange rates (Belgium and Denmark).[13] In general, changes in these real exchange rates have been smaller during the last two years than in the previous phase of the EMS. This suggests that over this more recent period there may have been a greater convergence in the inflation performance of EMS members. Table 13.2 shows that in fact in the last three years both the average rate of inflation for the EMS countries combined and the dispersion among the countries were substantially reduced. This was undoubtedly a major achievement.

It is, of course, difficult to establish the direction of causation in this respect: whether the increased discipline of nearly fixed exchange rates has fostered convergence in inflation rates, or whether the latter has been instrumental in allowing the maintenance of fixed exchange rates. We are inclined to believe

13. These statements refer to real exchange rates as measured by indices of relative consumer prices adjusted for changes in bilateral nominal exchange rates. They are, however, broadly supported by the available evidence on movements in relative unit labor costs.

*Table 13.1 Adjustments of EMS central rates[a]*

|  | BF | DKr | DM | FF | IR£ | Lit | DFl |
|---|---|---|---|---|---|---|---|
|  |  |  | In Percent |  |  |  |  |
| **1979** |  |  |  |  |  |  |  |
| Sept. 24 | – | -3.0 | +2.0 | – | – | – | – |
| Nov. 30 | – | -5.0 | – | – | – | – | – |
| **1981** |  |  |  |  |  |  |  |
| March 22 | – | – | – | – | – | -6.0 | – |
| Oct. 5 | – | – | +5.5 | -3.5 | – | -3.5 | +5.5 |
| **1982** |  |  |  |  |  |  |  |
| Feb. 22 | -8.5 | -3.0 | – | – | – | – | – |
| June 14 | – | – | +4.25 | -5.75 | – | -2.75 | +4.25 |
| **1983** |  |  |  |  |  |  |  |
| March 21 | +1.5 | +2.5 | +5.5 | -2.5 | -3.5 | -2.5 | +3.5 |
| **1985** |  |  |  |  |  |  |  |
| July 20 | +2.0 | +2.0 | +2.0 | +2.0 | +2.0 | -6.0 | +2.0 |
| Cumulative changes vis-à-vis EMS countries from March 13, 1979 to December, 1985[a] | -12.10 | -14.4 | +27.2 | -11.3 | -5.7 | -23.9 | +11.4 |

*Note:* a. In terms of effective exchange rates (weighted by trade shares). The symbols used are respectively: BF: Belgian franc; DKr: Danish krone; DM: deutsche mark; FF: French franc; IR£: Irish pound; Lit: Italian lira; DFl: Dutch florin.

*Source:* Thygesen (1984). The table has been updated by the authors to reflect the July 20, 1985 realignment.

that both factors played a role. The strength of the US dollar, notably vis-à-vis the deutsche mark, in recent years has eased potential strains within the EMS both through its effect on capital flows and, perhaps more importantly, by moderating the impact of the real appreciation of the currencies of EMS members with higher rates of inflation, vis-à-vis those with lower inflation, on their overall competitive position. Strains within the EMS have apparently been increasing since the last quarter of 1985, as the US dollar has weakened substantially, and have required stepped-up intervention by the Central Banks participating in the arrangement.

The deceleration of inflation in the EMS members since 1981-82 is undoubtedly in part a reflection of favorable external influences – in particular the decline in international prices – which partly offset the rise in the dollar during the same period. Also important, however, has been the pursuit in recent years of monetary policies aimed toward a steady deceleration in the growth of the monetary aggregates, supported in most instances by incomes policy measures. Table 13.3 shows the rates of growth of the most relevant monetary aggregates in the EMS countries. The dispersion among these growth rates has been significantly reduced from the inception of the EMS. The deceleration in the rate of growth of broad money has been especially marked in

*Table 13.2 Inflation rates in EMS countries[a]*

| | 1978 | 1979 | 1980 | 1981 | 1982 | 1983 | 1984 | 1985[b] |
|---|---|---|---|---|---|---|---|---|
| Germany | 2.7 | 4.1 | 5.4 | 6.3 | 5.3 | 3.3 | 2.4 | 2.2 |
| France | 9.1 | 10.7 | 13.8 | 13.4 | 11.8 | 9.6 | 7.4 | 5.7 |
| Italy | 12.1 | 14.8 | 21.2 | 17.8 | 16.5 | 14.7 | 10.8 | 9.1 |
| Belgium | 4.5 | 4.5 | 6.6 | 7.6 | 8.7 | 7.7 | 6.3 | 4.8 |
| Netherlands | 4.2 | 4.2 | 6.5 | 6.7 | 5.9 | 2.8 | 3.3 | 2.3 |
| Denmark | 10.1 | 9.6 | 12.3 | 11.7 | 10.1 | 6.9 | 6.3 | 4.2 |
| Ireland | 7.6 | 13.2 | 18.2 | 20.4 | 17.1 | 10.5 | 8.6 | 5.5 |
| Average EMS[c] | 6.5 | 8.0 | 11.1 | 10.9 | 9.8 | 7.7 | 5.9 | 4.9 |
| Measures of dispersion[d] in relation: | | | | | | | | |
| to average | 3.5 | 3.9 | 5.3 | 4.2 | 3.9 | 3.9 | 2.8 | 2.1 |
| to lowest | 3.8 | 3.9 | 5.7 | 4.6 | 4.5 | 4.9 | 3.5 | 2.7 |

*Notes:* a. The inflation rates are measured by year-on-year percent changes in the consumer price index.
b. Third quarter 1985 over third quarter 1984.
c. Weighted by annual shares of each country's GDP (in US dollars) in total GDP of EMS.
d. Weighted arithmetic averages of absolute difference from reference points, weights as in footnote c.

*Source:* IMF, *International Financial Statistics.*

the countries (Italy, France, Ireland) with relatively higher rates of inflation, while the growth of M2 broadly stabilized or accelerated slightly in the lower inflation countries, with the exception of Denmark.[14] At the same time, incomes policy measures aimed at moderating the growth of labor costs were introduced in a number of EMS countries.[15]

## B. Convergence in the Fiscal Area

The increased convergence in monetary policies has, however, not been matched by a greater convergence in fiscal performances. Table 13.4 presents some summary indicators of fiscal performance (with reference to the general government) in the EMS countries since the inception of the system. On balance, it appears that dispersion has tended to increase if fiscal performance

14. Measuring convergence of monetary policy in terms of convergence in the growth of the monetary aggregates is open to dispute as equal growth rates of monetary aggregates in member countries may not guarantee exchange rate stability given potentially widely different structural characteristics of the demand for money between EC countries.
15. See Commission, *Annual Report*, various issues, for a description of these measures.

## Table 13.3 Growth of money in EMS countries

| | Definition | 1979 | 1980 | 1981 | 1982 | 1983 | 1984 |
|---|---|---|---|---|---|---|---|
| | | | | End of period | | | |
| Belgium | M2 | 6.2 | 3.3 | 6.4 | 7.1 | 8.3 | 4.4 |
| Denmark | M2 | 10.8 | 8.1 | 9.6 | 11.8 | 25.5 | 17.8 |
| Germany | M3 | 5.8 | 6.2 | 5.1 | 7.2 | 5.6 | 4.7 |
| France | M3 | 14.2 | 9.5 | 11.0 | 11.2 | 10.8 | 8.0 |
| Ireland | M3 | 19.0 | 17.7 | 17.4 | 12.9 | 5.6 | 10.1 |
| Italy | M3 | 23.2 | 17.3 | 16.0 | 17.2 | 14.6 | 13.9 |
| Netherlands | M2 | 6.9 | 3.8 | 6.3 | 7.8 | 10.3 | 8.4 |
| Average EMS[a] | | 11.4 | 8.9 | 9.3 | 10.5 | 9.9 | 8.2 |
| Measures of dispersion[b] in relation: | | | | | | | |
| to average | | 5.6 | 3.5 | 3.7 | 3.1 | 3.7 | 3.7 |
| to lowest | | 5.6 | 5.6 | 4.2 | 3.4 | 4.3 | 3.8 |

*Notes:* a. Weighted by shares of each country's GDP (in US dollars) in total GDP of EMS.

b. Weighted arithmetic averages of absolute differences from reference points, weights as in footnote a.

*Sources:* National publications; IMF staff.

is measured in terms of the ratios of the general government balances to GDP. More specifically, fiscal deficits rose in relation to GDP in all EMS countries during the early years of the arrangement, but the extent of the increase varied substantially among the countries. Over the 1979-82 period the greatest fiscal deterioration occurred in Denmark, Belgium, Italy, the Netherlands and Ireland. From 1982 to 1984 the deficits declined in all the countries with the exception of Italy and to a much lesser extent France.

In other to ascertain to what extent differences in fiscal performances have reflected different cyclical positions, it is useful to look at cyclically adjusted budget balances. Available estimates from the EC and the OECD suggest that the degree of convergence in fiscal performances is not significantly higher when measured in terms of cyclically adjusted balances. This may be explained by the fact that cyclical changes were largely synchronous for the EMS countries except for Italy which lagged both the recession and the recovery in these countries.

A more important factor behind the differences in fiscal performances among EMS countries is the interaction between the stock of public debt and the rate of inflation. This is a factor that had not attracted much attention until recent years. Ratios of central government debt to GDP ranged at the outset of the EMS from around 15 percent in France and Germany, to around 25 percent in Denmark and the Netherlands, to 50 percent in Belgium, to 70 percent in Italy, and to nearly 90 percent in Ireland (Table 13.5). As some of the high debt countries have also been characterized by relatively high rates of inflation (Table 13.2), interest payments on the public debt have tended to rise rapidly in relation to GDP in these countries. Therefore, it is not surprising that the

## Table 13.4 Indicators of fiscal performance[a]

| | 1979 | 1980 | 1981 | 1982 | 1983 | 1984 |
|---|---|---|---|---|---|---|
| | | | In Percent | | | |
| **Financial balance/GDP** | | | | | | |
| Germany | − 2.6 | 2.9 | − 3.7 | − 3.3 | − 2.5 | − 1.9 |
| France | − 0.7 | 0.2 | − 1.8 | − 2.7 | − 3.1 | − 2.8 |
| Italy | − 9.5 | − 8.0 | −11.8 | −12.5 | −12.4 | −13.5 |
| Belgium | − 7.4 | − 9.3 | −13.4 | −11.9 | −12.8 | −11.4 |
| Netherlands | − 3.7 | − 4.0 | − 5.5 | − 7.1 | − 6.5 | − 6.3 |
| Denmark | − 1.5 | − 3.0 | − 6.9 | − 9.0 | − 7.1 | − 4.3 |
| Ireland | −10.6 | −11.5 | −12.3 | −13.3 | −11.5 | −11.2 |
| Weighted EMS average | − 3.6 | − 3.4 | − 5.4 | − 5.8 | − 5.6 | − 5.4 |
| Measures of dispersion: | | | | | | |
| (a) from average | 3.4 | 3.5 | 4.6 | 4.7 | 4.6 | 4.9 |
| (b) from minimum | 2.9 | 3.6 | 3.6 | 3.1 | 3.1 | 3.5 |
| **Cyclically and inflation-adjusted balance/GDP[b]** | | | | | | |
| Germany | ... | ... | − 3.7 | − 1.4 | − | 0.4 |
| France | ... | ... | − 1.3 | − 1.9 | − 1.4 | − 0.3 |
| Italy | ... | ... | − 9.0 | − 7.7 | − 4.6 | − 6.2 |
| Belgium | ... | ... | − 8.4 | − 5.4 | − 5.5 | − 4.1 |
| Netherlands | ... | ... | − 5.7 | − 5.1 | − 3.5 | − 3.4 |
| Denmark | ... | ... | − 4.2 | − 7.3 | − 5.0 | − 2.5 |
| Ireland | ... | ... | −11.1 | − 9.6 | − 6.1 | − 4.5 |
| Weighted EMS average | ... | ... | − 4.4 | − 3.5 | − 2.0 | − 1.7 |
| Measures of dispersion: | | | | | | |
| (a) from average | ... | ... | 3.1 | 3.0 | 2.3 | 2.7 |
| (b) from minimum | ... | ... | 3.1 | 2.1 | 2.0 | 2.1 |
| **Financial balance/gross private savings** | | | | | | |
| Germany | −12.8 | −15.0 | −19.3 | −17.1 | −12.5 | − 9.8 |
| France | − 3.4 | 1.2 | − 9.9 | −15.4 | −17.5 | −15.5 |
| Italy | −34.2 | −31.2 | −46.3 | −49.4 | −51.5 | −55.6 |
| Belgium | −35.2 | −44.8 | −61.9 | −57.0 | −55.1 | −49.9 |
| Netherlands | −18.8 | −21.8 | −27.2 | −31.5 | −29.2 | −26.2 |
| Denmark | −10.7 | −21.8 | −45.4 | −51.0 | −39.1 | −24.8 |
| Ireland | ... | ... | ... | ... | ... | ... |
| Weighted EMS average | −15.3 | −15.5 | −25.0 | −26.7 | −25.6 | −24.2 |
| Measures of dispersion: | | | | | | |
| (a) from average | 10.6 | 12.4 | 17.5 | 17.7 | 17.6 | 18.1 |
| (b) from minimum | 11.9 | 16.7 | 15.1 | 11.3 | 13.1 | 14.4 |

*Notes:* a. All indicators refer to the general government (national account basis).

b. Estimates of cyclically and inflation-adjusted budget balances are taken from the 1984 EC *Annual Report*, and for 1983 and 1984 reflect provisional estimates.

*Sources:* OECD, *Economic Outlook* and *National Accounts Statistics*; EC Commission, *Annual Report*; IMF, *World Economic Outlook* and calculations by the authors.

variance in fiscal performances among EMS members is reduced somewhat when measured in terms of inflation-adjusted deficits (Table 13.4).

*Table 13.5 Central government debt in EMS countries*

|  | 1979 | 1980 | 1981 | 1982 | 1983 | 1984 |
|---|---|---|---|---|---|---|
|  |  |  | In Percent of GDP |  |  |  |
| Germany | 14.5 | 15.6 | 17.8 | 19.4 | 20.4 | 20.9 |
| France | 15.7 | 15.9 | 16.8 | 19.8 | 22.0 | 23.6 |
| Italy | 70.1 | 67.0 | 70.0 | 76.2 | 84.6 | 91.3 |
| Belgium | 50.3 | 56.0 | 67.0 | 78.2 | 88.7 | 94.8 |
| Netherlands | 25.4 | 27.5 | 33.0 | 41.6 | 50.4 | 58.1 |
| Denmark | 24.7 | 33.7 | 46.7 | 59.5 | 69.7 | 74.0 |
| Ireland | 88.2 | 87.7 | 94.0 | 103.9 | 117.1 | 126.1 |
| Average EMS | 27.6 | 29.0 | 32.3 | 36.7 | 41.2 | 44.6 |
| Measures of dispersion in relation: |  |  |  |  |  |  |
| to average | 24.8 | 24.8 | 27.3 | 30.6 | 34.8 | 37.6 |
| to minimum | 13.1 | 13.4 | 15.5 | 17.3 | 20.8 | 23.7 |

*Source:* National publications.

While, however, measures of so-called structural deficits (cyclically and inflation-adjusted) may represent better indicators of the fiscal stance and its direct impact on domestic demand and output than conventionally measured deficits, they are less appropriate for an assessment of potential conflict between fiscal and monetary policies. Ultimately, both the cyclical and inflation-related components of the fiscal deficit need to be financed, thereby adding to either the money supply or the stock of government debt in the hands of the non-bank public, with the consequences discussed in Section II above.

Ratios of public sector deficits to domestic savings provide a better indication of the degree of absorption of savings by the government than the ratios of the deficits to GDP for countries with significantly different rates of domestic savings. This is clearly the case for EMS members, where domestic saving rates have ranged from 22 percent of GDP in Germany to 16 percent in Ireland on average during the period 1979-83. Table 13.4 shows that the ratios of general government deficits to gross private savings have varied substantially among countries in the EMS, ranging from a low of about 10 percent in France for the 1979-84 period to a high of 50.7 percent in Belgium for the same period. For Italy that ratio has averaged 44.7 percent but it has been growing over the years, reaching 56 percent in 1984. Divergence in performances in this respect among EMS members has tended to increase over time. Specifically, the absorption of savings by the public sector, after increasing in most EMS countries in the early years of the arrangement, has declined since 1982 in Germany, the Netherlands and, more significantly, in Denmark and Belgium. Instead, it has tended to increase in France and, especially, in Italy.

One perhaps disturbing aspect in this supply-side era is the fact that until recently fiscal correction has been in general more a reflection of increases in revenue than of retrenchment in expenditures. The ratios of total revenues and especially tax revenue to GDP have risen steadily in most EMS members; the degree of dispersion in tax ratios has tended to narrow, especially on account of the sharp increase of the tax burden in Italy (9 percentage points) and Ireland (over 8 percentage points) over the 1979-84 period. If high tax rates have the negative effects emphasized by supply-siders, this is not a change that one would cheer about. Ratios of expenditures to GDP have also tended to increase in most EMS countries, with a deceleration in this growth (and marginal declines in some instances) only in evidence in the last two years. For expenditure, the degree of dispersion has generally grown over the period. In general, the increase in expenditures has reflected both the growth of interest payments on the public debt and that of non-interest expenditures. However, there have been marked differences in the rates of growth of these two categories of expenditures among EMS members.

In summary, the record of fiscal performances in EMS members does not point to a generalized trend of convergence over the period of existence of the arrangement. On balance, the smaller countries, notably Belgium and Denmark, have made a substantial effort toward reducing their fiscal deficits over the last three years or so. The absorption of domestic savings by their general governments remains, however, still high compared with Germany. In France, after a significant deterioration in the early 1980s, the fiscal position has tended to stabilize but the gap in relative rates of absorption of domestic savings vis-à-vis Germany has widened. The largest and still growing divergence in fiscal performance is now between Italy and Germany; by 1984 the general government absorbed five times as large a proportion of private savings in Italy as in Germany.

## C. Consequences of Non-Convergence in the Fiscal Area: The Case of Italy

In analyzing the impact of divergent fiscal performances on interest rate developments in EMS members, we shall focus on differentials between the rates in Germany and those in other EMS countries. We thus implicitly assume that external monetary shocks are transmitted within the EMS through the 'filter' of the policy response of Germany. This hypothesis, which reflects the growing role of the DM as an alternative reserve currency in international portfolios, has been supported by empirical evidence.[16] An analysis of developments in nominal and real short-term interest rate differentials between Germany and the other EMS members shows that the divergence in fiscal-monetary policy mixes has been reflected in a marked increase of both nominal and real interest rates in Ireland and Denmark as compared with those of

16. See, e.g., Micossi and Padoa-Schioppa (1984), and Padoa-Schioppa and Papadia (1984). Padoa-Schioppa and Papadia argue that there is a process of currency substitution at work promoted by the better quality of the deutsche mark as a result of the German policies.

Germany over the period 1981-83. Improved convergence in fiscal performance, against the background of easier monetary policies, contributed to some relative decline in differentials in these interest rates in more recent years. Differentials have fluctuated more narrowly in Belgium and especially the Netherlands, probably reflecting the closer economic and financial integration of these countries with Germany. In France, interest rate differentials with Germany declined through 1980, increased markedly in the period through mid-1983 reflecting, inter alia, the worsening of the fiscal performance, and fluctuated around a broadly stable trend thereafter.

Space limitations prevent a more thorough and detailed analysis of individual countries' developments in this context. Nevertheless it may be illustrative to review the Italian experience in greater detail, since, as indicated above, divergences in the fiscal-monetary policy mixes have been especially pronounced between Germany and Italy. There is little doubt that, despite the existence of a wider band and repeated modifications in Italy's central rates, participation in the EMS has placed constraints on the use of the exchange rate as an instrument of external adjustment in Italy. An indirect evidence of this is provided by the substantial real appreciation of the lira vis-à-vis the DM from the inception of the system to the third quarter of 1985 (about 25 percent in terms of relative prices and 20 percent in terms of relative unit labor costs).[17] The counterpart of the reduced flexibility in the exchange rate has been the increasing role of monetary policy in the adjustment process.

Following a short-lived expansionary phase through mid-1980, monetary policy was progressively tightened and remained relatively restrictive through 1983. At the same time, institutional weaknesses in the control of public expenditures, as well as discretionary boosts to spending, pushed the fiscal deficit to unprecedented highs, despite a large increase in the tax ratio. The monetary authorities responded to the difficulties posed by the divergent stances of financial policies by increasing the independence of monetary management, through institutional changes, notably the so-called divorce[18] between the Treasury and the Bank of Italy, refinements in the instrumentation of monetary policy (see Bank of Italy Annual Reports, various years) and especially through increased flexibility in interest rates, which rose steeply in real terms during the early 1980s. The real interest rate differential between Italy and Germany increased from a negative 9 percent in mid-1980 to a positive 2 percent in 1983.

These efforts resulted in a substantial shift in the composition of financing of

---

17. The competitive position of the lira at the beginning of the EMS was particularly strong as the authorities allowed a significant depreciation of the lira over the six months or so preceding the entry into the system.
18. The legal provision requiring that the Bank of Italy act as the residual buyer at treasury bill auctions was repealed in 1981.

the fiscal deficit, with the share of the central government deficit financed by the Bank of Italy declining from nearly 27 percent in 1980 to 1.5 percent by 1983. The share of debt to the Bank of Italy in total public debt declined from over 23 percent in 1980 to below 17 percent by 1984, and there was a decline in the share of the debt held by other banking institutions as well, at a time when the debt was rising by the equivalent of about 24 percentage points of GDP. The resulting sharp increase in holdings of government securities by the non-bank public was accompanied initially by a decline in the average maturity of the debt (from about 14 months in 1979-80 to 9 months in 1981-82) as treasury bills of maturity up to one year became the preferred form of government paper. The average maturity of the debt increased once again − to about 18 months − in the two subsequent years, reflecting, on the one hand, some decline in inflationary expectations and, on the other, increasingly pervasive indexation of rates of interest on medium- and long-term securities to those on short-term paper. Thus, holding longer-term Treasury bonds became much less risky while these bonds became more negotiable and thus more liquid. By 1984 the share of medium- and long-term securities in total public debt had nearly doubled from the 1981 level (to over 37 percent) but indexed bonds represented an overwhelming proportion of these securities.

The most recent experience of Italy, especially in 1985, shows the difficulty of maintaining substantially different stances of monetary and fiscal policy over extended periods of time. Concern over the costs of the steady and steep rise in real interest rates − in terms of the growth of domestic demand and the size of the interest burden on the public debt − has led the authorities to ease somewhat the stance of monetary policy, allowing a significant increase in the share of the deficit financed through monetary base creation. The easing of financial policy was accompanied by a devaluation in mid-1985 and by further pressures on the exchange rate in the later months of the year.

IV. CONCLUDING REMARKS

The main conclusions of the paper can be summarized briefly. Adherence to a system of relatively fixed exchange rates, such as the EMS, requires consistent monetary and fiscal policies on the part of the Member Countries. It was shown that the EMS has brought about more coordinated monetary policies but that, so far, its impact on fiscal policies has been much more limited. Such a situation will inevitably bring about periodic and possibly frequent adjustments in the exchange rates of the Member Countries, thus in a way neutralizing, at least in part, the advantages of a system of fixed rates. These periodic adjustments have costs associated with them.

The paper has mentioned but not emphasized the possibility that the authorities may utilize capital controls as an additional policy instrument. This

353

possibility was not emphasized because of the efficiency costs involved. When this instrument is utilized, monetary policy can be used to reduce the rate of inflation while capital controls can be used to prevent the appreciation of the real exchange rate in the face of an expansionary fiscal policy. This approach has been suggested by some prominent economists but the authors of this paper doubt that it is a viable alternative except in the very short run.

Another issue that could have been analyzed in detail, if more space had been available, is whether it is necessarily country B (the one with the higher rate of inflation and the more expansionary policy) that should adjust its policies to make them more consistent with those of country A. Why shouldn't country A adjust *its* policies to B's? This argument is made by those who believe in a more active economic policy for the promotion of shorter-term or stabilization objectives. They believe that the pursuit of a more expansionary fiscal (and perhaps monetary) policy by A could bring benefits to the whole group. Thus coordination of policies for short-run objectives may be different from that for longer-run objectives. As the emphasis in the paper has been over the medium term, we have not been able to deal with this aspect. But obviously, if we have to choose between policies that bring about higher inflation and those that bring about lower inflation, we shall choose the latter unless there are clear benefits in terms of real growth and employment associated with the former policies.

In 1962 Robert Mundell put forward his influential proposition that 'in a country which considers it inadvisable to alter the exchange rate or to impose trade controls . . . monetary policy ought to be aimed at external objectives and fiscal policy at internal objectives.' More specifically 'monetary policy should be reserved for attaining the desired level of the balance of payments, and fiscal policy for preserving internal stability . . .' (op. cit., p. 77). Of course Mundell's concept of fiscal policy was essentially a Keynesian one based on two important assumptions: first that fiscal policy is strictly cyclical so that deficits occur in a recession and surpluses in a boom; second, fiscal policy is always a powerful tool for regulating the economy. In recent years the second of these assumptions has been subjected to sharp criticisms by the so-called rational expectation school. In addition, it is now realized that sustained fiscal deficits may have a negative impact on the private sector and may thus reduce, if not totally neutralize, the stimulative power of fiscal policy. Higher (non-cyclical) fiscal deficits may at times even reduce aggregate demand.

The dichotomy suggested by Mundell cannot be extended to the longer run as, over the long run, fiscal and monetary policies become progressively more intermingled. It thus becomes more difficult to follow his prescription that: 'policies should be paired with the objectives on which they have the most influence' (op. cit., p. 77). Take interest rates for example. In the short run, *monetary* policy is the driving force in changing their level. However, these short-run changes are likely to be around a trend that is determined by long-run *fiscal* policy. This intermingling of monetary and fiscal policy is now most obvious in the Italian case.

Membership in the EMS requires that monetary policies be coordinated so that inflation rates do not diverge much and thus allow the countries to adhere to the fixed exchange rates. It also requires fiscal policies that *over the long run* do not diverge considerably as these divergencies will make difficult the adherence to fixed exchange rates either through their effect on monetary policy or through their direct effect on the economy (investment, interest rates, liquidity, etc.).

In recent years the EMS members have pursued policies that have become progressively more coordinated. Thus there is evidence that the exchange rate commitment has had a disciplinary effect on policies. Although the evidence is not beyond controversy, this effect is so far more evident in the monetary than in the fiscal area and more in some countries than in others. It is hoped that not just the monetary authorities but also the fiscal authorities will come to see the need for this coordination.

Barro, Robert J. 'Are Government Bonds Net Wealth?' *Journal of Political Economy*, 82, 1974.

Boskin, Michael J. 'Taxation, Saving and the Rate of Interest.' *Journal of Political Economy*, 86, 2, 2, 1978.

Boskin, Michael J. and Kotlikoff, Lawrence J. 'Public Debt and U.S. Saving: A New Test of the Neutrality Hypothesis.' *Mimeograph*, 1984.

Commission of the European Communities. 'Documents relating to the European System.' *European Economy*, 12, 1982.

Economic Planning Agency (Japan). *The Japanese Economy in 1983: Review and Prospects*. Tokyo, 1983.

Friedman, Benjamin. 'Debt and Economic Activity in the United States.' In Friedman, B. (ed.). *The Changing Roles of Debt and Equity in Financing U.S. Capital Formation*. Chicago University Press, 1982.

Friend, I. and Hasbrouch, J. 'Saving and After-Tax Rates of Return.' *The Review of Economics and Statistics*, 65, 1983.

Goldsmith, Raymond W. 'The Stability of the Ratio of Nonfinancial Debt to Income.' *Banca Nazionale del Lavoro Quarterly Review*, September 1984.

Gylfason, T. 'Interest Rates, Inflation, and the Aggregate Consumption Function.' *Review of Economics and Statistics*, 63, 1981.

Ludlow, Peter. *The Making of the European Monetary System*. London: Butterworths European Studies, 1982.

Masera, Rainer. 'Monetary Policy and Budget Policy: Blend or Dichotomy?' In Masera, Rainer S. and Triffin, Robert (eds). *Europe's Money: Problems of European Monetary Coordination and Integration*. Oxford: Clarendon Press, 1984.

Micossi, Stefano and Padoa-Schioppa, Tomasso. 'Can Europeans Control Their Interest Rates?' Centre for European Studies, 17, 1984.

Modigliani, F., Japelli, T. and Pagano, M. 'The Impact of Fiscal Policy and Inflation on National Saving: The Italian Case.' *Banca Nazionale del Lavoro Quarterly Review*, June 1985.

Muller, Patrice and Price, Robert. 'Public Sector Indebtedness and Long Term Interest Rates.' *Mimeograph*, 1984.

Mundell, Robert. 'The Appropriate Use of Monetary and Fiscal Policy for Internal and External Stability.' *IMF Staff Papers*, 9, 1962.

Padoa-Schioppa, Tomasso and Papadia, Francesco. 'Competing Currencies and Monetary Stability.' In Masera, Rainer S. and Triffin, Robert (eds). *Europe's Money: Problems of European Monetary Coordination and Integration*. Oxford: Clarendon Press, 1984.

Phelps, Edmund S. 'The Real Interest Rate Quiz.' *Atlantic Economic Journal*, 13, 1985.

Sargent, T. and Wallace, N. 'Some Unpleasant Monetarist Arithmetic.'

*Federal Reserve of Minneapolis Quarterly Review*, Autumn 1981.

Tanzi, Vito. *Inflation and the Personal Income Tax: An International Perspective*. Cambridge University Press, 1980.

Tanzi, Vito (ed.). *Taxation, Inflation, and Interest Rates*. Washington DC: International Monetary Fund, 1984a.

Tanzi, Vito. 'Fiscal Harmonization.' *Economica*, VIII, 1984b.

Tanzi, Vito. 'Fiscal Deficits and Interest Rates in the United States: An Empirical Analysis, 1960-84.' *IMF Staff Papers*, 32, 1985.

Tanzi, Vito and Sheshinski, Eytan. 'Behind the Strange Behaviour of U.S. Saving.' *IMF Survey*. November 26, 1984.

Thygesen, Niels. 'Exchange-Rate Policies and Monetary Targets in the EMS Countries.' In Masera, R.S. and Triffin, R. (eds). *Europe's Money: Problems of European Monetary Coordination and Integration*. Oxford: Clarendon Press, 1984.

Ungerer, H., Evans, O. and Nyberg, P. 'The European Monetary System: The Experience 1979-82.' *Occasional Paper*. Washington DC: International Monetary Fund, May 1983.

van Ypersele, Jacques and Koeune, Jean-Claude. *The European Monetary System*. Brussels: Commission of the European Communities, 1985.

# Participants

*Emile a Campo*, European Communities, Brussels, Belgium
*Julian S. Alworth*, Bank for International Settlements, Basel, Switzerland
*Norbert Andel*, Saarland University, Saarbrücken, Germany
*Brian T. Bayliss*, University of Bath, United Kingdom
*Richard M. Bird*, University of Toronto, Canada
*Piervincenzo Bondonio*, University of Turin, Italy
*Jan H. Christiaanse*, Erasmus University Rotterdam, Netherlands
*Sijbren Cnossen*, Erasmus University Rotterdam, Netherlands
*Albert M. Dierick*, Rabobank, Utrecht, Netherlands
*Lutz Fischer*, University of Hamburg, Germany
*Francesco Forte*, University of Rome, Italy
*Malcolm Gillis*, Duke University, Durham, North Carolina, USA
*Richard Goode*, Brookings Institution, Washington DC, USA
*Karl Häuser*, Johann Wolfgang Goethe University, Frankfurt, Germany
*Flip A. de Kam*, Social and Cultural Planning Bureau, Rijswijk, Netherlands
*John A. Kay*, Institute for Fiscal Studies, London, United Kingdom
*Michael J. Keen*, University of Essex, Colchester, United Kingdom
*Han A. Kogels*, Philips, Eindhoven, Netherlands
*Maurice Marchand*, University of Louvain, Belgium
*Paul R. McDaniel*, Boston College, USA
*Charles E. McLure, Jr.*, Hoover Institution, Stanford University, California, USA
*Kenneth C. Messere*, Organisation for Economic Co-operation and Development, Paris, France
*Andy Murfin*, London School of Economics and Political Science, United Kingdom
*Peggy B. Musgrave*, University of California, Santa Cruz, USA
*Richard A. Musgrave*, H.H. Burbank Emeritus Professor of Political Economy, Harvard University, USA
*Fritz Neumark*, Emeritus Professor of Public Finance, Baden-Baden, Germany
*Satya Poddar*, Department of Finance, Ottawa, Canada
*Albert J. Rädler*, University of Hamburg, Germany
*Jozef J.M. Ritzen*, Erasmus University Rotterdam, Netherlands
*Manfred Rose*, University of Heidelberg, Germany
*David Rosenbloom*, Caplin and Drysdale, Washington DC, USA
*Karl W. Roskamp*, Wayne State University, Detroit, Michigan, USA
*Carl S. Shoup*, McVickar Emeritus Professor of Political Economy, Columbia University, New York, USA
*Gerardo P. Sicat*, World Bank, Washington DC, USA
*Roger S. Smith*, University of Alberta, Edmonton, Canada
*Pieter Stek*, Ministry of Finance, The Hague, Netherlands
*Vito Tanzi*, International Monetary Fund, Washington DC, USA

*Teresa Ter-Minassian*, International Monetary Fund, Washington DC, USA
*David Ulph*, University of Bristol, United Kingdom
*Dirk J. Wolfson*, Erasmus University Rotterdam, Netherlands

360

# Name Index

364

366

# Subject Index

Ad valorem versus specific rate,   34, 87, 94-106
Agricultural levies and subsidies,   26, 65, 82, 121-123, 328
    *see* Common Agricultural Policy (CAP)
AID Ltd.,   177, 189, 192
Alcohol taxes:
    harmonization of,   7, 14, 32-33, 47, 85-109
    and optimal taxation,   123-124
    rates of,   33, 86
    revenue aspects of,   30-31
Allegiance rule,
    *see* Residence principle
Arm's-length rule,   73, 202, 218


Bank of England,   183, 192
Belgique Auto,   183, 192
Benefit principle:
    and corporation taxes,   205, 233
    and motor vehicle taxes,   141-142, 146-147, 148-149
    and value-added taxes,   69-70
Border controls,   9, 34-36, 47, 74-81, 82
Border tax adjustments:
    administrative aspects of,   72-73
    for excises,   7, 82
    for turnover taxes,   6, 28, 61-62
    for value-added taxes,   3, 28-29, 47, 61-62
British Labour Statistics,   182, 183
Bundesministerium der Finanzen,   302
Bundesverband des Deutschen Guterfernverkehrs,   153, 156, 159, 160, 169
Bureau Européen des Unions Consommateurs (BEUC),   171, 172, 173, 174, 176, 177,
    179, 192


Canadian Royal Commission,   236, 242, 251
Canadian Tax Foundation,   154, 169, 237, 249
Capital-export neutrality,   205-207, 233, 241
Capital gains, tax treatment of,   269, 296-297
Capital income, taxes on:
    coordination of,   214-220
    criteria for,   201-208

Court of Justice of the European Communities, 2, 13, 27, 32, 42, 45, 53, 78, 86, 110, 123, 149, 169, 329
CSO, 182, 183, 192
Customs duties:
  abolition of, 3, 25-27
  cost of, 59
  for 'own resources', 26, 47, 65
  revenue aspects of, 26
  and single document, 3, 36


Debt in EMS-countries, 350
Deferred payment scheme, 35, 74-76, 79-81
Department of Employment (United Kingdom), 182, 183, 192
Depreciation, tax treatment of, 260-264, 291-294, 327-328
Deringer Report, 25, 35, 53
Destination principle:
  and border tax adjustments, 67
  concept of, 28
  versus origin principle, 67-74
  and removal of border controls, 35, 74-81
Direct versus indirect taxes, 14, 25
Dividend withholding taxes, 4, 14, 38, 39, 229, 230-231
Double taxation:
  of dividend income, 38, 39, 222, 230-231, 237
  of employment income, 42, 44, 300, 302, 303, 324
  of investment income, 206, 215, 259-260, 261, 299-300

Economic and Monetary Affairs Committee, 88, 92
Economic and Monetary Union, 4, 49
Economic Planning Agency (Japan), 341, 356
Economic and Social Committee of the European Communities, 2, 143, 144, 149, 150, 169
Economist, The, 144, 146
Economist Intelligence Unit, 183, 193
Efficiency:
  and border tax adjustments, 70-71
  and corporate investments, 212
  and labor income taxation, 308
  *see* Capital-export neutrality; Locational neutrality
Employment income,
  *see* Labor, income taxes on
Entitlement rule,
  *see* Interjurisdictional equity
Equity:
  intertaxpayer, 207-208, 309-310
  *see* Interjurisdictional equity